AF607977

SACRED BOUNDARIES

Keith P. Luria

SACRED BOUNDARIES

Religious Coexistence and Conflict in Early-Modern France

The Catholic University of America Press
Washington, D.C.

The paper used in this publication meets the minimum requirements of American National Standards for Information Science—Permanence of Paper for Printed Library materials, ANSI Z39.48-1984. •

∞

LIBRARY OF CONGRESS CATALOGING-IN-PUBLICATION DATA
Luria, Keith P.
Sacred boundaries : religious coexistence and conflict in early-modern France / Keith P. Luria. — ed.
p. cm.
Includes bibliographical references and index.
ISBN 13: 978-0-8132-1411-5 (cloth : alk. paper)
ISBN 10: 0-8132-1411-4 (cloth : alk. paper)
1. France—Church history—17th century. 2. Catholic Church—Relations—Huguenots. 3. Huguenots—Relations—Catholic Church. I. Title.
BR845.L87 2005
274.4′ 06—dc22
2004014866

FOR MARY

CONTENTS

ACKNOWLEDGMENTS

Writing books and creating religious coexistence have, at least, this much in common: they both require collaboration and institutional support. The institutional, that is to say financial, support for this book came from North Carolina State University, the National Endowment for the Humanities, the National Humanities Center, and the American Philosophical Society. I am grateful to them for providing me with the means to undertake the research for and to complete the writing of this book.

I also wish to thank the staffs of the institutions in which I carried out research, including those of the Archives Départementales de la Charente-Maritime, Archives Départementales des Deux-Sèvres, Archives Départementales de la Vienne, Archives Nationales, Bibliothèque Municipale d'Orléans, Bibliothèque Municipale de Poitiers, Bibliothèque Nationale de France, Bibliotheque du Protestantisme Français, Bibliothèque Provinciale des Capucins, and Bibliothèque de Sainte-Geneviève. It is the professionalism of these people, along with their interest in scholarship and their willingness to help researchers, that makes the study of French history possible.

I am grateful to audiences that listened to and commented on parts of this work. I found receptive listeners at East Carolina University, Portland State University, Rutgers University, the University of Kentucky, the University of Memphis, the National Humanities Center, the University of New South Wales, and the Research Centre on Religion and Society at the University of Amsterdam. I have also benefited a great deal from an ongoing exchange with a group of scholars, whom Wayne te Brake has organized into a workshop entitled "Accommodating Difference: The Politics of Cultural Pluralism in Europe."

Bringing a project such as this to completion depends not just on the efforts of an author but on a network of family, friends, and colleagues who offer support, advice, and the hard work of reading the manuscript as it progresses. For their help, I want to thank Harold J. Luria, Edwin Bezzina, Robert Chanaud, Carolyn Lougee Chappell, Natalie Z. Davis, Barbara Diefendorf, Nicholas Doumanis, Sandria Freitag, Gregory Hanlon, Lynn Hunt, Joseph Klaits, Yves Krumenacker, Florence Mirouse, Kathleen Nicholson, Bodo Nischan, Jeremy Popkin, William Ray, Peter van der Veer, and Dale Van Kley. Those who have given time and effort to reading the manuscript include David Gilmartin, Daniel Hickey, Anthony La Vopa, Jonathan Ocko, Steven Vincent, as well as other colleagues in the History Department of North Carolina State University. In particular, for their painstaking and perceptive readings, I must offer special thanks to Philip Benedict, Katherine Stern Brennan, S. Amanda Eurich, and Raymond A. Mentzer. I have also greatly appreciated the efforts of David J. McGonagle, Theresa Walker, and Philip G. Holthaus, who have overseen the book's publication. A previous version of chapter 3 appeared in *French Historical Studies* 24, no. 2 (Spring 2001): 185–222. My greatest debt of gratitude is to my wife, Mary D. Sheriff. She has read the work too many times to count and offered long, unwavering encouragement. In addition, through her own scholarship, she has provided an inspiration and example to many, not the least to me. This book is dedicated to her.

ABBREVIATIONS

ADDS	Archives départementales des Deux-Sèvres
ADV	Archives départementales de la Vienne
AN	Archives nationales
BMP	Bibliothèque municipale de Poitiers
BCP	Bibliothèque provinciale des capuçins
BPF	Bibliothèque du protestantisme français

INTRODUCTION

Religious rivalry, persecution, and violence have bedeviled so many societies past and present that confessional difference often seems an unavoidable source of conflict. Religion ostensibly breeds loyalties so deep and feelings of particularism so strong that enmity between faiths comes to seem inevitable and natural. Even if conflicts have other causes—socioeconomic antagonism, political competition, kin group or personal feuds—they can most readily be explained as religious in origin if believers of different groups are involved. The list of contemporary areas beset by such strife is all too familiar: South Asia, the Middle East, the Balkans, Ireland; and on it goes. The level of religious violence in such places—or our understanding of the violence as religiously inspired—speaks all too powerfully of our belief in the power of faith to create gulfs between neighbors and imbue their relations with hostility. Or, at least, we believe religion to have such power if it is not tamed by laws and political structures that separate religion from public life and consign it to the reputedly private realms of the family and individual conscience. Those of us who live in societies that have supposedly succeeded in setting such hedges around religious conflict look with dismay at others we think have not while feeling, nonetheless, the need for constant vigilance against attempts to break down the barriers. The historical memory of violence in the name of religion or against groups identified by religion remains too fresh to take tolerance for granted.

In places we think have not managed to privatize and compartmentalize religious belief and identity, violence appears so inevitably the result of religious differences that peaceful coexistence between religious groups seems startling. Yet close examinations of societies that appear ridden by confessional conflict often show coexistence not to be exceptional; if we look for examples of good relations among those groups we assume to be bitterly opposed, we frequently find them.[1] People of competing faiths can and do get along in daily life. The lesson is hopeful, but in thinking about religiously mixed societies and the coexistence or conflict within them, we are left with a problem. How can we explain both coexistence and conflict, which frequently appear at the same time? Do religions necessarily shape the social identities and attitudes of their adherents so as to make them inevitably hostile to those of other faiths? Do faiths necessarily create irreconcilable differences that lead only to conflict? Or have we overestimated the power of religion to override what people hold in common across confessional divides that separate neighbors who might otherwise be intent on living together peacefully?

This book raises such questions and provides a means for thinking about them by looking at one of the most historically notable examples of a society torn apart by religious rivalry, that of early-modern France. Violence between French Catholics and Protestants in the sixteenth-century Wars of Religion epitomized for centuries thereafter the horrors that religious division could provoke. Indeed, the work of historians in recent decades has reinforced our understanding of this strife as based on religious hostility rather than, as earlier historical interpretations stressed, aristocratic rivalries or the political weaknesses of the French monarchy.[2] Scholars of the confessional conflict, such as Natalie Zemon Davis and Denis Crouzet, have, in different ways, described an enormous cultural gulf that opened between Catholics and Huguenots.[3] Each side feared the other as a false religion, a threat to social order, and a source of contami-

1. For recent examples that describe good relations in societies known for religious violence, see Ashutosh Varshney, *Ethnic Conflict and Civic Life: Hindus and Muslims in India* (New Haven, Conn., 2002), and Robert J. Donia and John V. A. Fine Jr., *Bosnia and Hercegovina: A Tradition Betrayed* (New York, 1994).

2. Mack P. Holt, "Putting Religion Back into the Wars of Religion," *French Historical Studies* 18, no. 2 (Fall 1993): 524–51.

3. Natalie Zemon Davis, "The Rites of Violence," in *Society and Culture in Early Modern France* (Stanford, Calif., 1975), 152–87, and Denis Crouzet, *Les guerriers de Dieu: La violence au temps des troubles de religion, vers 1525–1610*, 2 vols. (Seyssel, 1990). Davis describes the legitimation given religious violence by reference to Scripture, doctrine, rituals, and judicial procedures. Crouzet emphasizes the eschatological sense of doom that promoted confessional bloodshed. See also Barbara B. Diefendorf, *Beneath the Cross: Catholics and Huguenots in Sixteenth-Century Paris* (New York and Oxford, U.K., 1991).

nation in the society of true believers. The perpetrators of horrible violence imagined religious difference as excluding their victims from a shared national community, culture, and even humanity. Each confessional group ensured its purity and defended its beliefs by attacking its opponents as polluting heretics or unbelievers. Such an interpretation proceeds from our understanding of religion as having extraordinary power to determine belief and behavior and to provoke hostility toward those of different creeds. Religious distinctions appear absolute; they provoke the deepest apprehensions and the most radical reactions.

Cultural anthropologists have taught historians to think of religion not only as a body of theological doctrines accompanied by a set of rituals but also as a symbol system that imbues social life with meaning.[4] Historians of sixteenth-century religious violence have used these anthropological ideas effectively to explain how the contrary beliefs of Protestants and Catholics fashioned different cultures and led to hostility. The historiography describing these two religiously shaped, warring cultures has provided a compelling explanation for sixteenth-century confessional strife, and it has influenced the study of religious violence in other times and places.[5]

We must be cautious, however, about assuming that two irreconcilable cultures were at war in France. Certainly, Protestant and Catholic disagreements over doctrine were of fundamental importance. But can we suppose that doctrines fixed the substance of everyone's beliefs and practices? This view overestimates the stability of cultural meanings and underestimates the ability of individuals to take and reshape elements of a

4. Such as in the classic works of Mary Douglas, *Purity and Danger* (Harmondsworth, U.K., 1966) and *Natural Symbols* (New York, 1973); Victor Turner, *The Ritual Process: Structure and Anti-Structure* (Ithaca, N.Y., 1969) and *Dramas, Fields, and Metaphors: Symbolic Action in Human Society* (Ithaca, N.Y., 1974); and Clifford Geertz, "Religion as a Cultural System," "Ritual and Social Change: A Javanese Example," and "Deep Play: Notes on a Balinese Cockfight," all in *The Interpretation of Cultures* (New York, 1973), 87–125, 142–69, 412–53. For an overview, see Catherine Bell, *Ritual Theory, Ritual Practice* (New York, 1992).

5. In drawing on the work of Davis, Mack P. Holt has used the term "two cultures" to describe Catholic-Protestant differences (*French Wars of Religion, 1562–1629* [Cambridge, U.K., 1995], 87). For an example of the historiography's influence outside the study of early-modern Europe, see Sandria B. Freitag, *Collective Action and Community: Public Arenas and the Emergence of Communalism in North India* (Berkeley and Los Angeles, Calif., 1989), 3, 5.

cultural repertoire to suit their own purposes. Furthermore, if we judge early-modern Catholic-Protestant differences from a wider geographical perspective, can we say that their cultural dissimilarity was as great as that between Europeans and other people they were encountering in these years, such as those in the Americas? Here we find truly striking cultural differences and mutual incomprehension. Montaigne famously drew this comparison precisely to reflect upon what his Catholic and Protestant countrymen shared, even if in his ironic observation the French of either faith suffered in comparison to New World cannibals.[6]

Another history of early-modern French religious relations is possible, especially if we shift our focus from the period of the Wars of Religion to that after the promulgation of the Edict of Nantes in 1598. At the end of the wars, France sat poised between two possibilities: the continuation of confessional conflict or the construction of a society in which the rival religions would live together. After almost four decades of confessional strife, the prospects for coexistence did not look good, and yet the desire for peace was often strong enough, both nationally and within localities, to counter the impulse toward violence. It is precisely the tension between coexistence and conflict and the process by which French Catholics and Huguenots tried to construct a means to live together that is the subject of this book. That this process was possible at all calls into question the idea that the two groups were divided by an unbridgeable cultural gulf. And, in turn, it raises questions about the nature of confessional-group, family, and individual religious identities, all issues that require examination to understand conflict and coexistence in religiously divided societies.

Despite their disagreements, what Catholics and Huguenots shared in their common culture was considerable: family attitudes, economic practices, notions of honor, political ideas, concepts of social order. They also possessed a common Christian background, as the more irenic-minded among them willingly acknowledged. In a sense, the argument for two antagonistic cultures implies that common Christian beliefs could no longer play their traditional role in generating bonds of community,

6. Michel de Montaigne, "Of Cannibals," in *The Complete Essays of Montaigne*, translated by Donald M. Frame (Stanford, Calif., 1958), 150–59.

neighborliness, and kinship. But it remains possible that shared religious values created social bonds across the confessional divide. As Catholics and Huguenots sometimes told their priests and ministers—much to the clerics' dismay—people could be saved in either faith, so long as they remained good people.[7] Thus we can still think of early-modern culture as profoundly shaped by religious belief and practice, even while questioning the idea that France's two religions necessarily created separate and opposed cultures.

The uncovering of numerous examples of peaceful coexistence between people of the two confessions, not only in the period after the Edict of Nantes, but also during the Wars of Religion, further challenges the notion of two irreconcilable cultures.[8] Despite the religious tensions, Catholic and Huguenot neighbors found grounds on which to cooperate and negotiate local reconciliation. Historians of seventeenth-century France have not always paid much attention to these examples of coexistence between the religious groups. Instead, a preoccupation with conflict and persecution has long dominated the historiography. In large part, that focus comes from a tradition reaching back to the seventeenth century of Protestant historians producing confessional history that criticized Catho-

7. Bernard Dompnier quotes examples in which Catholics told missionaries and priests that "heretics are not outside the path to salvation . . . as long as they live in conformity with the profession of their Calvinist faith" or that "one could be saved in any sort of religion" (*Le venin de l'hérésie: Images du protestantisme et combat catholique au XVIIe siècle* [Paris, 1985], 153–54).

8. See, e.g., Elisabeth Labrousse, *"Une foi, une loi, un roi?": Essai sur la révocation de l'Édit de Nantes* (Geneva, 1985), chap. 4; Gregory Hanlon, *Confession and Community in Seventeenth-Century France: Catholic and Protestant Coexistence in Aquitaine* (Philadelphia, 1993); Hanlon, *L'univers des gens de bien: Culture et comportements des elites urbaines en Agenais-Condomois au XVIIe siècle* (Bordeaux, 1989), 229–32; Robert Sauzet, *Contre-réforme et réforme catholique en Bas-Languedoc: Le diocèse de Nîmes au XVIIe siècle* (Louvain, 1979), chap. 5; and Louis Pérouas, *Le diocèse de La Rochelle de 1648 à 1724: Sociologie et pastorale* (1964; reprint, Paris, 1999), 143–44. See also Philip Benedict, "*Un roi, une loi, deux fois:* Parameters for the History of Catholic-Reformed Co-existence in France, 1555–1685," in *Tolerance and Intolerance in the European Reformation*, edited by Ole Peter Grell and Bob Scribner (Cambridge, U.K., 1996), 65–93. For sixteenth-century examples of cross-confessional cooperation, see Olivier Christin, *La paix de religion: L'autonomisation de la raison politique au XVIe siècle* (Paris, 1997), 103–34; and Thierry Wanegffelen, *Ni Rome ni Genève: Des fidèles entre deux chaires en France au XVIe siècle* (Paris, 1997), 307–29.

lic oppression and defended Protestant resistance.[9] Their early-modern Catholic counterparts produced an equally polemical history detailing Protestant cruelty, though their modern descendants are hardly eager to excuse religious intolerance.[10]

Only lately have historians begun to question the historiography of conflict and persecution by looking closely at the examples of peaceful relations between the confessional groups. As Bernard Dompnier has pointed out, "all recent studies of religious history examining regions of confessional coexistence emphasize that conflicted relations between the Catholic and Protestant faithful were far from being the rule." Historians have found many examples of "pacific attitudes" and "even amiable behavior" in both lay and ecclesiastical milieux.[11] They have generally focused on specific localities or regions in which day-to-day interactions can best be investigated. Gregory Hanlon surveyed the "strategies of conciliation, cooperation, and avoidance of conflict" that operated in one southwestern biconfessional town. Robert Sauzet examined how coexistence in Nîmes grew out of the minority Protestants' domination of the city for much of the century. Elisabeth Labrousse's work on biconfessional communities in the southwest explored how local Catholic and Huguenot elites found common ground in their concern with dominating their social inferiors.[12] As will become apparent, this book is deeply indebted to the work of these scholars.

These studies are a welcome counterpoint to those stressing unmitigated hostility and frequent violence between the two confessions, and

9. See Elie Benoist, *Histoire de l'Edit de Nantes contenant les choses les plus remarquables qui se sont passées en France avant & après sa publication . . .*, 5 vols. (Delft, 1693–1694). This tradition lives on, for example, in the work of Janine Garrisson; see *L'Édit de Nantes et sa révocation: Histoire d'une intolerance* (Paris, 1985).

10. Though one can find a hint of it in Jean-Robert Armogathe's *Croire en liberté: L'église catholique et la révocation de l'Édit de Nantes* (Paris, 1985) with its attempt to diminish the Catholic Church's role in the Revocation of the Edict of Nantes and its contention that Protestant historians have exaggerated the violence Huguenots suffered. Early-modern martyrologies were a type of history writing that enumerated each side's grievances against the other. See Brad S. Gregory, *Salvation at Stake: Christian Martyrdom in Early Modern Europe* (Cambridge, Mass., 1999).

11. Dompnier, *Venin de l'hérésie*, 139, 152.

12. Labrousse summarizes her findings in *"Une foi, une loi, un roi."* Also see Sauzet, *Contre-réforme et réforme catholique;* and Hanlon, *Confession and Community.*

they are in keeping with more general trends in the study of confessional relations in early-modern Europe.[13] In their effort to stress religious tolerance over violence, however, they also leave us with certain conceptual difficulties. Sometimes underlying their explanation for good relations is a simple notion of popular ecumenicism: left to their own devices people will get along. Bob Scribner described such an attitude in sixteenth-century Germany as the "tolerance of practical rationality" in which "ordinary people . . . made little fuss about difference in belief" and shared a mistrust of both clergies.[14] But if so, how are we to understand the impact of religious difference on social relations? What had happened to each religion's capacity to produce a sense of its own absoluteness, and of the radical difference, the impurity, indeed the satanic nature, of the other? What had happened to the deep fears of contamination and of pollution, which the historians of sixteenth-century religious violence have so brilliantly described?

Furthermore, the older Protestant confessional historiography—with its descriptions of seventeenth-century incidents of property destruction, grave desecrations, riots, and deaths—was not wrong. France in the 1600s did not repeat the massacres of the Wars of Religion, but violence did not simply disappear in the face of a practical willingness among people to get along. Nor is it acceptable simply to blame outbreaks of hostility on the instigation of militant clerics, though, as we will see, they certainly bore much of the blame. If people were truly as tolerant, peaceful, and anticlerical as some have thought, rabble-rousing Huguenot pastors or Catholic missionaries would not have whipped them up so easily. We cannot romanticize communal coexistence; people did not always get along. Competing religious observances or political rivalries between the groups could be sources of great tension or even flashpoints for violence.[15]

13. See the essays in Grell and Scribner, eds., *Tolerance and Intolerance*, and Jean Bérenger, *Tolérance ou paix de religion en Europe centrale (1415–1792)* (Paris, 2000).

14. Bob Scribner, "Preconditions of Tolerance and Intolerance in Sixteenth-Century Germany," in Grell and Scribner, eds., *Tolerance and Intolerance*, 32–47, esp. 38. See also Elisabeth Labrousse, "La conversion d'un huguenot au catholicisme," *Revue d'histoire de l'église de France* 64, no. 172 (January–June 1978): 55–68, and 64, no. 173 (July–December 1978): 251–52.

15. As Benedict has put the matter: "A full picture of Protestant-Catholic relations needs to make room at once for the evidence of frequent, cordial interaction between

The historians of coexistence, concerned though they are with emphasizing good over bad Catholic-Protestant relations, are well aware that interconfessional cooperation did not prevent the eventual suppression of the minority. The older Protestant historiography, written in the shadow of the Reformed Church's brutal repression after 1685, placed the blame for persecution squarely on the Catholic Church and the monarchy. No one would dispute the role each played in the Revocation of the Edict of Nantes and the violence that accompanied it. But in recent work, the monarchy's impact has been, to a certain extent, set aside as historians have stressed less state power and more a dynamic of differentiation inside each church and each group in biconfessional communities. Church leaders sought to impose on their flocks more rigorous adherence to prescribed doctrines and practices. In doing so, they hoped to make a clear distinction between the religions. Locally, priests, ministers, and their allies strove to ensure that church requirements were obeyed. The result was "a powerful cultural dynamic [that] worked to heighten awareness of confessional differences. . . . The two confessions may have become increasingly sharply separated and self-enclosed communities as the century advanced."[16]

This impulse internal to both churches was one means by which, through "rivalry and emulation," churches "defined and enforced their particular versions of orthodoxy and orthopraxy, demonized their rivals, and built group cohesion and identity."[17] As a result, "barricades were erected around each church group."[18] But I will suggest here that impor-

members of the two faiths and for the recognition that a continuing sense of difference set them apart—differences that could, in certain situations, spark violence or panic" ("Catholic-Reformed Co-existence," 84). And Hanlon points out that "social relations are not fundamentally harmonious, conflictive, consensual, or repressive, but are *all* of these" (*Confession and Community*, 6).

16. Benedict, "Catholic-Reformed Co-existence," 89, 90. More recently Benedict has rephrased his understanding of this development as "a modest tendency . . . for the two confessions to become increasingly self-enclosed communities as the seventeenth century advanced" ("Confessionalization in France?: Critical Reflections and New Evidence," in *The Faith and Fortunes of France's Huguenots, 1600–85* [Aldershot, U.K., 2001], 309–25, see p. 324 for quotation).

17. Benedict, "Confessionalization in France?," 313.

18. "By restoring an efficacious ritual framework over Catholic society . . . clerics were consciously erecting boundaries between Catholics and Protestants" (Hanlon,

tant as the internal dynamic was, it does not alone account for the concretization of confessional identities. A clear sense of religious identity also depended on the means available to local Catholics and Protestants to orchestrate their dealings with each other. Coexistence was not built simply on the innumerable daily interactions between individuals getting along, but also on the careful, and sometimes painful, negotiation of local religious relations. The agreements that emerged had the effect of making group identities in biconfessional communities more, not less, distinct. Still, they established peaceful ways for Catholics and Protestants to live together. The negotiations were local, but they were often undertaken with the encouragement of royal officials and only within a legal framework the monarchy provided. Thus while acknowledging the importance of an internal dynamic in each group, we must realize that cooperation across the confessional divide also contributed to creating difference. And while focusing on the local nature of the process, we must reintroduce into our analysis the state's role in determining the nature of confessional relations.

The French state was, at different times during the seventeenth century, a promoter of either coexistence or intolerance. Recognizing the monarchy's role in furthering coexistence offers a perspective on the early-modern state different from that of historians who have seen it, particularly in German principalities, as an agent of "confessionalization." The term refers to the state's enforcement of religious conformity and disciplined social behavior as a means of increasing its power.[19] Certainly, un-

Confession and Community, 225). The Reformed Church sought the same goal by imposing consistorial discipline over its faithful. See Raymond A. Mentzer, "Morals and Moral Regulation in Protestant France," *Journal of Interdisciplinary History* 31, no. 1 (2000): 1–20, and "Marking the Taboo: Excommunication in French Reformed Churches," in *Sin and the Calvinists: Morals Control and the Consistory in the Reformed Tradition*, edited by Raymond A. Mentzer (Kirksville, Mo., 1994), 97–128.

19. The bibliography on confessionalization in Germany is far too long to list here. But for a recent overview, see Joel F. Harrington and Helmut Walser Smith, "Confessionalization, Community, and State Building in Germany, 1555–1870," *Journal of Modern History* 69 (March 1997): 77–101; Heinz Schilling, ed., *Kirchenzucht und Sozialdisziplinierung im frühneuzeitlichen Europa* (Berlin, 1994), and "Confessionalization in the Empire: Religious and Societal Change in Germany between 1555 and 1620," in *Religion, Political Culture and the Emergence of Early Modern Society: Essays in German and Dutch History* (Leiden, 1992), 205–45; Paul Warmbrunn, *Zwei Konfession en einer Stadt:*

der Louis XIV, the French monarchy acted in such a way to repress Protestantism as well as to increase its control over provincial society and its potentially restive inhabitants. But in the first several decades of the century, the state sought not confessionalization but carefully constructed coexistence. Admittedly there were limits; Huguenot military strength was destroyed in the 1620s, and Catholicism was reestablished everywhere as the legally dominant religion. But coexistence served the aims of state builders just as much as confessionalization would later. The agents the government sent into biconfessional communities in the century's earliest years to negotiate or dictate resolutions of confessional conflict increased the state's presence in local society just as did the better known *intendants*.[20] The Edict of Nantes helped pacify the kingdom and it made the monarchy the arbiter of confessional disputes. The king became the guarantor of religious peace and hence of civil order.

The dynamic behind the construction of confessional relations was thus simultaneously local and national, and any sharp distinction between the two is misleading. Catholics and Protestants constructed coexistence or created conflict in the communities they shared, but they could not order their relations with complete independence from the policies of their churches and, even more so, of their king with his legislative authority, judicial system, and enforcement powers. Local people might cooperate with or obstruct government policies, but they could never escape them. Therefore, even while focusing on communities, families, and individuals, this study pays close attention to the actions of a state that started the century by promoting coexistence but later turned to persecution.

Das Zusammenleben von Katholiken und Protestantischen in den Paritätischen Reichsstädten Augsburg, Biberach, Ravensburg und Dinkelsbühl von 1548 bis 1648 (Wiesbaden, 1983); Etienne François, *Protestants et catholiques en Allemagne: Identités et pluralisme Augsbourg, 1648–1806* (Paris, 1993); Peter G. Wallace, *Communities and Conflict in Early Modern Colmar: 1575–1730* (Atlantic Highlands, N.J., 1995), 2–3; and R. Po-Chia Hsia, *Social Discipline in the Reformation: Central Europe, 1550–1750* (London, 1989). On the use of the concept in France, see Benedict, "Confessionalization in France?"

20. Royal provincial administrators, whose activities contributed to government centralization. See James M. Collins, *The State in Early Modern France* (Cambridge, U.K., 1995), 53–54.

CONFESSIONAL BOUNDARIES

How, then, are we to arrive at a conceptual framework that can help us understand peaceful coexistence, continuing suspicion, and at least occasional violence between the two sides? And how can we include in this analysis roles for both the state and for people negotiating their local religious relations? The answer lies in shifting our interpretative focus away from opposed religious cultures toward an examination of how group identities were constructed and reconstructed, a process that led at *specific* times in *specific* places to greater peace or conflict. With such a reorientation, we no longer need assume either good relations or bad ones as the normal state of affairs between the confessional groups. Rather, we can think about how a variety of issues crucial to members of both faiths, including religious belief and practice, community concerns, and family interests, influenced the confessional situation and the formation of social identities.

Within communities, each group's sense of itself depended on its internal sociological makeup and ecclesiastical structures, as well as on its adherence to particular religious doctrines and practices. Thanks to work by social historians of religion we have a good understanding of these matters for both faiths during the seventeenth century.[21] But each confession's transactions with the other along the social boundary between them also molded its identity. Like all social groups, Catholics and Protestants engaged in "boundary work," which is to say that to define who they were, they created distinctions by separating themselves from those they

21. The bibliography for each church is too large to list here in its entirety, but for the Reformed Church, in addition to previously noted works, see Philip Benedict, *The Huguenot Population of France, 1600–1685: The Demographic Fate and Customs of a Religious Minority* (Philadelphia, 1991), and Raymond A. Mentzer and Andrew Spicer, eds., *Society and Culture in the Huguenot World, 1559–1685* (Cambridge, U.K., 2002). On the Catholic Reformation's impact on Catholic belief and worship, see, e.g., John Bossy, "The Counter-Reformation and the People of Catholic Europe," *Past and Present* 47 (May 1970): 51–70, and "The Social History of Confession in the Age of the Reformation," *Transactions of the Royal Historical Society*, 5th ser., 25 (1975): 29–38; Philip T. Hoffman, *Church and Community in the Diocese of Lyon, 1500–1789* (New Haven, Conn., 1984); and Keith P. Luria, *Territories of Grace: Cultural Change in the Seventeenth-Century Diocese of Grenoble* (Berkeley and Los Angeles, 1991).

construed as different.[22] Boundary building is an oppositional process; people "think themselves into difference," manufacturing an apparent similarity and coherence out of the variety within one group by opposition to the same process underway in the other group.[23] Belief systems teach people that the distinctions boundary building creates are normal, natural, and perhaps even divinely ordained.[24] We should not think of a social boundary as merely a reflection of underlying social structures.[25] It is a mental construct; it exists in the minds of those who live along it, who participate actively in its creation, and who share the meanings attributed to it. Ultimately, if a secure boundary is established, people hold fast to the distinctions it creates because they are thereby provided with a social identity that appears as the irreducible core of their selfhood. To question such distinctions puts their identities and sense of self at risk.

Sociologists, anthropologists, and social psychologists have devoted great effort to explaining how and why people construct boundaries, and in so doing, of course, they have created boundaries between themselves.[26] Some, following a Durkheimian approach that emphasizes shared communal beliefs as essential to boundary building, have focused on the role of human cognition: "human beings name and classify things and people. They create labels through contrast and inclusion."[27] Others place less emphasis on individual cognition and more on creating identity by

22. As Cynthia Fuchs Epstein notes, "A belief in difference permeates our lives. . . . Groups . . . rely on distinctions to create a 'we'-and-'they' boundary to define themselves" ("Tinkerbells and Pinups: The Construction and Reconstruction of Gender Boundaries at Work," in *Cultivating Differences: Symbolic Boundaries and the Making of Inequality*, edited by Michèle Lamont and Marcel Fournier [Chicago, 1992], 232–56, see pp. 232 and 234 for quotations).

23. Anthony P. Cohen, *The Symbolic Construction of Community* (London, 1985), 117.

24. Epstein, "Tinkerbells and Pinups," 237.

25. Nicola Beisel, "Constructing a Shifting Moral Boundary: Literature and Obscenity in Nineteenth-Century America," in Lamont and Fournier, eds., *Cultivating Differences*, 104–28, see esp. 107.

26. I follow here the summary of different sociological views of boundary construction that Lamont and Fournier provide in their "Introduction" to *Cultivating Difference*, 1–17. They reasonably point out, however, that the distinctions between different schools of thought on boundary construction can, in practice, be quite fuzzy.

27. Lamont and Fournier, "Introduction," 2.

means of social processes that define inclusion and exclusion.[28] Yet others emphasize the political or economic dimension to boundary building. People live in groups that are mobilized in the pursuit of power or greater access to wealth. Marxists emphasize class conflict and the role of the state in fabricating forms of consciousness that maintain political domination over subordinate classes.[29] Weberians look at how status groups pursue their interests and compete for resources. Poststructuralists uncover the power relations that lie behind the definitions of difference and describe the socially constructed nature of all such definitions. Yet each approach relies on the notion that a "logic of distinction" always operates in social life; individuals and groups inevitably participate in it.[30]

In contemporary American scholarship, those working on the construction of difference in terms of race, class, and gender have drawn from work (particularly poststructuralist work) on boundaries to show how they create distinctions that are not inherent or natural to human beings but that can become powerful forces for social discrimination. Historians thinking about boundaries have relied less on poststructuralism and more on Weberian or Marxist approaches to examine ethnic-group rivalries, nationalism, or the construction of territorially bounded nation-states.[31] Scholars working on religion have not been as attracted to such ideas as a means of explaining how religion can create social difference, though its effects are all too apparent in our daily news reports.[32] I hope in this study to bring concepts of boundary work and boundary management to the historical study of religious conflict and coexistence. But my understanding of social boundaries is eclectic. I acknowledge the importance of boundary construction both as an ongoing means of investing groups

28. The approach associated with social psychology and symbolic interactionism. See Lamont and Fournier, "Introduction," 3.

29. Cohen, *Symbolic Construction of Community*, 71.

30. Lamont and Fournier, "Introduction," 4–6. They take the idea of a "logic of distinction" from Pierre Bourdieu, *Distinction: A Social Critique of the Judgement of Taste*, translated by Richard Nice (Cambridge, Mass., 1984).

31. For an example of a historian's use of boundary ideas in discussing the nation-state, see Peter Sahlins, *Boundaries: The Making of France and Spain in the Pyrenees* (Berkeley and Los Angeles, 1989).

32. But see, e.g., Varshney, *Ethnic Conflict and Civic Life*, though he prefers to characterize Hindu and Muslim identities as ethnic rather than religious.

with social identities and as a way of pursuing political ends (in this case, the goals of the Catholic and Reformed Churches and of the French state).

The use of boundary concepts to study early-modern French confessional groups centers our attention on their interaction rather than on their internal development, which has been the concern of much previous work. And it widens our perspective on their interaction beyond the focus on conflict and repression. We can use it to explore relations that ranged from amiable to forbearing to hostile. In turn, the study of Catholic-Huguenot relations raises an issue that scholars working on social boundaries have not much addressed. Whatever their particular approach, they focus on how boundary building creates identities that separate people from each other and how these perceptions of difference become concretized or naturalized in the minds and behaviors of the people they study. They tell us less about boundary crossing or about how boundaries may be effaced.[33] As we will see here, however, the confessional boundary in early modern France was permeable. Catholics and Huguenots crossed it often in a variety of daily interactions: they lived together, worked together, married each other, shared civic responsibilities, participated in each other's religious observances, and buried their dead together. In such exchanges the confessional boundary did not necessarily disappear, but it did not prevent people of the two faiths from living together.[34]

What explains this permeability is in part the complexity of social identity. Early-modern French people not only belonged to the Reformed or the Catholic Churches. They also belonged to families; to occupations; to cities, towns, or villages; to status or corporate groups; and so forth. Reli-

33. However, see the work of Fredrik Barth, a pioneer in the application of boundary ideas to the study of ethnic identities, who emphasizes the frequency and importance of boundary crossing. "Human activities perversely create . . . leakages through conceptual boundaries by reconnecting what has been separated. . . . Often one will find that while some do the boundary imposing, others look for loopholes" ("Boundaries and Connections," in *Signifying Identities: Anthropological Perspectives on Boundaries and Contested Values*, edited by Anthony P. Cohen [London, 2000], 17–36, see p. 29 for quotation).

34. Or as Barth points out regarding ethnic differences, "Interaction in . . . a social system does not lead to its liquidation . . .; cultural differences can persist despite interethnic contact and interdependence" ("Introduction," in *Ethnic Groups and Boundaries: The Social Organization of Culture Difference*, edited by Fredrik Barth [London, 1969], 10).

gious affiliation did not always determine their inclusion within or exclusion from those various groups or foci of identity. Other means of self-definition cut across those of confession and helped maintain ongoing connections between people of the two faiths, giving them shared concerns and interests that undermined a resolute confessional identity.[35] The creation of a strict religious boundary would depend on elevating confessional identity above these other crosscutting social definitions, abstracting it from the social mix, and concretizing it as the chief way people construed their places in French society. This was the objective of the churches and, at times, of the French state, but it was one they could never completely reach.

The permeability of the confessional boundary depended on the context *within* which and the issues *around* which it was erected. In a particular place and time, the barrier could be weakened or fortified in any of the numerous interactions between Catholics and Protestants.[36] And the boundary could take many forms. For analytical purposes, however, I suggest that Catholics and Protestants in the communities and families they shared drew the confessional boundary in three ways. The threefold distinction is, admittedly, schematic. On the ground, no doubt, confessional boundaries never took shape in quite so distinct a manner. But proposing a model of three boundary arrangements can help us understand both how confessional identities were constructed and how other social imperatives could temper them. Thereby it can also help us understand continuing conflict and coexistence between Catholics and Protestants.

35. On crosscutting identifications and for an example of Catholic-Protestant boundary building in a modern society, see Graham MacFarlane, "'It's not as simple as that': The Expression of the Catholic and Protestant Boundary in Northern Irish Rural Communities," in *Symbolising Boundaries: Identity and Diversity in British Cultures*, edited by Anthony P. Cohen (Manchester, U.K., 1986), 88–104. "The cross cutting identification of 'your own' as fellow community members has clear effects on the Catholic and Protestant boundary in people's minds. There is an idea that people who know each other in the round, and not just as Catholics and Protestants, are likely to 'get on better,' even if they are on different sides" (p. 97).

36. As David Nirenberg points out in discussing religious relations in medieval Spain, "religious boundaries were . . . multiple. Depending on the needs of the moment, people might attempt to invoke or efface a great variety of implications of religious difference" (*Communities of Violence: Persecution of Minorities in the Middle Ages* [Princeton, N.J., 1996], 127).

In the first form of boundary, the line between the religious groups was blurred as Catholic and Protestant neighbors subordinated religious allegiance to concerns for family alliances, business dealings, and civic affairs. When parents of one faith chose for their children godparents of the other, or when relatives of one faith participated in the family religious rituals (baptisms, marriages, funerals) of the other, or when Catholics and Huguenots buried their dead side by side in common cemeteries, familial interests overrode a sense of concrete and opposed confessional identities. This type of boundary is the hardest for us to trace because its very indefinability depended on day-to-day, and often unrecorded, sociability. But it was also the product of a certain attitude in which, locally, confessional difference was less important than the tolerance of practical rationality, which Scribner described. In certain circumstances, such as when someone made a temporary conversion for the sake of a cross-confessional marriage, it also depended on an understanding of confessional identity as malleable. An individual's church affiliation could be realigned to suit the social imperatives of family alliances. When this sort of boundary arrangement existed, nonconfessional crosscutting identities were at their strongest, confessional identity was at its weakest, and coexistence was more likely than conflict.

In contrast to this indistinct separation, a much clearer division could delineate the position of each group and, in David Nirenberg's useful formulation, reinforce a boundary that "contributed to the conditions that made possible the continued existence" of the minority in communities.[37] *This second form of boundary arrangement, a negotiated demarcation between the confessions*, was closest to what the Edict of Nantes envisioned and what the state encouraged in the early decades of the century. In biconfessional communities it promoted a situation in which the difference between the religious groups was clearly recognized and even fostered. Each group's worship was distinct: Huguenot psalm singing would not interrupt the celebration of the mass; Catholic processions would not pass by temples when Protestants gathered for worship. Sacred space was parti-

37. Nirenberg, *Communities of Violence*, 228. Nirenberg treats the relations between Jews, Muslims, and Christians in medieval Spain, but his discussion of practices that kept religious groups separate, yet integrated them into communities, opens possibilities for thinking about communal religious boundaries elsewhere.

tioned. Catholics regained their churches, chapels, and religious houses; Protestant temples might be moved but received an agreed-upon location in the community. Deceased Catholics and Protestants were no longer buried next to each other, but their separate cemeteries remained adjacent in arrangements both sides accepted. Positions on town councils were distributed according to quotas, and local militias enrolled carefully stipulated numbers of Catholics and Huguenots.

The confessional groups reached agreements over civic offices, times of worship, cemetery arrangements, and so forth through painstaking negotiations, frequently secured with written contracts. The state's role was crucial in many of these negotiations. Royal commissioners sent to the provinces to enforce the Edict of Nantes mediated or arbitrated the settlements. The contracts Catholics and Huguenots agreed to spoke of their desire to live in peace "under the king's edicts" or "because the king commanded it." But the success of the accords also depended on the willingness of local Catholics and Huguenots to reach accommodations. No doubt feelings of neighborliness and a desire for civic harmony underlay their negotiations, but we cannot assume that townspeople of the two faiths possessed a simple, natural willingness to get along. Their parleys were often quite strained. Tensions were apparent during the relatively peaceful years of Henri IV's reign but were even more evident during the two conflict-ridden decades that followed his death in 1610. It was vital for Catholics and Huguenots in biconfessional communities to reach accommodations to avoid violence. Indeed, as France returned to religious warfare in the 1620s, it became more pressing than ever to do so.

The agreements the two sides reached did not blur confessional difference; indeed it was underscored and confessional identity made more concrete. But the second form of confessional boundary limited conflict and maintained space in towns for both groups to live and worship. We should not assume that the accords always treated the religious groups equally and with complete fairness to the minority. And no doubt making religious identities clearer could lead to increased hostility and create an essential condition for a harsher and more discriminatory situation. Nonetheless, the boundary was constructed locally, by means of cooperation and accommodation. It was the process of negotiation as much as its result that maintained the integration of both groups into a community.

Setting up a clear boundary thus distinguished the groups without necessarily implying rejection and exclusion. But a clearer confessional definition could lead to *the third form of boundary, which separated the groups completely* and led to the ostracizing of Huguenots in the communities they shared with Catholics. Each church's effort to differentiate itself from the other and to impose more orthodox standards of belief and observance was an essential part of this process. But neither church was entirely successful. Much more effective in the construction of the third discriminatory boundary was the policy of persecution to which the state turned in the 1630s and then again under Louis XIV. Insofar as the state and the churches succeeded in constructing this stricter barrier, the distinctiveness of Huguenots as Huguenots and Catholics as Catholics was promoted over the other social identities they possessed. The old fears of social contamination rematerialized and broke the bonds between people of the two faiths. Protestant cemeteries, temples, and schools were expelled from towns or closed down, and thus symbolically Protestants were deprived of their membership in communities.[38] They were increasingly excluded from guilds, professions, and public posts. They lost the freedom to marry Catholics. Their children were sometimes taken away and placed in Catholic homes and orphanages. Only conversion to Catholicism assured the excluded readmission to their communities. Indeed, we can think of this most persecutory phase of boundary building as having two parts. The first was the enclosing of the minority within the strict confessional boundary that defined Protestant identity narrowly. And the second was the placing of great pressure on Huguenots to recross the rigid boundary by converting to the majority faith.

Regardless of the policy the monarchy followed, it could not simply impose its will. It could only encourage coexistence if Catholics and Huguenots were willing to cooperate. So, too, the state needed allies to harass

38. For discussions of the attack on Huguenot temples, see Bernard Dompnier, "La logique d'une destruction: L'église catholique, la royauté et les temples protestants (1680–1685)," in *Révolution française et "vandalisme révolutionnaire": Actes du colloque international de Clermont-Ferrand, 15–17 décembre 1988*, edited by Simone Bernard-Griffiths, Marie-Claude Chemin, and Jean Ehrard (Paris, 1992), 343–51; and Solange Deyon, "La destruction des temples," in *La révocation de l'Édit de Nantes et le protestantisme français en 1685: Actes du colloque de Paris (15–19 octobre 1985)*, edited by Roger Zuber and Laurent Theis (Paris, 1986), 239–59.

Protestants and encourage conversions. Local Catholics filed the lawsuits that led to the closing of Protestant temples, cemeteries, and schools, and they kept their eyes on Huguenot activities, looking for opportunities to register complaints with royal authorities.[39] But local people did not always cooperate with government policies. The state's efforts to encourage coexistence did not, in all cases, succeed in overcoming hostility between Catholics and Huguenots. And Catholics who maintained good relations with their Protestant friends and neighbors frustrated the later policy of persecution. Indeed, good relations could survive even the most intense persecutions, the *dragonnades* of the 1680s leading up to the Revocation of the Edict of Nantes and the repression that followed it.[40]

We should not think of the three possible confessional boundaries as succeeding each other in strict chronological sequence. Different forms could exist simultaneously. For example, neighbors of different faiths might divide cemeteries, thereby constructing the second type of boundary. At the same time, they might blur the confessional division through intermarriage, creating one more like the first. Nonetheless, the overall direction toward discrimination is clear. In some places the third form of boundary appeared quite early. The Catholic Church worked hard to restrict Protestant practices. It often found allies in the judicial system, especially in the *Parlements* (supreme law courts), which, in the years after Henry IV's death, sometimes issued decisions harassing Huguenots. But the state did not mount a concerted anti-Protestant campaign until the 1630s, after the final round of religious warfare. The campaign waned during the years of the *Fronde* (revolts of nobles and officials against royal

39. Historians of Germany have also recently noted the necessary role of local people in furthering confessionalization and thereby have deemphasized the state's role. See Marc Forster, *Counter-Reformation in the Villages: Religion and Reform in the Bishopric of Speyer, 1560–1720* (Ithaca, N.Y., 1992); Harrington and Smith, "Confessionalization in Germany"; and Heinrich Richard Schmidt, "Sozialdisziplinierung?: Ein Plädoyer für das Ende des Etatismus in der Konfessionalisierungsforschung," *Historische Zeitschrift* 265 (December 1997): 639–82.

40. Dragonnades were campaigns in which Louis XIV forced Protestants to convert to Catholicism by quartering mounted troops (i.e., dragoons) in their homes. Accounts of Huguenots who escaped France during the dragonnades of the 1680s make clear how important was the help of friendly Catholics. See, e.g., Jean Migault, *Le journal de Jean Migault: Les dragonnades en Poitou et Saintonge*, edited by N. Weiss and H. Clouzot (1910; reprint, Le Poiré-sur-Vie, 1988).

authority from 1648 to 1653), but efforts to create the third persecutory boundary intensified from the late 1650s to the Revocation of the Edict of Nantes in 1685 and beyond.[41]

SACRED BOUNDARIES

It is fitting that a book concerned with religious mixing should itself be mixed in its geographical focus and methodology. Many of the best recent works on Catholics and Protestants in early-modern France are regional or community studies.[42] *Sacred Boundaries*, by contrast, poses questions not about a specific location but about the process by which Huguenots and Catholics arranged the boundary between them, constructed and re-constructed their group identities by doing so, and found ways to live together despite confessional rivalry. Certain issues the book discusses—agreements between religious groups, the division of sacred space in communities, the management of religious life in confessionally mixed families—can best be examined through specific local examples. To do so I draw material from the western province of Poitou, where the interchange between the Catholic majority and a large and often-powerful Protestant population left documentation in communal agreements between confessional groups, petitions to government officials, court cases, royal orders, accounts of Catholic missionary work, family records, personal correspondence, memoirs, and fragmentary consistorial registers. Rarely does this documentation allow for the sort of quantitative analyses social historians have undertaken in tracing Huguenot demographic de-

41. Various recent works survey the increasing persecution. See Garrisson, *Édit de Nantes*, 119–262; Jean Quéniart, *La révocation de l'Édit de Nantes: Protestants et catholiques français de 1598 à 1685* (Paris, 1985), 101–33; Labrousse, *"Une foi, une loi, un roi,"* 125–95; and Brian E. Strayer, *Huguenots and Camisards as Aliens in France 1598–1789: The Struggle for Religious Toleration* (Lewiston, N.Y., 2001), 53–141.

42. Or even family studies. See Raymond A. Mentzer, *Blood and Belief: Family Survival and Confessional Identity among the Provincial Huguenot Nobility* (West Lafayette, Ind., 1994). For examples of regional or community studies, see Sauzet, *Contre-réforme et réforme catholique;* Yves Krumenacker, *Les protestants du Poitou au XVIIIe siècle (1681–1789)* (Paris, 1998); Stéphane Capot, *Justice et religion en Languedoc au temps de l'Édit de Nantes: La chambre de l'édit de Castres (1579–1679)* (Paris, 1998); Hanlon, *Confession and Community;* and Pérouas, *La Rochelle.*

cline or in mapping religious commitment through studies of baptism and consistorial injunctions against wayward church members.[43] But these sources do permit a close examination of the interactions between the confessional groups, which is this study's subject.

Poitou provides excellent examples of how the first and second forms of confessional boundary were constructed. But it was also a testing ground for the construction of the third form of boundary from the work of Catholic missionaries in 1617, to the legal offensive against Reformed worship in the 1630s, to the first dragonnade repressing Protestantism in 1681. Thus the example of Poitou reminds us that while Catholics and Protestants constructed the confessional boundary locally, they had to do so within a framework of opportunities and constraints the state and churches established. Government policies, the churches' disputes, the gendered nature of confessional polemics, and the meaning of conversion all contributed to the building of this framework—and all of these topics will be considered here. The sources used to examine them—royal legislation, polemical publications, conversion accounts—are best studied without being limited geographically, though we can certainly be aware of their local ramifications. Thus this book is not a local or regional study but moves between the local and the national to trace the means by which confessional boundaries were shaped.

Since each of the following chapters explores a specific topic or site in which Protestants and Catholics constructed the boundary between them, the book is methodologically diverse. Each chapter adopts the approach appropriate to the particular subject addressed and the sources used. It includes community studies, ritual analysis, family history, and examinations of the discourses of missionary rhetoric, gendered religious polemics, and conversion accounts. The sheer variety of topics and methods available—by no means exhausted here—demonstrate the richness of the material to be explored but also the impact the confessional boundary issue had on so many aspects of early-modern life. It should also be noted that, given its topical organization, the book does not present a chronological narrative of Catholic and Protestant history from the proclama-

43. See, e.g., Benedict, *Huguenot Population;* Mentzer, "Marking the Taboo"; and Philippe Chareyre, "'The Great Difficulties One Must Bear to Follow Jesus Christ': Morality at Sixteenth-Century Nîmes," in *Sin and the Calvinists*, 63–96.

tion of the Edict of Nantes in 1598 to its revocation in 1685.[44] Each chapter covers the timeframe relevant to its subject. While the first chapter does provide a starting point by discussing the construction of coexistence in the decades immediately following the Edict of Nantes, the others are bounded not by time but by the questions they pose and the availability of sources to provide answers. Similarly, chronological development does not govern the chapters' order. Instead, they are arranged in a way that traces the construction of the boundary in different spheres—one might think of them as levels—of confessional interaction, first in communities, then in households and gender attitudes, and finally in individual consciences.

Chapter 1 examines how local people and the state negotiated the uneasy balance of religious conflict and coexistence in biconfessional communities. It argues that, at least in its first decades, the Edict of Nantes offered the means by which the government and local religious groups could limit strife and arrive at, if not toleration, then a way for the rival faiths to live together. In some communities confessional relations were hostile and remained so. But in others tensions were eased and potential conflicts avoided by careful negotiations over issues including the holding of civic offices, times of religious observances, or access to schools and hospitals. The agreements the two sides reached did not blur the confessional boundary; instead, they contributed to making confessional identity concrete. The result was the second form of confessional boundary, the sort the Edict of Nantes envisioned. Conflict was averted, and space was maintained in towns for both groups to live and worship.

Chapter 2 looks at the program Catholic missionaries promoted to eliminate the first two forms of boundary in favor of the third. It takes as its example a Capuchin mission in Poitou, starting in 1617, which was the first full-scale anti-Protestant missionary campaign in France. The Capuchins wanted to erect an impermeable barrier around those they considered heretics, a barrier that would ostracize Huguenots and lure them to convert as the only means of reintegrating themselves into their commu-

44. Though it certainly draws on such narrative histories. See, e.g., Auguste-François Lièvre, *Histoire des protestants et des églises réformées du Poitou*, 3 vols. (Paris, 1856–1859); and Pierre Dez, *Histoire des protestants et des églises réformées du Poitou* (La Rochelle, 1936).

nities and the kingdom. Mission records described the Capuchins' impact as a shock wave that provoked a rupture between the religious groups. They conducted public rituals to strengthen Catholic fervor and alienate Huguenots; they combated Protestant ministers in debates; and they converted prominent Huguenot nobles. They also attacked the Huguenots' public presence in communities by reclaiming churches and cemeteries for Catholic use and by taking over civic spaces, such as markets, for their mission exercises. The missionaries did not rid the region of heresy, but they did demonstrate for future anti-Protestant campaigners how to pursue the third type of confessional boundary by concretizing religious identities, raising confessional tensions, and placing Huguenots on the defensive.

Chapter 3 considers the arrangement of cemeteries as an example of how the confessional boundary was manifested in communities. In these important civic spaces each of the different forms of confessional boundary took physical shape. Despite the Catholic prohibition on burying heretics in sacred ground, and despite the provisions of the Edict of Nantes, Catholics and Huguenots were often interred side by side in parish cemeteries. This mixing created an indistinct boundary of the first sort, in which religious affiliation was ignored in favor of placing the dead near their previously buried kin, regardless of their confession. Huguenots maintained access to a central communal institution and space, and they thereby continued to claim full membership in their communities. Furthermore, to display status and gain acceptance among Catholic neighbors, they often evaded the strict austerity Calvinist doctrine demanded and included in their funeral ceremonies elements resembling those in Catholic burials, a practice that also blurred the confessional border. The second form of boundary was established when officials or locals, insisting on a stricter separation, divided cemeteries into two adjacent burial grounds. Catholics and Huguenots would no longer be buried next to each other, but both groups maintained an agreed-upon place within communal sacred space. Pressure from Catholic authorities and eventually from the state led to the third form of boundary. Huguenot cemeteries were pushed outside of towns or closed down entirely. Royal legislation also placed stricter limits on the times and size of Protestant funerals, thus reducing their usefulness to Huguenots as a means of maintaining a public presence in their communities.

Chapter 4 shifts the focus from boundary construction in communities to that within families by discussing intermarriage and confessional relations in religiously mixed households. Seventeenth-century royal legislation and jurisprudence promoted strategies by which families consolidated wealth and increased social standing, such as through making socially advantageous marriages for their offspring. But when these strategies led to weddings between Catholics and Huguenots, they ran afoul of the churches' insistence on maintaining religious uniformity in households. For both churches, intermarriage signaled a dangerous permeability of the confessional boundary. As this chapter shows, however, mixed marriages could have a variety of consequences. A blurred boundary of the first sort resulted from family members of the two faiths participating in each other's rituals, such as baptisms, marriages, and funerals. Some families established the second form of boundary by means of a cooperative arrangement that maintained separate and distinct religious practices in the home. In others, religious disputes led to a tense atmosphere, and the third hostile boundary prevailed. Whatever the ultimate arrangement of the household confessional boundary, most mixed marriages depended on the conversion of one spouse, usually the wife, prior to the wedding. Often these converts returned to their original faith. Both churches found this malleability of individual religious identity disturbing, and eventually the monarchy outlawed relapses to Protestantism. It thereby sought to secure Catholic religious affiliation and undermine the Reformed Church. But in doing so it also obstructed the family strategies that lay behind intermarriage.

In mixed marriages, women's confessional identity was seen as dangerously insecure. But in the polemical battles between the faiths, women were more often criticized for being passionately attached to the wrong faith rather than for religious indeterminacy. Chapter 5 focuses on the portrayal of women as religious amazons or *femmes fortes* (powerful women) and the role these characterizations played in confessional boundary building. It examines the debate over women's religious activities and learning, as well as the controversies over prominent and powerful women of both churches who challenged accepted gender boundaries. I argue that depictions of women and their religious activities were equivocal. Not surprisingly, religious error was often associated with the feminine. Yet at the same time women were also championed as the "devout sex," naturally more pious than men and more apt to practice a heroic faith. Such gendered categorizations provided each church a means of celebrating its heroines while condemning the rival as a religion that gave women too much authority or too large a role in public life. The disputes over religious heroines raised the public prominence of women, whose subordination to men in religious life was usually unquestioned. But they also hardened the confessional barrier.

After tracing the construction of confessional boundaries in communities, families, and gender categories, this study turns in Chapter 6 to what, for the churches, was the ultimate arena of their struggle: personal conscience. Because conscience was seen as the locus of religious truth, it became the decisive site in which the confessional boundary had to be built. And here it was constructed through conversions. I examine in this chapter the accounts converts published of their religious changes. These accounts elaborated Catholic and Protestant models of the sincere conversion. By detailing the converts' wrestling with spiritual turmoil, their examination of rival doctrines, their acceptance of the true faith, and their rejection of the false one, these models sought to make conversions irrevocable and the confessional boundary impermeable. Once a convert had crossed the confessional frontier, there would be no going back. But as this chapter shows, the models did not always work; religious changes were not irrevocable. A number of those who abjured their original faith later returned to it. The motives behind relapses were complex, and the churches did not willingly accept them as sincere. But they often served family or political imperatives, and they thereby indicate how, despite the insistence of churches and the state, the demands of society continued to require flexible confessional identity and a traversable confessional boundary.

The topics covered in these chapters illustrate the process of boundary construction at work in communities, families, and individuals' lives. The religious situation in France, governed by the Edict of Nantes as well as by later and, often harsher, legislation, was not exactly the same as in other early-modern states, much less other countries at other times. Nonetheless, the way in which the two religious groups cooperated in the first boundary arrangement, accommodated each other across the second, and struggled when opponents of coexistence tried to establish the third provides an approach to thinking about religious relations and the formation of confessional identities elsewhere. The conclusions *Sacred Boundaries* draws about confessional boundary building will help those seeking to understand religious conflict and coexistence in early-modern Europe. But I hope they will also have resonance for those concerned with the many other times and places in which different religious groups have had to find ways to live together.

SACRED BOUNDARIES

Major Protestant Communities in Seventeenth-Century Poitou

PROTESTANTS, CATHOLICS, AND THE STATE

Constructing Communal Coexistence

IT MIGHT SEEM STRANGE to begin a history of Catholic-Protestant relations in seventeenth-century France by suggesting that the boundary between the two groups was anything but solid. After all, over three decades of vicious religious warfare should have more than sufficed to construct an impermeable confessional barrier. But in the years after the Edict of Nantes, the boundary was not so clear, nor the division between Huguenots and Catholics so strict. We have much evidence that in many communities they were willing to cooperate across the confessional divide, a willingness essential for the restoration of order. Yet, at the same time, we must acknowledge that confessional conflict did not disappear.

Explaining the presence of both strife and coexistence in biconfessional communities has proved difficult, and historians tend to emphasize one or the other by assuming either that religious conflict was unavoidable or that good relations inevitably grew out of daily interactions between Catholics and Protestants. Thus, in some accounts, Huguenots appear well integrated into their communities, living on good, neighborly terms with Catholics. Familial, social, business, intellectual, and political contacts produced shared concerns, evident, for example, in a desire for peace, and a common cultural code, such as in attitudes toward family honor.[1] In other studies, the two groups maintained a much stricter separation; they in-

1. This theme is common in recent works, such as Labrousse, *"Une foi, une loi, un roi,"* 68–88; Sauzet, *Contre-réforme et réforme catholique;* and Hanlon, *Confession and Community.*

termarried little, exhibited little comprehension or sufferance of each other's religious beliefs and practices, and fell frequently into conflict.[2]

The model of confessional boundary construction offered here can address this interpretative dilemma by focusing our attention on how coexistence or conflict was constructed in communities where the two religious groups lived together. It can illustrate the ways in which shared interests, daily interactions, and an emphasis on civic rather than confessional identity helped create good relations of the sort found in the first and most indistinct form of confessional boundary. But it also acknowledges that what looks like social harmony might often have been the result of the locally weaker group adapting itself to the dominance of the locally stronger group. Thus in places where the Protestants were weak, they often observed religious strictures that had no place in Reformed theology out of care not to offend Catholic sensibilities.[3] Similarly, in communities Huguenots dominated, Catholics sometimes found it hard to reestablish their worship, despite the Edict of Nantes's insistence on their prerogative to do so.[4]

The confessional boundary model can also explore the situation in which the two confessional identities were clear but both were accommodated. This second form of confessional boundary was constructed through negotiations over specific, often tense, issues: for example, local power sharing, competing religious observances, and the partition of communal sacred space. The day-to-day neighborliness of Catholics and Huguenots could not easily assuage conflicts over such matters, and often agents from outside the community had to intervene. It is easy to describe outsiders, like missionaries, as determined to embroil peaceful neighbors of the two faiths in their "enterprises of fanaticization."[5] And it is true

2. See, e.g., Pérouas, *La Rochelle*, 143–44, 175–77; and Gabriel Audisio, "Se marier en Luberon: Catholiqes et protestants vers 1630," in *Histoire sociale, sensibilités collectives et mentalités: Mélanges Robert Mandrou* (Paris, 1985), 231–45.

3. Philip Benedict argues that the relative local strength of the two groups and the degree of insecurity the local minority felt were often determining factors in confessional relations (*Huguenot Population*, 49, 84–85).

4. See the southwestern communities Gregory Hanlon examines in *Univers des gens de bien*, 229–32. Hanlon suggests that true tolerance might only have been possible where the religious groups were roughly equal (338).

5. Dompnier, *Venin de l'hérésie*, 154.

that they often provoked conflict. But other outsiders, such as royal officials, could help build good relations by mediating disputes, imposing agreements on community members, and reminding them that the king wanted them to live in peace.

The boundary model also shows that sometimes negotiations failed or were just impossible, which led to the third, harshest, form of confessional division. In communities where this boundary triumphed, good confessional relations suffered as the minority was excluded from full participation in communal life, denied the free and complete exercise of its religion, and forcefully pressured to convert. But, as was the case with the second boundary, the third was not the result of local interactions alone. Here too the king's role was crucial. When royal policy changed from encouraging accommodation to pursuing persecution through legislation, the courts, and, finally, military force, then the construction of the third boundary took on speed. That persecution did eventually become royal policy has made it seem inevitable to some historians.[6] But the monarchy followed another path in the early decades of the century when Henri IV and the religious settlement envisioned in the Edict of Nantes sought to construct the second (not the first, but also not the third) form of confessional boundary.

THE EDICT OF NANTES AND HENRI IV'S RELIGIOUS POLICY

The Edict of Nantes established a framework for interconfessional cooperation, but its complexity and ambiguities also laid the basis for future conflicts. It included four separate texts: the formal edict, consisting of a preamble and ninety-two articles (ninety-five in the original version); fifty-six "secret" articles; and two royal warrants.[7] Certain provisions in the se-

6. E.g., Garrisson in *Édit de Nantes.*

7. For a text of the document, see Catherine Bergeal and Antoine Durrleman, *Protestantisme et libertés en France au 17e siècle de l'Édit de Nantes à sa révocation, 1598–1685* (Carrières-sous-Poissy, 1985), 11–59, or Bernard Cottret, *1598, L'Édit de Nantes: Pour en finir avec les guerres de religion* (Paris, 1997), 361–84. The English translation of the ninety-two articles by E. Everard (published in 1681 in *The Great Pressures and Grievances of the Protestants in France*) along with a modern translation of the secret articles and the warrants can be found in Roland Mousnier, *The Assassination of Henri IV: The Tyranni-*

cret articles and warrants provided exceptions to or contradictions of the formal edict.[8] The two versions in which the law existed, one that the king signed in the spring of 1598 and the other that the Parlement of Paris ratified in February 1599, further complicated its enforcement. The Parlement refused to agree to certain parts of the original document and changed the wording of others.[9] Huguenots saw the unratified document as more favorable and insisted on its validity; their Catholic opponents held to the Parlement's version. Henri IV allowed the court's alterations to stand.

The edict and the policy of pacification it represented had to address a series of tension-ridden issues, including an amnesty for wartime offenses, the establishment of each church's worship, the organization of a justice system that could adjudicate Catholic-Protestant disputes fairly, the social integration of the minority, financial support of its church, and its military protection. Above all, for Henri's policy to succeed, it was essential to break the cycle of retribution for outrages committed during the wars. The edict declared "that the memory of all things passed" during the wars "shall remain extinguished and suppressed, such as things that had never been" (Article 1).[10] Of course, memories of bloodshed were not so easily disposed of, but the article stipulated that courts would no longer hear cases stemming from wartime violence.

Matters of religious practice had to be regulated in a way that would

---

cide Problem and the Consolidation of the French Absolute Monarchy in the Early Seventeenth Century, translated by Joan Spencer (New York, 1973), 316–63. I have modernized Everard's spelling. On the different texts, see Emile G. Léonard, *Histoire générale du protestantisme*, 3 vols. (Paris, 1988), 2:146.

8. E.g., to honor agreements Henri had made with the Catholic League prior to 1598 that prohibited Reformed worship in places where the edict would have allowed it.

9. Cottret shows the differences in *1598, L'Édit de Nantes*, 361–84. See also "Note sur les éditions de l'Édit," in Michel Grandjean, "Présentation," in *Coexister dans l'intolérance: L'Édit de Nantes (1598)*, edited by Michel Grandjean and Bernard Roussel (Geneva, 1998), 7–14, see esp. 14.

10. Mousnier, *Assassination*, 318. Also see Diane C. Margolf, *Religion and Royal Justice in Early Modern France: The Paris Chambre de l'Edit, 1598–1665* (Kirksville, Mo., 2003), 75–98; "Adjudicating Memory: Law and Religious Difference in Early Seventeenth-Century France," *Sixteenth Century Journal* 27 (1996): 399–418; and "The Edict of Nantes's Amnesty: Appeals to the *Chambre de l'Edit*, 1600–1610," *Proceedings of the Annual Conference of the Western Society for French History* 16 (1988):49–55.

ensure Protestantism's protection while guaranteeing Catholicism's status as the legally dominant religion. Catholic worship was permitted everywhere, and it was to be restored in places where Huguenots had halted it. Protestants could not obstruct the Catholic clergy in conducting religious observances, and they had to surrender any churches and other ecclesiastical properties they had taken during the wars. Nonetheless, in confessionally mixed areas, the majority faith would now have to share space with the religion it deemed a heresy. Huguenots were permitted "to live and dwell in all the cities and places of [the] kingdom . . . without being inquired after, vexed, molested, or compelled to do anything in religion, contrary to their conscience" (Article 6). But they could not publicly practice their religion everywhere. In towns with established Protestant congregations, the edict authorized Reformed worship either by "possession" or "concession." Huguenots "possessed" a legitimate exercise of their religion in locales where they had regularly exercised their faith in 1596 and 1597. They were also "conceded" public worship in the suburbs of one town in each *bailliage* or *sénéchausée* (intermediate-level court jurisdictions) where they lived (Articles 9 and 10).[11] But they could not build a temple on an ecclesiastical fief or in a city that was an episcopal seat. The edict also prohibited Huguenot worship in Paris and a five-league radius around it (Articles 11 and 14). Huguenot noblemen, who possessed the feudal privilege of "high justice," were permitted "fief" worship on their estates for their families, dependents, and other local coreligionists. Those nobles not entitled to "high justice" were only allowed private worship for their families and households with no more than thirty participants (Articles 7 and 8).

Within these restrictions, Huguenots could establish temples, cemeteries, and schools. They could send a deputy general to represent them before the king. They could maintain the governing structure of their church with its local consistories, regional *colloques* (conferences) and synods, and national synods, but they would no longer be able legally to hold

11. A privilege first granted them in the Peace of Bergerac (1577) and the "conference" of Fleix (1580); see Cottret, *1598, L'Édit de Nantes*, 356–57. See also Andrew Spicer, "'Qui est de Dieu oit la parole de Dieu': The Huguenots and Their Temples," in *Society and Culture in the Huguenot World, 1559–1685*, edited by Raymond A. Mentzer and Andrew Spicer (Cambridge, U.K., 2002), 175–92, see esp. 180.

political assemblies, such as those that had organized Huguenot military activities during the wars.[12] And they were forced to abide by certain regulations governing Catholic religious life that were contrary to Reformed teachings. They had to pay the local ecclesiastical tithe, an obligation so intricately bound to property ownership in French communities that it would have been difficult to exempt Huguenots from it (Article 25). They had to close their shops and do no work on Catholic festivals so as not to disturb Catholics observing the celebrations (Article 20). They did not have to decorate the fronts of their houses on such festivals, but they had to allow local authorities to do so (Secret Article 3). And they had to observe Catholic marriage rules regarding consanguinity and the prohibition of weddings during Lent (Article 23).

Reformed religious institutions and practices would thus distinguish the minority, but otherwise it was to be fully integrated into French society. All official positions were open to Huguenots, and so were professional corporations, craft organizations, universities, hospitals, and poor relief institutions. They paid the same taxes and conducted their family affairs as Catholics did. And they had the same guarantee of justice in the king's courts. To ensure that they received it, the edict set up (Articles 30 and 31) *chambres de l'édit* with a fixed number of Huguenot judges in the Parlements of Paris, Rouen, and Rennes and *chambres mi-partie* with equal numbers of Catholic and Protestant judges in the Parlements of Bordeaux, Grenoble, and Toulouse (actually located in Castres). The detailed attention the edict paid to these chambers and judicial matters in general was a testament to the importance in the peace process of settling confessional conflicts in institutions under royal authority rather than on city streets and battlefields.

Henri was caught in 1598 between Catholics who opposed concessions to the minority, such as many parlementary judges, and Huguenots who demanded more of them. That is why some of the law's most controversial components were listed not in the formal edict or its appended "secret

12. The king weakened this prohibition when he did not insist on the disbanding of the political assembly that had sat continuously during the negotiations of the edict and that would continue after its promulgation. In 1601 Henri allowed for the regular holding of assemblies to elect the Protestant representative to the court. See Garrisson, *Édit de Nantes*, 19–20; and Léonard, *Histoire générale*, 2:148.

articles" but in two *brevets*, or warrants, which the Parlements would not have to register.[13] One of these contained Henri's promise of financial support to the Reformed Church for ministers' salaries. In a sense, this offer compensated Protestants for their obligatory payment of the tithe. The other consisted of Henri's agreement to allow Huguenots to maintain "surety towns" in which they could keep military garrisons. Probably nothing in the edict proved to be as controversial as this concession, which threatened to create a Huguenot "state within the state." But the Huguenot military threat was too strong for the king to ignore. And unlike the edict's formal provisions, which Parlements registered and which were declared "perpetual and irrevocable," those of the warrants had a limited term of eight years.[14] In principle, Protestants would only be able to maintain a separate military force for that time, though in actuality they maintained it until Louis XIII's defeat of the final Huguenot rebellion in 1628.

The Edict of Nantes thus provided the foundation for peace but also the basis for future disputes. As a result, historians have been divided in their appraisal of the possibility it created for confessional coexistence. Some see the edict as advantageous for Protestants and as a major step in the direction of modern religious toleration and liberty.[15] Others have seen it as a victory for Catholicism, which spelled the eventual doom of legally protected Protestant worship in the kingdom.[16]

13. Mounsier, *Assassination*, 358–63; Bergeal and Durrleman, *Protestantisme et libertés*, 55–61.

14. The term "perpetual and irrevocable" was the source of future disputes. Protestants took it at face value and argued that later kings could not change the laws governing them. But an edict was perpetual and irrevocable only until a later royal edict, which the Parlements duly registered, overturned it. See Holt, *French Wars of Religion*, 163.

15. See, e.g., John Viénot's assessment that the edict posed "the principal of tolerance." "Artificial religious unity was broken in favor of liberty, and France had the honor of having proclaimed, for the first time in a public and official act, that souls are free to profess the religion that seems to them the best"; John Viénot, *Histoire de la réforme française* (Paris, 1926), 1:455, 461 (my translation), quoted in Dompnier, *Venin de l'hérésie*, 22–23.

16. Janine Garrisson's views are perhaps the most negative of all; see *Édit de Nantes*, 16, 18–22, and *L'Homme protestant* (Paris, 1980), 32. For others who have recently argued that the edict did not and was not intended to create religious toleration in France, see Mounsier, *Assassination*, 143, 148; Hanlon, *Confession and Community*, 21, 125; Michael Wolfe, *The Conversion of Henri IV: Politics, Power, and Religious Belief in Ear-*

To be sure, the Edict of Nantes did not create a tolerant or religiously neutral state.[17] It did not grant religious liberty in the modern sense of the term as based on individual right and the privacy of conscience. "Liberty of conscience" pertained to the faithful of the Reformed Church only as members of a group, not as individuals. Protestants were recognized as a *corps* (a collectivity) within the state, which, like other corps, had a royal grant of privileges. Toleration was not seen as a positive outcome of religious difference. In the common understanding of the term, to "tolerate" another religion meant to endure its existence only because its elimination was not possible.[18] Yet in recognizing the edict's limitations and in acknowledging that over the long run it did not prevent persecution, we may have deflated too much of the Edict of Nantes's potential for creating, if not toleration, then religious coexistence.

Coexistence was the immediate goal of the person responsible for the edict's enforcement: Henri IV. It is likely that he hoped Catholic unity would eventually be restored. The edict's preamble suggests this idea by stating: "But now that it has pleased God to give us . . . some rest, we think we cannot employ our self better, than to . . . provide that he may be adored and prayed unto by all our subjects: *and if it has not yet pleased him to permit it to be in one and the same form of religion, that it may be at the least be with one and the same intention.*"[19] The king's meaning here seems clear: he foresaw a time when all his subjects would be of one religion, namely, Catholicism.[20] Unity would come not from repression of the minority but from compromises between the two religions on matters of

ly Modern France (Cambridge, Mass., 1993), 182–83; and Cottret, *1598, L'Édit de Nantes*, 250.

17. Nor was the Edict of Nantes unique. On regimes of biconfessional parity or religious coexistence elsewhere in Europe, see François, *Protestants et catholiques en Allemagne;* Jean-Pierre Kintz and Georges Livet, eds., *350e anniversaire des Traités de Westphalie, 1648–1998: Une genèse de l'Europe, une société à reconstruire. Actes du colloque international tenu à l'initiative de l'Université Marc Bloch, Université des Sciences Humaines et de la Ville de Strasbourg* (Strasbourg, 1999); and Bérenger, *Tolérance ou paix de religion*.

18. Elisabeth Labrousse, "Religious Toleration," in *Dictionary of the History of Ideas*, 4 vols. (New York, 1973), 4:112–21; and Dompnier, *Venin de l'hérésie*, 24–25.

19. Quoted from Mousnier, *Assassination*, 317 (emphasis added).

20. See also Dompnier, *Venin de l'hérésie*, 24; and Holt, *French Wars of Religion*, 164.

doctrine and practice, perhaps arrived at by a general council of the French Church, an idea that *politiques*, some Gallican Catholics, and some Protestants had long promoted.[21]

But the immediate goal of pacifying the kingdom called for accommodations in which each group gained concessions, and it depended on the king's interpretation and enforcement of the edict. Recent historians, even those who see the edict as essentially unfair to Protestants, generally have had a positive assessment of Henri's balanced approach to enforcing it.[22] But it is better to think of him as tacking back and forth in a series of decisions that would mollify first one side, then the other, thereby gaining his immediate objectives: an armistice, an amnesty for acts committed during the wars, and the regulation of religious coexistence by which the majority faith would be restored throughout the kingdom and the minority faith protected. These were the goals of Henri's policy, and the Edict of Nantes provided the legal framework for pursuing them. They led essentially to the second form of confessional boundary. Neither the law nor the king envisioned a blurring of confessional identities. And neither promoted the suppression of the minority through force. Pending some future resolution of religious differences, each group's confessional identity was to be secure and embodied in its church's institutional organization, beliefs, and practices. But accommodations would allow each a legally recognized place in French society.

Temporary concessions such as the Huguenot surety towns aside, this confessional arrangement also furthered Henri's political interests by making the monarchy the arbiter of disagreements between Catholics

21. Politiques were Catholic moderates who sought to preserve the state in the face of religious conflict and to work peacefully to restore Catholic unity. In a manifesto issued at Châtellerault in March 1589, Henri spoke of a council as the "true road" to religious unity. In a declaration issued at Saint-Cloud in August of the same year, he promised to maintain the Catholic religion in France and expressed a personal desire to receive instruction from a "good, legitimate, and free national or general council." See Joseph Lecler, *Histoire de la tolérance au siècle de la réforme* (1955; reprint, Paris, 1994), 496–501. On Henri's beliefs, see also Wolfe, *Conversion*, 56–57, 155–58, 163–67; Wanegffelen, *Ni Rome ni Genève*, 397–406; and Ronald S. Love, *Blood and Religion: The Conscience of Henri IV, 1553–1593* (Montreal, 2001), 269–304.

22. Léonard, *Histoire général*, 2:148–49; Mousnier, *Assassination*, 153; Garrisson, *Édit de Nantes*, 26; and Labrousse, *"Une foi, une loi, un roi,"* 29.

and Protestants; by forcing them to bring their disputes before the king, his officials, and his courts; and by reducing religious violence.[23] As we will see in Poitou, religious coexistence also grew out of the interest of Protestants and Catholics in "getting along." But even locally constructed coexistence would depend upon the monarchy's enforcement of the edict. It was not the pursuit of religious conformity or confessionalization that helped build a powerful monarchy, as it did in the German states. Rather, the goal was achieved through creating a regime in which the government guaranteed and policed religious difference.

COEXISTENCE AND CONFLICT IN POITOU

The province of Poitou provides an excellent setting in which to examine confessional boundary building in communities the religious groups shared. We have much evidence of Catholics and Protestants cooperating, but we also know there were acts of intolerance, sometimes violent ones. The province proved to be a staging ground for the policies of the state and the Catholic Church toward Protestantism. It was the site of the first Catholic mission to convert Huguenots in 1617, and it endured repeated military campaigns during the religious warfare of the 1620s. The government established a special regional court there in the 1630s to target Protestant worship. And, in the 1680s, it suffered the first dragonnades, which led up to the Revocation of the Edict of Nantes in 1685. As with other areas in which the two faiths lived side by side, royal officials worked hard in Poitou in the years after 1598, enforcing the Edict of Nantes's provisions and negotiating religious relations. The effects of their work and of the spirit of cooperation found in many biconfessional communities survived into the harsher middle decades of the century up to the Revocation. Even during the 1680s and after, Huguenots could often count on their Catholic neighbors for help in escaping persecution.[24]

23. See Cottret, *1598, L'Édit de Nantes*, 215.

24. As the schoolteacher Jean Migault described the account of his escape from France; see *Journal de Jean Migault*, 133, 141, 151, 190–91. André Benoist presents examples of good relations during the middle decades of the century in "Les populations rurales du 'Moyen-Poitou' protestant de 1640 à 1789: Économie, religion, société dans une groupe de paroisses de l'éléction de Saint-Maixent" (Thèse de 3e cycle, Université de Poitiers, 1983), 231, and "Catholiques et protestants en 'Moyen-Poitou' jusqu'à la

Protestant ideas had first appeared in Poitou in the 1530s, spreading from La Rochelle and from Poitiers, after Calvin's brief stay there in 1534. The religion took root in rural wool-working areas in the west, in the towns of the province's center, and on noble estates.[25] In the 1580s perhaps as much as one-third of the province's population was Protestant.[26] Poitou was a prime arena for the violence of the religious wars, especially the first (1562) and the third (1568–1570).[27] However, the massacre of Saint Bartholomew's Day (1572) had a relatively small impact on the province. And by the mid-1570s, the Catholic-Protestant confrontation was giving way to a more complicated situation. Politique Catholics and Protestant leaders formed alliances, such as that between the Catholic François de Valois, duc d'Alençon and the Poitevin Huguenot military leader Claude de La Trémoille. Among the lower orders, revulsion against warfare, banditry, and rapidly rising taxes sparked popular opposition to both sides.[28] A 1575 petition to the king from Poitou made clear the inhabitants' sense of victimization: "As for the soldiers who come to our defense, considering their behavior, we see no difference between friend and foe." A local chronicler during these years described the pillaging of homes, food, and flocks: "everyone asks for mercy," and from everywhere came the same cry, "we are sick of it [*Nous sommes las*]!"[29]

Peasant rebellion in the 1570s foreshadowed social unrest during the

---

révocation de l'Édit de Nantes, 1534–1685," *Bulletin de la société historique et scientifique des Deux-Sèvres*, 2nd ser., 16, no. 1 (1983): 300, 318.

25. For accounts of the growth of Poitevin Protestantism, see Lièvre, *Histoire des protestants;* Dez, *Histoire des protestants;* Benoist, "Catholiques et protestants," 235–39, and "Populations rurales," 223–30, 320; Krumenacker, *Les protestants du Poitou*, 32–38; and Jacques Marcadé and Marie-Louise Fracard, "Le XVIe siècle: Le temps des crises," in *Le diocèse de Poitiers*, edited by Robert Favreau (Paris, 1988), 114–34.

26. Marcadé and Fracard, "Temps des crises," 120–21; and P. Boissonade, *Histoire de Poitou* (Paris, 1926), 201, 206.

27. For a discussion of the Wars of Religion in Poitou, see, in addition to the works noted above, Nicole Vray, *Protestants de l'ouest: Bretagne, Normandie, Poitou, 1517–1907* (Rennes, 1993), 77–104.

28. Philip Benedict, *Rouen during the Wars of Religion* (Cambridge, U.K., 1981), 240–43; and Holt, *French Wars of Religion*, 98–120.

29. Quoted in Boissonnade, *Poitou*, 214. Yves-Marie Bercé, *History of Peasant Revolts: The Social Origins of Rebellion in Early Modern France*, translated by Amanda Whitmore (Ithaca, N.Y., 1990), 97.

years of conflict between Henri IV and the Catholic League.[30] What became evident during these last stages of warfare was that social resentments could forge alliances across the confessional divide. Sectarian violence did not entirely disappear. The Catholic Leaguers committed one of the last atrocities of the Wars of Religion in Poitou: the August 1595 massacre of Protestants worshipping at La Brossadière, near La Châtaigneraie.[31] But this turn of the conflict from religious and toward social confrontation blurred the confessional boundary and created the possibility for establishing a coexistence largely founded on reaction against war and disruption.

Poitou would be an important testing ground for the construction of coexistence because of the size and power of its Huguenot population. At the beginning of the seventeenth century, the province had between 80,000 and 100,000 Protestants. Benedict estimated the Huguenot population of the province in the 1660s to have been around 77,500.[32] At that time, according to Louis XIV's intendant in Poitou, Charles Colbert de Croissy, Huguenots accounted for about 10 percent of the population.[33]

Thus Protestants were never more than a small minority, but their geographical and social distribution gave them a weight beyond their numbers, leading some Catholics, like the seventeenth-century Benedictine church historian Dom Liaboeuf, to think of Poitou as "one of the provinces the most infested with heresy in all of France."[34] We can conve-

30. As Benedict points out, peasant rebels sometimes came from both religious groups; see Benedict, *Rouen*, 240–42, 246n.1, 248n.1. Poitiers was a League stronghold, but otherwise the province was a center of the royalist cause; see Boissonnade, *Poitou*, 208.

31. A.-F. Lièvre, *Les martyrs poitevins* (1874; reprint, La Mothe-Saint-Héray, 1984), 50–55. See also Léonard, *Histoire générale*, 2:146n.3.

32. Samuel Mours, *Les églises réformées en France: Tableaux et cartes* (Paris, 1958), and *Essai sommaire de géographie du protestantisme français au XVIIe siècle* (Paris, 1966); Louis Pérouas, "La 'Mission de Poitou' des capuçins pendant le premier quart du XVIIe siècle," *Bulletin et mémoires de la société des antiquaires de l'ouest et des musées du Poitiers*, 4th ser., 7, no. 1 (1964): 349–62, see esp. 349n.3; Marcadé and Fracard, "Temps des crises," 132; and Benedict, *Huguenot Population*, 10. See also Philip Benedict, "La population réformée française de 1600 à 1685," *Annales: Économies, sociétés, civilisations*, no. 6 (November–December 1987): 1433–65.

33. Charles Colbert de Croissy, *État du Poitou sous Louis XIV: Rapport au roi et mémoire sur le clergé, la noblesse, la justice et les finances* (Poitiers, 1976), 22.

34. Quoted in Benoist, "Catholiques et protestants," 242.

niently examine the geographical distribution of Protestants in the province by following the administrative divisions into which the Protestant churches grouped themselves. The Poitou synodal province had, at the signing of the Edict of Nantes, thirty-nine churches and fifty-three other places of worship on the fiefs of Protestant seigneurs.[35] The province was divided into three colloques. The Haut-Poitou in the east had twelve churches, fourteen other places of worship, and around 1660 between 15,000 and 18,000 Huguenots.[36] Protestant communities were located mostly in towns: Poitiers, Châtellerault, Civray, Chauvigny, La Trimouille, Parthenay, Thouars, Lusignan, and Loudun.[37] In Poitiers, the provincial capital, Huguenots made up only about 5 percent of the town's 10,000 to 12,000 inhabitants. Precise numbers for the smaller towns are difficult to come by, but early in the century Lusignan and Civray had Protestant majorities, and others had sizable Huguenot groups.

The Moyen-Poitou, with its ten churches and thirteen fief exercises, was the stronghold of Poitevin Protestantism with well over 40,000 Huguenots.[38] Saint-Maixent had some 10,000, making up half the city. Niort

35. I take these numbers from Marcadé and Fracard, "Temps des crises," 133. Others give slightly different figures. Dez counts thirty-nine churches and fifty-four fief exercises; see *Histoire des protestants*, 231–33. M. Calmette puts the total at fifty, without mentioning a date ("Un épisode de la Contre-Réforme: La mission des capucins dans la province de Poitou," *Bulletin de la société polymathique du Morbihan* [1937]: 38–39). The discrepancies result from the list's instability. Because of financial pressures or changes in membership, the synod occasionally combined or separated neighboring churches. Over the course of the seventeenth century, legal procedures also closed many temples. Furthermore, some Poitou churches belonged to neighboring provincial synods. Hence Loudun fell under the jurisdiction of the Touraine synod, Rochechouart was in Limousin, and Villefagnon and Champagne-Mouton were eventually placed in the province of Angoumois. Because of their close association with Poitevin Protestantism, I include these places in this study.

36. Marcadé and Fracard, "Temps des crises," 133; Krumenacker, *Protestants du Poitou*, 43.

37. The information that follows on Protestant geographical distribution is compiled from a number of sources, including Benoist, "Populations rurales," 2:20, and "Catholiques et protestants," 243–44; Solange Bertheau, "Le consistoire dans les églises réformées du Moyen-Poitou au XVIIe siècle," *Bulletin de la société d'histoire du protestantisme français* 116, no. 3 (July–September 1970): 332–59, and 116, no. 4 (October–November 1970): 513–49, see esp. 332–35; Pérouas, "Mission de Poitou," 350, and *La Rochelle*, 130–39; and Colbert de Croissy, *État du Poitou*, 54.

38. Krumenacker, *Protestants du Poitou*, 43.

had over 3,000, or one-third of its population.[39] In Melle, 5,500 Huguenots made up a majority of the town's and its surrounding region's inhabitants.[40] Exoudun had a similar number, and in nearby La Mothe-Saint-Héray 3,000 Huguenots comprised one-quarter of the population.[41] Chef-Boutonne had 2,500 Protestants; Cherveux had 2,000; and the combined church of Aulnay and Chizé had somewhat fewer than 1,000. The Moyen-Poitou also had a large rural population of Protestants, especially in the countryside between Niort, Melle, Lusignan, and Champdeniers. In some places, such as Thorigné, Chavagné, and Pamproux, they comprised almost the entire population.

The Bas-Poitou in the west had seventeen churches, twenty-six other places of worship, and 17,000–18,000 Protestants. Fontenay-le-Comte's 1,000–1,100 Huguenots, at midcentury, made up only about 10 percent of its inhabitants, and in the area surrounding it they accounted for only about 8 percent of the population. But the Gâtine region had perhaps as many as 3,400 Huguenots (about 18 percent of the population). In some small towns, like La Châtaigneraie and Moncoutant, they comprised about half the inhabitants. Mouchamps, in 1622, was almost entirely Protestant.

Protestants could be found in all social groups from poor rural weavers to great aristocrats, but they came disproportionately from the higher social levels.[42] Huguenots were numerous among the urban and rural bourgeoisie, as professionals, merchants, craft masters, and landowners. Colbert de Croissy claimed in the 1660s that almost half the Poitevin noble families were Protestant.[43] At the top of Poitevin society sat the great Huguenot clans of La Trémoille, Rohan, and Saint-Georges (led by the mar-

39. L. Favre cites a 1610 report to the government from the city's governor Parabère that claimed Protestants to be half of the city's population, but he suggested that a decade later Protestants made up only one-third; see *Histoire de la ville de Niort depuis son origine jusqu'en 1789* (Niort, 1880), 220.

40. The town had approximately 1,500 Protestant inhabitants; see Bertheau, "Consistoire . . . du Moyen-Poitou," 3:335n.14.

41. The Protestant churches of Exoudun and La Mothe-Saint-Héray were distinct until 1665, after which they were united.

42. Bertheau, "Consistoire . . . du Moyen-Poitou," 3:347; Benoist, "Catholiques et protestants," 236, 243; and Pérouas, *La Rochelle*, 138.

43. *État du Poitou*, 22.

quis de Vérac). Below them were numerous Protestant seigneurs, some from old, landed, sword noble households, others from families that had risen to nobility through civic office in Poitiers, Niort, or La Rochelle. Because these seigneurs could maintain fief worship on their estates, they were crucial to the protection of the faith, especially when the anti-Protestant campaign succeeded in closing temples.

Protestant strength in Poitou weakened across the century, as it did throughout France. Sources that would allow a close, decade-by-decade study of the decline throughout the province are not available, but we have snapshots of it in certain communities. In Chef-Boutonne, the number of Protestants fell from 2,500 to 700 between 1598 and 1660. Chizé had 550 Huguenots in 1600 and only 200 in 1663.[44] Huguenots made up 41 percent of the 6,500 people in Loudun in the first decade of the century; at midcentury they were only 21 percent of 10,000; and in the 1660s they were down to 18 percent of 8,750 people.[45] As the state promoted the third form of confessional boundary from the century's middle decades on, conversion and emigration took their toll on Huguenot numbers. However, in some communities, such as La Mothe-Saint-Héray, Protestantism remained strong, if only because of the influx of Huguenots from places where Reformed worship was prohibited. In each community, confessional boundaries were renegotiated as the relative size and power of the groups changed. But royal law and policy established the framework for these local negotiations, and in the century's early decades they encouraged not discrimination but accommodation between the confessional groups.

THE CONSTRUCTION OF COEXISTENCE UNDER HENRI IV

Henri IV followed a policy of appeasing both sides in Poitou. He helped the Catholic Church regain ground, for example, by promoting the establishment of Catholic Reformation religious orders in the prov-

44. Benoist, "Populations rurales," 468. Such figures represent both an absolute and a relative decline, as the population of the Moyen-Poitou increased across the century. See Benedict, *Huguenot Population*, 70.

45. Benedict, *Huguenot Population*, 34–35.

ince. But Protestants were able to continue conducting synods, opening schools, and organizing propaganda efforts. Important posts went to those loyalists of both sides who were likely to moderate conflict in the province—for example, the governorship to the Protestant Sully, the diocese of Luçon to the Catholic Richelieu. The king allowed Poitevin Protestants to extend their control over their surety towns, due to expire in 1606. He also worked to increase his authority at the expense of both groups. He kept the troublesome Protestant noble Claude de La Trémoille in line by raising him to the peerage; he thereby made it clear to prominent Huguenots that they had to depend on him for preferment. And the king reined in the cantankerous Catholic bourgeoisie of Poitiers by restricting their municipal autonomy and establishing more control over their elections of mayors and *échevins* (city councilors).[46]

Enforcement of the king's will was the task of local royal officials or commissioners sent into the provinces to apply the edict and to adjudicate disputes between the faiths.[47] The commissioners toured their jurisdictions receiving complaints from the religious groups; settling disputes over cemeteries, schools, poor relief, or representation on town councils; establishing Protestant worship on its strictly limited grounds; and reestablishing Catholic worship everywhere. Royal orders to the commissioners granted them *"plein pouvoir, puissance, autorité,"* but their task was difficult.[48] They faced local opposition; their resources were limited; and

46. Boissonade, *Histoire de Poitou,* 219–20; Lièvre, *Histoire des protestants,* 274; and Dez, *Histoire des protestants,* 241. On the changes to the Poitiers municipality, see S. Annette Finley-Crosswhite, *Henry IV and the Towns: The Pursuit of Legitimacy in French Urban Society, 1589–1610* (Cambridge, U.K., 1999), 148.

47. Commissioners had also been used to enforce earlier settlements during the Wars of Religion. See Penny Roberts, "Religious Pluralism in Practice: The Enforcement of the Edicts of Pacification," in *The Adventure of Religious Pluralism in Early Modern France: Papers from the Exeter Conference, April 1999,* edited by Keith Cameron, Mark Greengrass, and Penny Roberts (Bern, 2000), 31–43. The best study of the commissioners' work is F. Garrisson, *Essai sur les commissions d'application de l'Édit de Nantes, première partie: Règne de Henri IV* (Montpellier, 1964). Elisabeth Rabut has examined the Dauphiné commission of 1599–1601 in *Le roi, l'église et le temple: L'exécution de l'Édit de Nantes en Dauphiné* (Grenoble, 1987), and has summarized her findings in "Vie religieuse et vie de la cité. Catholiques et protestants en Dauphiné au lendemain de l'Édit de Nantes," in *Renaissance européenne et phénomènes religieux, 1450–1650* (Montbrison, 1990), 317–24.

48. Rabut, "Vie religieuse et vie de la cité," 317.

their terms were often of short duration. In addition, they were enforcing an often vague law. Frequently they felt compelled to refer matters to the royal council for adjudication, and the council sometimes overruled decisions they had taken. Despite the problems, commissioners during the early decades of the century appear to have been largely successful in pragmatically managing the most urgent issues.[49] Their activities reinforced the message that union and harmony depended directly on the king.[50] Only through obedience to him could peace and social order be maintained. But the commissioners' success also speaks to the strong interest local people of both faiths had in negotiating their differences and preserving local peace.

The first commissioners for Poitou, appointed in May 1599, were the Catholic Martin Langlois and the Huguenot Jean Baudéan de Parabère, the province's lieutenant-general governor.[51] Their three-month commission included not just Poitou but also Angoumois and Aunis, which, with its capital of La Rochelle, was their major preoccupation. After finishing their work elsewhere, the commissioners visited the major urban centers of southern and western Poitou—Fontenay-le-Comte, Niort, Saint-Maixent, and Civray—before arriving in Poitiers.[52] As their royal instructions

49. Such is Garrisson's opinion *(Essai sur les commissions)*, as well as that of Rabut for the Dauphiné ("Vie religieuse et vie de la cité," passim, and *Le roi, l'église et le temple*, 42–47). It was also true for Poitou.

50. The message was explicit in the speeches that the Dauphiné's commissioners gave in each locality they visited. They stressed the obligation of Christians, of either religion, to obey the monarch. The king would ensure the kingdom's unity. Only God could restore religious unity. Thus peace would be achieved despite religious difference through the liberties the king granted to subjects of both faiths. See Rabut, *Le roi, l'église et le temple*, 209–21.

51. See Daniel Hickey, "Enforcing the Edict of Nantes: The 1599 Commissions and Local Elites in Dauphiné and Poitou-Aunis," in *Adventure of Religious Pluralism*, 65–83; Garrisson, *Essai sur les commissions*, 93–94; and Dez, *Histoire des protestants*, 234. Langlois was a Parisian *maître des requêtes* (official of the king's council) and *prévôt des marchands* (head of city government), who had endeared himself to Henri by his role in helping to defeat the League in the capital. The Protestant Parabère was a military commander and old comrade of Henri's, who had fought against the League in Poitou. He was rewarded with the governorship of Niort.

52. I base this section primarily on the work of Garrisson, who draws on a memoir, "Observations sur le procès-verbal de MM Parabère et Langlois," written in 1665 by a lawyer named Loride. See *Essai sur les commissions*, 96.

made clear, their primary task was to reestablish Catholic worship in areas Huguenots controlled, return Catholic clergy to places from which they had been expelled, and restore Catholic Church control of its property.[53] This charge meant, effectively, that the commissioners would be reintroducing Catholic worship into some places where it had ceased perhaps decades earlier. And they would be challenging local Huguenot political strength—as they did, for example, in Niort. There, Protestants were politically dominant, the mass had not been said since 1588, and Catholics had to baptize their children at a church outside the city walls.[54] The commissioners also ordered the return of the Catholic clergy to the Protestant-dominated towns of Maillezais, Fontenay, Saint-Maixent, Lusignan, and Civray.[55] We have no evidence of particular trouble at this time in any of these places; the restoration of Catholic worship did not immediately threaten Protestant power in them. Elsewhere, the commissioners did not succeed easily in restoring the mass. For example, the Catholic clergy who had left Mouilleron during the first of the Wars of Religion would not be able to return for yet another two years. And the Catholic Church did not always regain control of its local property. Witness the case of Maillezais: Catholics would still be complaining in 1618 that the former cathedral remained a Protestant fort.[56]

Just as provocative as the restoration of Catholic worship in Protestant strongholds was the establishment of Protestant worship in or near Catholic-dominated towns. The edict allowed two places of Protestant worship in each sénéchausée. In the jurisdiction of Fontenay, the commissioners chose the towns of Saint-Maxire and Coulonges-les-Royaux (today Coulonges-sur-l'Autize). In Civray's jurisdiction, they chose Sauzé and La Mothe-Saint-Héray. Montmorillon and Châtellerault also had sénéchausée courts, but the commissioners did not grant places of Protestant worship in either district. Their reasons for not following the edict's provisions in these places remain unclear. Perhaps the number of temples was

53. For the royal instructions, see Garrisson, *Essai sur les commissions*, 187.

54. Favre, *Histoire de la ville de Niort*, 220, 262.

55. Garrisson, *Essai sur les commissions*, 99.

56. On Mouilleron, see Vray, *Protestants de l'ouest*, 110; on Maillezais, see "Estat de la religion en Poictou," Archives Nationales (hereafter AN) TT 262 (8). Catholics also proved eager to hang on to Church possessions they had appropriated. See Benoist, "Catholiques et protestants," 301–23.

sufficient for the small Huguenot population in these regions. Or perhaps Protestants could not afford any others.[57] In Poitiers's sénéchausée a special provision applied. Secret Article 28 of the edict, recognizing a 1594 agreement Henri had made with the League, conceded only one place of Protestant worship in the jurisdiction, in Chauvigny, where it would otherwise have been prohibited because the place was an episcopal fief.[58]

Royal officials and those Poitevins working to construct coexistence had to contend with levels of confessional tension that varied considerably from location to location. In some places antagonism was so strong there seemed little hope of moderating it. Even the pressure officials exerted might not have much effect. In others, mediators could capitalize on a common desire for order or reserves of goodwill. In yet others, negotiations were difficult, and what success officials achieved may have only papered over continuing hostility. But as the following examples demonstrate, nowhere could confessional coexistence be taken for granted. It had to be constructed with painstaking care.

In Niort, royal commissioners were able to implement the edict's provisions by building on relatively peaceful confessional relations. At the very least, there is little evidence of severe tensions in the city at this time. Huguenots were politically powerful but not demographically dominant in Niort. People of the two faiths easily and frequently crossed the religious divide. For example, Niort's minister complained to the provincial synod at Couhé in 1601 about members of his congregation who danced with Catholics at the inaugural banquet of a new Catholic mayor. The minister also asked the synod whether he should punish those who had merely attended the banquet without dancing. His consistory was divided on the matter.[59] The episode suggests that apart from the minister and

57. According to Garrisson, the edict's provision was not always followed strictly in other regions where Protestants already had a dense network of temples; see *Essai sur les commissions*, 98–99.

58. For the article, see Mousnier, *Assassination*, 352; and Lièvre, *Histoire des protestants*, 1:262. Chauvigny's status as an episcopal fief would later serve as a pretext for closing down the temple there despite the edict's explicit permission for it.

59. "Synodes, Exercices de la RPR 1574–1680," AN TT 241 (4), 366; Bibliothèque du Protestantisme Français (hereafter BPF) Ms. 579 (1): Collection Auzière: Synodes et Colloques du Poitou, 36–37; and Solange Bertheau, "Consistoire . . . du Moyen-Poitou," 4:532–34. The synod refused to decide and turned it back to Niort's minister and elders to act as they thought best.

some elders, Huguenots in Niort were willing to get along well with their Catholic neighbors, and that the stricter members of the faith were unable to use the Reformed Church's political position in the city to enforce a complete separation. To some degree, relations characteristic of the first form of confessional boundary were apparent in Niort. This situation aided the commissioners in August 1599, when they sought to introduce the second form of boundary, along the lines the edict required, by restoring Catholic worship in the city. It also prevented explosions when the bishop of Poitiers, Geoffroy de Saint-Belin, arrived quickly in the commissioners' wake to consecrate the churches returned to Catholicism and celebrate the mass, or when Catholic preachers came during the next Advent.[60] To Huguenots, both acts were potentially provocative.

Perhaps what mollified Niort's Protestants was that they too benefited from the commissioners' work. They received permission to set up their own grammar school, in keeping with Secret Article 37 of the edict.[61] Furthermore, the restoration of Catholic worship did not alter local political arrangements, which favored the Huguenots. So confessional tensions did not noticeably increase. This situation would change during the much tenser 1610s and 1620s, when Niort's inhabitants of different faiths were quicker to complain about each other.

In other places where potentially serious conflicts existed, the commissioners were able to facilitate coexistence by mobilizing local feelings of neighborliness or, at least, a willingness to avoid further trouble. And they made it clear to both sides that the king, whose will they were to obey, commanded peaceful resolutions of problems. For instance, in 1599 the Catholics and the Protestants of Lusignan were in dispute over the bell at the Notre Dame church. Catholics claimed its exclusive use. Protestants argued that they had paid for it too, and they insisted on sharing it with the Catholics so they could ring it for their worship services and funerals.

60. Garrisson, *Essai sur les commissions*, 99; Vray, *Protestants de l'ouest*, 109; and Dez, *Histoire des protestants*, 237–38.

61. Evidence of this permission comes from a complaint of Niort's Protestants, presented to the commissioners in 1623, that they had been obstructed in founding the school the original commissioners granted them in August 1599. I will return to this subject below. See Lièvre, *Histoire des protestants*, 1:304. For Secret Article 37, see Mousnier, *Assassination*, 353.

The commissioners made a pragmatic decision. The bell would be left to the Catholics, but they, in turn, would contribute to the cost of another one for the Protestants. The decision's *procès-verbal* (official report) bespeaks the desire of Lusignan's inhabitants to get along. "The sieurs lieutenant-general, procurator and attorney of the king; the sieurs priors and curé of Lusignan; [Catholic] lawyers, merchants, and artisans; the ministers and a number of other members of Reformed Religion . . . have sworn before the commissioners to keep and observe the edicts and to look out for one another."[62] The settlement suggests that the commissioners, by arranging for separate bells, were working toward a mutually agreed-upon second form of confessional boundary. They knew that local coexistence could be nurtured to avoid its dissolving into reciprocal recriminations or worse. So, by insisting that the parties take an oath, they reinforced coexistence with their own authority and that of the king.

By contrast, in Poitiers, confessional relations always seemed hostile. Despite the 1594 agreement Henri reached with the League, Poitiers's Protestants were granted a place for worship. But a particularly aggravated dispute arose over choosing its location. There was no question that the temple would be outside the walls of this bishop's seat, but Protestants wanted it as close to the city as possible. Catholics opposed a temple near the city. The commissioners finally settled on a site at the extreme end of a suburb, in a place called Cueille-Mirebalaise, where they set up four stakes marking the emplacement, henceforth known as Quatre-Picquets.[63] While constructing the temple in November 1599, Protestants traveling between the city and Quatre-Picquets complained of being insulted and attacked. Their Catholic assailants had reportedly referred to the temple as a "pigsty," and when one Protestant objected that such speech was contrary to the edict, he was kicked in the face and his fellows were thrown into a pond.[64] On 20 July 1606, the city's Huguenots cele-

62. Quoted in J. Durand, *La réforme à Lusignan en Poitou des origines à la révolution (1559–1789)* (Paris, 1907), 37–38; and in Lièvre, *Histoire des protestants*, 1:265–66. In La Mothe-Saint-Héray, the groups shared the cost and the use of a new parish bell; see Dez, *Histoire des protestants*, 247. Rabut presents examples of such oaths in Dauphiné (*Le roi, l'église et le temple*, 81–83, 94–96, 106–7, 114–16, 118–19).

63. Garrisson, *Essai sur les commissions*, 97; Lièvre, *Histoire des protestants*, 1:265.

64. Dez, *Histoire des protestants*, 239n.3.

brated a fast day, during which they remained at the temple from 6:00 in the morning until 5:00 in the afternoon. A rumor spread that they were planning to take over the city. The mayor thought it advisable to deploy the militia, which only increased the panic. Eventually, magistrates in the city gained control over the situation, and their authority along with the return of the Protestants, unarmed, deterred bloodshed.[65] In 1609, Protestants complained that their pastor was being subjected to insults and that troublemakers threw stones at his windows on Catholic festivals. Local magistrates did not intervene, and it required direct orders from the royal court to put an end to the problem.[66]

Various factors contributed to the city's hostile atmosphere. Poitiers was an episcopal seat and a former League stronghold with a heritage of violence from the Wars of Religion. Huguenots were a small part of Poitiers's population, and they had no political power in the city. The city did have a group of politique Catholic humanists in the university and the law courts, but they did not succeed in moderating conflicts.[67] Outside authorities also had little success in easing confessional antagonism; the Catholic civic leadership and populace often simply ignored them. Protestants and their later historians blamed intolerance on the Jesuits and the Capuchins, who were established in Poitiers earlier than in most other Poitevin cities.[68] They were the spearhead of the anti-Protestant campaign in the province, and their arrival in Poitevin towns often led to increasing tension. But they were established in Poitiers and other cities only with the support of local lay elites. The city's Catholic leaders did not *learn* intolerance from Jesuit fathers and Capuchin friars: they *shared* it with them. In Poitiers, a confessional boundary closer to the third than the second form appears to have triumphed. Reformed worship would be forced outside the town. Nonetheless, the commissioners managed to prescribe a settlement by which the right of Protestants to live there was legally protected.

65. Lièvre, *Histoire des protestants*, 1:271–72; Dez, *Histoire des protestants*, 240.

66. Lièvre, *Histoire des protestants*, 1:274–75; Dez, *Histore des protestants*, 240.

67. Boissonnade, *Histoire de Poitou*, 220. On the earlier history of this group, see Robert Favreau, ed., *Histoire de Poitiers* (Toulouse, 1985), 183–85.

68. See the comments on the Jesuits in particular of Lièvre, *Histoire des protestants*, 1:274–75; and Dez, *Histore des protestants*, 240.

The confessional situation was also precarious at Parthenay, but here we see an example of how negotiations, with the participation of a royal official, could curb severe local friction. The issue here was establishing a place for Protestant worship in one of the few major Poitevin towns that was not a Protestant place of surety. The 1600 contract by which Catholics and Protestants came to an agreement reveals both the tensions and the desire for cooperation at work in the community. It contains competing claims and threats of violence alongside professions of friendship and declarations of peaceful intentions.[69] The document begins with a statement by the Huguenot representatives to the negotiations: they know that the prerogative of exercising their religion in the town displeases Catholics and "engender[s] divisions and enmities between them." Therefore, they had "voluntarily" desisted from worshipping in Parthenay and sought, instead, to locate their temple in the suburban seigneurie of their fellow Protestant Pierre Alloneau, seigneur de Saint Pardoux. He had the privilege of high justice, and thus could establish a temple on his fief. Catholics had opposed the use of Saint Pardoux's seigneurie by claiming that he did not possess the right of high justice, and hence it was not a legitimate locale for public Protestant worship. The Protestants found this Catholic opposition "severe and grievous," and were now appealing a previous ruling by the Catholic lieutenant-general of Poitiers, Louis de Sainte-Marthe (known for his politique views), which had supported the Catholic side. His decision had forced them to travel a considerable distance to worship, and it left their "wives, children, and families at the mercy of the weather . . . or deprived of the exercise of their religion and of instruction in piety."

The Catholic representatives argued that no one but the Dame de Parthenay (the redoubtable defender of Protestantism, Catherine de Parthenay, duchesse de Rohan) had a right of high justice in the area. She did not reside in Parthenay, and therefore the Huguenots were not legally permitted to establish public exercise of their religion in either the town or its suburbs. Nonetheless, the Catholics realized that their opposition to Protestant worship had provoked a "great altercation between the parties,

69. The contract was signed on 15 December 1600. A copy of it may be found in the Bibliothèque municipale de Poitiers (hereafter BMP) Fonds Fonteneau, vol. 79, 303–6, and another in BPF Ms. 869 (1). See also Dez, *Histoire des protestants*, 235.

such that each side was close to taking up arms to preserve its rights." So, "to avoid tumult and sedition and to nourish peace between the inhabitants, who for the past thirty years have unanimously maintained themselves in the king's service," they would now consent to public Protestant worship, "providing it was held neither in the town nor the suburbs." The Catholics stated that "to maintain friendship between them [and the Protestants], inasmuch as it is the king's intention that all live in peace under his edicts," they would offer to accept Protestant worship in one of three locations beyond the immediate suburbs. The Huguenot representatives, seeking to remain in friendship with their Catholic neighbors, "and not having great interest in which place they hold their worship," chose one of the three locations, a pasture.[70] Sainte-Marthe then enjoined all to conduct themselves as fellow citizens in the union ordered by the king's edicts, and he warned that anyone obstinate enough to oppose the agreement would be punished for being guilty of disturbing the peace and of *lèse-majesté* (treason).

Violent tensions seemingly lay close to the surface in Parthenay, but so too did a common interest in order, which could be encouraged. Protestants clearly did not achieve all that they had hoped for: a temple based on the legally solid ground of a fief exercise. But they were not as strong in Parthenay as they were in other Poitevin towns. Catholics managed to prohibit Huguenot worship in the town proper and in its immediate suburbs, but they could not deny their Protestant neighbors a temple. One suspects that outside pressure was exerted on the inhabitants of Parthenay, perhaps by the lieutenant-general Sainte-Marthe. Certainly the threat to treat any troublemakers as guilty of lèse-majesté was an unmistakable sign of the seriousness with which authorities approached the resolution of confessional conflict in a town like Parthenay and of their worries about just how difficult the task might be. Their fears were not misplaced. The document itself states that the inhabitants were ready to resort to violence. This admission seems odd in what was, after all, an agreement. It may have resulted from a certain brinksmanship in the negotiations; perhaps the threat of violence was not that evident. But the

70. The location was described as an "ouche," a Poitevin word that can be translated as a small pasture, vegetable garden, or orchard. See Pierre Rézeau, *Dictionnaire du français régional de Poitou-Charentes et de Vendée* (Paris, 1990), 103.

claim might also indicate circumstances in which the two groups were on the edge, ready to make peace but also ready to take up arms. So, too, the claims of long-standing friendship and a desire to avoid enmity might reflect good relations among the town's inhabitants (or perhaps only its biconfessional elite). Or Sainte-Marthe might have inserted the declarations of amity into the document, forcing them on reluctant rivals to encourage a state of affairs that did not exist. We cannot say that the situation here was one simply of confessional toleration or antagonism. The issue was far from decided in Parthenay or other Poitevin communities in 1600. Desire for peace existed alongside deep apprehension. The signals the community received from the king, his commissioners, and provincial magistrates would be crucial in pushing Poitevins in one direction or the other.[71]

The 1600 Parthenay agreement was far from establishing the most tolerant form of confessional boundary. Evidently, tensions ran too high in the town to allow for an easy mixing of the two groups in which confessional identity would be deemphasized. Nor did the contract encourage a boundary of the second sort. Protestant worship would not share civic space with that of Catholics. Protestants and Catholics would not mingle on their way to the temple or the church. As in Poitiers, the Parthenay settlement seems closest to the third and harshest type of confessional boundary, in which Protestant worship was pushed outside the town. However, it is important to remember neither judicial decision nor administrative fiat forced the temple out. The agreement favored the Catholics, but Protestants secured a right to worship, a right that resulted from negotiations between the groups. The result was not simply discriminatory, since the minority's position received legal recognition.

Nonetheless, we cannot assume that the effort to ameliorate hostility had a long-lasting effect. Available sources do not permit a close examination of confessional relations in the years that followed, but an incident in 1618 suggests that the earlier agreement had not succeeded in eliminating tensions.[72] On Christmas Eve 1618, Parthenay narrowly escaped an armed

71. Thus, I would not agree with Garrisson, who sees the 1600 Parthenay contract as "proof of peaceful confessional relations that confirm the ease with which the Edict of Nantes was applied" (*Essai sur les commissions*, 241).

72. "Procès-verbal de la prise d'armes des religionnaires de Parthenay, 1618" (29 December 1618), AN TT 261 (21).

fracas between the confessional groups. Catholics complained to the officials who investigated the incident that while they were at that night's vigil, Huguenots armed themselves and gathered secretly in various homes around the city. The Protestants claimed self-defense. A rumor had spread through their ranks that the Catholics were planning to massacre them. The investigation did not uncover what had provoked each side's fears. Perhaps the heightened religious atmosphere of the Christmas season contributed to the apprehension.[73] The episode ranks as perhaps the worst in any Poitevin community in these years. Yet, in the end, no violence was committed.

In this town, as in Poitiers, the disparity in the two groups' political and demographic strength may have undermined any impulse toward more peaceful coexistence. Lusignan and Niort present a different situation. There commissioners could build on a foundation of good relations and on the willingness of Catholics and Protestants to traverse the religious boundary in daily interactions. Despite their differences, the arrangements in each town accorded with the spirit of, if not always the letter of, the Edict of Nantes. Both religions were maintained, but their practice was separated. Protestants and Catholics would have different schools in Niort. In Lusignan they would have separate church bells. In Parthenay and Poitiers, Huguenots would have temples but outside the city. The confessional boundary in each town and the place of each confessional group thus were clearly defined. Such settlements were not always easy to reach, and they became that much more difficult in the politically troubled years following Henri IV's death.

BOUNDARY BUILDING IN A TIME OF CONFESSIONAL CONFLICT

The king's assassination in 1610 provoked another long period of political unrest. Although the regent, Marie de Medici, reaffirmed the Edict of Nantes in 1611, Huguenots worried about her commitment to concilia-

73. Festivals were often the occasion for violence during the Wars of Religion; see Davis, "The Rites of Violence," 170–73. It is also possible that the Capuchin mission, which had begun operating in the area the previous Christmas, provoked this Protestant reaction, but the *procès-verbal* makes no mention of it.

tion and the government worried about the Huguenots' obedience.[74] The confessional groups' suspicions of each other grew. Nonetheless, efforts toward constructing good relations did not disappear. People still sought ways to maintain coexistence locally, and officials from outside communities continued to encourage it through negotiation and adjudication of confessional disputes.

The divisions within each confessional group further complicated the political situation in the province. Poitevin Catholics split between hardliners with their Catholic League heritage and moderates descended from the politiques. The leading figure in the first group was Bishop Henri-Louis de La Rocheposay of Poitiers, who was eager to push the fight against Protestantism. The most notable Poitiers moderate was the magistrate Louis de Sainte-Marthe (negotiator of the Parthenay agreement).[75] Protestants were also divided. Philippe Duplessis-Mornay and Maximilien de Béthune, duc de Sully, led moderate loyalists. Militants looked to Henri, duc de Rohan, who put his followers on a military footing in 1612 and revived the dream (or nightmare, for the government) of an autonomous "Huguenot republic."

When Rohan led his followers into a series of rebellions in the 1620s, the Poitevin Protestant nobility divided again. Henri, duc de La Trémoille remained loyal, but a good number of the province's lesser Huguenot nobles joined Rohan.[76] The province's ministerial corps split, with some supporting Rohan and others not.[77] The provincial Huguenot bourgeoisie

74. Boissonade, *Histoire de Poitou*, 220. At a 1613 colloque held in La Mothe-Saint-Héray, Protestants declared their obedience and fidelity to the young king and his mother and hoped they would respond with "ample evidence of their *bienveillance* and affection." Quoted in Dez, *Histoire de protestants*, 245–46n.4.

75. Marcelle Gabrielle Formon, "Un évêque de la Contre-Réforme: La Rocheposay et le diocèse de Poitiers, 1612–1651" (thèse pour le doctorat, Université de Poitiers, 1951), 64–79. (I thank Edwin Bezzina for this information and for other references to this work.)

76. Benoist, "Populations rurales," 229.

77. Rohan's supporters included Pierre de La Vallade (Fontenay), Jacques Clémenceau (Poitiers), and Jacques Cottiby (Poitiers). Among those who likely did not were Pierre Pasquier (Champdeniers), Jean Vatable (Coulonges), Daniel Guérineau (Saint-Benoist), and Jacques Prunier (Talmond), though their precise political views are difficult to ascertain. See Dez, *Histoire des protestants*, 265; and Benoist, "Populations rurales," 231.

generally resisted joining their militant coreligionists; they had little to gain and much to lose from aristocratic rebellion and wartime depredations.[78] And they did not want to poison relations with their Catholic neighbors.

Once again biconfessional communities varied in their responses to the increasingly disturbed political and confessional atmosphere. Tensions ran especially high in Poitiers, where the city government refused to publish the regent's confirmation of the Edict of Nantes. Hostility boiled over on the night of 30 June 1610, during which Catholics sounded the tocsin, doubled the guard, and raised barricades on city streets, which they maintained for several days. Fearful Protestants mostly remained indoors, and when they ventured out to go to their temple the militia harassed them at the gates. Poitiers's magistrates did little to calm the situation until the regent, the provincial governor Sully, and his lieutenant Parabère all wrote to the city council insisting that it put an end to the disorders. The mayor finally complied on 19 July.[79]

Two years later Protestants in the city complained that Catholics had invaded their cemetery, tearing down its walls and knocking over tombstones. City officials prevented an assault on the temple, but students at the Jesuit college attacked the house of minister Jacques Clémenceau, breaking doors and windows. Again, Marie de Medici wrote to the city council ordering it to control such behavior.[80] Antagonism continued to mark confessional relations in Poitiers, though it did not break out into further violence until the beginning of the renewed religious wars. In 1622 Jesuit students again rampaged through the cemetery, and this time the king ordered the community to provide the Protestants with a new burial ground.[81]

This degree of hostility was not found everywhere. Although tensions were certainly rising in other towns, the religious groups, sometimes un-

78. Benoist, "Populations rurales," 231.

79. Lièvre, *Histoire des protestants,* 1:275–76.

80. Dez, *Histoire des protestants,* 245; Summary of a letter of 12 January 1612 from Marie de Medici to Poitiers's council in BPF Ms. 870 (1).

81. Dez, *Histoire de protestants,* 266. For a Huguenot complaint about the cemetery disorders, see *Le manifeste de Monsieur de Bouillon envoyé à messieurs de la religion* (n.p., 1622). I return to this incident in Chapter 3.

der pressure from authorities, made efforts to live together. In Luçon, Bishop Richelieu, the cathedral chapter, and the inhabitants of both faiths signed a letter addressed to Lieutenant-General Parabère in 1610 in which they assured him of their "resolution to live in peace . . . without regard to religion . . . according to their oath of fidelity to the king and the regent." Their oath followed a royal order enjoining the two confessional groups to get along. Richelieu provided further exhortation and pushed them to sign the agreement.[82] This effort by Luçon's inhabitants stood as a determined attempt, in the wake of Henri IV's assassination, to counter rising tensions. That Luçon did not experience the same degree of confessional hostility evident in Poitiers suggests that the act had some success. But the agreement in and of itself could not completely eliminate tensions. Each group's pursuit of its prerogatives or its religious practices would continue to aggravate the other. In 1609 Richelieu had stopped the construction of a temple in Luçon by insisting that it was too close to the cathedral and his episcopal palace. Eventually he offered the local Huguenots a small indemnity for their lost property and gave them a new site on which to build. However, Catholics continued to block the temple, and as late as 1627 Protestants were still petitioning commissioners for the right to exercise their religion publicly in Luçon.[83] Nothing, however, could overshadow local religious conflicts more than the threat of rebellion and warfare. No doubt, such a danger pushed the two groups in 1610 to their promise of peaceful coexistence. And in 1620, with war imminent, they again joined "to maintain and preserve themselves together." They agreed to mount a unified city guard corps, and to oversee security measures they set up a council of fifteen members, which included three canons from the cathedral and six Protestants.[84]

82. Copy of "Lettre addressée par le chapitre de Luçon et les habitants . . ." (24 May 1610), BPF Ms. 870 (1).

83. "Requête des protestants de Luçon aux commissaires du roi pour obtenir l'exercise public de leur religion, 6 mars 1627"; "Acte de Mr de Melleville commissaire en l'instance et poursuite par la religion prétendue réformée du rétablissement de l'exercise de leur religion au lieu de Luçon 28 mai 1627," in BPF Ms. 870 (1), 233, 235. Lièvre, *Histoire des protestants*, 1:273–74. The cemetery also remained a source of conflict, to which I return in Chapter 3.

84. "Acte" (21 July 1620) BMP Fonds Fonteneau, vol. 14, 213, quoted in Lièvre, *Histoire des protestants*, 1:289.

In these years of conflict it was all the more pressing for confessional groups in Poitevin towns to negotiate coexistence. Mutual suspicions strained the reserves of goodwill to the breaking point. But townspeople of the two faiths still had a common interest in trying to preserve order, as did the state, which once again played a direct role in adjudicating confessional conflicts. Under pressure from a Huguenot political assembly meeting in Poitou in 1611, Marie de Medici agreed to dispatch new commissioners to the provinces.[85] Available documentation allows us to examine their work in three Poitevin towns: Loudun, Saint-Maixent, and Niort. Confessional antagonism in these places is evident in the lists of grievances Catholics and Protestants compiled about each other and presented to the commissioners. These lists and the officials' responses demonstrate the way all three parties manipulated the framework the Edict of Nantes provided to reconstruct the confessional boundary.

Loudun

Loudun was a strategically important Protestant surety town. Catholics were not excluded from the city's government, but prior to the 1620s Huguenots dominated it.[86] The distribution of political power was a serious point of contention between the groups. Catholics complained to the commissioners in 1611 that, in contrast to what had previously been the case, the most recent election had chosen only Protestants to serve as échevins. They feared leaving political power solely in Huguenot hands. They also had grievances over religious issues.[87] Catholics were distressed

85. Those selected for Poitou were the Protestant Saint-Germain de Clan, an associate of the Duc de Bouillon, and the Catholic Méry de Vic, a president of the Toulouse Parlement, who had served as a commissioner of the edict in Dauphiné. See Lièvre, *Histoire des protestants*, 1:275–80; Rabut, *Le roi, l'église et le temple*, 14–15; and Garrisson, *Essai sur les commissions*, 149n.277.

86. Edwin Bezzina's current research will lead to a much more complete understanding of confessional relations in the city.

87. A copy of the Catholic complaints and the commissioners' responses can be found in "Articles contenants des plaintes des habitants catholiques de la ville de Loudun pour estre présentés à M.M. les commissaires députés pour l'exécution des edits" (1611), in BPF Ms. 869 (1). See also Lièvre, *Histoire des protestants*, 1:281–82. We have no Protestant response. It is not certain whether they saw no need to register complaints with the commissioners, which seems unlikely, or that they did so, but the document has not survived.

that Protestants opened shops on the days of Catholic festivals, did not allow the facades of their homes to be decorated during Corpus Christi celebrations, interfered with Catholic processions, buried their dead in Catholic cemeteries, and sold meat during Lent. Furthermore, Catholics complained that Huguenots refused to refer to themselves in public documents as the *"religion prétendue réformée"* (the so-called reformed religion), the title the Edict of Nantes prescribed. Protestants hated this obligation, a bitter reminder both of their minority status and of the refusal of the majority church to acknowledge any value in their religious beliefs. They avoided the phrase whenever they were not forced into compliance with the law.

Forcing compliance is essentially what the commissioners tried to do in Loudun. Rather than negotiate an agreement between the groups, they dictated their decisions with the backing of royal authority. The commissioners ruled that henceforth Protestants would have to use the despised label "religion prétendue réformée." They ordered Huguenots to close their shops on Catholic festivals and not even to work behind closed doors if Catholics could hear them outside. They were not to interfere with Catholic processions. They were to permit the city to decorate their houses, at municipal expense, on Corpus Christi, and they would not be allowed to sell meat during Lent. Protestants were also to return burial grounds to Catholics, with the one exception being the cemetery of the Saint-Pierre-du-Marché parish church. On the political issue, however, Catholics would receive no gratification. The commissioners insisted that they had no authority to overturn election results, and so the Protestant city government would stand.

Another ongoing conflict increased ill will in Loudun. In 1594 Henri IV had rebuked the Protestant governor of the city, Marc-Antoine Marreau de Boisguérin, who, despite orders from the court, had refused to allow two Jesuits into the château where the order had its local home. The regent admonished him again in 1610 and 1615 to stop harassing the Jesuits. The governor was worried about security; he objected to Jesuits moving freely in and out of the town and argued that royal edicts prevented Jesuits from celebrating the mass or residing in Protestant surety towns, such as Loudun. This argument had no legal foundation, but the governor's stance certainly had the backing of his coreligionists. In 1607 the Jesuits opened a college in Loudun, but since their building was not yet completed, they asked one Sieur de Pigarreau, a Protestant, for the temporary use of a vacant college his ancestors had founded. Huguenots saw the presence of Jesuits as a provocation, and, not surprisingly, Pigarreau refused the request. He barricaded himself inside the building at the instigation, or so Catholics claimed, of his fellow Huguenots. Judicial authorities ruled against him and authorized forcible entry into the building if necessary.[88]

Given the attitude of the Huguenot governor and the conflict with the Jesuits, any decision the commissioners made that favored Catholics was likely to provoke trouble. Here as elsewhere they appealed to the edict's authority, and in keeping with its provisions granted a number of the Catholic demands, such as those concerning festivals and selling meat during Lent. And yet they did not apply the law with absolute rigor. Catholics could claim cemeteries as ecclesiastical properties, which, according to the edict, were to be returned to them. But the commissioners conceded to Protestants the continued use of one.[89] And, for the time being, Huguenots remained in political control of the city. Confessional resentments were growing in Loudun. But by offering benefits to each side, likely based on a sense of what the groups would accept as an accommodation of their disputes, the commissioners were able to constrain potential conflict by means of the second form of confessional boundary. For the moment, at least, the commissioners succeeded in keeping the peace.[90]

Saint-Maixent

Saint-Maixent was a Protestant surety town with a Protestant governor, but its échevins and its militia captains were Catholics. Huguenots do not appear to have objected publicly to this situation prior to 1610; perhaps having a coreligionist as governor was sufficiently reassuring. But in

88. See the copy of "Lettres adressées de 1585–1625 à Marc-Antoine Marreau de Boisguérin, governeur de Loudun" [letters of 7 November 1610 and 6 July 1615] and notes on the "Mémoires" of René de Brilhac, Sieur du Parc, in BPF Ms. 870 (1).

89. Chapter 3 will present a more detailed examination of the cemetery issue.

90. As Chapter 5 will show, matters changed during the affair of the Ursuline nuns in the 1630s.

the changed atmosphere after Henri IV's death, they were no longer content with their exclusion from the city's leadership. In 1610 Sully and the city's governor, Monglas, negotiated with Catholics the entry of two Protestants onto the council along with a promise that in the future candidates would be chosen without regard to religion.[91] It is difficult to know if the agreement signaled the willingness of the Catholic inhabitants to maintain a harmonious relationship with Protestants or if Sully forced their compliance.

The agreement was not enough to satisfy the Huguenots. The secret and illegal political assembly Protestants held in the city in 1611 seems to have stiffened the resolve of their local coreligionists, even if their own minister, Jonas Chaigneau, had been reluctant to participate in it.[92] The list of grievances the Huguenots presented to the commissioners in 1612 reveals a combative attitude and suggests considerable confessional and political tension in the town. They complained that Catholics obstructed the free exercise of their religion, though they offered no specific examples of their rivals doing so. They again raised the issue of admission to the posts of échevins and mayor and argued that, since Saint-Maixent was a surety town, it should have a Protestant mayor as did Niort. Huguenots further complained that city officials always appointed them as tax assessors and collectors. The tasks were burdensome, and collectors could be held liable for uncollected revenues. The Huguenots wanted to open their shops on Catholic festivals, an activity the Edict of Nantes expressly prohibited (Article 20). And they insisted on an exemption from contributing to church repairs, which the edict expressly granted (Secret Article 2). Finally, they demanded the liberty to eat meat in the city's hostelries on Fridays, when Catholics could not.[93] This was a long-standing dispute be-

91. Lièvre, *Histoire des protestants*, 1:277. Similar political arrangements were made in other communities. For examples, see that of Châtellerault (Formon, "Évêque de la Contre-Réforme," 239–40); Layrac (Hanlon, *Confession and Community*, 39–72); and Gap (René Debon, "Religion et vie quotidienne à Gap," in *Le protestantisme en Dauphiné au XVIIe siècle: Religion et vie quotidienne à Mens-en-Trièves, Die et Gap (1650–1685)*, edited by Pierre Bolle [Poët-Laval, 1983], 91–170, see esp. 105–6).

92. Benoist, "Populations rurales," 229, 232.

93. "Remonstrances addresses par les religionnaires de ladite ville de St. Maixent à Messieurs de Vic & de Saint-Germain (15 April 1612)," BPF Ms. 869 (1), n.p.

tween the confessions. In 1601 the minister had complained to a provincial synod that the Catholic mayor was entering the Huguenots' homes to see if they were eating meat on days prohibited to Catholics, even though the Edict of Nantes did not oblige them to observe the Catholic fast.[94]

Catholics responded with their own grievances in which they accused the "religionnaires" of "revolt and violence." They claimed that Protestants openly contravened the provisions of the Edict of Nantes, actively seeking to create scandal and division. They resisted the orders of proper authorities "with vehemence and indiscretion," and they threatened to raise all their churches in rebellion. The Huguenots' more specific offenses included keeping their shops open on Catholic festivals and publicly selling meat to anyone on prohibited days. They had refused to follow the decision of the 1599 commissioners to build a wall around a cemetery to separate it from that of Catholics, and they had appropriated parts of the Catholic burial ground. After Henri IV's death, they had ignored letters from the regent and Sully urging them to live in concord with the Catholics. Instead, they created an uproar in the city by taking up arms. They continued to demand positions as échevins and half of the city's militia captaincies. And Catholics claimed that, to force the issue, Huguenots had stolen the keys to the city's gates and taken the mayor prisoner.[95]

In a second response to the Huguenots, Catholics insisted that Saint-Maixent was not a surety town, though the edict did list it as such. Furthermore, they claimed to have always been faithful servants of the king, who had never contravened the edict in their conduct of municipal elections. They had accepted all candidates qualified to serve, without consideration of religion. Protestants who now complained about election results had never asked to be admitted to office. Instead, after the king's death, the Huguenots had raised the alarm, assaulted the city hall, tried to seize command of the city from the mayor and échevins, and then con-

94. Synodes et Colloques du Poitou, BPF Ms. 579 (1), Collection Auzière, 31. After later complaints about mayoral investigations of Protestants eating meat, civic governments were ordered not to bother them in their own homes.

95. "Requête des maire, échevins, bourgeois, et habitants catholiques de la ville de Saint-Maixent au sujet de la révolte et violence des religionnaires, présenté à nos seigneurs les députés par sa majesté en ce pays et province de Poitou," BPF Ms. 870 (1). This copy of the Catholics' complaints is undated, but presumably would have been presented around the same time as the Protestants' grievances in April 1612.

strained the city's Catholic leaders to promise that henceforth Protestants would have two seats on the city council as well as the right to nominate six candidates for them.[96]

If we are to believe the grievances of both sides, Saint-Maixent was on the brink of violence in the politically confused period of the early regency. Neither side appears to have complied with either the edict or the royal conciliation policy. Threats were flying, arms taken up, and officials held captive. Relations between the confessional groups could hardly have been worse. But the language of the grievances was also inflated as each group tried to gain the rhetorical high ground. Catholics insisted they had been faithful servants of the former king; they had tried to maintain harmony as he intended. Protestants claimed to be the victims of intolerance and of the authorities' failure to enforce the edict properly. Some complaints dealt directly with religious differences: for example, meat eating, cemetery sharing, and shop opening on festivals. But the issue that appears to have provoked the most tension, namely, the question of representation in city government, tied religious difference to political power. These lists, in other words, did not simply record the groups' complaints. Rather, Protestants and Catholics depicted each other in the worst possible light so as to gain an advantage in the commissioners' hearings. It was these officials who had the means to reorder the relations of confessional groups in the city.

The commissioners did not fall prey to either side's supercharged rhetoric. As was their practice elsewhere, they stuck as close to the edict as possible; they prohibited the mayor from investigating what Protestants ate in their homes or inns, and they exempted Protestants from having to pay for church repairs. But they also acceded to the Protestants' political demands. Henceforth some échevins would be Huguenots (though the commissioners did not specify how many or how they would be chosen), and henceforth Catholics and Protestants would share the burdens of tax assessing and collecting.[97] Catholics were no doubt displeased with the

96. "Réponse des habitants catholiques aux plaintes de ceux de la r.p.r. . . ." (12 May 1612), BPF Ms. 870 (1). See also another version of the Catholic response in BPF Ms. 869 (1).

97. "Réponse des députés" (16 July 1612), BPF Ms. 869 (1); Garrisson, *Essai sur les commissions*, 231n.32.

changes in their political standing. But when we consider their position in the city and the region, the commissioners' decision does not appear unreasonable. Saint-Maixent was a Huguenot surety city, with a Huguenot governor, in a region that was Poitou's Huguenot bastion. Catholics maintained the majority on the council in an area where they were otherwise relatively weak. The commissioners had found a way to make concessions to powerful Protestants, while preserving Catholic authority in the important town. Relations between the religious groups in the city were not good; the confessional boundary required careful patrolling. But by accommodating both groups, the commissioners had created a means for Catholics and Protestants to avoid violence and continue living together in difficult times.

Niort

The tensions of the years after Henri IV's assassination also threatened confessional relations in Niort, where the groups had reached earlier accommodations. Here too coexistence was bent considerably as each side tested the other by means of commissioners' adjudications. Strains appeared, for instance, during the Prince de Condé's revolt against the regent in 1615, when the city was obliged to billet soldiers, always a fearsome responsibility for seventeenth-century households. Parabère, Protestant governor of the city, presented the Catholic inhabitants with a request that they forgo their exemption from troop lodging and accept soldiers, as would the Protestants. As an acknowledgment of Parabère's authority and as a statement of obedience to the king, they agreed. As always, submission to royal authority provided a political reference point that helped maintain an atmosphere of compromise in the city.[98]

Over the next decade, however, that atmosphere began to deteriorate. Here, as elsewhere, the arrival of Catholic religious orders provoked Protestant suspicions. In 1611 Niort's Catholics obtained the site of a former priory outside the city for a Capuchin home.[99] The Oratorians came in 1617, and their appearance in the city provoked the sort of incident that

98. "Assemblée généralle et extraordinaire des maire, échevins, et pairs du corps et college de Niort . . . 6 septembre 1615," in BMP Fonds Fonteneau, vol. 68, 312; Favre, *Histoire de la ville de Niort*, 237–39.

99. Favre, *Histoire de la ville de Niort*, 228.

could trouble peaceful relations. Reportedly, the town's Protestants intended to buy a building from one of their coreligionists, the nobleman Saint-Gelais. An Oratorian, Jacques Gastaud, also had his eye on the building as a residence for his order. Knowing that Saint-Gelais would never sell it to him, he set up a scheme by which an attorney from La Rochelle, named Tuffet, bought the building from the nobleman. Tuffet ceded it immediately to a Sieur Auboineau, who then promptly claimed that he had purchased it with money provided by Gastaud, who intended to use it as an Oratorian house.[100] Catholics saw the establishment of the Oratorians as in keeping with the Edict of Nantes's guarantee that their religion would be practiced everywhere; Protestants saw the scheme as the sort of chicanery that was contrary to the edict's spirit if not its letter.

Despite such incidents, it still proved possible to reach accommodations even over provocative issues such as Catholic processions. In 1618 Niort's curés testified before the city's judicial officials that the minister Jacques Chauffepied with some of his fellow Huguenots had blocked the Catholics' Ascension Day procession as it passed the Protestant temple.[101] The Huguenots objected to the procession parading in front of the temple even though they had finished their service and most of the congregation had returned home. The curés claimed that they had felt constrained to turn back and lead the procession by another route for fear of being "*offensés*." Protestants demanded that no procession pass by the temple, despite commissioners' orders that Catholics had the right to do so outside the times Protestants worshipped. The curés requested judicial intervention to ensure that Catholics had full liberty to practice their religion. More immediately, Catholics wanted assurance that they could undertake a procession on the upcoming Feast of the Trinity. They intended to march between 6:00 and 7:00 in the morning, so as to avoid the hours of Protestant worship.

The judicial officer Isaac Tesserteau was assigned the task of ascertaining Chauffepied's intentions. He tracked the minister down at the home of a Protestant échevin and militia captain, Nicholas Gallet, sieur de la

100. Favre, *Histoire de la ville de Niort*, 243.

101. "Procès-verbal . . . donné à Niort . . . aux catholiques de faire une procession," AN TT 260 (10), 1097–1116.

Roche.[102] Several others were also present, including the mayor, Jean Gratien (or Gracien), sieur de Gerbaudnot.[103] Chauffepied insisted that Catholic processions were permitted to pass the temple only four times a year. If the Catholics tried to direct any other procession past the temple, he would do his best to prevent trouble, as he had during his nineteen years as the town's minister. Chauffepied noted that the mayor had prudently forced the Ascension Day procession, which had entered the temple's street, to turn around and take another route. At that time, no Catholic had said it was necessary to pass in front of the temple, a claim that Tesserteau disputed. The minister added that Niort was hosting a provincial colloque of ministers and elders, which would complicate the problem. The Protestants would begin worship earlier than usual on the upcoming day that "the papists called Corpus Christi," so as to be finished before the Catholic procession passed the temple. No one, however, should be so brazen as to lead a procession there on any other than the four permitted days.

At the court's direction, Tesserteau returned to Chauffepied with a document showing that the commissioners had permitted Catholic processions to pass in front of the temple not only on the four appointed days but on any day, providing it was not during Protestant worship. The minister repeated that he was a man of peace; he had always prevented seditious activities, though he sometimes feigned great anger to keep his followers happy. Nonethless, if a Catholic procession passed in front of the temple, Protestants would oppose it.[104] The minister thought he had enough "credit" among his coreligionists to prevent trouble, but some of his followers were hotheaded, as were some of the Catholics. Tesserteau replied that if the Protestants were willing, it should be easy enough to reach some accommodation by which processions could be held and trouble avoided. He offered as a solution that Catholics would accept the time Chauffepied suggested for their processions. The minister responded that

102. La Roche's religion can be determined from the 1621 militia list, where he is named as one of the Protestant captains; see BMP Fonds Fonteneau, vol. 68, 357–59.

103. See the list of Niort's mayors in BMP Fonds Fonteneau, vol. 68, 239.

104. The minister was particularly worried about armed processions. Tesserteau insisted that the Catholics had never carried arms in their processions; indeed, Niort's Catholics could not carry weapons publicly.

because Protestants attending the colloque would be entering the temple at 5:00 in the morning (and presumably would be there all day), the Catholics could not be permitted to take a procession past the temple at all. It would not be either *"honnête"* (honorable) or *"sain"* (reasonable) for Protestants to encounter a procession on their way to the temple in the morning (or to be disturbed during their deliberations).[105] But on other days, processions could be permitted providing they passed the temple before or after the times of worship.

The procès-verbal provides an example of exactly how the rival religions could arrange a very sensitive matter, and, in this case, without a mediator from outside the city. But the citizens of Niort could not reach that settlement easily, for what was at stake was not just the important matter of the processions, but the whole set of issues that constituted relations between the two groups. The document mixes warnings with protestations of peaceful intent. Catholics threaten processions at an hour and in a place practically guaranteed to provoke trouble. Protestants threaten to do what is necessary to stop them. Each side appears to have its moderates, willing to seek accommodation, and its hotheads, who by their menace can actually push the moderates of both sides to compromise. Chauffepied appears as both; he threatens to take action against the processions, but he proclaims himself a man of peace working hard to restrain others. It seems a contradictory self-presentation, but the threats may have been intended to satisfy his more militant followers as well as to intimidate Catholics. Each group claimed liberties based on edicts or commissioners' decisions. But both could manipulate edicts and decisions by deliberately misreading or misinterpreting them to suit their purposes. For example, contrary to what the Catholics claimed, the commissioners had not permitted them to undertake processions by the temple on any day they wanted. Royal law and commissioners' adjudications set rules; they did not permanently settle disputes. Instead, they provided points of reference for the disputes' negotiation. Here the protagonists reached a pragmatic compromise. Religious violence was avoided and coexistence

105. I have added the remarks in parentheses, since they seem a reasonable interpretation of Chauffepied's argument, which otherwise suggests that because the Protestants would be arriving at the temple at 5:00 A.M., no procession could be allowed at any time during the day.

was preserved. But the underlying issues remained, and the king's arrival four years later presented new occasions to air them and renegotiate the way the two confessions would live together.

The political turmoil of the early 1620s, when Niort was caught in the center of renewed religious warfare, put to the severest test whatever goodwill Protestants and Catholics had remaining. Huguenots were apprehensive after Louis XIII's subjugation of their coreligionists in Béarn in 1620, and Catholics feared Protestant military organizing in La Rochelle in 1621.[106] The king's presence in Niort in 1622, during his campaign against Poitevin Protestant rebels, provided opportunities for bad feelings to crystallize in new lists of grievances. Catholics presented their complaints directly to the king in April 1622. The next year Protestants presented theirs to royal commissioners, who also received a Catholic rebuttal.[107] Each side's grievances zeroed in on issues that were major irritants in the city's confessional relations: the obstruction of religious practices, the Protestant school, the treatment of the Protestant poor, and the suggestion that Niort's Huguenots were in collusion with rebels outside the city.

Catholics objected to constraints on the free exercise of their religion, once again focusing on processions. They were permitted to undertake them only on certain days and along certain streets. Even then Huguenots often disrupted the processions and picked fights with participants. Protestants countered that, while earlier regulations permitted Catholic processions to pass in front of the temple only on particular days each year, the Catholics actually marched every Sunday and on other days dur-

106. A. Lloyd Moote, *Louis XIII: The Just* (Berkeley and Los Angeles, 1989), 124; Benoist, "Populations rurales," 230.

107. Copies of the Catholic and Protestant complaints and royal responses are found in BMP Fonds Fonteneau, vol. 68, 379, 405–17. The Catholic rebuttal was presented in two documents: "Délibérations des habitans catholiques de la ville de Niort pour répondre à la requête de ceux de la religion prétendue réformée" (19 July 1623) and "Les plaintes que mettent et fournissent pardevant . . . les commissaires . . . des maire, échevins, pairs, et habitans catholiques . . . contre les habitans de la religion prétendue réformée" (21 July 1623). The first text is actually dated the day before the Protestant complaints (20 July), suggesting Catholics drew them up with knowledge of the Protestant grievances but before the Protestants had officially presented them to the commissioners. The commissioners' decisions are found in marginal notes to the Protestant complaints. See also Favre, *Histoire de la ville de Niort*, 255–56. In what follows I combine material from the different documents.

ing Protestant worship. "Scandals and tumults" resulted as some of the participants made a point of banging on the temple door. Catholics also protested the treatment their clergy received. Huguenots had prevented a Jesuit preacher named Sicard from entering the city, and they had harassed Capuchins and Cordeliers. Protestants retorted that Catholic preachers incited disorder by addressing crowds in the public marketplace. The gatherings obstructed the commerce of Catholics as well as Protestants and disturbed their coreligionists whose homes opened onto the place. In response, Catholics cited royal letters-patent of May 1621, which allowed Catholic preaching in the marketplace.

Catholic sacred days also provoked a dispute. Huguenots refused to decorate their houses or allow them to be decorated on festivals, and Catholics accused them of working during the celebrations. Protestants objected to what they saw as the large and variable number of festivals they were obliged to observe by not working. The lack of certainty about which days were holidays left them open to frequent prosecution for working when they should not. Finally, the two sides quarreled over the display of a crucifix in the city's courtroom. Catholics claimed that Huguenots had prevented them from setting up the crucifix (referred to elsewhere as a painting of a crucifix) and from celebrating masses the king had endowed in the court's chapel. At issue here was the attempt to sanctify (for Catholics) or to Catholicize with an idolatrous object (according to Protestants) a building in which people of both faiths conducted business.

The two sides also clashed over the issue of a Huguenot school in the city. Protestants complained that, contrary to the decision of the first commissioners in 1599, they had been prevented from opening a public school for the teaching of grammar, Latin, and Greek.[108] Catholics, in turn, pointed out that the king had not given permission for it. Nonetheless, the Huguenot schoolmaster, a Scot named Jacques Wilson, continued to teach children in his home. And his lessons included material that was scandalous and critical of the Roman religion. Another dispute arose over admission to the city's *hôtel-dieu* (poor hospital). Protestants objected

108. They cited Secret Article 38 of the Edict of Nantes, but likely meant Article 37, which allowed Protestants to open such schools in places where their public worship was authorized.

to the exclusion of their poor coreligionists from it; they argued that all should have access to this important civic institution. They claimed that Catholics had made it impossible for Protestants to remain there by removing the rails that separated the hospital hall from a chapel, thereby incorporating the entire room into the chapel where the mass was celebrated. The Catholics insisted that the Frères de la Charité, who administered the hôtel-dieu, never excluded poor Huguenots because of their religion. The brothers were required to accept everyone, regardless of faith, who had the proper admission slip mayors issued. Furthermore, the rails separating the chapel from the hall had been dismantled only because the chapel was to be repaired; new ones would be installed.

Religious practices and municipal institutions were common targets in Catholic-Protestant disputes, but in Niort the political and military situation of the early 1620s gave Catholics an opportunity to level another sort of accusation against their Huguenot neighbors. Catholics insisted that their rivals were in collusion with rebels outside the city. They claimed that Protestants had set up a new cemetery against the city walls that blocked access to the city's fortifications.[109] And they held conventicles in taverns and private homes. Catholics asked the king to disarm Huguenots and remove them from posts in the civic militia. And they suggested that any civic officials who had joined the rebellion (presumably Protestants) be removed from their offices and replaced with "persons of probity" (presumably Catholics). Only in this way could the city be maintained in peace and obedience to the king.

Not surprisingly in a time of Huguenot revolt, the king's responses to the initial complaints in 1622 gave Catholics much of what they wanted, but he offered them little satisfaction on their accusations of Protestant sedition. He refused to consider the charge that the city's Huguenots were in collusion with rebellious coreligionists. He would not disarm them and he would allow the removal of town officials accused of rebellion only after proper judicial procedures had found them guilty. However, the king did order the city to choose a Catholic mayor or continue the present one in office. Complete Protestant control of the city would not be permitted. Otherwise he declared the Catholic clergy free to lead processions on

109. See below, p. 134.

whatever days they wanted and through whatever streets they chose without Protestant obstruction. He also commanded that all preachers the bishop approved would be received in the city, regardless of Huguenot objections. He instructed judicial authorities to investigate "insolences" committed against the Capuchins and the Cordeliers. He insisted that the crucifix be placed in the courtroom and the mass be celebrated according to his endowment. In addition, he refused to allow a Protestant college in Niort without his express permission. On the issue of Catholic festivals, the king followed exactly Secret Article 3 of the Edict of Nantes: he discharged Huguenots from any obligation to decorate their homes themselves, but they would have to permit civic authorities to install the decorations. Finally, he ordered all citizens of Niort, whether Catholic or of the religion prétendue réformée, to live together in "good union, concord, and friendship."

The next year the commissioners responded to the continuing complaints. They ordered the hospital to accept the poor of both religions and treat them all humanely. They insisted that Protestants observe Catholic festivals by not working. However, in a sign of how confessional hostility had even come to mark their own work, they could not agree on other issues.[110] They divided on the matter of the school. Chalas (the Protestant) said that, according to the Edict of Nantes, the school was permissible since Protestants could have schools wherever they enjoyed the liberty of public worship. Amelot (the Catholic), citing a royal ruling of 1611, insisted that a school could be set up to teach reading and writing only and that teachers should not be allowed to "dogmatize."[111] They referred the matter to the king, who sided with Amelot. The schoolmaster would be allowed to continue instruction but not to "dogmatize" or teach any scandalous doctrines. The commissioners also differed on processions. Chalas maintained that processions passed by the temple more often than Catholics admitted and that the 1599 commissioners, having good reason to be concerned about public order, had limited them to only four times a year. Their original order should be maintained. Amelot simply referred to the

110. This despite Protestant suspicions that Amelot (the Catholic), in selecting his own fellow commissioner, Chalas, picked someone who lacked fervor and was too conciliatory. See Lièvre, *Histoire des protestants*, 1:303.

111. I have found no such ruling.

king's decision of the previous year permitting the processions and added that magistrates should guarantee that no disorders ensued. On the matter of Catholic preaching in the marketplace, Chalas insisted that it was deliberately provocative. It was also unnecessary; the 1599 commissioners had ordered that preaching was to be done only in churches, cemeteries, and the temple. Amelot cited the royal letters-patent of May 1621, which gave permission to Catholics to preach in the marketplace. Any further decisions on these issues they left up to the king.

The complaints each side lodged against the other suggest that Niort's confessional groups were at each other's throats, with the threat of religious warfare exacerbating the antagonism. Protestants felt that the liberties granted them in the Edict of Nantes, which earlier commissioners confirmed—for example, that of having a school—were threatened. Catholics felt the threat of presumed Protestant collusion with the rebels. And each side continued to annoy the other on religious occasions. Huguenots kept their shops open on festivals; Catholic preachers whipped up crowds in the marketplace. Protestants made a point of interrupting processions and starting fights, while Catholics purposely routed their processions past the temple to disturb Protestant worship. The lists of grievances portray a community torn apart by confessional conflict.

But other evidence suggests a different picture. Niort's Huguenot bourgeoisie did not take the rebel side in the 1620s. They did, however, participate in the city's militia regiment, known as the Royal-Niort, which saw action in the king's siege of rebel-held Saint-Jean-d'Angély in May and June 1621.[112] The militia had an interesting organization. It was composed of twelve companies, of which six had Catholic captains and ensigns with Protestant lieutenants and sergeants and six had Protestant captains and ensigns with Catholic lieutenants and sergeants. Each company had equal numbers of Catholic and Protestant soldiers. The militia—an institution important for the city's defense, for its self-image, and for the civic pride of its bourgeoisie—was thus an example of confessional cooperation through a parity arrangement.[113] Niort's leading citizens appeared quite

112. Benoist, "Populations rurales," 231; Favre, *Histoire de la ville de Niort*, 257.

113. See "Establissement des gardes de la ville de Niort au service du roi" (30 June 1621) and a similar list from 23 January 1625, in BMP Fonds Fonteneau, vol. 68, 357–59, 431.

capable of cooperating across the religious divide. Indeed, the costs of war were great enough to remind them how much they had to lose in not working together.

How are we to reconcile such seemingly contradictory behavior, on the one hand, complaining bitterly to royal officials or the king and, on the other hand, cooperating in an important confessionally mixed civic institution? One possibility is not to regard the complaints and accusations as simply the reflection of intense hostility. Instead, they were a means for both groups to make use of outside authorities to jockey for position in the city. Through such negotiations confessional relations and the nature of the confessional boundary were being established. This is not to say that the offenses and insults of which each side accused the other were fabrications. Rather, it is to suggest that certain issues, such as the school or processions, were singled out to influence commissioners and the king precisely because they were potential flashpoints or because the Edict of Nantes addressed them specifically.

Louis XIII's presence in Niort in the early 1620s provided the religious groups with a means to settle their differences by recourse to the outsider with the greatest authority to regulate confessional relations in the city. Although the king's decisions favored the Catholics, he also offered Protestants continued protection under the Edict of Nantes, provided that they, unlike their rebel coreligionists, remained loyal. Confessional relations were not always good and neighborly in Niort and other towns, though certainly evidence of good relations exists. But in the province's biconfessional communities the religious groups managed to keep the peace by reaching accommodations on the very specific issues—political power and religious practices—that determined how they lived together. The government encouraged these negotiations, and sometimes arbitrated disputes, within the framework the Edict of Nantes provided. The results did not blur the confessional boundary. On the contrary, they constructed the second form of boundary in which confessional identities were clear but each group had a recognized and acknowledged place in the community. In one sense, the creation of distinct identities would prove ominous for the minority. When the government's policy of conciliation turned to one of persecution, the clear separation of the groups left Protestants in a situation where they could be readily ostracized. The wars of the 1620s, which permanently fixed the balance of power in favor of the king's religion, signaled the beginning of this change, and, as the next chapter shows, a Catholic missionary campaign in that decade worked hard to promote it by cementing the barrier between the groups. But the full weight of a discriminatory policy would not be felt until the 1630s or indeed the 1660s. Prior to that time the second confessional boundary was the key not to persecution but to coexistence.

CATHOLIC MISSIONS AND THE CONSTRUCTION OF THE CONFESSIONAL BOUNDARY

COEXISTENCE IN RELIGIOUSLY mixed communities depended on the willingness of Catholics and Protestants to traverse the confessional boundary in pursuit of common aims or to negotiate agreements across it. Such cooperation always had opponents among the clergy and militant members of both churches. To them, good relations between the groups signified a dangerous disorder in religious and social life. To combat it, the confessional boundary had to be closed by separating neighbors of different faiths and constructing a clear sense of difference between them. Border crossing would be stopped; each confession would be clearly differentiated and objectified to firm up group identity. No accommodations with the rival faith would be allowed. To accomplish this end, each church had to promote discipline within its group while mounting an attack on the other side.

The confessions pursued internal discipline through similar strategies of carefully regulating religious practice and social life. The Reformed Church sought to impose the control of consistories over their flocks.[1]

1. Among many works, see Benedict, *Huguenot Population*, 98–99; Mentzer, "Morals and Moral Regulation" and "Marking the Taboo"; Chareyre, "Great Difficulties One Must Bear"; Janine Garrisson, *Les protestants au XVIe siècle* (Paris, 1988), 51–78; Didier Poton, "Le consistoire protestant au XVIIe siècle: Un tribunal des moeurs?," in *Ordre moral et délinquance de l'antiquité au XXe siècle. Actes du colloque de Dijon, 7 et 8 octobre 1993*, edited by Benoît Garnot (Dijon, 1994), 411–17; and Poton, "Les déliberations consistoriales: Une source pour l'histoire de la violence au XVIIe siècle," in *Histoire et criminalité de l'antiquité au XXe siècle: Nouvelles approaches. Actes du colloque de Dijon-*

The Catholic Church followed the Council of Trent's program in trying to enforce greater conformity and clerical control over worship and moral behavior.[2] Both efforts belonged to what historians have called the "social disciplining" of Europe's people, or to the process of "confessionalization," which aimed at producing properly pious and obedient subjects of early-modern states.[3] The churches also made use of similar means of attacking each other—for example, through harsh polemical publications, which poured off the presses.[4]

The Catholic Church also had another tool useful both for promoting internal reform and attacking Protestantism—namely, the mission. Missions encouraged among Catholics a new understanding of and fervor for their faith. And mission promoters believed them to be well suited for destroying coexistence. They shocked people of the two faiths out of their habitual good relations. They undermined coexistence by attacking it in its most important sites: the shared sacred and civic spaces of communities, the ties of kinship and sociability that crossed the religious divide, and the often fluid confessional identities of individuals. Missions also exacerbated tensions between the groups by confronting and harassing the Protestant clergy and by propagating an image of Huguenots as deceitful, disloyal, and diabolical. In these ways, they laid the groundwork for a harsh confessional boundary. Missionaries could then reintegrate heretics into their communities by converting them. Huguenots would recross the confessional boundary through the only means left available to them: joining the majority faith. Missions thus proposed a two-stage process of, first, separation and, second, reconciliation through conversion.

Chenove 3, 4, 5 octobre 1991, edited by Benoît Garnot (Dijon, 1992), 67–73. I thank Daniel Hickey for referring me to Poton's articles.

2. Luria, *Territories of Grace*, 1–13, 53–58.

3. See above, p. 19.

4. Here Catholics had a clear advantage thanks to state support, greater resources, and a freer hand in publishing than their opponents had. For an inventory of polemical works, see Louis Desgraves, *Répertoire des ouvrages de controverses entre catholiques et protestants en France (1598–1685)*, 2 vols. (Geneva, 1984).

SEVENTEENTH-CENTURY MISSIONS

The Catholic Church in the early seventeenth century had little doubt about the effectiveness of missions; they had proven themselves during a century of winning converts, mostly in foreign lands. They had ardent practitioners, organizations devoted to their pursuit, established methods, and an increasingly sophisticated theoretical underpinning.[5] They also had a number of different forms.[6] To take only a partial list: in the Americas, a mission was a colonial settlement evangelizing and Europeanizing native inhabitants; in the Ottoman Empire, it was a chaplaincy associated with a European consulate ministering to local Christians; in China, it was akin to an embassy at the imperial court targeting the educated elite.[7] In Europe, a mission might be the enterprise of a charismatic, peripatetic preacher, urging repentance on Catholics.[8] Or it could be the sort of en-

5. Not all Catholics were convinced of the effectiveness of missions. One critic was Bishop Jean-Pierre Camus, who distrusted reports of large numbers of sincere converts won overseas and at home. He argued that missionaries worked up an enthusiasm in their listeners that was of short duration at best. See *Des missions ecclésiastiques* (Paris, 1643), 58–65; Louis Pérouas, "Missions intérieures et missions extérieures françaises durant les premières décennies du XVII siècle," *Paroles et mission* 7, no. 27 (15 October 1964): 644–59, see esp. 651; Marc Venard, "'Vos Indes sont ici.': Missions lointaines (et) (ou) missions intérieures dans le catholicisme français de la première moitié du XVIIe siècle," in *Les réveils missionaires en France du moyen-âge à nos jours (XIIe–XXe siècles). Actes du colloque de Lyon, 29–31 mai 1980*, edited by Guy Duboscq and André Latreille (Paris, 1984), 83–89, see esp. 89; Bernard Dompnier, "Mission lointaine et mission de l'intérieur chez les capuçins français de la première moitié du XVIIe siècle," in Duboscq and Latreille, eds., *Les réveils missionaires*, 91–106, see esp. 105–6.

6. Pérouas, "Missions intérieures et missions extérieures," 647. On French missions, see Guillaume de Vaumas, *L'éveil missionaire de la France: D'Henri IV à la fondation du Séminaire des Missions Etrangères* (Lyon, 1942), and Dominique Deslandres, *Croire et faire croite: Les missions français au XVIIe siècle (1600–1650)* (Paris, 2003).

7. On missions in the Ottoman Empire, see Bernard Heyberger, *Les chrétiens du Proche-Orient au temps de la réforme catholique (Syrie, Liban, Palestine, XVIIe–XVIIIe siècles)* (Rome, 1994); Charles A. Frazee, *Catholics and Sultans: The Church and the Ottoman Empire, 1453–1923* (Cambridge, U.K., 1983), 73–102; and Denise Thiollet, "Les capucins et la Congrégation de la Propagande d'après le mss 112 conservé chez les pères capucins (1624–1647)," *Revue historique* 280, no. 2 (October–December 1988): 387–93. The literature on American and Asian missions is vast, but R. Po-chia Hsia presents a useful overview in *The World of Catholic Renewal, 1540–1770* (Cambridge, U.K., 1998), 165–93.

8. On fourteenth- and fifteenth-century peripatetic missions, see Jean Delumeau, *Le catholicisme entre Luther et Voltaire* (Paris, 1979), 286; Louis Châtellier, *La religion des*

deavor with which this chapter is concerned, a group effort of itinerant evangelists devoted to winning Protestants for the Catholic Church.[9]

The differences among these types of mission were considerable in the living conditions missionaries faced, the languages they had to learn, and the degree of hostility or cooperation they could expect from local governments and people.[10] Yet early-modern missionaries preferred to stress the similarities in how they conceived of their work and organized it, as well as in the techniques they used. These similarities were to a large degree an artifact of a mission discourse shaped by a predetermined framework of imagery and rhetoric that mission reports reproduced in locale after locale. Missionaries in Europe read—in letters, reports, and chronicles—about the exploits and achievements of their brethren overseas.[11]

---

pauvres: Les sources du christianisme moderne, XVIe–XIXe siècle (Paris, 1993), 64–70; Raoul de Sceaux, "Le Père Honoré de Cannes: Capucin missionaire au XVIIe siècle," *XVIIe siècle* 7 (1958): 349–74; Jacques Maillard, "La mission du Père Honoré de Cannes à Angers en 1684," *Annales de Bretagne et des Pays de l'Ouest* 81, no. 3 (July 1974): 501–16; Charles Berthelot du Chesnay, *Les missions de Saint Jean Eudes: Contribution à l'histoire des missions en France au XVIIe siècle* (Paris, 1967), 12; and Louis Pérouas, *Ce que croyait Grignion de Montfort et comment il a vécu sa foi* (Tours, 1973).

9. See Jean Mauzaize, "Le rôle et l'action des capucins de la province de Paris dans la France religieuse du XVIIème siècle" (thesis, Université de Paris, 1977), 3 vols. (Lille, 1977), 3:1053; Father Cuthbert, O.S.F.C., *The Capuchins: A Contribution to the History of the Counter-Reformation*, 2 vols. (London, 1928), 2:282; Dompnier, "Mission lointaine et mission de l'intérieur," 103; and Robert Sauzet, "Prédication et missions dans le diocèse de Chartres au début du XVIIe siècle," *Annales de Bretagne et des Pays de l'Ouest* 81, no. 3 (July 1974): 491–500, see esp. 493.

10. They also had different institutional statuses. Missions to Catholics were under the supervision of local bishops, who granted missionaries the permission necessary to conduct their work in specific dioceses. Overseas missions were under the patronage of individual governments, though they also came under the supervision of the Congregation for the Propagation of the Faith (Propaganda fide) after it was established in 1622. Missionaries to Protestant areas were appointed directly by Rome rather than by local bishops, and were also placed under the Congregation's jurisdiction. See Pérouas, "Missions intérieures et missions extérieures," 649–52.

11. Especially in Jesuit publications. See Jean-Claude Laborie, *La mission jésuite du Brésil: Lettres et autres documents (1549–1570)* (Paris, 1998), 17; Philip M. Soergel, *Wondrous in His Saints, Counter-Reformation Propaganda in Bavaria* (Berkeley and Los Angeles, 1993), 95; Adriano Prosperi, "The Missionary," in *Baroque Personae*, edited by Rosario Villari (Chicago, 1995), 160–94, see esp. 163; and Margaret J. Leahey, "'Comment peut un muet prescher l'évangile?': Jesuit Missionaries and the Native Languages of New France," *French Historical Studies* 19, no. 1 (Spring 1995): 105–31.

They learned about the methods those colleagues used and assimilated their attitudes. Their missions at home, in turn, furthered the work of later foreign missions. For example, the Capuchin Père Joseph de Paris, founder of the Poitou mission to be examined here and prefect for all French Capuchin missions, thought of his Poitou campaign as a model for later Capuchin endeavors in France and overseas.[12]

When evangelizing among non-Christians in foreign lands or Protestants at home, missionaries sought a change in religion, marked by acceptance of the Catholic faith and the Church's spiritual authority. In contrast, when preaching to members of their own faith, missionaries urged a reformation of moral behavior and religious practice. Catholics signaled their change by making a general confession of past sins and resolving to lead a pious life.[13] Yet missionary discourse from both home and abroad depicted all people among whom missionaries worked—whether Native Americans, Protestants, or Catholic peasants—as pagans, mired in sin, and in thrall to demons.[14] Clerics in the southern French diocese of Gap echoed their colleagues overseas in worrying about local peasants worshipping the sun.[15] Capuchin missionaries in Poitou complained that the region "contains close to 2,000,000 souls of which the majority know neither prayers, doctrines, nor even how many gods there are."[16] Such comments became clichés of Catholic Reformation rhetoric, but they helped Catholics con-

12. As he wrote: "It is no small good fortune for the [Capuchin province of the] Touraine that since the mission of Poitou, all the [Capuchin] provinces of France have followed this good example by both domestic and foreign missions" (quoted in Mauzaize, "Rôle et l'action des capucins," 3:1296).

13. Pérouas, "Missions intérieures et missions extérieures," 656; and Bernard Dompnier, "Mission et confession au XVIIe siècle," in *Pratiques de la confession: Des pères du desert à Vatican II, Quinze études d'histoire* (Paris, 1983), 201–22. I thank Robert Chanaud for bringing this latter essay to my attention.

14. Dompnier, "Mission lointaine et mission de l'intérieur," 99, 104–5, and *Venin de l'hérésie*, 203; Manuel Morán and José Andrés-Gallego, "The Preacher," in Villari, ed., *Baroque Personae*, 126–59, see esp. 152–53; Prosperi, "Missionary," 178–82; and Jennifer D. Selwyn, "'Procur[ing] in the Common People These Better Behaviors': The Jesuits' Civilizing Mission in Early Modern Naples, 1550–1620," *Radical History Review* 67 (Winter 1997): 4–34, see esp. 10–11.

15. Dompnier, "Mission lointaine et mission de l'intérieur," 102.

16. "Recueils pour l'histoire generalle en abbregé de touttes les missions des capuçins depuis le commencement de la reforme jusques l'an 1673," Bibliothèque municipale d'Orléans, Ms. 916, 54.

ceive of the Church's missionary effort as one, unified, worldwide undertaking. Bishops and the leaders of religious orders often told aspiring evangelists that they had no need to go abroad: "Your Indies are here."[17]

The timing of the various seventeenth-century French missions also suggests they were seen as part of the same enterprise. In 1609 Jesuits went to Constantinople. In 1611 they were sent to Canada, where Recollets replaced them four years later. Capuchins sailed for Brazil in 1612.[18] Little in the way of organized missionary campaigns could be found inside France prior to 1610.[19] But in that decade and the next missionaries started work there, taking inspiration and borrowing techniques from earlier missions in Italy, the Comtat Venaissin, and the Duchy of Savoy.[20] In 1617 Père Joseph founded the Capuchin mission in Poitou and in 1620 expanded his efforts into the neighboring provinces of Angoumois, Aunis, and Saintonge. In the same decade he organized Capuchin missions in the Middle East.[21] Foreign and domestic missions were connected, in part, by political reasons. They were associated with the policies of Louis XIII's government: establishing colonies in Canada, expanding its diplomatic presence in the Ottoman Empire, and conducting military campaigns against Protestants at home.[22]

17. Venard, "'Vos Indes sont ici,'" 83–89.

18. Pérouas, "Missions intérieures et missions extérieures," 646; Vaumas, *Éveil missionaire de la France*, 39–112.

19. In 1570 Charles IX and the cardinal of Lorraine sent a group of Jesuits to Poitou and its surroundings to preach, catechize, and engage in debates with Protestants. Their mission lasted only three or four weeks and had little impact on the region's Huguenots. See Châtellier, *Religion des pauvres*, 35–36; and Marcadé and Fracard, "Temps des crises," 129. From other colleges scattered around the country, Jesuits undertook informal rural "missions"; see Berthelot de Chesnay, *Jean Eudes*, 4; and Châtellier, *Religion des pauvres*, 42. See also Dompnier, *Venin de l'hérésie*, 200–201.

20. The Capuchins and Francis de Sales conducted a series of campaigns starting in 1594 to convert Protestants in the area around Geneva. See P. Charles de Genève, *Trophées sacrés ou missions des capucins en Savoie, dans l'Ain, la Suisse Romande et la vallée d'Aoste, à la fin du XVIe et au XVIIe siècle*, edited by Félix Tisserand, 3 parts (Lausanne, 1976).

21. During these years, he also lobbied, unsuccessfully, in Paris, Rome, and Madrid for a crusade against the Ottomans. See L. Dedouvres, *Politique et apôtre: Le Père Joseph de Paris, Capucin: L'éminence grise*, 2 vols. (Paris, 1922), 139n.1; and Aldous Huxley, *Grey Eminence* (New York, 1941), 147–53.

22. As their promoters made clear, foreign missions were tied to diplomatic or overseas commercial concerns and to the expansion of French colonialism. Antoine de

In mission discourse, what also tied the different endeavors together was the conviction that missions were an effective agent of social and cultural change. To raise Mayans in the Yucatan or Hurons in Canada to a more "reasonable" level of civilization and thus achieve true conversions, missionaries targeted not only the natives' religious practices, in the narrowest sense of the term, but also their patterns of political authority, social organization, economic activity, even the spatial arrangements in which people lived.[23] In Europe, neither Protestants nor Catholics would have their lives so radically altered. But there too missionaries sought to win conversions through social transformation. Because missions were seen as dramatically disruptive of normal social patterns and effective in prompting deep emotional reactions, they could permanently change the way people thought and acted.[24] And if missions could bring about such profound changes, they could also be put to work erecting a confessional boundary between Catholics and Huguenots. Through their elaborate ceremonies, charismatic preachers, spellbinding sermons, rallying of Catholics, and demonizing of heretics, missions could confront Protestants, separate them from their Catholic neighbors, force them onto the defensive, and open them to an acceptance of Catholic truth.

THE POITOU MISSION

From the perspective of anti-Protestant campaigners, Poitou presented an excellent target for the shock of a mission. Here mixing between Catholics and Protestants appeared all too evident, and accommodations the

---

Montchrétien, in his *Traité d'économie politique* (1615), added, "If it is proper for some nation of the world to become involved there [Canada], then it is for the French, to which belongs, as is proper, glory in letters and arms, arts and civility, and, what is more, of true Christianity, to which others only pretend" (quoted in Vaumas, *Éveil missionaire de la France*, 33).

23. On this cultural campaign in the Yucatan, I have found useful Inga Clendinnen, "Landscape and World View: The Survival of Yucatec Maya Culture under Spanish Conquest," *Comparative Studies in Society and History* 22, no. 3 (July 1980): 374–93. Natalie Zemon Davis provides an overview of the Canadian situation in *Women on the Margins: Three Seventeenth-Century Lives* (Cambridge, Mass., 1995), chap. 2. On the Jesuit missionaries' understanding of "levels of civilization" and their role in conversion, see Selwyn, "Procur[ing] in the Common People," 8–9.

24. Châtellier, *Religion des pauvres*, 197–241.

confessional groups had reached allowed Protestantism to flourish. The "true faith" seemed to languish in subordination to a "false religion." In 1618 an anonymous Catholic observer sent the government a report on the province's religious situation entitled "Estat de la religion en Poictou."[25] The report was not an objective analysis of the provincial religious situation. Instead, it was a call for Catholic and government action composed during a time of increasing civil and religious tension. Its language was very close to the rhetoric of mission accounts in its depiction of a determined and dominant Protestant minority, of a demoralized and disordered Catholic population, and of a region heresy had devastated.[26]

According to the "Estat," Protestantism's power in the province rested on the social standing of its adherents and on the concessions the Edict of Nantes made to their military strength. As it pointed out, all of the major Poitevin cities, with the exceptions of Poitiers and Parthenay, were in Huguenot hands. The former cathedral in Maillezais was a Huguenot fort (232). In these towns, Catholics had trouble maintaining the liberty of worship the edict granted them (232). In the countryside, Protestant nobles obstructed Catholic worship on their estates (234).[27] The Church had lost control of many properties. The Protestant Sully possessed three important abbeys, and local noblemen of both religions held onto numerous

25. AN TT 262 (8), 232–35 (page citations will follow in the text). On the "Estat," see Daniel Hickey, "Le rôle de l'état dans la réforme catholique: Une inspection du diocèse de Poitiers lors des Grands Jours de 1634," *Revue historique* 307, no. 4 (October–December 2002): 939–61, see esp. 951–55. It is possible that the author was a Capuchin friar, perhaps associated with Père Joseph de Paris, if not Père Joseph himself. Other than the mention of the Capuchin mission at the end of the report, there is no evidence to support such a claim. But Père Joseph was well acquainted with religious conditions in the province, and he had begun his mission there some months before the report. Thus he was in a good position to compose it.

26. Some historians have either taken the "Estat" at face value or seen it simply as the exaggerated expression of Catholic intolerance, without paying attention to its connection with Catholic missionary rhetoric and with the beginnings of the anti-Protestant campaign in Poitou. See Gustave Fagniez, *Le Père Joseph et Richelieu (1577–1638)*, 2 vols. (Paris, 1894), 1:286–87; Mauzaize, "Rôle et l'action des capucins," 3:1030–31; Lièvre, *Histoire des protestants*, 1:290–93; and Dez, *Histoire des protestants*, 253–56.

27. This passage is ambiguous, and hence it is not clear whether it refers to Protestants obstructing Catholic "offices" or worship, or to the prevention of Catholics from holding seigneurial "offices" or positions.

parish benefices (232). They appointed their own servants to enjoy them, sold them at will, or gave them to daughters as dowries (233).

Wealthy Huguenot landholders ensured Protestant power in the countryside by buying up Catholic properties and establishing their worship on them (234). They forced their dependents to go to the temple, beating them with sticks if necessary (234), and in this way they spread the infection of Calvinism. Huguenot ministers, consistories, and nobles also colluded to pervert the workings of justice. They used their positions and power to intervene in investigations, to suborn witnesses, and to intimidate judges and accusers (235). Local authorities did nothing to prevent these outrages.

To be sure, the "Estat" was also very critical of Catholics and their clergy: "The priests, for the most part, are ignorant and vicious. They keep women and children in their homes openly. . . . Some have wed these women, following a tradition by which they claim that the marriage of priests is not prohibited" (233). These clergymen married off their children without hindrance, sometimes to their colleagues' offspring or into "honest households" attracted to such alliances by the dowries priests could offer (233). Given this appraisal of the clergy, it is not surprising that the report finds the Catholic laity, especially in the countryside, to be "quasi-indifferent in religion" (234).[28]

The "Estat" seemed believable to its Catholic readers because it made effective use of common rhetoric about Huguenot power. It presented charges against Protestant ministers, consistories, landowners, and nobles in keeping with the frequent allegation of Catholic propaganda that the minority was victimizing the majority. The report deployed its polemical discourse about both Protestant domination and Catholic shortcomings as part of a campaign to encourage the government to destroy Huguenot military and political strength and turn from a policy of coexistence to one promoting a strict confessional boundary. And in the final paragraph of the "Estat" the author points to the best means for accomplishing that

28. And in a statement that all historians who have worked with the "Estat" find striking, the report claimed that, according to the province's mothers, their daughters had no religion at all and would adopt that of their future husbands (234). See Benedict, *Huguenot Population*, 70; and Hanlon, *Confession and Community*, 215. I return to this issue in Chapter 4.

goal: "There is an effort to remedy these misfortunes by establishing all sorts of religious orders in Poitiers, by introducing Capuchins in all the towns of surety, and by missions that the bishop has procured . . . which have converted a great number of people" (235). A Capuchin mission would be the key to Catholic success.

The most complete description of the Poitou mission appears in a manuscript entitled "Recueils pour les missions en particulier de la province des capuçins de Touraine."[29] This anonymous chronicle, probably written in the 1670s, was compiled from earlier reports on the mission, such as those sent to the Congregation for the Propagation of the Faith in Rome starting in the 1620s. As with the accounts of other missions, the "Recueils" does not present a straightforward or objective relation of the mission's activities and accomplishments. It is, instead, an epic account of heroic missionaries struggling to achieve great victories for God and the Church against Satan and the heretics, as well as against Catholic lassitude and sinfulness. It reveals how the Capuchins understood their enterprise and legacy: the undermining of Huguenot strength in the region, the breaking apart of coexistence, the establishment of a rigid boundary between the two groups, and, finally, the enticing of Huguenots across that boundary through conversion.

The chronicle's reports of success can rarely be verified, though we should not assume that they were all exaggerated. As we will see, the friars never claimed to have eliminated heresy from the region. Nor can the account be challenged by means of a Protestant reaction to the mission. I have searched largely in vain for evidence of such a response. As always, the absence of evidence is difficult to interpret. The sources revealing a Protestant reaction may simply not have survived, but that seems unlikely given the records of Poitevin Huguenot complaints to the government during the mission's active years.[30] In their polemical publications, Protestant authors often vilified Capuchin missionaries (along with Jesuits), but

29. Subtitled: "Des missions generalles de toute les provinces pour exercer la charité et soustenir la foy." The manuscript is part of the "Recueils" (see note 16). Page citations will follow in the text. Other sources consulted here on the mission include polemical works and accounts of conversions published during the mission, as well as the correspondence of the mission's founder, Père Joseph de Paris.

30. Such as those from Poitou examined in Chapter 1.

did not single out the Poitou mission for mention.[31] Perhaps the most likely reason Protestants did not respond is because the mission never had as large an impact on them as the Capuchins claimed. Ultimately, as the account makes clear, the Capuchins' greatest achievement lay in shaping the anti-Protestant strategy through the mission program they established and bequeathed to later anti-Protestant campaigners.

Central to the Capuchins' strategy was the disruption of the easy social interchange between Catholics and Protestants. They also wanted to reverse the dependence of the "weaker" Catholics on the "stronger" Huguenots by restoring Catholic power in the region. One way to undermine Protestantism's strength was to attack its guardians: Protestant ministers and nobles. It was a commonplace of Catholic thought that Huguenots remained mired in heresy because they were in thrall to their clergy and subservient to powerful nobles. If missionaries weakened their prestige or attachment to the heresy, other Huguenots would convert to the true faith quickly. The Capuchin approach to destroying the authority of the rival clergy and the respect it commanded was to establish in people's minds a clear distinction between God's true servants and those of Satan. Toward this end, mission discourse glorified missionaries for their selflessness, suffering, and success. Missionaries proved their worth by defeating in public debates self-interested Huguenot clergymen incapable of defending their false beliefs. They thereby humiliated ministers and drove a wedge between them and their disappointed flocks. Catholicism's truth was further proven when some of those defeated ministers converted.

Nobles required different treatment. The mission did not attack them. Mission discourse instead celebrated their conversions. The noblemen we meet in the mission chronicle all converted. After consultations with the Capuchins had "resolved all [their] doubts" and "shown [them] the truth of the Catholic Church," they became such "good Catholic[s]" that they prohibited ministers from preaching on their estates and closed down Huguenot worship (59, 66). Noblewomen were a different story. Certainly women converted, but not powerful ones. Reasonable men reconciled

31. For criticisms of missionaries, see, e.g., *Manifeste de Monsieur de Bouillon;* Charles Drelincourt, *Avertissement sur les disputes et le procédé des missionaires* (Charenton, 1654); and Pierre Dumoulin, *Le capucin traitté auquel est descrite et examiné l'origine des capucins, leurs voeux, reigles, et disciplines* (n.p., 1641).

themselves to the Church, while stubborn women became the protectresses of the false faith. The best example, the Huguenot Catherine de Parthenay, duchesse de Rohan, is presented as a "sworn enemy of the faith," who obstructed the reinstatement of Catholic worship on her estate at Mouchamps (69–70).[32] Religious truth and error, as well as the anti-Protestant campaign, thus took on a gendered cast.

The missionaries also attacked the sites of religious mixing in urban space, households, and individuals' minds. In cities, the friars sought to reestablish Catholic control over sacred and secular space. The chronicle reported the restoration of "deserted churches . . . ruined by the heresy," and the expulsion of Calvinist worship from churches heretics had taken over (69, 70). Temples were destroyed "in quantity" (70). Huguenots lost the use of Catholic cemeteries, and their burial grounds were carefully separated from those of Catholics so that there would be no mixing of condemned heretics with the faithful. The physical structures and locations—of temples and cemeteries—by which the Reformed Church established its presence in communities were thus displaced from the centers of towns, pushed to the margins, or eliminated altogether. And the Capuchins also displaced Huguenot residents (at least symbolically) from central squares and marketplaces, which the friars took over for their mission activities.

Nowhere did religious mixing seem more threatening than in biconfessional households. "The marriages [Catholics] contracted with [Huguenots] without anyone feeling the least apprehension" (54) were one of the most troubling consequences of coexistence, and missionaries sought to stop them. The friars celebrated the conversions of those who were members of mixed households, such as the Dame de La Poste of Sanxay, who was described as "very firm in her [Protestant] religion," but who had a Catholic son.[33] Ministers and nobles who converted were pushed to bring their spouses and children with them. In some cases, the missionaries succeeded and family religious unity was maintained, but now in the Catholic faith. In other cases, however, when one spouse converted and the oth-

32. I discuss Rohan below; see pp. 211–15.

33. No Catholic spouse is mentioned. See Jacques Mestayer, *Conversions signalées depuis peu de iours par l'entremise des pères capucins de la mission de Poictou, d'un de plus anciens ministres et autres notables personnes de la R.P.R. . . .* (Paris, 1620), 47–49.

er remained a Protestant, the friars managed only to create newly divided families.

To achieve their aims, the missionaries had to make Catholicism's truth evident not only to Huguenots but also to Catholics, who, as is usual in the missionary rhetoric of the period, were considered ignorant of their own religion's beliefs. Catholics in Poitou "knew neither prayers nor what to believe; they were deeply influenced by the opinions of the heretics" (54). Bolstering the faith of Catholics and instructing them in proper doctrine and observance was just as much a goal as converting Huguenots. Indeed, as the chronicle makes clear, the two were inextricably linked.[34] Under the pretext of asking directions while traveling, the missionaries stopped people working in the fields and offered instruction "to convert them if they were heretics or to affirm their faith if they were Catholics" (56). One missionary, Père Raphael d'Orléans, was "never happier than when he could contribute to the conversion of a heretic or to the instruction of a poor, ignorant Catholic peasant" (53). Missionary sermons were directed to Catholics as much or more than to Protestants, and the friars spent much of their time at each stop on their itinerary hearing confessions and distributing communion (57). They also led Catholics on processions and pilgrimages, such as to the shrine of Notre-Dame des Ardilliers at Saumur.[35] Rallying Catholics was essential to constructing the confessional boundary; it raised awareness of their Catholic identity and increased the sense of separateness from their Huguenot neighbors.

In pursuing their objectives, the missionaries showed how the confessional boundary could take physical shape in the spaces of biconfessional communities between churches and cemeteries of the two faiths. They also demonstrated how it could be built figuratively between households.

34. For other examples of missions combining these goals, see Forster, *Counter-Reformation in the Villages*, 217; and Châtellier, *Religion des pauvres*, 77.

35. The Capuchins claimed that the devotion of Catholics at Thouars "forced [them] to lead a procession, of practically the entire city, and especially the most qualified, to Notre-Dame des Ardilliers. A number of heretics converted en route" (from a letter of Père Joseph de Paris to his mother in 1618, quoted in Raoul de Sceaux [Jean Mauzaize], *Histoire des frères mineurs capucins de la province de Paris, 1601–1660* [Blois, 1965], 453). Saumur was a Protestant stronghold under the governorship of Philippe Duplessis-Mornay. Louis XIII and other members of the royal family supported the shrine heavily.

And finally, they revealed how the boundary could be constructed in the minds of individuals—Catholics who reaffirmed their faith and Protestants who converted. Ultimately this last site of the boundary was the most important because conversion required, in the classic Christian understanding of the term, that individuals in the depths of their consciences separate themselves from their old lives. In other words, converts individually had to draw a confessional boundary between themselves and their former coreligionists. Thus the mission's program highlighted the various sites of interaction between the faiths where the confessional boundary would have to be built: biconfessional communities, religiously mixed families, gendered religious identities, and individual confessional loyalties.

The mission focused the attention of Catholic anti-Protestant campaigners on all these sites, but, according to the chronicle, the missionaries worked more actively in some than others. Those included the heroization of the missionaries, the humiliation of their minister rivals, and the re-Catholicization of urban space. The account also makes clear how the missionaries, in associating their program with the monarchy, lobbied the government to pursue the goal of religious uniformity in France. As a result, I will focus on these topics in this chapter. Other issues, such as the separation of cemeteries, religiously mixed families, and the gendered nature of the confessional polemical battle, require looking beyond the mission's activities. And while mission discourse celebrated the conversions the friars claim to have won, the meaning of conversions in the construction of the confessional boundary will also require separate examination. I will turn to these issues in the book's remaining chapters.

THE MISSION AND THE MONARCHY

In writings from the 1620s Père Joseph reminded readers that the best way to achieve conversions was not through coercion but through preaching and persuasion. The Protestants, he wrote, have set down deep roots: "it would be easier to tear [them] out by peaceful and gentle means and not with arms in hand, seeing that peace weakens their zeal and their courage while war only reignites and reheats both one and the other."[36]

36. "We must await from heaven the conversion of those who have gone astray" ("Discours d'Estat contenant les raisons pourquoy la France ne doit entrer en aucune

After all, true conversions were God's work, not that of kings or armies. However, in Poitou, Joseph and his missionaries realized that persuasion was much more effective when combined with coercion. Catholic polemicists drew support for this proposition from St. Augustine. In urging the state's repression of the Donatist heresy, Augustine had referred to the parable of the wedding feast (Luke 14:23) to argue for the notion of *compelle intrare*, compel them to come in.[37] If peaceful means did not win conversions, force could be acceptable.

By insisting that the mission served the state's interests as well as the Catholic Church's interests, Père Joseph was pushing for a change in royal policy toward Protestants from encouraging coexistence to pursuing repression. Catholics denied that Protestants could ever be loyal; heresy inevitably led to rebellion.[38] Rather than ensuring stability of the state through conciliation, as his father had done, and rather than strengthening royal authority by making it the arbiter of confessional disputes, Louis XIII was urged to take action against an inherently dangerous element in his kingdom. He did not, as some hoped, revoke the Edict of Nantes. But in the 1620s he destroyed Huguenot military and political power. And he encouraged conversions. The Poitou mission served both goals: it helped him to impose control over the rebellious west and it won converts.

Hence the monarchy offered the mission its support. When, in 1616, Père Joseph left for Rome to lobby Pope Paul V for authorization of the Poitou mission, the regent Marie de Medici had only recently made a tenuous peace with the Prince de Condé. He had gained the support of

---

guerre ny contre les Huguenots ny contre les Espagnols" [1624], quoted in L. Dedouvres, *Le Père Joseph polémiste, ses premiers écrits, 1623–1626* [Paris, 1895], 105–6). The "Discours" appeared anonymously in the *Mercure françois* (vol. 10, pp. 97–105), but Dedouvres makes a convincing case that Père Joseph was its author. See also Huxley, *Grey Eminence*, 203.

37. On the notion of *compelle intrare*, see Lecler, *Histoire de la tolérance*, 86–88, 252–53. On its use by Catholic polemicists to justify the repression of Protestantism, see Jean Orcibal, *Louis XIV et les protestants* (Paris, 1951), 114–15.

38. The argument appeared frequently in Catholic polemics and was especially forceful during the Interregnum in England, when the association of Calvinism with political rebellion seemed self-evident to French Catholics. Huguenot apologists worked hard to disassociate themselves from the politics of English Puritans and, in general, from any charge of disloyalty to the monarch. See Labrousse, *"Une foi, une loi, un roi,"* 39–41.

Poitevin Huguenot grandees, such as the Duc de Rohan.[39] In a letter to the pope, the government suggested that a mission would "provide the means to lead those who had gone astray back to the right path and to obedience, from which they were far too distanced." Louis XIII assisted the mission later in other ways. In 1620 he wrote the pope in support of the Capuchins' request for a renewal of their missionary "faculties."[40] And in 1621 he "favored [the Capuchins] with his royal authority so that they could preach freely without any obstruction in the marketplaces, public squares, crossroads, and other locations, even in places where the seigneurs were of the religion prétendue réformée."[41] The king also mobilized the state's judicial machinery and instructed magistrates to use their authority "against those who might try to oppose [the Capuchins]" (56).

The missionaries made it clear that they served the monarchy as well as the Church. The mission saw as one of its stated purposes maintaining the provinces of Poitou, Saintonge, and Angoumois in obedience to the king.[42] Joseph instructed friars leading processions to the mission exercises to chant litanies for the Virgin with a "Vive le Roi" after each reprise. And he ordered the saying of public prayers for the king and queen's prosperity. After the fall of Saint-Jean-d'Angely in 1621, Joseph preached in the town's principal church, taking as his subject "the obedience one owes to princes."[43] The mission's call for political allegiance provided a powerful inducement for Huguenots to abjure. The former Lusignan pastor Jacques Mestayer described his conversion at the mission's start in 1617 as

39. Mauzaize, "Rôle et l'action des capucins," 1032; Moote, *Louis XIII*, 86; Jeffrey K. Sawyer, *Printed Poison: Pamphlet Propaganda, Faction Politics, and the Public Sphere in Early Seventeenth-Century France* (Berkeley and Los Angeles, 1990), 73–83.

40. Dedouvres, *Politique et apôtre*, 160; Raoul de Sceaux, *Histoire des capucins*, 1436; and Mauzaize, "Rôle et l'action des capucins," 1037.

41. Catholics in Niort referred to these letters-patent in their dispute with Protestants in the early 1620s. See above, p. 41.

42. Lepré-Balain, "La vie du R. Père Joseph de Paris prédicateur de l'ordre des pères capucins, commissaire apostolique des missions étrangères, fondateur des religieuses reformées de S. Benoist sous le tiltre de la Congrégation de Nostre Dame sur le Calvaire," Bibliothèque Provinciale des Capuçins (hereafter BPC), Ms. 22, vol. 4, 261. The author was a friend of Joseph's Capuchin companion, Ange de Mortagne.

43. Lepré-Balain, "Vie du Père Joseph," 4:261, 264; Dedouvres, *Politique et apôtre*, 161. The "Recueils" (60) mention the litanies in the processions to Saint-Jean-d'Angély in 1623.

both an acceptance of religious truth and a return to political loyalty. He explained that a booklet circulating at the recent Huguenot political meeting at La Rochelle had disheartened him. Its purpose was to "prepare spirits for war against the king." He now wanted to "combat the resolutions of war and rebellion." His former religion "was no longer reformed but deformed by seditious movements and troubles, which lead only to confusion and anarchy." He detested "rebellions against the king and his state by ministers, who direct the public affairs of their churches, and he abhorred their scheming to corrupt good servants of the king and to ruin his state entirely."[44]

The sheer application of military force in Poitou during the 1620s was an even more powerful incentive for Huguenot conversions.[45] Many of the abjurations for which the missionaries claimed credit followed in the wake of royal victories. For example, Protestants in Maillezais converted in 1621 only after Louis had regained control of the city, removed the Huguenot garrison, and reestablished episcopal authority in this former bishop's seat.[46] The Duc de La Trémoille's conversion, which the Capuchin chronicle claims "should be attributed to the mission" (59), actually took place before Richelieu and Louis in the army camp besieging La Rochelle in 1628.

Even if the Capuchins wanted to appropriate such a notable success for themselves, they never denied their dependence on the king and their contribution to furthering his interests. Indeed, they made clear—to their Huguenot targets, Catholic supporters, and the king himself—the associa-

44. *La conversion du Sieur Mestayer cy-devant ministre du Lusignan, faicte en la ville de Poitiers le 23 jour de mars 1617* (Poitiers, 1617), 3, 8, 9, 18. It seems likely that Mestayer had converted before the mission began, but the chronicle suggests that the two events coincided. The conversion account was addressed to the provincial assembly of Poitevin ministers scheduled to meet at Thouars in April. See also Mestayer, *Conversions signalées;* and Lièvre, *Histoire des protestants*, 1:295.

45. In the summer of 1621, Louis led his army into the province in the first of several campaigns during the decade to suppress rebellion and Huguenot military power. See David Parker, *La Rochelle and the French Monarchy: Conflict and Order in Seventeenth-Century France* (London, 1980), xii–xiv, 10–12; Moote, *Louis XIII*, 124, 303; and Boissonade, *Histoire de Poitou*, 222–23. As Fagniez pointed out, "It is certain that Louis XIII's campaign in Poitou in 1621 . . . would much consolidate the mission's work" (*Père Joseph et Richelieu*, 1:295, 305).

46. Pérouas, "Mission de Poitou," 360.

tion between the mission and the monarchy. In a 1618 letter to his mother, Père Joseph wrote, "if [the mission] perseveres, you may well judge that God will be glorified, and the affairs of the king will advance no less because all these people who formerly hated him, are now beginning to love him greatly." God worked conversions, but he worked them through his devoted servants the king and the missionaries. Catholics repeated this lesson continuously. Louis XIII never took it as much to heart as his son, but within the discourse of the mission the concurrence between the king's goals and the missionaries' (and his support of their endeavor) was unquestioned. As Joseph explained to his mother, the people "believe he [the king] has sent them these men . . . [the Capuchins], who, as they say, appear to be from another world."[47]

MISSIONARIES AND MINISTERS

The "men from another world": this was a favorite description of Capuchin heroes in mission discourse.[48] The friars attributed much of their success as missionaries to their aura of otherworldliness. In missions to Protestants, the image also helped distinguish them from their rivals, Huguenot ministers, who were depicted as very much men of this world, unjustified in their claim to a divine vocation. Early Protestant reformers had attacked Catholic priests and monks for their incompetence, irresponsibility, and immorality. The anti-Protestant campaigners of the seventeenth century sought to turn the critique around. They wanted to show as false the Protestant clergy's reputation for learning, conscientiousness, and probity. Instead, the Catholic clergy was superior, and none more so than the members of orders dedicated to the Church's missionary work. The Capuchins cultivated a reputation through their mission activities (and burnished in their mission discourse) that could challenge that of the most renowned ministers. Drawing such a distinction between the clergies was, the missionaries were convinced, a very effective way of establishing a boundary between the religions.

47. Quoted in Dedouvres, *Politique et apôtre*, 161.

48. And an enduring one. See William A. Christian Jr.'s description of Capuchin missionaries in early-twentieth-century Spain (*Moving Crucifixes in Modern Spain* [Princeton, N.J., 1992], 29–37).

The Capuchins

The chronicle of a Capuchin mission, whether in Poitou or elsewhere, was hagiographical. It glorified missionary heroes by describing them with certain stereotyped characteristics that proved their holiness and ensured their effectiveness as missionaries (much as saints' biographies described their subjects with standardized motifs).[49] Individual evangelizers achieved success in winning converts because they possessed attributes thought necessary for, indeed infallible in, winning converts. The missionaries' reputation as holy men drew on long-standing motifs in Christian, and specifically Franciscan, tradition.[50] First and foremost were their lives of extreme austerity and privation. Capuchins possessed nothing other than their habits and begging sacks; they traveled barefoot; they ate little; and they practiced harsh discipline with frequent fasts and flagellations. For the French Capuchin mission theorist Yves de Paris, the friars' lives made them "perfect imitators of Christ and the Apostles in abandoning the things of this world," and in "the very strict observance of poverty." The Capuchin's "life and habit, the reform and retreat [he practices] preach even when he does not open his mouth."[51] François de Sales, who

49. Donald Weinstein and Rudolph M. Bell, *Saints and Society: Two Worlds of Western Christendom, 1000–1700* (Chicago, 1982), 139–64; Peter Burke, "How to Be a Counter-Reformation Saint," in *The Historical Anthropology of Early Modern Italy* (Cambridge, U.K., 1987), 48–62; and Jean-Michel Sallmann, *Naples et ses saints à l'âge baroque (1540–1750)* (Paris, 1994), 257–83.

50. Bernard Dompnier's work on the history of Capuchin missionaries in seventeenth-century France has been particularly important. In addition to his works cited above, see "Le missionaire et son public: Contribution à l'étude de la prédication populaire," in *Journées Bossuet: La prédication au XVIIe siècle. Actes du colloque de Dijon 2–4 décembre 1977*, edited by Thérèse Goyet and Jean-Pierre Collinet (Paris, 1980), 105–28; "Pastorale de la peur et pastorale de la séduction: La méthode de conversion des missionnaires capucins," in *La conversion au XVII siècle. Actes du XIIe colloque de Marseille (janvier 1982)*, edited by Roger Duchene (Marseilles, 1983), 257–81; and *Enquête au pays des frères des anges: Les capucins de la province de Lyon au XVIIe et XVIIIe siècles* (Saint-Etienne, 1993). See also Lazaro Iriarte, OFMCap, *Franciscan History: The Three Orders of St. Francis of Assisi* (Chicago, 1982), 282.

51. The quotations are taken from the following works of Yves de Paris: *La conduite du religieux* (Rennes, 1653); *Instructions religieuses tirées des annales et chroniques de l'Ordre de Saint François* (Paris, 1662); and *Les heureux succès de la piété* (Paris, 1634), all of which are quoted in Dompnier, "Mission lointaine et mission de l'intérieur," 97–98.

worked with Capuchin missionaries in the Duchy of Savoy, paid homage to the friars' austerity and its public impact: "The Capuchins have a severe and rigorous spirit; . . . it is a perfect contempt for the exterior world, all its vanities and sensualities. They want their example to induce in people contempt for the things of the world. The poverty of their habits serve this end, and by that means they convert souls to God."[52]

In late-seventeenth-century Capuchin missions among Catholics, such as those of Honoré de Cannes, this otherworldly image enabled missionaries to serve as mediators and peacemakers. They descended on cities as outsiders, devoid of the usual markers of social distinction and strangers to the solidarities and rivalries of local communities. Accounts of these missions highlight the missionaries' success in using their foreignness to reconcile conflicts and obtain restitutions from those who had improperly taken the property of others.[53] The eighteenth-century biographer of Père Joseph, Lepré-Balain, insisted that the Poitou missionaries also achieved "many reconciliations and a quantity of restitutions," but the "Recueils" and other early accounts of the mission say little about the Capuchins' role as peacemakers.[54] Assuaging enmity among Catholics could have furthered their goals by creating greater unity among Catholics, who would then have been better prepared to confront Huguenots. Perhaps the Poitou missionaries pursued this strategy, but their focus was elsewhere. They were less interested in healing the divisions of local society than in rearranging them along confessional lines. And in this aim too their otherworldly image was crucial.

We can see the attributes of the ideal Capuchin missionary crystallize in the person of Chérubin de Maurienne, hero of a Capuchin mission in Savoy.[55] This mission in the 1590s provided a model for the order's later endeavors in France. The mission chronicle depicted Chérubin as the epitome of Capuchin humility and tireless effort: "By day he gave himself to preaching, catechizing, and debates. At night he devoted himself to prayer

52. *Oeuvres complètes*, 6:226, quoted in Dompnier, *Venin de l'hérésie*, 206–7.

53. Raoul de Sceaux, "Père Honoré de Cannes," 367–69; Châtellier, *Religion des pauvres*, 61–74.

54. "Vie du Père Joseph," 4:261.

55. Described in Charles de Genève's chronicle of the mission, *Trophées sacrés*. Page citations are from Part 1 and will follow in the text.

. . . and to the study of Scripture and the Holy Fathers" (80). He was a learned disputant and preacher, renowned "not only for his talent in speaking and persuading but also for his vivacity and skill in treating points of doctrine that heretics [denied]" (70). His eloquence reportedly attracted thousands to his mission exercises.[56] Chérubin was also depicted as a courageous soldier battling heresy, a "valiant captain," a "brave champion of Jesus Christ . . . in the middle of a troop of heretics" (112). He was a healer and miracle worker who battled Satan in hundreds of cases of possession.[57] These cures too served a polemical purpose. The demons possessing the bodies of the unfortunate Savoyards always seemed to be Protestants. Like the heretics, they denied Catholicism until exorcised, after which they enthusiastically acknowledged its truth.[58] According to the account, many Protestants who witnessed the exorcisms converted. Soldier, scholar, charismatic preacher, healer, and humble ascetic, Chérubin is also described as a mother. In Annemasse, "he resolved to . . . suckle his new converts, his first spiritual children and very dear nurselings, so as to attract them to the preaching and to the divine sweetness of the . . . Catholic religion" (84).[59] The language emphasized the contrast between the Capuchin and the supposedly harsh (and strictly masculine) Protestant ministers more intent on imposing discipline than on nurturing their followers.

Chérubin's qualities made him heroic, but, according to the chronicler of his mission, Charles de Genève, they were typical of all Capuchin missionaries, and that is why the friars successfully defeated heresy. As he explained in a section of his chronicle entitled "A Brief Discourse Showing

56. According to the account, over 300,000 attended the jubilee he arranged in Thonon (111).

57. As Dompnier points out: "One can see how ambiguous their [Capuchins'] image was among the people. Wanting to be seen as divine men, they were perhaps perceived as *therapeuts* or men endowed with more or less magic powers" (*Venin de l'hérésie*, 207).

58. Professional exorcists, not Chérubin, performed the exorcisms. But the chronicle presents him as confronting the demons.

59. The maternal metaphors are reminiscent of the terms medieval writers employed to describe Jesus and Cistercian abbots. See Carolyn Walker Bynum, "Jesus as Mother and Abbot as Mother: Some Themes in Twelfth-Century Cistercian Writing," in *Jesus as Mother: Studies in the Spirituality of the High Middle Ages* (Berkeley and Los Angeles, 1982), 110–69.

the Reasons for Which the Capuchin Order Is Very Proper for the Conversion of Heretics":

> The ability of the seraphic order [Capuchins] to introduce itself among heretics has been ordered by God, who destined it for that purpose. The admirable conversions that one has seen in France, Germany, Flanders, and Bohemia have proven this to be true. . . . By the means of this order, God has worked and works everyday marvelous effects in the conversion of heretics and infidels in all the corners of the earth.[60]

The Poitou Capuchins did not have as good a publicist as did Chérubin de Maurienne, but the chronicle of their mission heroizes them, showing that they displayed many of the same attributes—charisma, austerity, piety, self-sacrifice—and pursued their ends with many of the same means. Primary position in the "Recueils" and all accounts of the mission is given to Père Joseph, its founder, administrator, and booster.[61] But Joseph was not only an administrator; he was also celebrated for preaching before and during the mission and for winning conversions.[62] Indeed,

60. *Trophées sacrées*, 1st part, 39–41. As the Capuchin writer Albert de Paris put it: "The vocation of the religious of Saint Francis is to apply themselves to the conversion of sinners, and . . . the mission is the most appropriate and efficacious means to arrive at that glorious end" (*Manual de la mission à l'usage des capucins de la province de Paris* [Troyes, 1702], 1, 8).

61. According to Lepré-Balain, the people proclaimed Joseph "the savior of Poitou." He states that Père Joseph first conceived of the mission in 1614 during a conversation with the guardian of Poitiers's Capuchin house ("Vie du Père Joseph," 3:209–10). Around this time, he composed an epic poem, the "Turciade" to promote another of his plans, a European crusade against the Ottoman Empire, for which he lobbied over the following years in Paris, Rome, and Madrid. The two projects were linked in his mind. Poitou is singled out in the poem because Calvin had lived there. See Dedouvres, *Politique et apôtre*, 139n.1; and Huxley, *Grey Eminence*, 147–53. Joseph wrote reports on the mission's accomplishments that he sent to Rome and to French supporters, such as Cardinal de La Rochefoucauld. See his letter to La Rochefoucauld, which is undated but likely was written around 1627, Ms. 3249, fol. 278, Bibliothèque Sainte-Genviève. See also Raoul de Sceaux, *Histoire des capucins*, 453, 454; and Mauzaize, "Rôle et l'action des capucins," 1036–37.

62. This brief account of Père Joseph's activities is compiled from the following: Lepré-Balain, "Vie du Père Joseph," Book 3, chap. 13; Dedouvres, *Politique et apôtre*, 1:274–85, 2:139–62; Fagniez, *Père Joseph et Richelieu*, 2:285–96; Huxley, *Grey Eminence*, 105–61; and Colette Piat, *Le Père Joseph: Le maître de Richelieu* (Paris, 1988), 34–39, 213–19. Père Joseph is also well known for his devotional writings, mystical piety,

it was his work as a renowned preacher that first brought him into close contact with Poitou. In 1606 he delivered sermons at places close to the province, in Le Mans, Angers, and the Huguenot stronghold of Saumur. In 1608 he was in Poitou at Pentecost to preach at Loudun. And he first encountered Richelieu, whom he would later serve famously as the *éminence grise*, in 1609 when the reform-minded bishop invited the Capuchins to conduct a Forty Hours devotion in Luçon.

However, perhaps because Joseph was often occupied with other duties as a Capuchin administrator and government advisor, the mission chronicle makes less effort to glorify him than the friars he selected to carry out the mission's work. The first six were Jean-Baptiste d'Avranches, Anselme d'Angers, Anastase de Nantes, Louis de Champigny, Eutrope de l'Isle Bouin, and Hubert de Thouars (52).[63] They had received the special training necessary for Capuchin preachers and missionaries, including "the study of *controverses* [religious polemic] and holy languages . . . so that they could render themselves capable of being good missionaries and of appearing with honor before ministers."[64] According to the *facultates*, or powers they received, they could resolve cases of simony (normally reserved for higher ecclesiastical officials), hear confessions, and read Protestant books (so as to be able to refute them). Most importantly, they could absolve heretics. Their authority was "apostolical," a means of comparing the Poitou missionaries to the Apostles but also a technical distinction indicating that their orders came directly from the Holy Office in Rome and

---

and leadership role in the French Capuchin order. He also helped establish the convent of the Filles du Calvaire in 1612, which situated itself in Poitiers in 1617. See Jacques Marcadé and Marie-Louise Fracard, "Le XVIIe siècle: Un triomphe difficile," in Favreau, ed., *Diocèse de Poitiers*, 135–55, esp. 140. He often urged the nuns to pray for his various enterprises, including the Poitou mission. At the time of the siege of La Rochelle, he instructed the nuns to "ask for the ruin of the heresy in this region" (quoted in Piat, *Père Joseph*, 115–16). He also had a controversial political career as Richelieu's *éminence grise*.

63. Fagniez substitutes for the last two on this list, Eutrope de Nantes and Georges de Paris, but he was apparently mistaken (*Père Joseph et Richelieu*, 289). It is possible that they became Poitou missionaries when the mission was expanded in 1625. See also Dedouvres, *Politique et apôtre*, 150; and Raoul de Sceaux, *Histoire des capucins*, 437–39.

64. From the 1616 order of the Capuchin procurator-general, Père Clement de Noto (quoted in Dedouvres, *Politique et apôtre*, 2:148).

hence intermediate authorities could not interfere with them.[65] The direct link to Rome would be further strengthened in 1622, when the mission was placed under the jurisdiction of the newly founded Congregation for the Propagation of the Faith.

No doubt because of the war atmosphere in Poitou during much of the mission's heyday in the 1620s, the chronicle and other accounts of the mission highlight certain standard missionary attributes more than others. The Capuchins are not described as mothers, as was Chérubin de Maurienne; nor did they apparently heal those suffering from possession or other illnesses. But they are portrayed as soldiers, a military association that came easily to mind when royal troops were attacking Protestant-controlled cities in the province. The warfare they waged was spiritual but compared easily to what troops were doing. When Père Joseph consulted Poitiers's bishop La Rocheposay about the mission, the prelate reportedly said that he worried about the Capuchins' project of going to the cities and towns of his diocese preaching against Protestantism, instructing heretics, undertaking debates, and maintaining the truths of the faith against ministers. He feared that it would be reckless for the friars to endanger their lives in such a way. Given the power that heretics had in the province and their hatred for those who tried to free people from their deception, the missionaries could not be safe without a special heavenly aid. But he acquiesced in Joseph's design since he had come to believe that the only means of attacking this fort of heresy and of bringing in some light was to employ good preachers. "Go then . . . to these people uprooted from the Church and torn from its beliefs, who have rendered themselves so terrible by their rebellion. Despoil and pillage them quickly."[66]

According to the mission chronicle, Capuchins were "involved in all the royal army's sieges of the Huguenots" (58, 61). They accompanied troops in the trenches, urging them "to fight for the faith and for their prince against the heretics." At the siege of Saint-Jean-d'Angély, Ambroise de Reims heard confessions and exhorted the soldiers:

65. Dompnier, "Mission lointaine et mission de l'intérieur," 100. Dompnier also cites the seventeenth-century Capuchin mission theorist Yves de Paris, who frequently compared the friars' work to that of the Apostles.

66. This text is found in slightly different versions in Dedouvres, *Politique et apôtre*, 149–50, and Raoul de Sceaux, *Histoire des capucins*, 438–439. Dedouvres sees in La Rocheposay's directive, "Go to these people . . ." a paraphrase of Isaiah 18:2.

> Notwithstanding the great danger from the city's cannon, . . . he went among the soldiers to assist promptly those who were wounded and to encourage others to fight for the faith, for their prince, and against the heretics. He always marched first at the head of the Beaumont regiment, with a crucifix in his hand, fearing nothing. . . . The admirable Père Hubert de Thouars confessed [wounded] soldiers in the trenches, looking for those still breathing so as to give them absolution, and although he was continually under fire and often the closest [to the enemy], he was never wounded.

When the city fell, the missionaries and other priests marched into the town in a procession with military-like trappings and precision: "solemnly, all in rank, bearing two hundred banners and crosses" (58, 60, 67).

The Capuchins ran great risks, but then suffering martyrdom was an important component of their sense of mission. According to the chronicle, in this province where Huguenots were powerful and belligerent, martyrdom was a constant possibility for the missionaries.[67] The ministers were "so angered by the good these fathers did in converting their people that they often lay in wait along the roads to attack [the friars] and set up ambushes in the countryside to kill them" (55). Others reportedly were attacked during debates with ministers. In Loudun, in 1618, Jean-Baptiste d'Avranches and Athanase de Nantes debated the minister of Fontenay, Pierre de La Vallade. In the Capuchin report, the Huguenot jumped onto a bench as the dispute turned against him. He yelled that the missionaries were doing him harm and called for his people to protect him. "Immediately the chamber was filled with bared swords, and [the Protestants] threw themselves on [the missionaries,] holding swords to their throats, beating them, and throwing them on the floor" (55). Such behavior was nothing less than readers of mission accounts expected of their heroes. They had to display courage in the face of death at the hands of armed heretics and nefarious ministers, who could only respond with violence to the truth preached openly and simply.

Nonetheless, descriptions of the Capuchins as combatants may not have been entirely appropriate for these apostolical men. Other meta-

67. None actually suffered martyrdom at Huguenot hands. The account glosses over the protection the missionaries had from the military and provincial Catholic magistrature.

phors were more peaceful. One of the most common in mission accounts was the comparison of missionaries to agricultural workers. Catholic rhetoric described areas with large heretic populations as deserts; they were sterile lands, choked with weeds and thorns. They could only be made productive through assiduous cultivation, described in language that came easily to Christians well acquainted with agricultural life but also with the New Testament parables of the sower or of the wheat and the tares.[68] The chronicle of the Savoy mission described how the Capuchins had "indefatigably cleared the fields newly acquired for the Church, tearing out the thorns and thistles of error and vice, turning them over with the plough of God's word to bring to light the . . . roots of [the heretics'] bad beliefs and habits, and to carry to them the fruits worthy of a holy conversion and a salutary penance."[69] Louis XIII endowed missions to follow in the wake of his military campaigns in the south so that, in the words of Père Joseph, "the fathers could clear the lands so long neglected and which have need of good and faithful workers."[70] Missionaries were the sowers, laborers, and harvesters of souls through conversions.[71] In a letter to his mother, Père Joseph wrote that "Poitou lacks only harvesters." When the friars set to work, preaching, catechizing, and conducting processions and Forty Hours ceremonies, the "fruit" of their harvest "appeared extraordinary in a short time." "Piety blossomed as recompense for its long captivity."[72]

The Capuchins' carefully constructed personae of selflessness, fearlessness, austerity, and piety combined to give them, if we believe their own accounts, a powerful charisma. Proof of their holiness was found in the conversions they won, but also in how people perceived them as popular saints. For example, Raphael d'Orléans died in such a great "odor of sanctity" that after his death a crowd (at Le Mans where he was buried) cut pieces of his habit and his hair to preserve as relics (53–54). Jean-Baptiste

68. Dompnier, "Missionaire et son public," 109.

69. Charles de Genève, *Trophées sacrés*, 1st part, 269.

70. Quoted in Sauzet, *Contre-réforme et réforme catholique*, 281–82.

71. Berthelot du Chesnay paraphrases the imagery: "the mission is the harvest of the Gospel with its workers, far too few in number, who sow, plant, and collect the fruits" (*Jean Eudes*, 66).

72. In the words of Joseph's biographer, Lepré-Balain, "Vie du Père Joseph," 3:210, 215.

d'Avranches, one of the original members of the Poitou mission, died as a result of a vein that burst while he was preaching "with great fervor." As he expired, he received one last conversion, that of a Huguenot noble. After his death, God "produced various signs of his sanctity" (68). Anselme d'Angers also died in a "great odor of sanctity" (69). Another missionary, Michel Ange d'Angers, who assisted soldiers at the siege of La Rochelle, died with "universal esteem for his sanctity" (65). Illuminé de Malicorne, Benoît de La Boulleraye, and Louis de Champigny were also revered for their efforts among the troops and, in particular, for their conversion of Protestant soldiers during the La Rochelle campaign (65–66). Gervais de Reims worked "with such fervor that he never preached without stirring many consciences. He gained so many hearts that at his death people wanted to kiss his feet and cut his habit for relics" (66).

Protestants too could not help but respond favorably to the friars. As the mission chronicle put it, the missionaries were sure to be "cherished and loved . . . by the Huguenots as well as the Catholics" (67). In describing the missionaries' impact, Lepré-Balain wrote that "their austerity, modesty, fervor, and public mortification of their bodies astonished the Huguenots as much as it edified Catholics."[73] In their self-sacrifice, they compared favorably with the Protestant clergy. Ministers, Père Joseph claimed, started to desert their congregations when they had trouble collecting their salaries. Capuchins, by contrast, impressed Huguenots as "men without money."[74] Indeed, mission accounts emphasize that they surpassed the Protestant clergy not only in their disdain for material rewards and comfort but in everything that signified a truly divine pastoral vocation. The Capuchins' rivals were a false clergy, as their religion was false, and the missionaries demonstrated the point at every opportunity to show the people of Poitou the unmistakable boundary between the faiths.

The Ministers

Catholic militants saw the Protestant clergy as diabolical, venal, malicious, and duplicitous: the lies ministers spread about Catholicism prevented people from seeing the truth and ensnared them in heresy. The ar-

73. Lepré-Balain, "Vie du Père Joseph," 3:215.

74. Quoted from a letter of June 1618 from Père Joseph to his mother, in Lepré-Balain, "Vie du Père Joseph," 4:267.

dent anti-Protestant campaigner François Véron insisted in his *La règle générale de la foi catholique* (1645) that it was necessary to "represent Catholic doctrine in the simple beauty of its faith against the trickery of ministers, who by the false colors in which they paint it render it so completely disfigured and hideous that it deserves to be forsaken. By that means more than any other, they maintain in schism those who follow them."[75]

When ministers failed to hold their followers in check through sheer deceit, they resorted to force and intimidation. According to the mission chronicle,

> The ministers, having seen the great éclat of the mission and the great fruit it had already started to bear . . . began to have a horror of the Capuchin missionaries, menacing them and secretly mistreating the new converts. . . . They [spied] on all their people and tried to intercept any message sent to the missionaries. . . . They used their power . . . even to separate husbands from their wives and wives from their husbands. . . . They warned others not to approach Capuchins because [the friars] were enchanters and gave away charms like sorcerers. . . . The ministers, seeing that the missionaries astonished their people so much and so aroused their consciences, tried to slander the Capuchins by all sorts of artifices but were so quickly routed [that their efforts] served only to advance the conversion of many who [saw] the malice, ignorance, and falseness of their ministers in all they said about religion. (54, 63)

Unlike the friars, who were valiant warriors, the ministers were deceitful spies acting secretly to prevent preaching of the simple truth. By drawing the contrast, missionaries sought to drive a wedge between Huguenot clergymen and their flocks. Once released from the power of their pastors and exposed to Catholic verities, Protestants inevitably would abjure.

The best way to weaken the ministers was to humiliate them, impugn their honor, show their doctrine to be false, and attack their confident belief that they were more learned in Scripture than the Catholic clergy. The

75. Quoted in Dompnier, *Venin de l'hérésie*, 105. Véron was a former Jesuit, who, in numerous publications, expounded his own approach to converting Huguenots. Nicknamed "la Véronique" method, it consisted of aggressively challenging ministers to produce the explicit scriptural passages supporting articles found in the Reformed Church's *Confession of Faith*. On Véron, see Dompnier, *Venin de l'hérésie*, 177–84.

means to do this—a means for which both the missionaries and many of their Protestant opponents were well prepared—was the public debate. In the decades following the Edict of Nantes, debates between Catholic and Protestant clerics were a familiar sight throughout France.[76] Ostensibly, the purpose of these encounters was to provoke or prevent conversions. They were often staged at the invitation of someone who supposedly was considering changing confessions. Each side hoped to attract potential converts or hold on to followers who might abjure by defending its beliefs and disputing those of the other side through reasoned argumentation. In many cases, however, the abjuration had already occurred. And accounts of the debates suggest that they were not just learned exchanges but also contests for defending honor and humiliating opponents, similar in some respects to duels. Even the participants remarked on the similarity. According to a Catholic report, the Poitevin minister Pierre de La Vallade tried to avoid a debate in 1620 by comparing it to a duel, which the king prohibited. The Catholic side harried him by insisting that the "king permitted certain duels, when performed in due order, so as to prevent worse evils; private debates with ministers are no less useful."[77]

Like the code of the duel, that of the doctrinal debate was reformulated in the late-sixteenth and early-seventeenth centuries.[78] Rules were fixed for its procedures, witnesses, and challenges. And, as in the duel, the debate relied on the threat to personal honor to induce participation from the side receiving the challenge. A debater claimed victory not just because of his superior learning or skill but because of his opponent's embarrassment and dishonor. Or, at least, this is how debates appear in published versions of them. Each side eagerly printed accounts of these encounters, which are the basis for the following discussion.[79] Since de-

76. The most complete study of these debates, unfortunately unpublished, is Emile Kappler, "Conférences théologiques entre catholiques et protestants en France au XVIIe siècle," 2 vols. (Thèse de 3e cycle, Université de Clermont II, 1980), 2:214–16. For a succinct discussion of the debates and of their rise and fall in the seventeenth century, see Dompnier, *Venin de l'hérésie*, chap. 7.

77. Cited in Kappler, "Conférences théologiques," 1:249, 2:216, and for other comparisons with duels, see 1:248–50.

78. On the duel, see François Billacois, *Le duel dans la société française des XVIe–XVIIe siècles: Essai de psychologie historique* (Paris, 1986), 97–111.

79. Though I will refer also to the mission chronicle. We never have, to my knowledge, independent descriptions of the encounters, only each side's reports and claims

bates actually resulted in few conversions and combatants rarely admitted defeat, the importance of the encounters lay in one side's or both sides' proclamation of success in defending doctrine and embarrassing their opponent. Thereby the debates aided the process of creating two clearly defined rival communities divided by a rigid boundary. By both emphasizing doctrinal differences and humiliating Protestant ministers, Capuchin debaters could claim to have strengthened Catholics' sense of a separate confessional identity and to have undermined the authority embarrassed ministers had over their flocks.

The procedural issues in such "duels" included the choice of location, moderators, secretaries, and verifiers who would check the debaters' assertions against Scripture, the *juge des controverses*. Indeed, the question of Scripture—of what constituted it, of how to interpret it, and of who had mastered it—was the central concern in many of these encounters. Resorting to the Bible as the juge des controverses raised two conflicts not easily resolved. One was the Catholic-Protestant argument over vernacular translations of the Bible (and the inclusion of certain apocryphal books).[80] Sometimes a disputant would agree, in a manner reminiscent of a gallant dueling gesture, to use the other side's Bible so as to disprove the opponent on his own ground. But more often one side would attack the authenticity and authority of the other's version.

The other dispute was over the Protestant belief in *sola scriptura*. The Reformed Church's *Confession of Faith* (1559) declared Scripture to have "proceeded from God, from whom—and not from men—it takes its authority. It is the measure of all faith. . . . It is not lawful for men . . . to add, diminish, or change anything in it."[81] Scripture was the sole source of doctrinal truth. Catholics countered by pointing out that not all doctrines

---

of victory. For a list of the publications, see Desgraves, *Répertoire des ouvrages de controverse*.

80. Roland H. Bainton, "The Bible in the Reformation," in *The Cambridge History of the Bible*, 3 vols., vol. 3: *The West from the Reformation to the Present Day*, edited by S. L. Greenslade (Cambridge, U.K., 1975), 1–37, see esp. 6–9; and Kappler, "Conférences théologiques," 1:151–55. Protestants did not generally recognize the canonicity of the apocryphal books, such as Maccabees, in which Catholics found scriptural support for purgatory. Translation differences could also become doctrinally significant and the source of contention in disputations.

81. Quoted in Kappler, "Conférences théologiques," 1:150.

could be found plainly stated in Scripture. The often-used example was the Trinity, on which Catholics and Calvinists agreed but which had no explicit scriptural warrant.[82] Catholics looked to the apostolic tradition of the Church. Scripture needed interpretation, which implied the need for an infallible interpreter, without which no infallible doctrine could exist. Only the Catholic Church, through the authority of its popes, could claim such a role. Thus, in debates, the claims of each side often rested less on actual interpretation of Scripture (though that too was at issue) than in the attempt by one side to force the other to recognize that only it had an accurate Bible and an authoritative means of divining its message. The Bible, then, was not just a reference for, or judge of, debates. It was a weapon of the debate itself, a means of demonstrating a rival's defeat and dishonor by his failure to impose a choice of text, by his inability to adopt a consistent approach to it, or by his total embarrassment in front of it.

In a debate staged at Civray four years before the beginning of the Capuchin mission, the Jesuit Etienne Moquot challenged the writings of the local minister, Jacques Crozé, who had published, in 1611, a book entitled *Le juge des controverses*.[83] In a sermon the Jesuit challenged his rival to show by Scripture that the French Genevan Bible was accurate. Crozé's response came in writing (the debate was conducted in writing for four months prior to the public encounter); he insisted that Scripture, in its original Hebrew and Greek, was divinely inspired and the supreme refer-

82. As the abbess of Poitiers's Sainte-Croix convent wrote in 1628 to her Protestant sister, the Duchesse de La Trémoille: "I would say to you . . . that you believe as we do in the Holy Trinity, one God in three persons, and yet it is not spoken of in Scripture" (copy of letter of 18 December 1628 in BPF Ms. 870 [1]).

83. Jacques Crozé, *Le juge des controverses de ce temps* (Poitiers, 1611). I am following here Kappler's discussion of the debate; see "Conférences théologiques," 2:127–32. Both debaters published accounts of the dispute: Etienne Moquot, *La fuite de Jacques Crozé, soy-disant ministre de Civray . . .* (Poitiers, 1613); Moquot, *Eclaircissements que l'impudence du ministre Crozé n'avoit pas permis au missionaire de dilater* (Poitiers, 1613); Crozé, *Traicté de la perfection suffisante, clarté luisante, salutaire lecture et sommaire doctrine de l'Escripture pour antidote aux sermons du jésuite Moquot* (Niort, 1613); Moquot, *L'examen et censure des bibles de la confession de foy des églises prétendue réformée de France . . .* (Poitiers, 1617). Poitou had already witnessed debates between the minister Pierre de La Vallade and the Capuchin Ange de Raconis at Fontenay in 1609 and between the minister Jean Chauffpied and the Capuchin Père Valentin at Niort in 1611 (see Kappler, "Conférences théologiques," 2:108–9, 121–23).

ence for truth. Therefore, it had to be translated into the "familiar mother language of everyone." Moquot's demand that scriptural proof be offered concerning the French Bible's veracity was absurd; the Bible could not possibly contain the words "the Bible of Geneva is without fault." The Jesuit, in turn, pointed out that successive editions of the Genevan Bible (those of 1561, 1566, and 1608) had corrected the 1535 Pierre Robert Olivétan translation, thereby showing all these translations to be false.[84] The minister responded by asking his opponent to demonstrate that the Latin Vulgate was faultless, something that humanist textual criticism had made impossible. The public meeting between the two quickly ended in disorder as each refused to respond to the other's challenges. Moquot insisted this was what happened when ministers pretended to base their faith on an inauthentic Bible. Crozé claimed that the Jesuit had shamefully fled the field, and, further, that when he had received the minister's writings, he "became livid, his teeth chattered, his lips trembled, and his tongue stammered." Catholics produced similar descriptions of Protestants in other debates; faced with clear truth, the opponent reacted viscerally. The evidence of victory was not the superior logic or scriptural basis of one's arguments but the opponent's loss of physical control, a sign everyone could recognize unmistakably.

Capuchins made the same argument in debates during the mission. One of their first Poitevin converts in 1617 was the minister of Lusignan, Jacques Mestayer, who became a disputant for the Catholic cause. Five days after the mission's official start on Christmas of 1617, Mestayer, accompanied by two Capuchins, debated Châtellerault's minister, Paul Geslin de La Piltière. The encounter's ostensible purpose was the instruction (and potential conversion) of a Protestant widow. According to Geslin's account, the minister challenged Mestayer to find a scriptural passage supporting the invocation of saints.[85] The recent convert agreed, but first demanded that the Huguenot produce a passage clearly showing that only Scripture (rather than Scripture and the Church) could justify an article of

84. On the different editions, see R. A. Sayce, "Continental Versions to c. 1600: French," in *Cambridge History of the Bible*, 3:113–22, see esp. 117–18.

85. I rely here on Kappler's discussion of Geslin's account of the debate in his *Bref et veritable discours de se qui s'est passé en la conférence . . .* (Saumur, 1618). See "Conférences théologiques," 2:159–63.

faith. Geslin saw no need to respond since, he insisted, Mestayer and his two Capuchin handlers were the debate's initiators.

Mestayer countered that he would offer his proof only if the participants agreed on an approved Bible. Geslin proposed Arias Montanus's Hebrew text, a gesture of bravado since it was a "Catholic" Bible.[86] But its choice embarrassed the Catholic. He complained that the debaters could not use a Hebrew Bible because the widow could not understand Hebrew. The Protestant pointed out, however, that Mestayer could not understand it either, a comment that, as he reported, "left most of the audience laughing." Mestayer then proposed the Latin Vulgate published in 1581 by Leonard Wild of Venice, to which Geslin would only agree if it was verified by Hebrew or Greek texts. Mestayer refused, and Geslin offered a Louvain-approved Greek New Testament.[87] Mestayer replied that the edition was not authentic. The session ended having resolved nothing. The next day the Protestant was again summoned to prove the authenticity of his proposed New Testament, or else he would be held "as deserting his cause." Geslin contended that it should be acceptable for Catholics to hold the Genevan Bible as authentic in arguing against Protestants and for Protestants to consider a Catholic Bible as authentic against Catholics. The debate disintegrated with each side boasting of success.

Mestayer became the Catholic reporter for other debates, and, not surprisingly, in his accounts the Capuchins always triumphed. Their success came from their infallible means of converting heretics; they needed only "shock" them into realizing that their "ministers had given them false Bibles" and hence "a false church."[88] In Pouzauges in 1620 the missionary Anastase de Nantes challenged the minister Jean de La Place by offering to argue publicly that Protestantism was not scripturally based.[89] The Ca-

86. This was the Royal Antwerp edition, printed by Christopher Plantin in the 1570s. It is possible that Mestayer objected to an edition that some Catholic theologians treated with suspicion, despite papal approval in 1572. See Basil Hall, "Biblical Scholarship: Editions and Commentaries," in *Cambridge History of the Bible*, 3:38–93, see esp. 54–55, 57, 58. This Bible was actually a polyglot one, but the debate referred only to its Hebrew text.

87. Published by Plantin in Antwerp in 1574.

88. *Conversions signalées*, unpaginated preface.

89. Kappler bases his discussion on *Extraict du success de quelques rencontres et conferences despuis peu de iours entre les P.P. Capucins de la mission & quelques ministres du Poitou* (Poitiers, n.d.) ("Conférences théologiques," 2:214–15).

puchin insisted that one could not find in Protestant Bibles, in explicit terms, the articles of the Huguenot *Confession of Faith*. Furthermore, the Bibles that Protestants used were not canonical. The *Confession of Faith* taught that canonical books were recognized "not so much by the accord and common consent of the Church but by the evidence and persuasion of the Holy Spirit."[90] According to Mestayer, the minister had to claim either that he, Jean de La Place, was personally inspired by the Holy Spirit to determine the validity and meaning of biblical books, or he had to admit that the Holy Spirit spoke in the "common consent of the Church," thereby confirming the Catholic position. It was a dilemma from which the Huguenot could not possibly emerge with honor. The minister was trapped, and the result, the Catholic account claims, was an armed scuffle that ended the encounter.

The outcome was similar at Fontenay-le-Comte, where Anastase de Nantes and his colleague Jean-Baptiste d'Avranches debated the minister Pierre de La Vallade over the same issue. According to an anonymous Catholic report, La Vallade, rather than replying directly to the challenge, resorted to a long discourse—"fertile in calumny and illusions"—against purgatory, images, and the invocation of saints. The Capuchins returned the debate to their theme by citing Huguenot authors—Philippe Duplessis-Mornay, André Rivet, and La Vallade himself—to the effect that Protestant translations were uncertain.[91] The Huguenots "were in agony," and responded by drawing weapons and assaulting the missionaries. A royal judge, the mayor, and soldiers from the local garrison intervened on the missionaries' behalf and restored order. According to their account, the Catholics' claim to victory seemed clear. Here, as in Pouzauges, Protestants unable to argue their case according to the Bible were reduced to violence.[92]

Catholics reported that, in other encounters, Capuchin mastery of

90. Article 4 of the *Confession of Faith*, quoted in Kappler, "Conférences théologiques," 1:150. See also Paul Romane-Musculus, "L'église réformée de Pouzauges de l'Édit de Nantes à sa révocation," *Bulletin de la société d'histoire du protestantisme français* 125 (1979): 9–46, see esp. 13–14.

91. The specific writings and statements of these authors are not reported. Rivet, a professor at Leiden, was formerly chaplain to the La Trémoille family in Poitou.

92. Kappler, "Conférences théologiques," 2:214–16. La Vallade was a veteran of such encounters, having debated another Capuchin in 1617; see Kappler, "Conférences théologiques," 2:158–59.

Scripture so overwhelmed Huguenots that they feared to refer to it at all. Mestayer described a 1620 debate between the Capuchin Anselme d'Angers and the minister of Parthenay, Nicolas Belin. They met around the sickbed of a Parthenay Protestant innkeeper named La Verdure.[93] Here the question was which church the Bible supported; according to the Catholic account, the debate centered on one particular scriptural passage. The Capuchin asserted that, clearly and formally, Paul's Epistle to the Romans approved and recommended the Roman Church with its salutation: "To all God's beloved in Rome who are called to be saints . . . your faith is proclaimed in all the world" (Romans 1:7–8).[94] The minister acknowledged that everyone proclaimed the faith of the Romans in the time of St. Paul; however, they had believed in justification by faith, not works. According to the Catholic account, after "having run through a rhapsody of so-called differences between the primitive and present Roman churches, it became apparent that [Belin] had no scriptural text that approached directly or indirectly the formal question." The friar asserted that Belin, in denying Paul's explicit teaching that faith alone does not justify, convicted himself of heresy. The necessity of works was a straightforward matter; the minister need only open the Bible and see what it said.

The Protestant, however, would not just open the Bible. The innkeeper complained that his pastor had not produced clear and explicit scriptural passages to back up his arguments. Instead, he became bewildered and "envelop[ed] himself in a labyrinth of long and obscure repetitions." The next day the Capuchin again summoned his opponent to show by "formal texts" that the Roman Church was not the true church, and that the one St. Paul praised was not the same as today's. Minister Belin admitted that he could not do so "by the letters, words, and syllables of Scripture, but he could prove the point by equipollence." The invalid did not understand this term of logical argumentation. The friar explained that ministers, supposedly as an article of faith, renounced all resort to "sagesse humaine," such as Scholastic logic and Aristotelian subtleties like equipollences. St. Paul had cautioned us against being taken in "by philosophy, vain fallacies, and the traditions of men."

93. Mestayer, *Conversions signalées*, 18–25; Kappler, "Conférences théologiques," 2:212–14.

94. I rely here on the Revised Standard Edition translation.

The Capuchin had delivered what seemed a very telling blow. He claimed the authority of Scripture and left his rival floundering in the vanities and fallacies of Scholastic argumentation. The early Protestant reformers had scored points against their Catholic opponents by mocking the excessive intricacies and artificialities of such reasoning. Now the Capuchins were turning the tables. They ridiculed Protestants for losing themselves in the labyrinths of "human wisdom." The accusation was disingenuous. Debaters on both sides were generally well educated in, and understood that their debates would be ordered by, the principles of Scholastic disputation. Indeed, missionaries sometimes found it advantageous to criticize their opponents for not having mastered the techniques of Scholastic debate. As the Jesuit Pierre Coton pointed out, it was by using successfully the form of Scholastic debate in a public setting that one could truly master an opponent. "Only in the public dispute . . . are you constrained to stand your ground, firm within the bounds of reason, of logic, of syllogism. . . . There one can really see what you are made of."[95] But, in debates over Scripture, a better strategy lay in demonstrating that the opponent was, like Minister Belin, lost in a "forest of consequences and equipollences," while the Capuchin relied on simple, clear, and explicit biblical proof by offering La Verdure three specific passages in which Paul had approved the Roman Church. The friar asked him if he would not rather embrace the faith of Paul and the Church than rely on the "spurious imagination of a private, faulty man, who was sustained only by his own ideas without any proof in Scripture." The innkeeper promptly renounced Calvinism.

Other ministers too would be afraid to open their Bibles. After one debate, the Capuchin Anastase de Nantes converted a Poitevin nobleman named Piraneau, who "seeing that Père Anastase had confused his minister" in two encounters, "announced in everyone's presence: 'I am convinced by these truths [the Capuchin's arguments]. I will leave my minister and become a Catholic.'" The consistory elders upbraided their pastor for not having performed better. Why, they asked, did he not refer to the Bible to confirm their beliefs and prove the Catholic ones wrong? Accord-

95. P. Coton, *Apologétique quatriesme* (Avignon, 1600), quoted in Kappler, "Conférences théologiques," 1:64; see also 1:125–27 and 2:195. On the use of Scholastic reasoning in these debates, see Dompnier, *Venin de l'hérésie*, 172–79.

ing to the mission chronicle, he responded: "I would rather lose this one convert than in opening my Bible risk losing a hundred others" (62).

At Saint-Jean-d'Angély, Coulonges, and Champdeniers, fearful Huguenot clergymen refused to appear in public against the Capuchins (57, 64). On the Isle de Ré (Aunis) and at Barbezieux (Angoumois), ministers were so terrified they could not sign their names to the debate proceedings (63–64). In all these places people disappointed with their pastors' performances quickly converted. The bold and learned minister of Saint-Claude assured his congregation that he could rout the Capuchins, but as the time for the debate approached he was "so intimidated in his soul . . . that . . . the elders and deacons of the consistory had to go to his house and threaten to depose him if he did not come to where everyone was assembled." Once there, "he fell into such confusion . . . and he became so sick . . . that he had to resign his ministry." His followers abandoned him and "many converted" (69).

Needless to say, Protestant accounts of debates, when they exist, present a very different picture, another indication that these contests were useful as a way of furthering the polemical conflict between the churches. The propaganda battle was weighted heavily in the Catholics' favor. The Reformed Church did not lack for ardent debaters, but they had less access to printing presses than their opponents, who could also count on greater financial support for their publications and less interference by royal censors. Eventually Protestant synods advised ministers against entering into debates; they were a losing proposition. Catholics also developed doubts. Even Père Joseph pointed out that the majority of conversions "arrive like a lightning bolt and not after debates." In the 1630s Vincent de Paul suggested that debates served little purpose: "they produce more noise than fruit." In the next decade Bishop Jean-Pierre Camus argued that "conversation" with Protestants was more effective than "ill-tempered" disputes.[96] After 1630 the frequency of debates fell considerably.[97]

The critics may well have been right. Missionaries claimed that debates

96. Fagniez, *Père Joseph et Richelieu*, 1:291; and Dompnier, *Venin de l'hérésie*, 186–89.

97. They enjoyed something of a revival, however, in the years preceding the Revocation of the Edict of Nantes.

produced abjurations, but there is little evidence that these were numerous. Indeed, accounts of the disputations suggest that their immediate purpose was less the winning of converts than the attacking of the rival clergy. Mission discourse portrayed the Capuchins as easily defeating ministers in debates, which, in turn, led to Huguenot abjurations. Père Joseph wrote in 1618 that ministers were scolding elders for not keeping watch over the flock more closely. Elders responded that they could not constantly be leaving their shops to "do nothing else but go after those who wanted to convert." "If the ministers wanted to be believed, they should be more like the Capuchins, but they [the ministers] would quit the ministry before they would act like Capuchins."[98] Drawing a sharp distinction between the true and the false clergy and the true and the false churches made the confessional boundary clear. In Catholic mission discourse, the only means left to cross it was through conversion. But to make the dividing line secure, it had to be established not just between clergymen but also between neighbors of the two faiths. And doing so required hardening the confessional boundary in the communities they shared.

THE CONTEST OVER SPACE

Catholic missionaries knew well that their religion was tied closely to specific locations in a sacred landscape: churches, religious houses, cemeteries, shrines, and so forth. But even mundane spaces could take on religious significance, as, for example, city streets when processions moved through them on saints' festivals or when priests carried the viaticum to dying parishioners. The respect spectators paid processions and the reverence they offered the Eucharist made sacred and nonsacred spaces indistinguishable, at least temporarily. As we have seen, Catholics and Huguenots could reach agreement on the sharing of public spaces, but the expansion of Catholic sacrality into shared public space could also set off confrontations between them. And then, despite the Edict of Nantes's stipulations, Huguenots might obstruct processions or refuse to remove their hats when they encountered a priest carrying the Host. The bitter

98. Letter of June 1618, quoted in Lepré-Balain, "Vie du Père Joseph," 4:268; and in Dedouvres, *Politique et apôtre*, 2:154–55.

complaints each side registered with royal officials suggest how tense these disputes could become.

Calvinists, in principle, had a very different understanding of space.[99] They did not invest buildings (e.g., temples) or locations (e.g., cemeteries) with sacredness. However, they did have a very acute sense of the importance of religious spaces and structures in towns they shared with Catholics. The presence of their temples and cemeteries, and their marching through the streets on the way to worship or to funerals, anchored them in civic space and ensured, as the Edict of Nantes guaranteed, their membership in the communities in which they lived. Their religious life and their social interactions with Catholic neighbors in markets and squares made them fully a part of their communities. They saw the Catholic appropriation of shared places as a threat. For the Capuchins, the mixture of religions in shared spaces was a problem, and they made the re-Catholicization of space in biconfessional communities one of their principal mission strategies. If they were to construct a strict boundary between Catholics and Protestants, they would have to separate the groups in daily social life, force Protestant religious activities to the margins, isolate Huguenots, and reclaim for Catholicism territory that heresy had laid to waste.

A Ruined and Barren Land

In making his case to Pope Paul V for a mission to Poitou, Père Joseph described the region in 1616 as

> formerly very Christian, but now one can see only the effaced image of Christianity. Holy places are desolated, altars profaned, sacred vessels carried off, crosses broken, images rent. The stones of sanctuaries are scattered in the streets. . . . Or they remain standing but are put to profane uses. . . . As for vicars, those who are good are persecuted; the others are without virtue and have no understanding of their duties. They . . . leave those around them . . . in ignorance and immorality. Catholics, having no one to give them the bread of the true word of God, all go to the [temple], where they and their children swallow the poison of

99. For a discussion of the different Catholic and Protestant senses of urban space, see Natalie Zemon Davis, "The Sacred and the Body Social in Sixteenth-Century Lyon," *Past and Present* 90 (February 1981): 40–70.

> heresy. Those who wish to serve God almost always have to hide themselves. The true daughter of heaven is persecuted; the servants have become the masters.[100]

The mission chronicler made use of essentially the same rhetoric in describing the province on the eve of the mission:

> Since they [Huguenots] were in the majority, all the churches were in ruins, without bells, without priests, and without sacraments. Catholics were constrained, in each of the parishes where there was a church, to receive the sacrament of the Eucharist only on the day of Easter, without any preparation or confession. . . . The province contained close to 2,000,000 souls of which the majority knew neither prayers, doctrines, not even how many gods there are. (54)

One can easily question the exaggerations in these reports—Poitevins do not even know how many gods there are![101] But the descriptions draw upon the commonplaces of anti-Protestant invective to depict physical and spiritual desolation, a land heresy and immorality have devastated. A region infected with false religion lay in ruins, devoid of Catholicism's physical markers—altars, crosses, images—which nourished spiritual life. Nothing good could grow in the barren soil heresy polluted. Thus La Rochelle was a "seedbed [only] of libertinage." And Latillé—a community with, according to the chronicle, only two or three Catholic families (and a Huguenot seigneur)—was one of "the most ruined, most deserted, and most abandoned" in Poitou. "Heresy had rendered it . . . savage" (56, 67). In part, the destruction the accounts portrayed—holy places desolated, stones of sanctuaries scattered in the streets—may well have been real even twenty years after the end of the Wars of Religion. But physical ruins signaled a more profound problem: the sorry state of spiritual life and social morality due to the overweening presence and power of the heresy.

The normal order of the world was overturned; the "servants have become the masters." The "master" here could refer to the cowed Catholic clergy, unable to exercise its traditional authority and supervision over re-

100. From Lepré-Balain, "Vie du Père Joseph," 3:12.

101. The claim resembles the one that Catholic missionaries made about the people they encountered in the Americas. The rhetoric is also typical of the Church's campaign against "popular religion." See Luria, *Territories of Grace*, introduction.

ligious life. Hence the good vicars "are persecuted." But the phrase also implies that with Huguenot domination no proper moral order can be sustained. The boundary between the true and the false faiths has collapsed. Catholics attend Protestant worship rather than the mass; their children absorb heresy rather than the teachings of the Catholic catechism. Many are left in "ignorance and immorality." The account of the Savoy mission in the 1590s described the problem even more explicitly, and colorfully, than Père Joseph or the Poitou chronicler: "the heretics' minds . . . wallow in the darkness of error and in the shadows of eternal death." They think nothing of severing the sacred union of marriage (a frequent Catholic accusation against Protestant authorization of divorce). They easily break oaths, contracts, and testimony sworn on Holy Scripture, for which they have no real regard. And they have contempt for the Ten Commandments.[102] Heretics could not be trusted to maintain the bonds necessary to the proper functioning of society—all the more reason why Catholics had to break off social communication with them.

Only returning the region to the Church could revive morality. Catholic religious life had to be rebuilt physically and spiritually. A land heresy and sin had made barren would be restored through assiduous cultivation. As we have seen, the Capuchin missionaries described themselves as tireless builders and planters. Their tools were not hammers and plows but the ceremonies and preaching of their mission. With them, the friars would sanctify the region and tear out the thorns of heresy by expelling Protestantism from the spaces Catholics and Huguenots shared and in which they carried on normal social interactions with each other. In other words, Poitou would have to be re-Catholicized or resacralized.

The Forty Hours and the Resacralization of Social Space

Through their mission exercises, the Capuchins pursued a confrontation over space that echoed Christianity's earliest conflicts with pagan temples. More recently, sixteenth-century missions in Latin America had demonstrated the importance of such struggles to Catholicism's expansion. Franciscans working in the Yucatan recognized, in Inga Clendinnen's words, "the efficacy of a minutely regulated environment in shaping be-

102. Charles de Genève, *Trophées sacrés*, 1st part, 49, 311.

havior into desired forms." To win conversions, they sought to transform Mayan lives by destroying the traditional spatial arrangements of their villages and constructing new ones more like those in Europe.[103] The Capuchins in Poitou had no need for anything quite so radical. But they too faced a rival religion embedded in townscapes that were "thickly inscribed with the social and sacred meanings of a way of life."[104] And they too sought to combat that religion by removing its presence from shared civic spaces, transforming them into purely Catholic locations.

The most effective means to achieve this end was to take over public space and fill it with Catholic ritual, sacred objects, and preaching, all of which were part of the spectacular Forty Hours devotion, the hallmark of Capuchin missions in France. The Forty Hours originated in Milan in the 1520s, and it could take a number of forms.[105] The basic ceremony consisted of a vigil performed over three days before the consecrated Host exposed on a church altar. Confraternities, such as those of the Blessed Sacrament, celebrated it in a relatively private fashion in their chapels with members taking turns two-by-two before the altar. Nuns also ob-

103. They replaced temples, village chiefs' courtyards, and multiple-family dwellings with churches, municipal buildings, and single-family houses; see Clendinnen, "Landscape and World View," 376, 379. For modern examples of the Christian missionary effort to remake "mystical geograph[ies]," see Terence Ranger, "Taking Hold of the Land: Holy Places and Pilgrimages in Twentieth-Century Zimbabwe," *Past and Present* 117 (1987): 158–94, see esp. 166; or to establish "mastery of the mundane map of lived space," see Jean Comaroff and John Comaroff, *Of Revelation and Revolution: Christianity, Colonialism, and Consciousness in South Africa*, 2 vols. (vol. 1: Chicago, 1991), 1:202. Early-twentieth-century Capuchins, working in northern Spanish towns and villages, organized the parishes in which they worked as "sacred territories" to combat socialism and anticlericalism (Christian, *Moving Crucifixes*, 29).

104. Clendinnen, "Landscape and World View," 379.

105. The general of the Capuchin order, Bellintani da Salò, introduced it to Paris in 1572. See Ann W. Ramsey, *Liturgy, Politics, and Salvation: The Catholic League in Paris and the Nature of Catholic Reform, 1540–1630* (Rochester, N.Y., 1999), 76. On the history of the Forty Hours devotion, see Bernard Dompnier, "Un aspect de la dévotion eucharistique dans la France du XVIIe siècle: Les prières des Quarante-Heures," *Revue d'histoire de l'église de France* 67 (January–June 1981): 5–31; and Ronald F. E. Weissman, *Ritual Brotherhood in Renaissance Florence* (New York, 1982), 229–33. I have also discussed it in "Rituals of Conversion: Catholics and Protestants in Seventeenth-Century Poitou," in *Culture and Identity in Early Modern Europe (1500–1800): Essays in Honor of Natalie Zemon Davis*, edited by Barbara B. Diefendorf and Carla Hesse (Ann Arbor, Mich., 1993), 65–81, see esp. 69–72.

served it in their convents, as did those of the Sainte-Croix home in Poitiers in 1627, who performed a Forty Hours to pray for the conversion of the Protestant Duchesse de La Trémoille, Charlotte-Brabantine de Nassau, sister of their abbess, Charlotte-Flandrine de Nassau.[106] The ceremony also could be expanded and used as a large, public, expiatory rite to appease God's anger in the face of epidemics or military threats. And it could be used to rally Catholic morale, as in Catholic League-controlled Paris during Henri IV's siege in 1590.[107]

Capuchins used it to open (and sometimes close) their missions; they theatricalized the rite to provide the sort of shock the mission needed to disrupt the usual patterns of daily existence and focus all attention on their evangelizing efforts. They felt the showy, baroque ceremony would revive the faith of Catholics, whom Huguenots had intimidated, and promote the Catholic Reformation style of worship. It was performed under the clergy's careful supervision, and it could be used to counter traditional practices, as in Italy where Forty Hours were arranged to coincide and compete with Carnival celebrations, of which Tridentine reformers disapproved.[108] The Forty Hours also promoted the Eucharistic cult, a central concern of the Catholic Reformation's program of devotional reform. The Eucharistic focus also made the Forty Hours valuable for polemical use against Protestantism. The vigil before the Host proclaimed the truth of the Real Presence, which Calvinists denied. Indeed, Capuchins found Forty Hours devotions so potent a polemical weapon that they conducted them at the same time and in the same places as Reformed Church synods. The Catholic faithful gained a greater sense of proper doctrine and practice. The distinctions between their faith and the heresy became clearer.

On Huguenots, the Forty Hours had a double effect of separation and

106. Letter of 28 December 1627, "Lettres de Flandrine de Nassau, abbesse de Sainte-Croix de Poitiers à Charlotte-Brabantine de Nassau, duchesse de La Trémoille, sa soeur," in *Archives historiques du Poitou*, vol. 1, edited by P. Marchegay (1872), 203–96, see esp. 286. I will return to this issue below, see pp. 231–32.

107. Ramsey, *Liturgy, Politics, and Salvation*, 76.

108. Keith P. Luria, "The Counter-Reformation and Popular Spirituality," in *Christian Spirituality: Post-Reformation and Modern*, edited by Louis Dupré and Don E. Saliers, volume 18 of *World Spirituality: An Encyclopedic History of the Religious Quest* (New York, 1989), 93–120, see esp. 115–16.

attraction. Gathering large numbers of Catholics in squares or markets literally excluded Protestants from spaces to which they normally had access. Ministers and consistories would only have increased this segregation by insisting that Protestants not participate in the mission's idolatrous ceremonies or listen to missionaries preach. Huguenots should not have been joining their Catholic neighbors in the vast outpouring of emotion the mission exercises provoked. However, the friars believed that the ceremony's baroque spectacle attracted the ritually deprived Protestants. Anti-Protestant campaigners were convinced that Calvinism's attempt to strip away the sensory aspects of religious practice was doomed to failure; it impoverished the senses or the imagination, both considered vital in provoking truly profound religious feelings. Thus after having created a boundary between Catholics and Protestants, the Forty Hours could open the way for Capuchins to reach Huguenots through their preaching and entice them to abjure.

According to the Capuchin mission theorist Yves de Paris, the friars could gain "authority over the minds of people" who attended their missions because they "believe what they see and give themselves to truths proven as much by impression and example as by reason."[109] A contrast between reason and emotion was central to how the Capuchins constructed their mission exercises and their preaching. Although the missionaries were well trained in the reasoned argumentation of theological disputation, which they put to use in debates with ministers, they judged the strength of their effectiveness to lie in an appeal to their audience's senses. The chronicler of the Savoy mission explained that the Capuchin order "is the most proper and powerful remedy against the spiritual infirmity of heretics and sinners, who always and everywhere prefer sensual appetites." Heretics were trapped in "sensual appetites," which led them into sin. Yet the Capuchins would have to reach them precisely through their senses rather than through reason. Truth's impact was physical not just intellectual. "Heresy liquefies and melts away gently before the burning splendor of Catholic verities."[110] The belief was based on a widespread understanding of human emotion, will, and intellect in conversion. De-

109. Quoted in Dompnier, "Mission lointaine et mission de l'intérieur," 97.

110. Charles de Genève, *Trophées sacrés*, 1st part, 40.

feating Protestants through reasoned argument was important but insufficient for moving souls. That required an assault on the senses, which would provoke a deep-seated emotional response and thereby impel the will to accept the truth.[111] Capuchins organized their missions to exploit this understanding of human psychology to the fullest extent possible.

Mission accounts made much of the sheer emotional power of Capuchin preaching. The friars were masters at combining the right place and time with the right rhetorical flourishes to produce dramatic effects. They gathered their listeners in the large central spaces of markets, squares, and cemeteries, or in darkened churches at dusk. Their props—skulls or whips for flagellation—were intended to provoke fear of damnation. And the preachers were adept at using natural occurrences, such as thunderclaps, lightning, or accidents.[112] During the Forty Hours in Saint-Jean-d'Angély, Jean-Baptiste d'Avranches positioned himself in the Protestant cemetery, where he mounted a Huguenot tomb and took for his text the words of Ezekiel: "Ossa arida audite verbum domini" ("Oh, dry bones, hear the word of the Lord"; Ezekiel 37:4). While he preached, the tomb suddenly gave way and sank into the ground "to the great astonishment of all those present, and a heretic who was there was so keenly touched that he cried out loudly: 'I want henceforth to be a Catholic,' which he did immediately after having been instructed by this father" (61). The setting and the theme of the friar's message matched perfectly. The missionary was quick on his feet and able to make good use of the unexpected dramatic event (presuming, of course, that the collapse was not staged).

The account of the Savoy mission describes the Capuchins' baroque Forty Hours devotions at their most spectacular. At Thonon in 1598 Chérubin de Maurienne covered a public square with large pieces of linen that protected the space from the weather but that also rendered it more

111. The idea was a commonplace in Catholic thought about the effects of good preaching in the early seventeenth century. Protestants too believed that faith was strengthened through moving the will emotionally as much as intellectually. See Morán and Andrés-Gallego, "The Preacher," 128–30, 134–36, 152–56; Prosperi, "The Missionary," 184–87; and Dompnier, "Mission et confession," 208–9.

112. The Capuchin development of these techniques reached its peak later in the century with the work of Honoré de Cannes. But earlier missions to convert Protestants also made use of them. See Raoul de Sceaux, "Père Honoré de Cannes," 363–65.

"venerable" by its "lights and shadows." He also constructed a temporary church, in which he set up a variety of theatrical effects to highlight the tabernacle and the Host. Immediately upon entering the structure the participants "could see shining the splendor of the lights set up above, below, and all along the walkways that led to the altar on which the ciborium stood." The entry was decorated with paintings and garlands of foliage and the interior with rich tapestries of gold and silver cloth. In a second celebration held in a church newly reclaimed from the Protestants, Chérubin de Maurienne decorated the nave with tapestries of gold, silver, and purple velvet. A series of Doric columns led from the entrance to the altar, the focal point of which was the tabernacle for the Host. They supported a vault painted azure with stars that reflected candlelight from below, creating the illusion of a starry sky. At the bottom of the steps leading up to the altar were large skeletons, "painted so well that they seemed to be throwing themselves out of their niches." Outside the church, a large artificial volcano shot flames "of love and charity toward heaven" and waters flowed from its base representing "clear and salutary doctrine." From a mock château, artillery fired on an attacking ship and filled the square with smoke.[113]

According to the Savoy chronicle, tens of thousands of Catholic participants witnessed the first Forty Hours celebration. Protestants were displaced from the central areas of the town they had dominated. They watched from the margins, along with coreligionists from Geneva, Lausanne, and Berne. The ceremony had its intended effect. It inspired "a great devotion among many [Protestants], who saw the respect Catholics had for, and the great solemnity with which they treated, God's service." Many Protestants converted, saying: "certainly we now know that faith [Catholicism] is true."[114]

The Poitevin Forty Hours were not as elaborate as those in Savoy, but they were conducted with similar exercises, and the Capuchins claimed similar results. According to the mission chronicle, the ceremonies burst upon Poitou with every bit as much éclat as the Savoy celebrations. The first was held at the mission's opening in Lusignan during Christmas of

113. Charles de Genève, *Trophées sacrées*, 1st part, 221–22, 235–36, 239–40.

114. Charles de Genève, *Trophées sacrées*, 1st part, 217–18, 222.

1617.[115] Staging the Forty Hours at this moment joined it to an already holy time, doubling the sacralizing effect of the large, Catholic observance. Local Protestants, by contrast, would likely have observed Christmas with a solemn communion. The missionaries were very conscious of the timing of their endeavors and of the need to organize time for the mission's benefit. By disrupting participants' daily routines and engaging them in a variety of mission exercises, normal secular time was transformed into a heightened, intense sacred time, which reordered communal life for days and sometimes, in the case of missions to Catholic communities, for weeks.[116] The concentration and energy of the participants were turned away from their usual occupations, considered at least a potential source of sin, and focused instead on the charismatic missionaries, the sermons they preached, the activities they organized, and the exemplary conversions they achieved. In making the days of the Forty Hours ceremony a sacred time, the Poitou mission thereby created a break for Catholics from their daily routine in which coexistence with Huguenots was normal.[117]

Every aspect of the celebration was designed to appeal to Catholic sensibilities in a way Calvinists supposedly found antipathetic. People arrived for the celebration in orderly processions "from cities, towns, and villages, nearby and distant, notwithstanding the snow and the cold of the season." They chanted litanies for the Virgin, and sacred songs were sung set to popular tunes. The marchers carried banners, standards, candles, torches, and crucifixes. The Blessed Sacrament was paraded from church to church and vigils conducted before it. The chronicle reports that processions came from towns and country parishes throughout the province. "From . . . Poitiers came forty Capuchins leading with a raised cross more than 4,000 people. Processions also came from Saint-Maixent . . . Niort, . . . Parthenay, and Châtellerault. . . . Each of these processions had three

115. Lepré-Balain suggested that Lusignan was chosen because it was a heavily fortified place "important to the plans [Huguenots] were preparing to establish a republic in this monarchical state" and because it sat along a strategically important route into Saintonge and Aunis ("Vie du Père Joseph," 3:210).

116. Raoul de Sceaux, "Père Honoré de Cannes," 362–71.

117. "The mission, though it sometimes might coincide with a specified holy time, derived much of its power from being outside that time, an ellipsis. . . . Missions were a break from routine" (Christian, *Moving Crucifixes*, 45).

or four thousand people led by a missionary."[118] The public mobilization of Catholics in these cities was intended to demoralize local Huguenots and reinforce a sense of Catholic separation from them. In one remarkable example, the missionary Hubert de Thouars encountered in a village the chronicle does not name a poor Huguenot alone and deserted; his neighbors had all departed to attend a Forty Hours ceremony at Latillé. The ceremonies' occupation of public space in cities was provocative. In 1621 the Capuchins received the king's official permission to use markets and squares for mission exercises, but they had commandeered these places since the mission's beginning in 1617. Large, enthusiastic, Catholic crowds were potentially dangerous to Huguenots, who complained about the "furor of people excited by preachers."[119]

During the succeeding years, the Capuchins staged Forty Hours devotions in Poitiers, Latillé, Thouars, Sauzé-Vaussais, Coulonges, Fontenay-le-Comte, Pouzauges, La Châtaigneraie, Saint-Jean-d'Angély, and Saumur.[120] Each attracted large crowds of participants. Of course, the numbers of those attending could easily be exaggerated, but the image of a vast Catholic mobilization taking over urban public spaces in response to the Capuchins' call was an essential part of mission rhetoric. It demonstrated the missionaries' success in reviving Catholic identity and fed the Church's sense of triumph. The processions that arrived in mission towns were cru-

118. Although mission accounts portray the Capuchins as undertaking an intrepid incursion into enemy territory, it is clear from the numbers of friars involved in these processions and the places from which they came that the order was well established in the province. Over the decade prior to the mission's beginning in 1617, Capuchin houses had been established in Poitiers, Fontenay-le-Comte, Châtellerault, Niort, Saint-Maixent, Les Sables d'Olonne, and Loudun. Luçon, Parthenay, and Thouars established them in the next few years. Five of the seven initial houses were in Protestant towns of surety. See "Memorabilia provincia turonensis capucinorum," BPC Ms. 43, fols. 109, 151, 159; untitled Ms. 180, fols. 92, 154; Dedouvres, *Politique et apôtre*, 2:145; Pérouas, "Mission de Poitou," 351–52; Raoul de Sceaux, *Histoire des capucins*, 236; and Mauzaize, "Rôle et l'action des capucins," 1029.

119. *Manifeste de Monsieur Bouillon*, 15.

120. In addition to the "Recueils," this list is compiled from Pérouas, "Mission de Poitou," 357–58, and from *La saincte messe restablie a Mouchamp & Vanderene par les pères capucins de la mission de Poictou, & de l'authorité du roy ou elle n'avoit esté dite depuis soixante ans. Avec la conversion de Madame de Rohan de messieurs des anfans & d'un grande nombre d'huguenotz* (Fontenay, n.d. [1622]), 8. Despite the title, neither Rohan nor her children converted.

cial to their resacralization: the 15,000–16,000 who converged on Saumur in 1618; the 50,000 who came to Lusignan where "there was such an abundance of people that it was necessary to have preaching in almost all the squares and crossroads" (52–53); the 6,000 or 7,000 in Latillé, the "place rendered so savage by heresy" that only two or three Catholic families remained in it (56); the 10,000 who gathered at Poitiers, where over a hundred Capuchins marched with the Blessed Sacrament in a torchlight procession from their residence to the cathedral, where the vigil took place (57).[121] So marginalized were Huguenots during the Forty Hours in the Protestant stronghold of Saint-Jean-d'Angély that they seemed invisible. An "infinity of people" watched as four hundred priests marched with two hundred banners and crosses. It was as if by commanding the city's space and time, the Forty Hours had made the large Protestant population disappear. "One would have said that there were no more Huguenots in this city." They "hid themselves from the shame of having to see so many beautifully ordered processions and so much devotion" (60).

The missionaries coupled preaching with these impressive vigils, processions, masses, confessions, and communions. In Latillé, Jean-Baptiste d'Avranches preached in a market square to over 10,000 listeners, while at the same time his colleague Anastase de Nantes delivered sermons in the large church of Saint Pierre, which was totally full. In Saint-Jean-d'Angély, Jean-Baptiste d'Avranches preached some thirty times in three days, and, on the last day, the crowds were so great that three preachers were needed, each delivering his exhortation at the same time to separate audiences all gathered near the market (57). The same was true elsewhere, such as Coulonges in 1620, where the attendance was such that even three missionaries preaching simultaneously were not sufficient; a fourth had to set himself up in a nearby field "to satisfy the huge assembly famished for the truth of the Gospel" (57).

The sacred objects the missionaries carried, such as the crucifix and the Blessed Sacrament, turned public spaces the confessions had shared or that Protestants had dominated into theaters of Catholic ritual. Calvinists considered the crucifix just another example of papist idolatry, but it be-

121. The Saumur figures come from a letter of Père Joseph to his mother in June 1618, quoted in Dedouvres, *Politique et apôtre*, 2:154.

came a potent symbol of re-Catholicization. The Capuchin Hubert de Thouars carried the crucifix like a "standard" into Latillé (56). After the fall of La Rochelle, Capuchins, marching at the head of royal troops, entered the city "carrying crucifixes, before which the Huguenot inhabitants got down on their knees and cried out for mercy" (68). The friars received their reward for their missionary work and their role in the siege when the king turned over to them for a new Capuchin house a fortification Huguenots called "the bastion of the Gospel." "The entire court was present for the planting of the crucifix for the new edifice" (65).

Of course nothing was as effective a riposte to Protestantism as the consecrated Host. Its movement through cities declared them Catholic territory, despite their large Protestant populations. And Huguenots reportedly succumbed to its sacred power. The "Blessed Sacrament, which had been hidden as in the times of the greatest and bloodiest persecutions, now marched in triumph in the cities heresy had dominated, and piety blossomed as recompense for its long captivity."[122] The Host produced conversions of both Protestant heretics and Catholic sinners. During the Forty Hours at Poitiers, the Blessed Sacrament moving in a large procession from the Capuchin church to the city's cathedral inspired such piety and devotion that "a quantity of conversions resulted and there was such a press [of people] wanting to make confessions and take communion that there were not enough priests and friars to satisfy them" (57). At Saint-Jean-d'Angély Protestant converts gave evidence of their new devotion to the Blessed Sacrament by asking for the right to carry it in processions (60).

The friars' success in gaining important converts aided their efforts. The Capuchins in Sanxay "touched so deeply" the Huguenot seigneur that he abjured after being instructed by Père Joseph. He showed such zeal for his new faith

> that he was no longer willing to allow the minister to preach in the local marketplace . . . where the seigneur himself had attended preaching before his conversion. When the minister returned, . . . the missionaries encouraged the seigneur so much that he went to the market, where the heretics had gathered and the minister was in his pulpit . . . and he prevented them from continuing, declaring that he would no

122. Lepré-Balain, "Vie du Père Joseph," 3:215.

longer suffer their conducting worship there. The missionaries took possession [of the market] for the Catholic religion, and the [seigneur] also deprived [the Huguenots] of the cemetery they had taken. The greater part of the inhabitants, his subjects, then converted to the Catholic faith. (59)

The Capuchins claimed the same success, in almost the same words, at Thouars, where the seigneur was the Huguenot grandee Duc Henri de La Trémoille. According to the chronicle, the duke "confessed that he was extremely pleased to watch from the windows of his château the large concourse of people" who gathered in Thouars, coming in devout processions from so many places. He was so deeply touched that he "resolved in his heart from that moment to return to the bosom the Church" (59).[123] After his conversion, the duke would

> no longer permit the minister [of Thouars] to preach in the marketplace, . . . where the duke himself had attended before his conversion. This minister had absented himself during the mission . . . and upon his return had wanted to preach [in the market] as he ordinarily did, despite warnings to give [the place] up. The missionaries so encouraged the seigneur that he went to the market, where the heretics had assembled and the minister was in his pulpit . . . and he prevented them from continuing, declaring that he would no longer suffer their conducting worship there. The missionaries took possession [of the market] for the Catholic religion. The seigneur also deprived [the Huguenots] of the cemetery they had taken. The greater part of the inhabitants, his subjects, then converted to the Catholic faith.[124]

123. In this way the Capuchins claimed a share of glory for Henri de La Trémoille's abjuration. However, the Thouars mission was conducted long before the duke's conversion during the siege of La Rochelle in 1628. The mission chronicle does indicate that La Trémoille converted in the presence of Richelieu, but it also states that Jean-Baptiste d'Avranches, one of the Poitou missionaries, instructed him.

124. This incident at Thouars is reported in a document of the Bibliothèque municipale d'Orléans, Ms. 1436, p. 49, quoted in Raoul de Sceaux, *Histoire de capucins*, p. 455. But its language is essentially the same as that describing what had happened at Sanxay reported in the "Recueils." That coincidence, plus the collapsing of the time between the mission at Thouars and the duke's conversion, raises the possibility that two manuscripts are recording the same incident and assigning it to two different towns, but La Trémoille is clearly named for the Thouars case while the Sanxay seigneur remains unnamed.

An alliance between the missionaries and converted seigneurs led to the shutting down of heretical worship and the removal of its signs and physical structures from public space. As we will see in Chapter 4, in Thouars at least, the story was more complicated; La Trémoille did not simply turn against local Huguenots. And there is little evidence that many in Thouars or Sanxay converted. But since Catholic polemicists insisted that nobles coerced their dependents into heresy, the abjuration of seigneurs was bound to provoke conversions among their subordinates.[125] The descriptions also claimed great success for the mission's strategy of expelling Huguenots from the gathering points for local economic, political, and religious life into which they had been integrated.

Elsewhere the Capuchins regained control of sacred space for Catholicism without converting the seigneur (though with the help of local magistrates). For example, in October 1622 Jean-Baptiste d'Avranches assembled Catholics from the surrounding area for a mission in Mouchamps, an estate of the Duchesse de Rohan, a "sworn enemy of the Catholic Church" (69). The duchess ordered her local officers and subjects to act circumspectly; the minister absented himself. Jean-Baptiste d'Avranches took over the church, which had been "profaned by the preaching of ministers for more than sixty years." He and his followers threw the minister's pulpit and the congregation's benches out of the church and Richelieu's grand vicar celebrated mass there. The Capuchin then led a procession from the church to the market, where he delivered a sermon. The missionaries also turned their attention to nearby Vendrennes and "solemnly reestablished the mass [there even though the chapel] was in the courtyard of that lady's [Rohan's] château, and notwithstanding all her efforts to prevent it." The Capuchins had carried the battle over sacred space not only to the heart of the enemy's territory, the seigneurial possessions of the Rohan family, but even into their château.[126]

With their temples and cemeteries under attack, with their Catholic neighbors ostracizing them, with the large numbers of Catholics crowding into their towns, and with the mission's ceremonies proclaiming the

125. After a military commander named Traversay converted he had "the catechism taught to his attendants and neighbors, which was the cause of many others receiving absolution" (66).

126. "Recueils," 69–70; *Sainncte messe restablie a Mouchamp & Vanderene.*

truth of Catholicism, Huguenots were supposed to feel the isolation that a secure confessional boundary imposed. Such was the mission's design. However, its ultimate goal was not just the construction of the boundary but also the conversion of heretics. The mission presented Huguenots with a way to recross the new sacred boundary. The missionaries would lure them back to abjure. According to the mission rhetoric, Protestants could not resist the attraction. It was so strong that they could not "separate themselves from the preachers' audiences notwithstanding that their ministers would excommunicate any who attended" (61). Huguenots attended the mission exercises as spectators and eventually as participants. The baroque observances appealed as much to them as to the Catholic faithful. Some who, the chronicle reports, feared approaching the missionaries to make their abjurations, mingled in the Catholic crowds listening to the sermons. They then pressed their way forward and "oblige[d]" the missionaries "to interrupt their preaching to receive" their professions of faith (53). Once they had abjured, the former Huguenots took on an exemplary role. One, a convert from Parthenay, insisted on marching at the head of a procession to give public testimony to his recent profession of faith (56–57). And others "were so animated for their own salvation by the grace of the Holy Spirit, which touched them so strongly, that they afterward took on the office of missionary to others of their sect" (53). The converts thus became models of what the mission had sought to achieve. Threatened with exclusion by their refusal to recognize the true faith, they had, with the missionaries' help, reintegrated themselves into their communities and the Catholic nation through conversion.

CONVERSIONS

The chronicle reports: "From all the most exact accounts . . . it appears that up to the year 1632, our missionary fathers had given absolution to more than 10,000 heretics, of which our archives are sure. This is the minimum number" (69).[127] A different Capuchin account claims that the mis-

127. It continues: "And if one wants to include the absolution of all those who converted following public debates and preaching or from the renown of these Capuchins, and who have received absolution from Capuchins in various places and cantons of our province of Touraine, the number would mount to 20,000 or even more,

sion achieved 12,000 abjurations in its first five and a half years.[128] The funeral oration for Père Joseph cited a figure of 50,000 over the course of the mission.[129] Even the largest figures make clear that the Capuchins never claimed to have converted all or even a majority of the region's Huguenots. Of course the chronicler was not a statistician, and while the numbers were important to him and to the recipients of his report, his purpose was not simply that of record keeping. The numbers are presented as part of the hagiographical narrative of the missionaries' accomplishments. Thus Hubert de Thouars converted more than 740 in various places. Louis de Champigny gave absolution to more than 500 (66–67). Anselme d'Angers gave absolution to 1,200 heretics while working in Poitou, and Jean-Baptiste d'Avranches converted 7,000 (68).[130]

without any exaggeration" (69). The date the mission ended is unclear. Pérouas, drawing on the "Recueils," says the mission continued up to 1640, but the chronicle mentions "relations" sent from the Poitou mission in 1642 and 1643 (70), though it gives few details for the years after 1630. It is possible that the missionaries switched their efforts to the La Rochelle region after the city's fall. See "Mission de Poitou," 354, 358n.34.

128. *Le nouveau restablissement de la ville de Sainct-Jean-d'Angely . . .* (Paris, 1623), 3, cited in Pérouas, "Mission de Poitou," 358. Historians have provided various figures for the conversions. J.-H. Mariéjol suggests 50,000 in his *Histoire de France illustrée*, vol. 6, part 2 (Paris, 1926), 208. The Franciscan Ubald d'Alençon gives a figure of 40,000 in *Leçons de l'histoire franciscaine* (Paris, 1918), 216. Both are cited in Pérouas, "Mission de Poitou," 358n.34.

129. Fagniez, *Père Joseph et Richelieu*, 1:292. The funeral orator apparently drew on a number contained in a letter from Joseph to his mother in which he said that 50,000 "took communion." Obviously this does not mean that they were all converts, though Fagniez still thinks it a reasonable approximation. Pérouas, who has examined the numbers most closely, suggests that the total for the first six friars who began the mission in 1617 should be between 7,000 and 8,000. With the addition of smaller results obtained by those friars who joined the mission in 1626, the total in 1627, the eve of the fall of La Rochelle, should be less than 10,000, or somewhat less than 10 percent of the province's Protestant population. Pérouas bases his totals on the Capuchin order's "Relatio generalis Missionis Pictaviensis," which, in turn, was based on accounts that the missionaries provided Père Joseph ("Mission de Poitou," 359).

130. The "Recueils" also lists Ambroise de Reims with 250 (though some number of these came from the Isle de Ré outside Poitou), Martinien de Saintes with 100, Fabien de Vierzon with 100, Eutrope de l'Isle-Bouin with 150, and Ignace de Nevers with 150. Gustave Fagniez, drawing on another report that apparently covered the same years, added to this list Anastase de Nantes with 250, Gervais de Rennes with 200, Jean-Baptiste d'Angers with 200, Ambroise de Rennes with 200, and Tranquille d'Angers with 150 (*Père Joseph et Richelieu*, 1:293).

The numbers of abjurations glorified the missionaries and advertised the success of their enterprise. Missions had their skeptics in the seventeenth century. Critics questioned the sincerity of the seemingly quick conversions of so many people; they doubted that the converts' emotional responses would be long-lived.[131] The Capuchins were sensitive to such criticisms. They argued that the converts' sincerity was evident in their actions. Père Joseph claimed in a letter to his mother that the converts "are so fervent and so devout that one can see the hand of God at work in their hearts and not any human considerations, which, to the contrary, would have prevented them [from converting]."[132] Jean Guillemard, who served as minister in various Poitevin churches, came to seek instruction from Joseph because he felt "burdened in his conscience" (58). A nobleman of Champdeniers abjured because he felt "tortured in his conscience" after his minister's defeat in a debate (57). An apostate priest, captured during the siege of La Rochelle and condemned to death, requested that the missionary Martinien de Sainctes "pray and supplicate [the Virgin] for me, since the anguish of my heart and the remorse of my conscience does not permit me to pray freely." He then renounced the heresy and made his profession of faith (67). Examples such as these demonstrated that the conversions the Capuchins won were not superficial but true movements of the heart and conscience.

The chronicler, writing in the 1670s, makes one further point about the conversions the Capuchins won. He remarks that the mission's effects "have continued and are continuing right up to the present with much fruit of conversions" (69). In other words, the mission's impact lived on; the approach the Capuchins set out in their mission of reviving Catholic identity, undermining the Huguenots' practice of their faith, and ostracizing them was continuing to lead Huguenots to convert. Other anti-Protestant campaigners—among the Church's clergy, the provincial Catholic elite, and the royal judiciary—would prove quite adept, indeed more so than the Capuchins, at following the strategies the missionaries had developed. In that sense, the friars could claim to have accomplished their goal,

131. See above, note 5.

132. Quoted in Lepré-Balain, "Vie du Père Joseph," 4:268. I will examine the meaning of these conversions below, see pp. 256–61.

even if only a minority of the Huguenot population converted during the mission. They had shown how the strict confessional boundary could be constructed. That part of the Capuchin program was a success. The Capuchin chronicler might well have thought that the other part of the Capuchin vision, the conversion of all the region's Huguenots, would soon be fulfilled as well. It was the failure to achieve that end that prompted the much harsher repression of French Protestantism in the years after he wrote. Yet long before that anti-Protestant campaigners were hard at work building on the Capuchins' strategy to undermine Protestantism by constructing a strict confessional boundary in civic space, in households, and in the minds of converts.

SEPARATED BY DEATH?

Cemeteries, Burials, and Confessional Boundaries

IN THE CIVIC SPACES Catholics and Protestants shared, their daily interactions could provoke conflict but also present opportunities for cooperation. The most sensitive of these locations were those constituting communal sacred space—Protestant temples and Catholic churches, chapels, religious houses, and processional routes—in which the religious groups undertook their devotional activities. In or around these places the possibility for strife was at its greatest, but so too was the potential for religious mixing across the first type of confessional boundary or negotiated accommodations along the second. Through these interactions the confessional boundary took literal, physical shape. This process of confessional boundary building was most visible in cemeteries. Here Catholic anti-Protestant campaigners sought to exclude Huguenots from communal burial grounds, while they, in turn, defended their access to them. As a result, within cemeteries we can see each of the different forms of confessional boundary being fashioned as the contest over communal space, which the Capuchin missionaries had dramatized, unfolded.

Fierce, sometimes violent, conflicts broke out over disputed cemeteries and the ceremonies that took place in them. What lay behind these confrontations was the heritage of the Wars of Religion, during which burial grounds and corpses were focal points for some of the bitterest strife. A 1597 "*Plaintes des églises réformées*" charged that Catholic authorities and royal courts condoned, even ordered, Huguenot remains disinterred, reburied, or sometimes just thrown by the roadsides.[1] Catholics, like the Jesuit Louis Richeome, insisted that Huguenots had relentlessly "demolished thousands of tombs . . . by pure animosity . . . [and] disinterred the bodies of saints and disturbed their bones' rest." "Was this," he asked, "a means of reforming the living by digging up the dead and clowning around over their ashes or playing with their remains?"[2]

We have learned to explain such violence as ritual-like behavior in which each religious group ensured its purity by attacking the pollution emanating not only from living heretics but also from their dead.[3] However, evidence from confessionally mixed communities in the seventeenth century indicates that in cemeteries, Catholics and Protestants often achieved remarkable cooperation, reaching agreements on sharing space, attending each other's funerals, and sometimes burying their dead side by side. The confessional boundary (i.e., the first type of boundary) was blurred when Protestants disregarded the austere funerals Calvinist doctrine demanded and instead sought a ceremony somewhat more akin to that of their Catholic neighbors. Burying Catholics and Protestants side by side also indicated an unclear confessional boundary and an indistinct recognition of confessional identity. The presence of Huguenot remains in the cemetery, an important civic space, signaled the religious minority's continued membership in a community.

A confessional boundary of the second type, which clearly acknowledged confessional difference, could also take shape in cemeteries. It was apparent in communal decisions to share cemeteries through their partition into two adjacent burial grounds. The careful articulation of space still made it possible for both groups to secure their place in the community. Maintaining this boundary distinguished the groups without necessarily implying rejection and exclusion.

1. "Plaintes des églises réformées de France sur les violences et injustices qui leur sont faites en plusieurs endroits du royaume . . ." (1597), which Charles Read reproduces in "Cimetières et inhumations des huguenots principalement à Paris aux XVIe, XVIIe, et XVIIIe siècles, 1563–1792," *Bulletin de la société d'histoire du protestantisme français* 11 (1862): 132–50, 351–59, see esp. 138–49.

2. Louis Richeome, *L'idolatrie huguenote figurée au patron de la vieille payenne divisée en huict livres & desdiée au roy très chrestien de France et de Navarre Henry IIII* [sic] (Montpellier, 1607), 157–61.

3. Davis, "Rites of Violence"; Crouzet, *Guerriers de Dieu.*

But a clearer confessional definition and demarcation of sacred space led to the third form of boundary. Each church sought to impose more orthodox standards of religious behavior by distinguishing its funeral practices from those of its rival. The churches had limited success in differentiating themselves in this way until the monarchy's policy toward the minority shifted from encouraging peace to pursuing persecution. When that happened royal courts and legislation started making the boundary in cemeteries and funerals absolutely clear and discriminatory. The policy tried to break the bonds between neighbors of different faiths by invoking the old fears of social contamination. Strict limits were placed on the public manifestation of Huguenot funerals: they were restricted to certain hours and the number of mourners was limited. Huguenot cemeteries were pushed outside towns, expelling Protestant funerals and the dead from communal space, and thus symbolically depriving Huguenots of their membership in communities.[4]

The examples of Protestant burial practices presented in this chapter come from around the country. When Huguenots continued or adopted burial practices not in keeping with the Reformed Church's *Discipline*, they came to the attention of national synods, royal investigations, and polemicists from the churches, which provide the documentation on funeral activities. Much of the evidence of shared cemeteries comes from Poitou, where they existed in over eighty communities.[5] Many were in the

4. As Penny Roberts puts it: "By excluding Protestant burial, the previously communal churchyard, the repository of a collective ancestry, became symbolic of the confessional rift in society" ("Contesting Sacred Space: Burial Disputes in Sixteenth-Century France," in *The Place of the Dead: Death and Remembrance in Late Medieval and Early Modern Europe*, edited by Bruce Gordon and Peter Marshall [Cambridge, U.K., 2000], 131–48, see esp. 140). However, Roberts feels Protestants accepted this separation. The campaign also pursued the moving of Huguenot temples outside towns or their destruction. See Dompnier, "La logique d'une destruction"; and Deyon, "La destruction des temples."

5. I have compiled this number from the lawsuits Benoist discussed in "Catholiques et protestants," 343–44, and "Populations rurales," 2:326. Further information comes from Jean Filleau, *Décisions catholiques ou recueil general des arrests rendus dans toutes les cours souveraines de France en Éxécution, ou interpretation, des Edits, qui concernent l'exercise de la religion pret. reformée . . .* (Poitiers, 1668), 26, 162–63, 234–322; Archives départmentales de la Vienne (hereafter ADV), C 49; BMP Fonds Fonteneau, vol. 64, 673, and vol. 78, 407, 415; BPF Ms. 869 (1), 870 (1); Lièvre, *Histoire des protestants*, 1:301–6; Raoul de Sceaux, *Histoire des capucins*, 455; Durand, *Réforme à Lusignan*, 43–44;

"Moyen-Poitou," where Huguenots often dominated local communities and could thus strongly influence cemetery arrangements. But shared burial grounds were also found in other parts of the province, where Protestants were fewer, weaker, and therefore had to reach agreements with their Catholic neighbors. We have little in the way of quantitative studies from other regions, but shared cemeteries were not just a Poitevin phenomenon. Historians have found them in Normandy, Agenais, Dauphiné, Orange, and Béarn.[6] Jean Filleau, in his massive 1668 compilation of anti-Protestant laws and legal cases, *Décisions catholiques*, cites lawsuits over common cemeteries from various other places, including Brittany, Saintonge, Maine, Angoumois, and Vendômois.[7] In these places the confessional boundary Catholics and Protestants constructed in cemeteries and funerals depended on their local relations. But they did not live in a vacuum. Church doctrines concerning the dead put limits on their accommodations. The state, with its legislative authority, judiciary, and enforcement powers, set the legal framework within which their negotiations proceeded. When it came to determining where and how deceased Catholics and Huguenots would be buried, a complex dynamic was at work.

CEMETERIES

For Calvinists, the notion that cemeteries were sacred ground, hallowed by the bones of the faithful, was just another example of Catholic superstition. The Huguenot historian Elie Benoist wrote that we are "not so obstinate as to continue to believe the vain prejudice that one piece of

---

and Marc Venard, "L'église catholique bénéficiare de l'Édit de Nantes: Le témoignage des visites épiscopales," in Grandjean and Roussel, eds., *Coexister dans l'intolérance*, 283–302, see esp. 293. Unless identified otherwise, the examples in this chapter come from Poitou.

6. Christian Desplat has counted more than sixty communities in Béarn in which the dead of the two religions were buried together or common cemeteries were divided ("Sépulture et frontière confessionelle: Protestants et catholiques de Béarn [XVI–XVIIe siècle]," *Revue de Pau et du Béarn* 23 [1996]: 67–75, see esp. 75n.21). See also Garrisson, *Essai sur les commissions*, 11–13, 235–49; Hanlon, *Confession and Community*, 44, 154, and *Univers des gens de bien*, 233; and Marc Venard, *Réforme protestante et réforme catholique dans la province d'Avignon au XVIe siècle* (Paris, 1993), 781–82.

7. *Décisions catholiques*, 270, 273, 295.

land is holier than another."[8] Thus Protestants should have been indifferent to the location of their burial grounds, so long as their bodies were treated with dignity. But Huguenots' insistence on being buried in parish cemeteries near their kin belied the Calvinist refusal to grant graveyards special significance.[9] They demanded continued access to communal graveyards and tombs in which their ancestors were interred.

The sharing of burial grounds with Protestants was anathema for Catholics. As Filleau put it: "The false beliefs of the *religionnaires* . . . render them unworthy of burial in Catholic cemeteries . . . and they are mistaken in choosing such places [for burials], which can only increase their troubles and punishments; their criminal souls will be deprived of the approbations of the Church . . . for all of eternity."[10] To be sure, burial grounds were a concern for the Catholic Reformation Church quite apart from the fear that heretics' bodies might desecrate them. They were also the focus of a contest between Catholic reformers and the laity. While parishioners sought to maintain local control over the sacred spaces and institutions in their towns and villages, including cemeteries, bishops wanted to establish securely the clergy's authority over these places. Burial grounds could then be purged of profane activities, such as fairs, assemblies, grazing, and dancing.[11] Evicting Huguenots eliminated another source of profanation. But doing so was particularly important because it furthered the anti-Protestant campaign's goal of ostracizing the minority in communities they shared with Catholics.

8. Benoist, *Histoire de l'Edit de Nantes,* 1:232. As the sixteenth-century preacher Pierre Viret had put it: "It is both a great superstition and idolatry to think that the ground itself confers some sort of sanctity" (quoted in Bernard Roussel, "'Ensevelir honnestement les corps': Funeral Corteges and Huguenot Culture," in Mentzer and Spicer, eds., *Society and Culture in the Huguenot World,* 193–208, see esp. 199).

9. Roberts found that sixteenth-century Huguenots wanted to be "buried with their ancestors in the customary way" but eventually sought separate cemeteries near their temples ("Contesting Sacred Space," 139–40). I suggest that their desire to be buried with kin remained strong.

10. "It is therefore unreasonable that sacred ground, destined to receive only the bodies of those who died in the true belief of the Church, remain open to and profaned by the reception of the bodies of those who separated themselves from the Church and, while alive, condemned its mysteries and holiness" (Filleau, *Décisions catholiques,* 263, 289).

11. Luria, *Territories of Grace,* 70–71.

The Edict of Nantes sought to allay the tensions and prevent the violence conflicting Calvinist and Catholic views could provoke. It ordered royal officers "to see to it that no scandals are committed at funerals."[12] It granted Catholics the sole use of their sacred buildings and spaces and commanded the two groups' cemeteries be completely separated or, at least, clearly divided. Thus it did not seek to blur confessional identities. But the edict's application was contentious because its different versions (the original document and the one the Paris Parlement ratified) allowed for different policies regarding cemeteries.[13]

Article 28 dealt with the separation of cemeteries by stipulating that "for the burial of the dead of those of the said religion . . . our commissioners . . . will promptly provide them with the most convenient place possible. And those cemeteries which they formerly held but which were taken from them during the troubles will be returned to them."[14] Protestants claimed that the original version of the article also included the provision that if royal officers delayed or avoided giving Huguenots new cemeteries, it would be permissible for them "to bury their dead in Catholic cemeteries in cities or places where they possess them and to do so until they are given their own."[15] The Assembly of the (Catholic) Clergy had insisted on dropping this clause. The "secret" articles appended to the edict ordered that no one would be prosecuted for Huguenot burials in Catholic cemeteries prior to the edict and prevented the Catholic clergy from any further disinterments of Huguenot remains to purify contaminated cemeteries.[16] But the Catholic clergy would not stomach further profanations, the Paris Parlement agreed, and Henri IV acceded to the change. Huguenots complained about the situation created by the Parlement's changes and the confusion over the provision of separate cemeteries. If the royal commissioners did not furnish them with new burial

12. This was from Article 29, which also ordered them to grant Huguenots new cemeteries within fifteen days of a request. See Bergeal and Durrelman, *Protestantisme et libertés*, 24.

13. See above, p. 4.

14. Bergeal and Durrleman, *Protestantisme et libertés*, 23–24.

15. The text can be found in Read, "Cimetières et inhumations" (1862), 353, and in Jacqueline Thibaut-Payen, *Les morts, l'église et l'état: Recherches d'histoire administrative sur la sépulture et les cimetières dans le ressort du parlement de Paris aux XVIIe et XVIIIe siècles* (Paris, 1977), 162.

16. Read, "Cimetières et inhumations" (1862), 149–50.

grounds, they could be left "not knowing where to bury their dead, except in places and in a manner both extraordinary and scandalous."[17] As late as the 1680s the Huguenots of Saint-Savin (Berry) complained that the denial to them of a burial ground left the bodies of their dead being treated like those of "criminals and wrongdoers."[18]

The edict was also vague about how the new Protestant cemeteries were to be financed. Article 28 stipulated that Huguenots would receive new burial grounds "for free." The king assured them that in practice the proviso would mean that they did not have to pay for new cemeteries themselves; entire communities would bear the expense. Catholics did not always do so willingly, but courts in the early years of the century often backed the Protestants. For example the bailliage court of Issoudun (Berry) in 1604 commanded the inhabitants of both religions in the town of Argenton to pay for a new Protestant burial ground.[19] The *siège royale* court (a local royal tribunal) of Saint-Maixent in 1623 ordered a new graveyard purchased for the Protestants of Augé at the "common expense of all the Catholic inhabitants."[20] But at about this time the Catholic argument against sharing these costs was finding powerful support, and Henri's guarantees were being swept aside. *Avocat général* (king's attorney) Jacques Talon, relying on the ratified version of the edict, contended before the Paris Parlement in 1622 that the former king had never intended to permit Huguenots to continue burials in Catholic cemeteries. And he insisted that they were to pay for their own new burial grounds.[21] The Parlement favored Talon's arguments, which provided the basis for much of the later jurisprudence on the financial issue.

17. From the complaints of the Huguenot assembly of Châtellerault (1599), quoted in Françoise Chevalier, "Les difficultés d'application de l'Édit de Nantes d'après les cahiers des plaintes (1599–1660)," in *Coexister dans l'intolérance*, 303–20, see esp. 306.

18. "Placet pour les habitans de St. Savin en Berry de la R.P.R." (1682), AN TT 271 (24), 2. Since Catholics deemed them heretics, Huguenots joined a list of other groups excluded from Catholic burial grounds including lepers, plague victims, and the unbaptized. See Roberts, "Contesting Sacred Space," 139.

19. The sentence is included with the documents concerning disputes over this cemetery in 1684; see AN TT 232 (7) 2, 7.

20. Archives départmentales des Deux-Sèvres (hereafter ADDS), Siège royal de Saint-Maixent Civil Divers 1631–1666 [*sic*] (unclassified).

21. For Talon's arguments, see Filleau, *Décisions catholiques*, 283–95. On Talon, see Thibaut-Payen, *Morts*, 162n.206, 170.

Given the uncertainties over the edict's meaning and the king's intentions, much of the law's effectiveness depended on its local interpretation and application. Thus its effect on the construction of confessional boundaries through cemeteries and funerals varied from place to place. The expulsion of Huguenots from parish cemeteries was just not always practical, especially if the means could not be found to buy a new one for them. During Henri's lifetime royal commissioners, whose tasks included the separation of cemeteries, sometimes had to allow Protestants, at least temporarily, to continue burials side by side with Catholics.[22] The result was precisely the sort of communal religious situation in which confessional boundaries remained blurred. If, in other places, commissioners did order separate cemeteries, financially strapped localities could avoid the expense by dividing an old one and giving Protestants the part furthest from the church. A hedge, a ditch, or a wall, if the inhabitants could afford one, would mark the division. The divided cemeteries provided for a clear but not exclusionary separation, which corresponded to the second form of boundary. It rested on the interpretation of the edict that Protestant leaders found most reasonable. Each faith would be given its place within local communities. The Catholic Church objected to such divisions, since Protestants would be buried in what had been sanctified ground, where Catholic remains resided.[23] But for royal officials and for neighbors of both faiths, partitioning solved the problem of providing different graveyards. As in the case of mixed cemeteries, divided ones also required cooperation between the religious groups. Separate but adjacent burial grounds pro-

22. See Read, "Cimetières et inhumations" (1862), 354; Thibaut-Payen, *Morts*, 162, 164; and Desplat, "Sépulture et frontière confessionelle," 73–74. A 1606 royal response to the grievances of the Protestant deputy general seemed to support the Huguenot claim that the king's intention was to allow them to continue sharing Catholic cemeteries until they were provided with new ones. See Benoist, *Histoire de l'Edit de Nantes*, 1:287–89, 436.

23. Benoist, *Histoire de l'Edit de Nantes*, 1:364. Under canon law, a wall separating contiguous cemeteries could prevent the pollution of one by the other; see Thibaut-Payen, *Morts*, 79n.341. However, this ruling may not have applied because of previous Catholic burials in what would now be profaned ground. In protesting the division of old cemeteries between Protestants and Catholics, Filleau argued that the sections given to the "heretics" would contain "the relics of many faithful Catholics which were venerated." Such remains were a *"precieux depost"* for the Church (*Décisions catholiques*, 283, 316).

moted a clearer sense of religious difference than mixed cemeteries. Nonetheless, each group still maintained a connection to the old parish cemetery and, through it, a position in the community acknowledged by all. The confessions were distinct but neither was expelled from the community.

Shortages of funds, however, only partially account for shared cemeteries. The notion remained powerful that a parish graveyard was common ground, used by all members of a community, who buried their dead in familial tombs or in graves near predecessors, even if they had been of the opposing faith.[24] Huguenots staked their claim to parish cemeteries on their sense of belonging by right of birth and inheritance to local communities and to the nation as a whole. As they argued in their 1597 "*Plaintes*," "our fathers had rights to [parish cemeteries] . . . that were public and common. Have we not inherited their rights just as much as this French air we breathe, the cities we frequent, and the homes we inhabit?" This sense of belonging, not religious affiliation, determined one's place of burial. Catholic polemicists responded to this claim by insisting that Huguenots were not really French precisely because they were heretics.[25]

Of course, the cemetery's arrangement might depend less on the wishes of a community's inhabitants than on the desires of local power-holders. Protestant seigneurs continued to use tombs in which their Catholic ancestors were buried. They claimed a right of burial in chapels of which their families were patrons by "ancient foundations; others had longstanding rights over tombs in parish churches."[26] Patronage claims remained powerful, despite the efforts of Catholic Reformation bishops,

24. In late-sixteenth- and early-seventeenth-century Münster, city magistrates continued to permit the burial of Protestant burghers in city churches and parish cemeteries, despite the objections of Catholic clerics. Protestants retained this right because of their citizenship in the city. See R. Po-chia Hsia, *Society and Religion in Münster, 1535–1618* (New Haven, Conn., 1984), 129–16. Forster presents similar examples from villages in the diocese of Speyer; see *Counter-Reformation in the Villages*, 100.

25. "Plaintes des églises réformées," in Read, "Cimetières et inhumations" (1862), 142. For the Catholic riposte, see Henri de Sponde, *Les cimetières sacrez* (Lyon, 1598), 187–88.

26. Benoist, *Histoire de l'Edit de Nantes*, 1:364. The "Conseil souverain" of Béarn, which protected Protestant interests in the principality, protested to Henry IV in 1601 that "the desire to be buried in tombs of ones' fathers is a natural right" (Desplat, "Sépulture et frontière confessionelle," 72).

who sometimes sought to override the inherited rights of even Catholic patrons in churches and cemeteries. For Protestants and Catholics, tombs were strong symbols of familial power, status, and continuity over time, all aspects of an aristocratic ethos that defied Protestant denials of significance to burial grounds and Catholic fears of profanation by heretics' remains.[27] The inhabitants of communities felt obliged even to Huguenot patrons. In Chalamont (diocese of Nevers), parishioners associated the church with its patronal family despite the former seigneur's Protestantism. They resisted their bishop's orders in 1612 to exhume his body from the church by claiming they wanted to ensure that the "divine service would continue in the church." Remembering "the good treatment" they had received from him, they "felt very obliged to his memory." For these inhabitants, the continuation of the divine service depended on honoring the memory of a noble patron, even if he was a Protestant. For the bishop, it depended on removing a heretic's polluting body from the church, which he eventually succeeded in doing.[28]

The Catholic clergy was successful in winning court cases against Huguenots burying their dead in churches. For example, Philippe de Choiseul of Presigny (diocese of Langres) was ordered in 1602 to disinter his wife from the parish church. And a Baron des Etangs of Messignac (Angoumois) was forced in 1620 to dig up his mother from a chapel.[29] Nonetheless, Huguenot nobles were willing to resist efforts to prevent them from using family tombs in churches. Catholics sometimes accused them of using force to do so, as happened in Luçon, where Huguenot nobles broke down a church door in 1613 to bury a coreligionist.[30]

27. Hanlon, *Confession and Community*, 166–67; and Read, "Cimetières et inhumations" (1862), 355.

28. Quoted in Thibaut-Payen, *Morts*, 173. See also Benoist, *Histoire de l'Edit de Nantes*, 2:97.

29. For the Presigny case, see "Le clergé de Langres et les enterrements huguenots (1602)," *Bulletin de la société d'histoire du protestantisme français* 47 (1898): 523–24. For the Messignac case, see Benoist, *Histoire de l'Edit de Nantes*, 2:308. For other examples, see two cases from the Chartres region in 1600, in which Protestants were forced to disinter children from the parish churches of Saint-Georges-sur-Eure and Chanceville ("Le clergé de Chartres et les enterrements huguenots (1600)," *Bulletin de la société d'histoire du protestantisme français* 47 [1898]: 524–25).

30. "Deposition des [*sic*] la rupture d'une porte de l'eglise de Boufferé par des gentilhommes protestants pour faire l'inhumation d'une religionnaire, 27 mai 1613," BMP

While custom, kinship ties, and seigneurial power could dictate sharing in some communities, in others it resulted from carefully constructed compacts to establish peace between the two religious groups. These agreements were counterparts to those discussed in Chapter 1, by which Catholics and Protestants reached accommodations on other issues, such as civic office sharing or the timing of public religious activities. Given the potential for conflict between the groups over cemeteries, it was important to negotiate their arrangement. And like the other agreements, cemetery settlements depended not only on the willingness of local groups to cooperate but also on the role of royal officials who sponsored or ordered the agreements. Even if the contracts did not follow strictly the letter of the Edict of Nantes's provisions concerning cemeteries, royal commissioners supported or, indeed, wrote them as a way of preventing occasions for violence. Thus, in 1599, commissioners gave the Huguenots of Marans (Aunis) a portion of the Catholic cemetery rather than a separate one. And they made certain to add a warning to the order prohibiting "Catholics from troubling [the Huguenots] in their exercises."[31]

Through the commissioners, the weight of the king's authority was brought to bear on biconfessional communities. In Castelmoron (Agenais) Catholic and Protestant inhabitants consented in 1609 to continue sharing the local cemetery so as to avoid disorder and maintain obedience to the king's religious settlement. The Huguenots stated that:

> Since the beginning of [religious] troubles in France, . . . the inhabitants of this city . . . by God's favor, have comported themselves so agreeably toward each other under the tolerance of the king's edicts that they have had neither debates nor contention among them over . . . the burial of the dead of one or the other religion. . . . On the contrary . . . the inhabitants of each religion have buried their dead in the parish cemetery in their predecessors' tombs without anyone object-

Fonds Fonteneau, vol. 14, 233. Benoist relates other cases, for instance, one from 1620, in which the widow and heirs of the Sieur de Lallier of Lonlai were accused of having "carried arms and used violence" to bury him in the parish church (*Histoire de l'Edit de Nantes*, 2:308).

31. "Le proces-verbal fait par Messieurs les commissaires deputez par le roy pour l'exécution des edits de pacification du pays d'Aulnis du 13 aoust 1599," AN TT 251 (40). This report is mentioned in a later undated collection of documents made during an investigation of Protestant worship in Marans.

> ing. . . . And [the Catholics stated] that they agree that those of the said religion will continue to use, just as they will, the parish cemetery. [Protestants] can bury their dead there, each family in the tomb of its predecessors, as much one religion as the other, just as has been done up to now, following the agreement made before messieurs the commissioners deputed by the king for the execution of His Majesty's edicts for the pacification of the troubles.[32]

The settlement in Marans established a confessional boundary of the second type in which the old graveyard was divided into two separate but adjacent cemeteries. But the Castelmoron agreement allowed for Catholic and Protestant burials to continue side by side. Here religious mixing characteristic of the first sort of boundary remained possible.

Although most such cemetery accommodations date from the first two decades of the seventeenth century, they can be found from later, and harsher, times. Witness the agreement Catholics and Protestants of Saint-Gelais reached in 1635, a moment when lawsuits brought by the leadership of the Poitevin Catholic Church and its allies in the provincial judiciary were putting a stop to cemetery sharing. In this town both groups used the graveyard around a priory, which served as the parish church. Given the coincidence between the contract's date and the sitting of the temporary royal commission in Poitiers that heard many of the cemetery cases, it seems likely that someone on the Catholic side (perhaps the recently arrived curé or perhaps his diocesan superiors) objected to the common burial ground. The Protestants agreed to accept a new site, "completely separated from the cemetery around the church." The location chosen was a vineyard outside the town. However, this place was adjacent to a new cemetery the Catholics had purchased to replace the one around the priory, which was now too small for them. Here both groups would have new cemeteries, next to each other. A wall would separate them. Despite the location of the new Huguenot burial ground outside the town, this agreement, amicably reached, suggests a confessional boundary of the second sort. Saint-Gelais's Catholics now also would be

32. "Usage en commun d'un cimetière entre catholiques et protestants en 1609," *Bulletin de la société d'histoire du protestantisme français* 2 (1853): 502–5. In nearby Layrac, inhabitants made a similar declaration to royal commissioners in 1602. See Hanlon, *Confession and Community*, 44, 54, 154.

burying their dead outside the town. The two cemeteries would be clearly separated but still contiguous.[33]

The contracts that established shared cemeteries are not always extant but can be inferred from the records of the court cases that later outlawed them. In lawsuits, Protestants looked back to these contracts for support and claimed that the practice persisted of burying the dead of both religions "promiscuously" because of *convention[s] particulière[s]* between the inhabitants. "No one had complained about them until now, . . . and Catholics had in no way suffered."[34] Documents from the cases speak of the communal consent to sharing. At Augé, in 1623, Protestants claimed that they had always shared the cemetery with Catholics not by "convention" but by "common consent." The 1611 commissioners, Saint-Germain de Clan and Méry de Vic, had, they said, maintained them in that right.[35] Loudun's Huguenots, seeking to defend their access to a Catholic cemetery in 1633, insisted that "since the establishment of their religion in this city . . . the alliances and friendship between the Catholics and them could not suffer the separation of their burials."[36] And Catholics too could claim that "amitié ancienne" had previously governed their sharing of the cemetery with Huguenots, as they did in Saint-Maixent.[37]

33. The contract is found in ADDS B, Siège royal de Saint-Maixent Civil, 1635, No. 680, quoted in R. Durand, *Saint-Gelais au péril des dragons, 1681–1981* (Niort, 1981), 83–84. Durand suggests that the agreement was made behind the curé's back, but he is listed among the Catholics agreeing to the contract.

34. "Sommaire des raisons que ceux qui font profession de la religion refformée ont de se plaindre de l'arrest du seiziesme septembre 1634 donné par nos seigneurs du parlement tenants les grands jours en la ville de Poictiers . . . ," ADV C 49, 1.

35. Now the *siège royal* court at Saint-Maixent insisted on a new burial ground for the Huguenots. But, as we have seen above, following the edict, it ordered Catholic inhabitants to pay for it. See "Procès-verbaux of 30 mars and 20 septembre, 1623," ADDS, Siège royal de Saint-Maixent, Civil Divers, 1631–1666 [*sic*] [unclassified].

36. AN TT 250, pièce 40 (22 December 1633). A decision of the royal council in the same year claimed that Loudun's Huguenots had simply abused the king's generosity and the tolerance of Catholics (ibid.).

37. The phrase "amitié ancienne" comes from the 1635 complaint of the curé and churchwardens in Saint-Maixent against Protestants for constructing a new wall that would increase the size of the Protestant portion of a shared cemetery. Its use in this context might have exaggerated the previous friendship between the groups in order to cast the Catholics as victims. Nonetheless, their words suggest there had been some previous sense of agreement between the groups (Benoist, "Catholiques et protestants," 343).

The language of friendship and alliance suggests good confessional relations existed in these communities or, at least, had existed in the decades prior to the 1630s. But it is difficult to know if we can believe these claims, especially when the minority Protestants made them in the context of lawsuits that led inexorably to their loss of rights in communal cemeteries. In a 1607 judicial investigation, the Protestants of Saint-Savin (Berry) insisted that they "had always lived amicably with their neighbors of the Roman religion." But the attempt of one Sulpice Dauvergne to bury his wife, Huguenot Rachel Léau, in the cemetery had provoked a complaint from the parish's churchwardens. They opposed the burial and brought the case to court. The community was ordered to name three notables from among its principal inhabitants of both religions to find another place for the Protestants to bury their dead.[38] Thus claims to long-standing friendship, while no doubt sometimes true, cannot always be taken at face value.

Another possibility is that rather than see such statements as simply an accurate reflection of good confessional relations in communities, we should instead remember the tutelary role that royal officials could play in trying to preserve peaceful relations through carefully negotiated agreements.[39] As we have seen, a common interest in maintaining order existed in many confessionally mixed communities despite the rising religious tensions of the 1610s and 1620s. Officials encouraged this interest by exerting pressure on neighbors of different faiths to reach accords on matters such as cemetery use. They could insist on inserting claims of friendship into the documents as a means of nurturing coexistence and preserving peace. In some cases, however, it seems that commissioners worked out cemetery sharing not with the cooperation of local Catholics but against their wishes. Despite the opposition of the curé and his parishioners in Fresne (Normandy), commissioners in 1612 "maintained . . . those of the said religion [in the right of] burying their dead in the place at the end of the cemetery . . . at the charge of separating that part of the cemetery, and they prohibit anyone from troubling them."[40] The minority faith would

38. AN TT 271 (24), pièce 4.

39. See above, pp. 24–25.

40. In 1611 the same commissioners had overcome Catholic objections and made the same arrangement in Courseulles. See Garrisson, *Essai sur les commissions*, 244n.69.

keep part of a divided parish graveyard. In a case such as this, royal officials were trying to prevent disorder by dictating a settlement that reflected the royal policy of accommodation, despite local Catholic opposition.

In reproducing documents from the cemetery lawsuits, Filleau refers to such arrangements only to denounce them as falsifications of the Edict of Nantes. He felt that the commissioners or judges who sponsored the accommodations had been misguided. At issue was the interpretation of Article 28 and its ambiguity over two matters: whether entire communities or just the local Huguenots were to pay for new Protestant cemeteries, and whether Huguenots could continue using Catholic burial grounds until provided with new ones of their own. Filleau followed the legal arguments of Jacques Talon: Protestants had to finance new cemeteries themselves, and they could not bury their dead in Catholic ones. But royal commissioners and courts had not always agreed.[41]

Thus, while under the provisions of the Edict of Nantes commissioners should have been engaged in separating completely Protestant and Catholic cemeteries, they appear in various places to have allowed instead the (at least temporary) sharing of common ones or, more often, they sponsored the division of old cemeteries into two adjacent burial grounds. In other words, they were actively engaged in helping to construct coexistence in localities either by blurring confessional identities or by carving out recognized and accepted spaces for both confessions in communities. The lack of clear distinction in cemeteries outraged Catholic anti-Protestant campaigners; the leaders of the Reformed Church, who, in principle, invested burial grounds with no sacredness and who wanted to maintain the position of the Reformed Church in communities, had no particular doctrinal reason to be opposed. But they did worry about the indistinct burial customs that their coreligionists practiced in indistinct burial grounds, and this concern their Catholic rivals shared.

41. See, e.g., Filleau's comments on cases from Villefagnon and Couhé, where commissioners had agreed with the Protestants' interpretation of the edict and allowed them continued use of parish burial grounds, or from Coupe-Chaignée, where they had divided the cemetery and ordered the portions separated by a hedge. In Couhé, as Filleau himself notes, the curé and inhabitants had agreed to the arrangement. In each case, the Protestants were evicted from the disputed graveyards. See *Décisions catholiques*, 289–93, 321–23.

FUNERALS

Catholicism and Calvinism disagreed profoundly over both rituals for interring the dead and beliefs concerning the fate of their souls.[42] The differences make any similarities in funeral ceremonies all the more surprising. For Catholics, the souls of the dead in purgatory remained closely connected with the living. To speed their release from purgatory, those who had the means left money in their wills for the saying of masses, or they left charitable bequests to the poor who, in turn, prayed for their benefactors. City men joined confraternities that saw to the decent interment of their deceased brothers and the saying of memorial masses. The urban and rural poor procured such benefits as they could afford, but they too felt a close contact with the dead through the observance of All Souls' Day in parish cemeteries (popularly thought to be the physical location of purgatory). The dead constituted, in Natalie Davis's words, "a kind of 'age group' to put alongside the children, the youth, the married, and the old."[43] If the connections between the living and the dead were broken by neglect or circumstance, then the ghosts of the deceased were likely to haunt their survivors.

Protestants rejected the Catholic doctrine of purgatory and the variety of intercessory practices it spawned, such as masses for the dead, testamentary almsgiving, and indulgences. Calvinists, in particular, believed that the soul was saved or damned immediately upon death.[44] Costly rituals aimed at rescuing souls from purgatory were thus mere superstition that increased the power and riches of the clergy. The Genevan ecclesiasti-

42. On the medieval funeral, see Paul Binski, *Medieval Death: Ritual and Representation* (Ithaca, N.Y., 1996). For Lutheran ideas on purgatory and the burial of the dead, see Craig M. Koslofsky, *The Reformation of the Dead: Death and Ritual in Early Modern Germany, 1450–1700* (New York, 2000), 19–39.

43. Natalie Zemon Davis, "Ghosts, Kin, and Progeny: Some Features of Family Life in Early Modern France," *Daedalus* 106 (Spring 1977): 87–114, see esp. 92–93. On the belief in purgatory's location in the cemetery, see Edward Muir, *Ritual in Early Modern Europe* (Cambridge, U.K., 1997), 49; Andrew Spicer, "'Rest of their Bones': Fear of Death and Reformed Burial Practices," in *Fear in Early Modern Society*, edited by William G. Naphy and Penny Roberts (Manchester, U.K., 1997), 167–83, see esp. 167. A related view had the soul staying near the body for the first month after death. See Roberts, "Contesting Sacred Space," 133.

44. Roberts, "Contesting Sacred Space," 134.

cal ordinances of 1541 held those who carried bodies to the gravesite responsible for ensuring that no "superstitions contrary to the word of God" occurred.[45] Calvin also objected to the elaborate funerals by which Catholics honored the dead of wealthy families and satisfied their survivors' taste for social distinction. All souls were equal and all human remains were equally insignificant. Pierre Dumoulin, one of French Protestantism's leading seventeenth-century theologians and polemicists, put the matter succinctly: "We don't fleece [*tondons*] people for burials."[46]

The *Discipline* of the French Reformed Church dictated a very minimal funeral ceremony: "To avoid all superstitions . . . no prayers or preaching will be offered nor public alms given at burials. Those who accompany the body will be exhorted to conduct themselves with modesty during the funeral procession, meditating . . . as much on the miseries and brevity of this life as on the hope for a happy life. . . . So that mourning . . . remains heartfelt, the faithful will . . . reject all ambition, hypocrisy, [and] vanity."[47] To discourage any belief that linked the soul's fate to ritual practice, the Huguenot funeral would be austere and testify to the confidence born of placing one's fate entirely in God's hands.[48]

More than the *Discipline*, however, was involved in dictating simple and severe Huguenot funerals. Catholics also kept a close eye on them. Local Catholic militants were eager to report any "scandal" of which they could accuse Huguenots. And royal officials worried about Huguenot funerals provoking violence.[49] The state had regulated Protestant funerals during

45. Geoffrey Rowell, *The Liturgy of Christian Burial: An Introductory Survey of the Historical Development of Christian Burial Rites* (London, 1977), 81–82; Claire Gittings, *Death, Burial and the Individual in Early Modern England* (London, 1984). Calvin did, however, feel that a burial service was useful as an argument against pagan denials of the resurrection.

46. Quoted in Paul de Félice, *Les protestants d'autrefois: Vie intérieure des églises, moeurs et usages*, 4 vols. (Paris, 1896–1898), 1:272.

47. Chapter 10, Articles 5 and 6, in François Méjan, *Discipline de l'église réformée: Annotée et précédée d'une introduction historique* (Paris, 1947), 260–61.

48. Catholics also sometimes requested simple funerals, which were seen as extraordinary acts of self-denial and personal piety, often associated with monastic discipline. See Roberts, "Contesting Sacred Space," 137.

49. As happened at Tours in 1621, when Catholic boys and artisans attacked a Huguenot cortege, leading to three days of rioting. See "Extrait de l'assemblée [de Niort] du vendredi dernier jour d'avril 1621: Lettres du roi à Mr. de Parabère," BMP Fonds Fonteneau, vol. 68, 349.

the Wars of Religion, prohibiting daytime burials and limiting the size of corteges.[50] The Edict of Nantes did not include any such restrictions, but Louis XIV would reinstate them in the 1660s.[51]

Despite their church's insistence on simple funerals, French Protestants resented the interference; they claimed that under different political conditions, Calvinist funeral practice was not always so constrained. As Parisian minister Charles Drelincourt complained:

> [Catholics] mock us because of our lack of ceremony and pomp, and this mockery has led to an infinity of disorders and inhumanities . . . but where our religion has full liberty, burials are not conducted as they are in this kingdom, where the misery of the times obliged our fathers to practice this simplicity. There are places where pastors deliver a public discourse for the consolation of the afflicted; they take the occasion of the death to exhort those present to live well in order, one day, to be able to die well. This is a holy and praiseworthy custom.[52]

In these comments, Drelincourt was certainly not longing for baroque-style, Catholic funerals; Calvinist ministers consistently urged austerity. Instead, he was complaining about the political conditions under which French Protestants lived. Nevertheless, he argued that different political circumstances could lead to somewhat more, not less, elaborate funerals, suggesting that practice did not always correspond to doctrine.

Evidence from areas with dominant Calvinist churches indicates he was right. In Scotland, the Reformed Church fought long and not very successfully against the burial of the socially prominent inside churches. For Calvinist ministers, this practice was a superstition, a survival of the custom of burying the privileged near altars and relics to shorten their souls' stay in purgatory. The Dutch Reformed Church acquiesced in church burials, satisfying itself with eliminating funeral processions and

50. A December 1563 edict ordered Huguenots to conduct funerals only between sunset and dawn and limited mourners to thirty (Roberts, "Contesting Sacred Space," 143). As Roberts points out, such restrictions could also protect Protestants participating in the funeral. The Peace of Saint-Germain (1570) ordered nighttime funerals with corteges of no more than ten. See André Stegmann, ed., *Édits des Guerres de Religion* (Paris, 1979), 72.

51. I return to the ordinances of the 1660s below.

52. Charles Drelincourt, *Avertissement*, 71–72.

sermons. Funeral feasting and bell ringing also continued in some Dutch cities and rural areas.[53]

But the comparison on Drelincourt's mind was between the Protestant situation in France and that in German Calvinist localities, particularly Heidelberg, where he had passed some of his youth. The German situation also illustrates how, where Protestantism was politically dominant, funeral practices could vary considerably from the doctrinal rule. German Protestants, both Lutheran and Calvinist, wanted to ensure that funerals would instruct people in proper living rather than encourage them to pray for the souls of the dead.[54] But their funerals were not devoid of ceremony. Lutherans included Bible readings, prayers, canticles, bell ringing, and sermons.[55] In principle, German Calvinists rejected all of these practices, but they often resisted the absolute simplicity their pastors sought. Drelincourt remembered hearing mourners gracefully singing the canticle of Moses, a practice that he applauded since it "excellently presented the fragility of human life and the brevity of our days."[56] Families often insisted on funeral sermons; for a minister to refuse them was a humiliation. Some Calvinist principalities even encouraged sermons by regulating their themes. Use of the "commendation of souls" to God's mercies continued even though Reformed Churches rejected it (no commendation was necessary if the soul was immediately saved or damned). And despite ministers' objections to recounting the deceased's life at a funeral, the practice spread, at first among the aristocracy. Indeed, everywhere the rich continued to seek funerals more elaborate than local consistories allowed.[57]

None of these examples suggests that one would have confused a

53. Spicer "'Rest of their Bones,'" 170–76. Old customs could, at least, be explained in new ways. The Reformed Church of Utrecht allowed bell ringing as a means of expressing communal grief rather than as a reminder to pray for the dead. On the continuation of elaborate funerals among English Calvinists, see Gittings, *Death, Burial and the Individual*, 55, 89.

54. For Lutherans, see Koslofsky, *Reformation of the Dead*, 31–54.

55. Rowell, *Liturgy of Christian Burial*, 80.

56. Drelincourt, *Avertissement*, 72.

57. Roussel, "Funeral Corteges and Huguenot Culture," 197; Bernard Vogler, "La législation sur les sépultures dans l'Allemagne protestante au XVIe siècle," *Revue d'histoire moderne et contemporaine* 22 (April–June 1975): 191–232.

Calvinist with a Catholic funeral. Rather, they demonstrate a considerable discrepancy between church teachings and practice in areas where the Reformed faith was dominant. It might seem that the close alliance between state and church in these Calvinist principalities would have ensured more, not less, conformity to doctrine, but the difficulty of enforcement, the weight of custom, and the pressure of elites on pastors and consistories all worked against conformity. In German Calvinist areas, state and church were allies in a not very successful struggle to impose doctrinal conformity. In France, one might think, Calvinists would be held to simple funerals by doctrine and the need to distinguish themselves from majority Catholics, but also, and perhaps more significantly, by the state's restrictions. Although the French monarchy and the Protestant clergy became bitter opponents, they worked, albeit with different motivations, toward breaking the bonds of easy familiarity between neighbors of different faiths. While ministers sought to establish a more disciplined confessional group, the state wanted to isolate and increase the pressure on the religious minority.

However, even in France, the sought-after simplicity was not so easily obtained. Descriptions of funerals suggest that even if Huguenots never demanded burials as elaborate as those of Catholics, they still expected some ceremony and display. The reason lay not only in the ineffectiveness of consistorial or government enforcement but also in the particular situation of the minority. Absolute austerity was hard to enforce because Calvinist funerals, like Catholic ones, had to respond not only to doctrinal beliefs about the fate of souls but also to social imperatives.[58] Huguenots sought to continue or to adopt some practices that fostered good relations with the majority, preserved their integration and public presence in communities, and maintained ties with ancestors, even those of the other faith. The funeral's role in displaying social prestige, demonstrating family ties, and building a sense of community (at least among the living if not between the living and the dead) did not readily disappear. Burial rituals provided both Catholics and Protestants a means to cope with death and

58. Although Roussel presents evidence of such imperatives at work, he argues, nonetheless, that Huguenot funerals were in accordance with the *Discipline* ("Funeral Corteges and Huguenot Culture," 194–97). On social imperatives and "confessional ambiguity," see Hanlon, *Confession and Community*, 219–20.

with the breech it caused in a community's social fabric. As Penny Roberts points out, Calvinist insistence on a simple funeral could offend Catholics both because it was a denial of their beliefs and because it could seem a rejection of the community's collective piety "which brought the community together at the death of one of its members."[59] The result could be the increased isolation of the minority. Even the theologian Drelincourt had complained: "[Catholics] mock us because of our lack of ceremony and pomp, and this mockery has led to an infinity of disorders and inhumanities." These social functions of funerals remained important for French Protestants and Catholics alike. Indeed, as the minority, it was necessary for Protestants to use funerals to stake a claim for recognition and acceptance in their communities. Simple burials put at risk social standing and connections and perhaps also kinship ties in religiously mixed families. Huguenot funerals, and the consistories and synods that regulated them, were therefore caught between the demands of strict Calvinist discipline and the concerns of Calvinists living beside their Catholic neighbors.[60]

Faced with requests from provincial delegations to allow for more funeral ceremony, national synods found it difficult to insist on simplicity. For instance, the question of whether ministers should be present at funerals proved troublesome. In principle, they were to attend only as friends or relatives of the deceased. Some synods discouraged their presence in a pastoral role as a means of preventing any hint of excessive ceremony; others left the decision to individual pastors. In some areas ministers were accustomed to giving funeral "remonstrances," if not at the cemetery, then in front of the deceased's house. The 1596 Saumur meeting would not agree to these addresses, which resembled funeral sermons, but the 1603 Gap synod responded to a request from Bas-Languedoc by saying that ministers were to use their discretion.[61] In 1631, at

59. Roberts, "Contesting Sacred Space," 137. Catholic polemicist Florimond de Raemond criticized Huguenot funerals for failing to restore social order through the use of funeral display. See Roussel, "Funeral Corteges and Huguenot Culture," 200.

60. Roussel notes the Huguenots' determination "to maintain their beliefs and worship without . . . abandoning their social position and all that it entailed." They "sought not to compromise their integration into French society." See "Funeral Corteges and Huguenot Culture," 199, 207.

61. Calvin had been hostile to funeral sermons. They smacked of ceremony, and since priests had traditionally received payment for sermons, the rich benefited from

Charenton, deputies from Normandy reopened the issue, seconded by those from Burgundy, who pointed out that such sermons could be turned to a polemical purpose against Catholics. However, the minister of Béziers revealed another reason behind the request. He insisted that Catholics held Protestants in contempt because they did not give funeral sermons, and he added that the lack of exhortations also offended many of the faithful. His concern, in other words, was not to combat religious rivals but to avoid imposing an obligation on Huguenots that marked them out in a humiliating way from their Catholic neighbors. The synod decided to leave alone those provinces where the practice existed, while prohibiting any new ones from taking it up.[62]

Synods worried about "papist ceremonies" slipping into burials. For example, it was a widespread practice to exhibit the deceased in front of their houses before carrying them to the cemetery. The ringing of bells during funeral processions continued in some areas, despite the complaints of provincial synods that the practice was superstitious.[63] Even the funeral procession was controversial. If a cortege followed the *Discipline's* requirements, it could stand as a rebuke to Catholics. The mourners would include only relatives and friends of the deceased; they would be dressed in black and march two-by-two with a meditative air, first the men (perhaps with the consistory elders leading) and then the women. But apparently this rule was not always followed, and synods were caught between local practices and the goal of imposing austerity. The 1637 Alençon meeting decided that "without permitting the introduction of any new custom regarding funeral corteges, for the consolation of the families of the deceased . . . the Company permits to those which have long had their own form and practiced it with edification to continue to observe their own order."[64]

---

them more than the poor. See Vogler, "Législation sur les sépultures," 202. The Scottish *Book of Discipline* (1560) forbade sermons because they opened the way to social distinctions in funerals. See Rowell, *Liturgy of Christian Burial*, 82; and Gittings, *Death, Burial and the Individual*, 138.

62. Charles Read, "Cimetières et inhumations des huguenots principalement à Paris aux XVIe, XVIIe, XVIIIe siècles (1563–1792)," *Bulletin de la société d'histoire du protestantisme français* 12 (1863): 33–41, 141–48, 274–84, 367–75, see esp. 144–45.

63. Félice, *Protestants d'autrefois*, 1:249–72.

64. Read, "Cimetières et inhumations" (1863), 144–45.

Evidence from the south suggests synods were correct in fearing that local customs merged Protestant practices with those of Catholics. Robert Sauzet found that in Nîmes the baroque funerals so popular among the wealthier Catholics of the Midi were also attractive to Huguenots. Provincial synods complained that people insisted on being buried in tombs that displayed family coats of arms. Consistories condemned the use of large retinues, hired mourners, and ornate tombstones. Likewise they disliked having corteges of wives carry the bodies of wives, children carry children, and unmarried women carry unmarried women. The 1601 national synod of Gergeau had condemned as a "novelty" the flower garlands Languedocian women wore while accompanying the deceased to the cemetery. The synods also worried about pastors, who, instead of resisting questionable ceremonies, sometimes participated in them.[65] And this problem was not confined to the south. Filleau reports a case in which the daughter of Caen's minister, Jean Bellache, was carried to her gravesite in a coffin covered by a white cloth on which were strewn wreaths and garlands of rosemary. Four girls held the cloth, and each carried a stem of rosemary.[66]

Sauzet felt such funeral pomp was newly introduced among the Protestants of Languedoc. But in general it is difficult to say if these practices were innovations, which thwarted Calvinist insistence on simple funerals, or surviving traditions, which consistories could not root out. In either case, they are evidence of the Huguenots' desire to bury their dead in ways that responded to social imperatives, even those Calvinist teaching on funerals rejected. This is not to suggest that members of the minority were simply trying to fit in by acting like Catholics.[67] Rather,

65. Sauzet, *Contre-réforme et réforme catholique*, 74–75. On Languedoc corteges, see Félice, *Protestants d'autrefois*, 1:258–59, 263–64. Synods did allow craft guilds to carry their former members to the grave. On women wearing flowers while carrying deceased women, see Read, "Cimetières et inhumations" (1863), 144.

66. Filleau reports the 1664 decision of the Chambre de l'Édit of the Rouen Parlement, which considered this incident and prohibited Huguenots from carrying such cloths and "from having any pomp or funeral ceremony at their funerals" (*Décisions catholiques*, 1:313–14). Also reported in documents concerning Protestant worship at Saint-Quentin in AN TT 271 (21), pièce 4.

67. For somewhat different views on this question, see Benedict, *Huguenot Population*, 86, 103; and Hanlon, *Confession and Community*, 151.

through the open ceremonial presence of their funerals on the streets of their towns, they demonstrated consideration for their neighbors' feelings and a demand to be seen as respectable members of communities.

At the very least, Protestants and Catholics were well aware of the other's funerary practices and participated in them. Since the confessional line often ran right through families, people of each faith inevitably participated in the rival religion's ceremonies. Even the Protestant *Discipline* despaired of preventing the faithful's presence at Catholic funerals, and instead allowed them to attend if they avoided all idolatry and superstition: they could not enter the church, they could only follow the procession at a distance, and they could not go to the meals that followed the burial.[68] Consistories faced cases such as that of Marthe Brun of Melle, who, in 1665, marched in the procession of her Catholic husband's funeral. She repented and was readmitted to communion.[69] In 1673 Isaac Maigneron apologized to the Melle elders for having attended the Catholic funeral of one of his daughters. The consistory acknowledged his repentance and admonished him not to do it again.[70] Incidents such as these indicate what consistories were up against in confessionally mixed communities. What real force could admonitions such as those to Brun and Maigneron have, when not only their neighbors but also their kin were of the opposite faith?

Given the privileged orders' preoccupation with securing honor and social standing through public display, it is not surprising that the most frequent contraventions of Calvinist simplicity came from members of the Huguenot elite, who sought funerals and funerary commemoration commensurate with their status. When the great were buried, the *Discipline's* rules were most likely to be frustrated—for instance, on the issue of monuments. Although the walls of Protestant cemeteries did sometimes carry biblical inscriptions, the *Discipline* discouraged tombs and tombstones.[71] But on this matter too synods had to wrestle with local usages and with the Huguenot elite's assertion of their status. At the 1603 Gap

68. Félice, *Protestants d'autrefois*, 1:267–68.

69. ADDS 2J 35 (1), p. 13 (Melle consistory, 25 September 1665).

70. BPF, 1500/6/c, p. 83 (Documents Maillard, Melle consistory, 7 April 1673).

71. Read, "Cimetières et inhumations" (1863), 143–47; Roussel, "Funeral Corteges and Huguenot Culture," 207.

synod, the Saintonge delegation asked if it were permissible to have decorated tombs elevated on pillars. The assembly responded that "for tombs each should maintain the simplicity of ancient Christianity without appropriating for himself anything in particular."[72] Social distinctions after death were precisely the sort of Catholic "abuse" from which Calvinism sought to distinguish itself. But Calvinist simplicity was hard to maintain when it conflicted with the status-conscious sensibility of family honor.[73]

The problem of funerary display was most acute in the Parisian Huguenot community, since the capital was home to high-ranking Protestant nobles and officials. For example, the funeral and the grave of Claude Arnauld, buried in 1603, was certainly in keeping with his important position as a financial officer of the Crown and with the rising reputation of the Arnauld family. A procession with fifty horses accompanied the carriage that brought his body to the Huguenot Saint-Pères cemetery. His tomb, consisting of a large black marble slab with an engraved epitaph listing his official positions and praising his virtue, attracted much attention. It was, wrote memoirist Pierre L'Estoile, "a new and unusual thing among those of the religion."[74] The comment suggests observers were aware that strict disciplinary regulations were being bent in the service of other interests. Perhaps such an innovation was not so surprising in a prominent and confessionally mixed family such as the Arnaulds. But it provoked resentment, and not just among Arnauld's coreligionists. Two or three weeks after the tomb's construction, it was covered in plaster for fear, according to L'Estoile, that it would become a target for Catholic crowds. During the period between the tomb's construction and its plas-

72. Read, "Cimetières et inhumations" (1863), 145.

73. And with the financial needs of Huguenot congregations. Amanda Eurich reports that, after 1643, the consistory of Pau (Béarn) started permitting the burial of wealthy members in the temple in return for a fee. Magistrates' families seized "this renewed opportunity to establish visual markers of family influence within the temple." See "'Speaking the King's Language': The Huguenot Magistrates of Castres and Pau," in Mentzer and Spicer, eds., *Society and Culture in the Huguenot World*, 117–38, see esp. 136.

74. Quoted in Jacques Pannier, *L'église réformée de Paris sous Henri IV: Rapport de l'église et de l'état, vie publique et privée des protestants* (1911; reprint, Geneva, 1977), 396–97. See also Alexander Sedgwick, *The Travails of Conscience: The Arnauld Family and the Ancien Regime* (Cambridge, Mass., 1998), 27.

tering, the Gap synod decided against allowing raised and ornamented tombs.[75] The efficacy of that ruling is questionable, however, given that seven years later the Charenton consistory had to order the dismantling of other tombs in the Saint-Pères cemetery "that various people have set up there, since they serve nothing other than to reintroduce papist ceremonies and superstitions."[76] Protestant authorities had trouble enforcing such orders and not just in Paris. A 1633 ordinance of the Council of State, which divided the mixed cemetery of Saint-Pierre-du-Marché in Loudun into Catholic and Protestant portions, accused the Huguenots not only of burying their dead with Catholics, but also of imitating them in building "raised sepulchers, epitaphs, and inscriptions."[77]

A 1680 Catholic memoir from Saint-Quentin (diocese of Noyon) reported that Protestants there had for decades been placing their dead in marble tombs inscribed with at least simple epitaphs: "In this tomb lies the flesh and bones of those whose names live on earth and among the souls in heaven"; or "This marble is placed here in the memory of Maître Pierre Cromelin and others of his family whose souls are gathered in heaven and whose bodies repose here below awaiting their very fortunate resurrection." These inscriptions were not as elaborate as Arnauld's, but they still provoked controversy among Saint-Quentin's Protestants. An elder, Jacques Le Serurier, complained to the consistory in 1679 about the tombs and epitaphs. When his local colleagues refused to take action against them, he appealed to the provincial synod, which ordered that no future tombs be allowed.[78]

In both shared cemeteries, such as that of Loudun, and separated cemeteries, such as that of Saint-Quentin, the practices of Huguenots and Catholics seemed to contemporaries hard to distinguish. It was a problem for consistories and synods worried about the intrusion of papist superstitions into the religious activities of Protestants. But it was also a problem for Catholic authorities eager to construct a more rigid wall between the confessional groups. The report on Saint-Quentin led the bishop of Noy-

75. Pannier, *Église réformée de Paris*, 398.

76. Quoted in Read, "Cimetières et inhumations" (1863), 147. See also Félice, *Protestants d'autrefois*, 1:269–70.

77. AN TT 250, pièce 39 (29 November 1633).

78. "Mémoire concernant le cimetière et les epitaphs des gens de la RPR de St. Quentin," AN TT 271 (21).

on to write the local intendant requesting an ordinance forbidding Protestants from raising tombs and inscribing them with epitaphs. They were "scandalous to the [Catholic] faithful who alone should enjoy after their deaths this honorable and public proof of a holy communion during their lives."[79] By the 1670s the beleaguered leadership of the Reformed Church may have been more insistent than ever on strict adherence to disciplinary rules, but it had less and less ability to enforce them. The Catholic clergy, however, had a powerful ally. The state's governance of Huguenot funerals and cemeteries, which had been growing increasingly harsh for decades, was far more effective than the actions of the churches in building barriers between the faiths.

CONSTRUCTING THE THIRD BOUNDARY IN FUNERALS AND CEMETERIES

The state's anti-Protestant campaign sought to prohibit Huguenot use of burial practices that resembled those of Catholics. Protestants would be forced to live not only within the *Discipline's* bounds but also within the state's more severe restrictions. These restrictions became increasingly harsh after midcentury, when both the central government and local authorities began to respond readily to the urging of the Catholic clergy that the Edict of Nantes be interpreted and applied in the strictest possible way.[80] The scope of the campaign is evident, for example, in Jean Filleau's huge volume *Décisions catholiques*, of which a sizable part is devoted to cemeteries and burials. He denounced similarities between Catholic and Protestant practices:

79. "Copie de la lettre escrite par M. l'Evesque de Noyon le 9 avril 1680 à M. l'Intendant . . ." and "Memoire pour Monsieur l'Evesque de Noyon contre ceux de la RPR de la ville de St. Quentin," AN TT 271 (21), pièces 8 and 9. The prolific Jesuit polemicist Bernard Meynier criticized the Protestant use of epitaphs, and Catholics cited his work in the Saint-Quentin case. See his *De l'exécution de l'Edit de Nantes en Guienne et en Poitou* (Cahors, 1665) and *De l'exécution de l'Edit de Nantes dans les provinces de Guyenne, Poitou, Angoumois, Xaintonge et Aunis . . .* (Poitiers, 1665). On Meynier, and on the works he and others, like Filleau, published to promote a more intransigent anti-Huguenot policy, see Labrousse, *"Une foi, une loi, un roi,"* 129–31.

80. See Pierre Blet, *Le clergé de France et la monarchie: Étude sur les assemblées générales du clergé de 1615–1666*, 2 vols. (Rome, 1959), 1:99–110, 2:342–88.

> Our time has seen with astonishment the enterprise of those of the R.P.R. [religion prétendue réformée] who, having denied all the ceremonies of the Church, nevertheless want, in some fashion, to imitate them by conducting their dead in the middle of the day [to the cemetery], with a great assemblage of people, marching in order, and what is more, by displaying bodies before the doors of their homes, in the form and manner of Catholic practice. . . . This new enterprise is full of presumption and condemned by the policies that permit this religion, or rather irreligion, to exist in France only by the tolerance, indulgence, and kindness of our kings. Their dead . . . should be buried only in the darkness of night because the exterior honor rendered to the dead should belong only to those who have a legitimate right to it by professing the true faith.[81]

For Filleau, Protestantism's danger lay not only in its rejection of, but also in its hypocritical imitation of, Catholicism. Protestants appeared not as a threat from the outside but, more insidiously, as one from within. Rooting them out required restricting them to funerals that were clearly differentiated from those of Catholics. The monarchy, whose "tolerance"—which is to say sufferance—of the heretics had allowed them to blur the distinction between the confessional groups, now would have to enforce a stricter boundary between them.

The government fulfilled such wishes with legislation that proved more effective in regulating Protestant funerals than the rulings of consistories and synods. According to the royal declaration of 1666 (reinforcing a 1663 order of the Council of State and various local ordinances), Huguenots could no longer display their dead before their houses, nor could ministers make funeral exhortations "in the streets." In seigneuries where Huguenot nobles had a right to private worship, burials could only take place at dawn or dusk and no more than ten people, all friends or relatives of the deceased, could attend. Elsewhere, Protestant funerals could be held, from April through September, only at 6:00 A.M. or at 6:00 P.M. precisely, and from October through March at 8:00 A.M. or 4:00 P.M. Corteges, consisting of relatives only, would be limited to thirty.[82]

81. Filleau, *Décisions catholiques*, 299.

82. "Déclaration du roy le 2 jour avril 1666," Articles 22–25, in Bergeal and Durrelman, *Protestantisme et libertés*, 92; Filleau, *Décisions catholiques*, 299–306.

Huguenots objected to the obligation of burying their dead at these times; it gave their funerals a furtive air.[83] In Melle, the consistory elders had tried to organize a protest of Huguenots in nearby Poitevin communities against the 1663 order on burial times. No evidence exists of their success, but perhaps that was because local Protestants simply were not following the council's decision. Compliance is difficult to assess. Certainly Filleau, admittedly not an objective observer, complained to the council in 1663 that disobedience was widespread in Poitou and asked it to reinforce the prohibitions.[84]

Such complaints may have led to the more sweeping and precise 1666 declaration. There was, however, a certain irony in a policy of harassment that intensified the strictures placed on Protestant worship. In a sense, the government was enforcing the Reformed Church's own doctrinal preference for simplicity in funerals, though admittedly going further than even the strictest consistory. The lack of public ceremony in a burial at dawn or dusk, with no display of the deceased, no ministerial exhortation, and a limited number of mourners, all helped ensure the Calvinist rejection of purgatory and honor paid the dead. In the words of the Protestant historian Paul de Félice, "a great silence would reign at burials." The "*Discipline* had found an auxiliary more powerful than it."[85]

As for expelling Huguenots completely from Catholic cemeteries, no further legislation was necessary. In the view of Catholic anti-Protestant campaigners, the Edict of Nantes, by calling for separation of burial grounds, provided a legal apparatus sufficient for the task, if courts interpreted it in the strictest sense possible. Increasingly, they found courts sympathetic to their cause. In communities where cemeteries were shared, either by indiscriminate burials or by partitioning, common ground became disputed territory as complaints were raised and lawsuits filed to force the complete separation of burial grounds or the expulsion of Protestant graveyards from towns.

It is often difficult to know with certainty who provoked the disputes. The documents from legal cases generally list the Catholic inhabitants of

83. Pannier, *Église réformée de Paris*, 383.

84. ADDS 2J 35 (1), p. 7 (Melle consistory, 18 February 1663); Filleau, *Décisions catholiques*, 305.

85. Félice, *Protestants d'autrefois*, 1:257.

a locality as being parties to a suit, without it necessarily being the case that they initiated it. In some instances, the two confessional groups do appear to have been at odds. In others, curés triggered the cases that led to Huguenots losing rights to a cemetery. In 1635 the Protestants of Cherveux blamed their expulsion from a burial ground on the hatred the local priest had for them. Their Catholic neighbors, they said, had always consented to sharing the graveyard.[86] But in some suits it seems that the instigators were diocesan officials or their lay allies like Jean Filleau. In 1622 the vicar-general, syndic, and deputies of the Catholic clergy of the diocese of Luçon brought a suit to deprive that city's Protestants of a cemetery they had used in common with Catholics.[87] Bishop La Rocheposay of Poitiers filed suits against Huguenots using Catholic cemeteries in a number of communities, including Villefagnan, La Mothe-Saint-Héray, Vouillé, and Nanteuil.[88]

When the courts decided in favor of Catholic plaintiffs, they dismantled the delicate earlier agreements or compromises on cemetery sharing and ordered complete separation and removal of Protestant burial grounds outside of cities and towns. We can see the process at work in Latillé, where cemetery arrangements moved progressively through each of the three stages of confessional boundary configuration. Early in the century royal commissioners sponsored an accord by which the parish cemetery remained common to both religions. But a 1619 lawsuit separated burial grounds, despite the Protestant claim that the earlier agreement had never provoked any conflicts among the inhabitants. The curé offered the Protestants another piece of church property at no cost; he did so, he declared, "to honor God and for the good of peace." The new cemetery would not be adjacent to the old, but it still offered Huguenots a clearly defined site within the community. The arrangement seemed perfectly ac-

86. In this case the dispute was over dividing a cemetery, to which the curé objected because a Catholic was buried on what would be the Protestant side (ADDS B Siège royal de Saint-Maixent, 13 septembre 1635, cited in Benoist, "Catholiques et protestants," 344 and note 115).

87. "Ordonnance du lt.-gen. de Fontenai-le-Comte [Fontenay-le-Comte] aux fins de donner aux protestants dans le bourg de Luçon une sépulture separée de celle des catholiques (3 janvier 1622)," BMP, Fonds Fonteneau, vol. 64 (2), 673.

88. These cases date from the 1640s; see Filleau, *Décisions catholiques*, 322. The bishop was also the seigneur of some of these localities.

ceptable to the people of Latillé—even to the Catholic priest. However, another suit three decades later broke the carefully negotiated agreement and denied Protestants their cemetery because it was on church-owned land. They were forced to seek another location outside the town.[89]

Protestants in Loudun suffered a similar fate. In the parish cemetery of Saint-Pierre-du-Marché, Catholics and Protestants were buried side by side. In 1611 Catholics complained about this "usurpation" to royal commissioners, who responded by ordering a wall constructed, at the city's not just the Huguenots' expense, which would divide the cemetery in two. That still left the matter of a cross standing on what would now be the Protestant side, but the commissioners ordered the Catholics to maintain it and forbade the Protestants from touching it.[90] Through these provisions, the officials sought to maintain "the peace and contentment" among the city's "principal inhabitants," which suggests that the cemetery dispute had divided Loudun's elite. The arrangement lasted two decades. In 1633 the king's envoy to Loudun, Jean Martin de Laubardemont, ordered the Huguenot burial ground out of the city. The Protestant pastor, Daniel Couppe, objected: "The alliances and friendship between the Catholics and them [Protestants] . . . could not suffer the separation of their graves. . . . The divided cemetery offered no inconvenience to the Catholics." Laubardemont rejected the Huguenot argument. The pastor may have been right that the religious groups had lived peacefully with each other in earlier years, but Loudun in the 1630s was caught up in the affair of the demon-possessed Ursuline nuns, which provoked confessional tension in the city. From a previously strong position in Loudun, the Huguenots found themselves increasingly on the defensive and excluded from communal life.[91]

Protestants sometimes defied orders to partition shared burial grounds.

89. Filleau, *Décisions catholiques*, 293–95. Filleau's account does not give the date of the first agreement. Benoist's version of this dispute is essentially the same despite his very different view of Catholic actions; see *Histoire de l'Edit de Nantes*, 3:92.

90. In other places, the Protestants would be given a place distant from such objects, which they considered superstitious.

91. AN TT 250, 814–22. "Procès-verbal de messieurs les commissaires pour l'exécution de l'Edit de Nantes" (11 December 1611) (pièce 31); "Extrait des registres du conseil d'estat du roy" (29 November 1633) (pièce 39); Laubardemont's orders (22 December 1633) (pièce 40). I return to the Ursuline affair below, see pp. 232–44.

As we have seen in Chapter 1, Catholics in Saint-Maixent accused Huguenots in 1612 of having refused to follow commissioners' orders, issued originally in 1599, to build a wall around their cemetery separating it from that of the Catholics.[92] And Huguenots also resisted attempts to force them into new cemeteries. In Niort, the two groups had clearly separate cemeteries within the city. But in 1623 Catholics complained to royal commissioners about the Huguenot cemetery. It was new, built during "the recent upheavals." And, although the Huguenots had enclosed it, the wall and gate obstructed an important public thoroughfare. Catholics insisted that Protestants should restrict themselves to the cemetery they had been granted outside one of the city's gates. Protestants objected to having their burials pushed outside the city, which was contrary to the order of earlier commissioners that permitted them a cemetery inside the walls. Now the commissioners split along confessional lines. The Protestant sided with his coreligionists. Catholics, he stated, were motivated only by "passion" and were trying to "molest" Huguenots by dumping rubbish before the cemetery gate. He insisted that the graveyard presented no great inconvenience to the community, and so Huguenots should be allowed to use it peacefully. The Catholic commissioner disagreed. The cemetery was contiguous to city walls and a gate; it blocked an important artery. Protestants had no need for two burial grounds and should be content with the spacious one outside the city. With the decision split, the commissioners referred the matter to the king. But they did, at least, reach a temporary compromise: the Protestants would be left their inside cemetery, providing they would agree to open a passage at one end of it if public necessity required. Perhaps influenced by the tense situation of impending religious war in the province, even the Catholic commissioner was not willing to force the most exclusionary form of cemetery arrangement on Niort's Huguenots.[93]

The tide turned definitively against Protestants in the 1630s, when the

92. "Requête des maire, échevins, bourgeois, et habitants catholiques de la ville de Saint-Maixent au sujet de la révolte et violence des religionnaires, présenté à nos seigneurs les députés par sa majesté en ce pays et province de Poitou," BPF, Ms. 870 (1). See also "Fonds du legs Alfred Richard," ADV F 183, 436. See the discussion of confessional relations in Saint-Maixent above, pp. 32–36.

93. "Les plaints . . . [des] habitans catholiques contre les habitans de la r.p.r." (1623), BMP Fonds Fonteneau, vol. 68, 415–17; Lièvre, *Histoire des protestants*, 1:304. The cemetery was one of a number of issues in dispute. See above, pp. 36–46.

royal judiciary undertook a major assault on Protestant use of Catholic cemeteries. In the western provinces, a *Grands Jours* court, which opened in Poitiers in 1634, provided the major weapon.[94] One of the court's most important tasks was hearing cases in which Catholics accused Huguenots of contravening the laws governing them. Mixed and shared burial grounds were obvious targets. The court considered suits from Poitou, Angoumois, Saintonge, Aunis, and the Vendômois.[95] Over the next two years, it ordered the complete separation of sixty-nine cemeteries in Poitou alone.[96] Those that escaped faced lawsuits in later years. The court's rulings were an attack on full Huguenot inclusion in their communities, and in some places they were also an attack against local Protestant power. For instance, the Protestants, who dominated Melle, had a separate cemetery, but the case before the Grands Jours court accused them of continuing to use the Catholic burial ground by force. They were ordered confined to their own graveyard, a blow to the exercise of their political strength in the town.[97]

In another setback to Protestant power, the court also prosecuted Huguenot seigneurs for burials in Catholic churches and tombs. The clerical deputies to the Estates General in 1614 asked for a prohibition on Protestant seigneurs enjoying their patronage rights over Catholic burial sites.[98] Jacques Talon aided their cause by arguing before the Paris Parlement in 1626 that since Huguenots denied that the souls of the dead could benefit from the "fruit of the . . . prayers" of the living, Huguenot patrons should not be able to claim burial in churches. Elie Benoist, who relates Talon's argument, rejected it by insisting that the prerogatives of a noble, whose ancestors had acquired the right of burial in a church, should be preferred

94. Grands Jours courts consisted of parlementary magistrates assigned temporarily to repress lawlessness and impose the royal will in regions where the local judicial system seemed incapable of doing so. See Marcel Marion, *Dictionnaire des institutions de la France aux XVIIe et XVIIIe siècles* (New York, 1968), 268; and Hickey, "Rôle de l'état," 939–45.

95. Filleau, *Décisions catholiques*, 263–323. Filleau also reports cemetery cases heard elsewhere, such as Languedoc.

96. Benoist, "Catholiques et protestants," 343. The author also lists nine decisions by the siège royal of Saint-Maixent for 1635 as well as four from other years.

97. Filleau, *Décisions catholiques*, 278.

98. "Les articles proposez . . . deputtez du clergé," BMP, Fonds Fonteneau, vol. 79 (1), 281–88.

to the avarice of priests.[99] But in the courts the Catholic economy of salvation and the purity of hallowed ground took precedence over seigneurial privilege. Poitevin nobles, such as Louis de Saint-Georges, sieur de Boissec of Exoudun and the Dame de La Tarbarrière of Chantonnay, were prohibited from burying family members in chapels. In these cases, the court ordered the demolition of walls, which had been constructed to close off these spaces from Catholic use. The chapels would be resanctified for Catholic worship.[100]

As a result of court decisions, Protestants had to find other burial grounds and bear the expenses themselves.[101] They also had to exhume any bodies newly interred in Catholic cemeteries.[102] Their new graveyards required express approval from royal officials so as not to obstruct "commerce," which is to say the daily activities of local Catholics. This stipulation served as a pretext for pushing the Protestant cemeteries as far as possible from the center of communal life. Anti-Protestant campaigners also sought to increase Catholics' suspicion of their Protestant neighbors. Official permission for the cemeteries was necessary, Filleau argued, because without close surveillance new, separate burial sites might provide Huguenots with a place to hide murdered corpses. What more could one expect from people who conducted their funerals at night with so little ceremony (this despite the fact that royal legislation, as Filleau had urged, insisted on Protestants conducting their funerals under such conditions).[103]

In principle, the Protestant clergy had no reason to object to separate burial grounds, and for Elie Benoist, "there seemed something perfectly

99. He was referring to the expenses the cult of purgatory imposed on Catholics. See *Histoire de l'Edit de Nantes*, 2:473.

100. In Exoudun the chapel was in the parish church; in Chantonnay it may have been separate. See Filleau, *Décisions catholiques*, 163.

101. E.g., the Huguenots of Marans (Aunis), whom commissioners granted a part of the Catholic cemetery in 1599, were forced to raise funds in 1630 to purchase themselves a new one (see AN TT 251 [40]).

102. Filleau, *Décisions catholiques*, 26. They could be assessed fines starting at 1,000 livres, though in some cases the fines were much larger. In 1633 an ordinance of the Council of State threatened Loudun's Huguenots with a 3,000-livres fine for using Catholic cemeteries. See "Extrait des registres du conseil d'estat du roy, (29 novembre 1633)," AN TT 250, pièce 39.

103. Filleau, *Décisions catholiques*, 297.

equitable in a regulation that left Catholics masters of their cemeteries on the condition that they gave others" to the Protestants.[104] Accepting them could settle disputes with the Catholic clergy and keep Huguenots obedient to the king's law. And Huguenots had, at times, shown themselves willing to agree to the strict interpretation of the Edict of Nantes by moving to a new cemetery. As the Protestants of Mollans (Dauphiné) reportedly said to the local bishop in 1600, they were happy to accept a separate burial ground "since it was the king's will."[105] Indeed, in 1611, the Huguenot leadership assembled at Saumur urged the royal commissioners to hasten the demarcation of new Protestant cemeteries, which would, at least, regularize the legal situation of Huguenot burials.[106] But for other good reasons Huguenots frequently resisted the separations, especially if they meant locating new burial grounds outside town walls. The removal would not only make funerals inconvenient, it could also pose two other problems for Huguenots: it could disassociate their cemeteries from their temples, and it could deny Protestants an important symbol of their place in the community.

Since Calvinists did not believe cemeteries were sacred ground, detaching them from temples should have caused no problem. Indeed, doing so could promote precisely the sort of desacralization of the cemetery that Calvinist ministers desired.[107] If Protestant burials were completely separated from those of Catholics, then Huguenots would have less contact with Catholic funeral rituals. And if they were no longer burying their deceased in parish graveyards, they would be less likely than their Catholic neighbors to believe that the ghosts of souls in purgatory lingered in

104. Benoist, *Histoire de l'Edit de Nantes*, 1:289.

105. Venard, "L'église catholique bénéficiare," 295.

106. Chevalier, "Difficultés," 310.

107. On this point, see Vogler, "Législation sur les sépultures," 231–32. German Lutherans moved cemeteries outside of towns to break the connection between graveyards and the cult of purgatory. The difference between their stance and that of French Calvinists suggests that the issue was less doctrinal than political. In areas Lutherans controlled, they did not have the same stake Huguenots had in maintaining inside cemeteries as signs of community membership. See Koslofsky, *Reformation of the Dead*, 46–54. For Roberts, seeking to detach cemeteries from temples was part of the Huguenot strategy for gaining permanent burial places (see "Contesting Sacred Space," 147–48).

them. But one has to wonder if Huguenots so resolutely rid themselves of their Catholic neighbors' and ancestors' beliefs in ghosts.[108] In England, as Keith Thomas has shown, ghost beliefs persisted among seventeenth-century Protestants at all social and educational levels.[109] If they did among Huguenots as well, then such beliefs would have been another motive for them to hold on to churchyards shared with their Catholic neighbors.

French ministers, however, associated cemeteries and temples for a different reason, one that had nothing to do with purgatory but everything with pedagogy. For Pierre Dumoulin, keeping cemeteries and temples adjacent to one another was useful so that while crossing the cemetery on the way to worship, the faithful could meditate on death and thus be reminded of their sinfulness. "The custom arose of putting cemeteries around temples so that one could pass by the graves before appearing in front of God, . . . one could present oneself to death before going to seek life, and thereby recognize ourselves as mortals and by consequence as sinners before beseeching God's grace."[110] Thus moving a cemetery or a temple could break different sorts of links, one with ancestors or their ghosts, which some Huguenots might be unwilling to give up, and another with a useful instructional device, which reminded them that while Protestants were not to participate in the purgatorial cult of the dead, death and their final ends were never to be far from their minds.

The tenacity with which Protestants struggled to defend their rights to old cemeteries suggests that, even if they rejected "superstitious" beliefs, they still invested burial grounds with great importance. A cemetery outside a town might be a perfectly suitable burial place, but it could leave local Huguenots with the sense that their dead, and hence they as well, were being expelled from the community. The famed Protestant Hellenist

108. Davis points out that late-sixteenth-century ministers and synods warned the faithful against beliefs in ghosts, but she feels that by the seventeenth century "the new Protestant sensibility" concerning the dead and funerals "took hold" ("Ghosts, Kin, and Progeny," 95).

109. Keith Thomas, *Religion and the Decline of Magic: Studies in Popular Beliefs in Sixteenth- and Seventeenth-Century England* (Harmondsworth, U.K., 1973), 701–18.

110. Quoted in Françoise Chevalier, *Prêcher sous l'Édit de Nantes: La prédication réformée au XVIIe siècle en France* (Geneva, 1994), 164. For a similar instructional link made between cemeteries and Protestant churches in Germany, see Vogler, "Législation sur les sépultures," 217–23.

Isaac Casaubon commented tellingly on the feeling after attending a funeral outside Paris in 1602: "It was the first time I had seen the place reserved for our burials. We are banished from the city; we are thrown out like rubbish in I don't know what sort of place. So be it! Our place is with God. Our city is in heaven."[111] The assault on the communal symbol of a shared cemetery created a stigma for Huguenots that they had to fight to remain part of local society. Benoist pointed out that since Catholics were prohibited from burying in their cemeteries anyone who the "councils or popes had declared a heretic," Protestants had to demand "with great insistence that they share the same cemeteries with Catholics." Huguenots "could not suffer a distinction in burials that would mark them with an odious stain"; to accept a separate burial ground would be to accept that they were heretics.[112]

Of course, Benoist was writing from a post-Revocation perspective, when the results of the state and Catholic Church campaign against Protestantism were clear. As we have seen, Huguenots were willing to accept, at least, divided cemeteries and perhaps separate ones if they were not pushed out of communities. His claim illustrates, however, that the separation of cemeteries could reflect and also create a barrier between the two religious groups in a community. He insisted that "Protestants could never live in peace with those who were allowed to carry hatred for them beyond the grave. They could share nothing in life with those who denied them the honor of a common burial ground. One could not treat without contempt, or frequent without horror, people whose corpses, one believed, profaned the ground in which they were buried."[113] If Catholics became convinced that sharing a graveyard with their Protestant neighbors threatened their eternal fate, then how could a sense of community survive and how could peace exist?

The Huguenots were fighting a losing battle, as became clear from the

111. Quoted in Read, "Cimetières et inhumations" (1863), 34.

112. According to Benoist, because the Edict of Nantes did not treat them as heretics, they should not be denied burial in the same ground as Catholics; see *Histoire de l'Edit de Nantes*, 1:232, 364. Technically, the edict treated Huguenots as "schismatics" not "heretics." See Chevalier, "Difficultés," 316; and Labrousse, *"Une foi, une loi, un roi,"* 99–101.

113. Benoist, *Histoire de l'Edit de Nantes*, 1:232.

1630s on. But the losses intensified during Louis XIV's reign, and culminated in the 1680s as the numbers of Huguenot abjurations grew. Now Protestants found themselves losing access not to old Catholic cemeteries; that issue had long since been decided. Instead they lost cemeteries to those who had formerly been of their faith. In 1683, the intendant in Poitou, Nicolas Lamoignon de Basville, ordered a division of the Protestant cemetery in La Mothe-Saint-Héray. The Huguenots would be left one-seventh of their burial ground, and the rest would belong to Catholics, a division based on the growing numbers of new converts. These ex-Protestant families outnumbered their former coreligionists, whom, they insisted, now comprised only one-seventh of the community's three hundred families. The cemetery division was necessary to "prevent in the future the confusion and mixing of Catholic bodies with those of the R.P.R." The Protestants disputed the numbers, claiming seventy-two families. And they argued that they had legal right to the site because the local seigneur had given it to them along with an adjacent piece of land for their temple, which had been demolished the year before.[114] But the Catholics presented a list of new converts to support their tally of abjurations. And they knew the Protestant decline would not be reversed. As they explained in a revealing remark, further conversions were to be expected. And since "it is legal to re-enter the Catholic Church but His Majesty has prohibited Catholics from joining the R.P.R.," one-seventh of the cemetery would certainly be sufficient. The division proceeded and markers were placed along the cemetery's new boundary.[115] The next year a magistrate ordered a similar division of the Protestant cemetery of Chenay. According to the official investigation, Chenay had only some thirteen remaining Protestant families as opposed to the one hundred and seventy who had converted. The magistrate left the Protestants with only one-fifteenth of the original space.[116] By the early 1680s France's Huguenots were rapidly losing ground, figuratively and literally.

Cemeteries were mirrors and shapers of communal confessional rela-

114. On the Parlement's interdiction of the temple in 1681 and its destruction in 1682, see ADDS 1I 1 (dossier 21) and ADV F 184.

115. ADDS 1I 1 (dossier 20).

116. The new Catholics' request to Lamoignon claimed that only three or four Protestant families remained in the parish, but the investigator's report put the number at thirteen. The request and the report are found in ADV C49 (10 juin 1684).

tions. They reflected the nature of the confessional boundary in the sacred space of biconfessional communities, and they contributed to its construction in each of its various forms. In communities where the two religious groups were most completely integrated, Protestants buried their dead in family tombs and shared cemeteries with their Catholic neighbors. They modified Calvinist funerary practice by including ceremony and funerary display that the Reformed Church's *Discipline*, in principle, did not allow. In these ways, they laid claim to an enduring position in their confessionally mixed communities. Admittedly, Huguenots sometimes forced their way into Catholic cemeteries, but in many places examples of shared burial grounds suggest a commonly accepted, nonantagonistic commitment of both confessional groups to an important communal institution. Practical requirements (usually a lack of funds for separate cemeteries) blurred the borderline between the faiths, but so too did familial or neighborly concerns as well as a desire to maintain peace.

The second form of confessional boundary is most apparent in communal agreements, which royal officials often sponsored and enforced, to share cemeteries not through side by side burials of Catholics and Protestants but through their division into two adjacent burial grounds. The careful articulation of a space for each group made possible the integration of both into the community. Even if we cannot always accept at face value the agreements' claims of friendship between the groups, we can understand the accords as settlements that permitted the minority continued access to an important communal institution, and hence to a recognition of their membership in the community.

The anti-Protestant campaign aimed at building the confessional boundary in a third, discriminatory way by breaking the communal bonds between neighbors of different faiths. It did so by invoking the fears that had often ignited confessional violence, namely, that members of the minority religion, both dead and alive, were social contaminants and that heresy threatened to pollute the body of true believers. Protestant cemeteries were forced outside towns. Huguenots were constrained to conduct simple funerals not only by the rules of their *Discipline*, but by the dictates of royal law, which forced their funerals into the hours before dawn or after dusk. Insofar as the campaign succeeded in constructing this rigid confessional boundary, Huguenots were isolated from the communal life they had shared with their Catholic neighbors. The pressure on them grew to erase the boundary through what was increasingly the only means available: conversion to the majority faith. But lawsuits, court decisions, and royal declarations would be hard-pressed to enforce the strictest form of boundary since the two faiths mixed not only in the sacred space of communities but also within families. If it was difficult to separate Catholics and Protestants after death, it was even harder to break the bonds between them when they were still alive and living in the same households.

DIVIDED FAMILIES

The Confessional Boundary in the Household

THE COMMUNITY'S SACRED SPACES were one arena in which Catholics and Protestants constructed and contested the confessional boundary. But there was another even more fundamental to early-modern conceptions of social order, political organization, and spiritual life: the family and its household. For political and religious authorities, the proper functioning of families was essential to collective harmony, political stability, and the spiritual development of its members, as well as to their social and economic betterment. Royal power drew one its most effective metaphorical justifications from the ideal of the properly ordered family, and through its legislation and jurisprudence the state sought to impose its model of political authority on the individual household. This concern allied it with propertied families preoccupied with the transmission of inheritances and social ascension. The monarchy supported what Sarah Hanley has aptly titled the "family-state compact," which promoted a "family model of socioeconomic authority under patriarchal hegemony."[1] Families were placed under the firm control of husbands and fathers,

1. Sarah Hanley, "Engendering the State: Family Formation and State Building in Early Modern France," *French Historical Studies* 16, no. 1 (Spring 1989): 4–27, see esp. 15. Hanley has also described the construction and operation of the compact in "Family and State in Early Modern France: The Marriage Pact," in *Connecting Spheres: Women in the Western World 1500 to the Present*, edited by Marilyn J. Boxer and Jean H. Quataert (New York, 1987), 53–63; "Women in the Body Politic of Early Modern France," *Proceedings of the Annual Meeting of the Western Society for French History* 16 (1989): 408–14; and "Social Sites of Political Practice in France: Lawsuits, Civil Rights, and the Separation of Powers in Domestic and State Government, 1500–1800," *American Historical Review* 102, no. 1 (February 1987): 27–52.

whose governance of their wives' property and activities, their children's marriage choices, and the distribution of family wealth was strengthened. Royal law and policy thus sought to preserve both the patrimonial lineage's financial capital (property and offices) and its symbolic capital (honor and status).[2]

The pursuit of these aims could set families in opposition to the churches that also exercised great influence over how they functioned. It sometimes led them to make marriage alliances for their offspring across the confessional divide. An advantageous marriage was an advantageous marriage, even if it transgressed the religious boundary. Families of the lower ranks found their marriage markets likely to be geographically restricted, which might make the choice of spouses from the rival faith a necessity. Such matches were important to cement local social and political positions, to accumulate needed capital, or simply to survive. Aristocratic and bourgeois families made mixed marriages for reasons of social ascension, political alliance, and economic improvement.[3] These incentives for cross-confessional matches were powerful and appealed even to stalwarts of the faith. Take, for example, the Huguenot Marie de La Tour d'Auvergne, duchesse de La Trémoille, whom her coreligionists considered a heroic defender of the Reformed Church. According to her granddaughter's memoir, the duchess considered a marriage between her daughter Marie-Charlotte and the "extremely rich" Duc de Meilleraye. But the

2. To be sure, the family-state model did not necessarily dictate how all families behaved. As Hanley and others have shown, wives retained some independence in matters of work and the disposition of family property. In addition to Hanley's work cited above, see Gayle K. Brunelle, "Dangerous Liaisons: Mésalliance and Early Modern French Noblewomen," *French Historical Studies* 19, no. 1 (Spring 1995): 75–103; Carol L. Loats, "Gender, Guilds, and Work Identity: Perspectives from Sixteenth Century Paris," *French Historical Studies* 20, no. 1 (Winter 1997): 15–30; Julie Hardwick, "Seeking Separations: Gender, Marriages, and Household Economies in Early Modern France," *French Historical Studies* 21, no. 1 (Winter 1998): 157–80, and *The Practice of Patriarchy: Gender and the Politics of Household Authority in Early Modern France* (University Park, Pa., 1998).

3. On the social imperatives behind intermarriage, see Barbara Diefendorf, "Houses Divided: Religious Schism in Sixteenth-Century Parisian Families," in *Urban Life in the Renaissance*, edited by Susan Zimmerman and Ronald F. E. Weissman (Newark, Del., 1989), 85; Labrousse, *"Une foi, une loi, un roi,"* 83; Dompnier, *Venin de l'hérésie*, 157; Benoist, "Catholiques et protestants," 328, Bertheau, "Consistoire . . . du Moyen-Poitou," 4:522–23; and Debon, "Religion et vie quotidienne à Gap," 141.

duke was Catholic, and the duchess worried that her daughter would adopt his religion. She came to change her mind: "she thought of the high place her daughter would occupy and hoped that this marriage would put straight all the affairs of our house." She hoped Marie-Charlotte "would not become a papist, and consoled herself with a thousand other worldly considerations."[4]

While the teachings of the churches supported the patriarchal family model, both were fiercely opposed to intermarriage. Just as the well-regulated household was seen as the means of ensuring stability in the state, so too it was seen as the locus of proper religious life and the fulfillment of God's intentions for, at least, most people (the celibate Catholic clergy being the exception). Rival theologians shared a view of marriage as the means to ensure mutual companionship and support for couples, as a social alliance to join families and produce children, and as a legitimate sexual union to combat concupiscence.[5] They drew on the same scriptural texts to describe marriage's origins and meanings, even if they did not necessarily agree on the lessons to be drawn from them. Both churches, for instance, described the marital state by referring to Genesis: "So God created a helper for Adam who was his equal and implanted such a great love and desire to be good to her that Adam said, 'This is now the bone of my bone and flesh of my flesh'" (2:23). For Protestant theologians, the Genesis text meant that marriage was the central institution in the divinely ordained social order; it was built on relations of mutual dependence between men and women. Catholics read the passage as emphasizing the indissolubility of marriage, an argument against the Protestant allowance of divorce. And they dwelled less on the married couple's mutual dependence than on family life as a means of saving men and women from sinful

4. *The Autobiography of Charlotte Amélie, Princess of Aldenburg, Née Princess de la Trémoille, 1652–1732*, edited by Aubrey Le Blond (London, 1913), 26–27. The marriage plan fell through when the duchess became ill and interpreted her malady as God's punishment for having consented to the wedding. Instead, her daughter married the Protestant Duke of Jena in 1662. The memoirist does not provide a date for this incident, but it would have occurred before Meilleraye married Hortense Mancini in 1661. See also Hugues Imbert, *Histoire de Thouars* (Niort, 1871), 268.

5. Though their ordering of these purposes might vary. Some stressed the emotional bond between husband and wife, others focused on procreation or avoiding sin. See Merry E. Wiesner, *Women and Gender in Early Modern Europe*, 2nd ed. (Cambridge, U.K., 2000), 27–30.

passions while directing their desires toward the lawful procreation of offspring.[6]

The two sides found further support for both the ideas they shared and those they did not in St. Paul's explanation of the succeeding Genesis verse to the Ephesians: "'For this reason a man shall leave his father and mother and be joined to his wife, and the two shall become one.' This is a great mystery, and I take it to mean Christ and the church" (Ephesians 5:31–32).[7] The passage describing marriage as a "mystery" was rendered in the Latin Vulgate as "hoc sacramentem magnum est," and, for Catholics, it supported the understanding of marriage as a sacrament. Protestants followed Luther in denying that marriage was a sacrament. As the seventeenth-century minister and theologian Charles Drelincourt explained: "To speak properly, [marriage] is not a sacrament of the Christian Church because God instituted it in the terrestrial paradise. . . . Before the coming of Jesus Christ, it was established in all the nations of the world." But despite their disagreement over the sacramental nature of marriage, both faiths conceived of it as a sacred bond and representation or figuration of Christ's union with the Church. According to Drelincourt, "Marriage represents well to us the union of Jesus Christ with his Church." The Catholic Nicolas Turlot explained that "the first alliance of Christ with his Church is made in the mystery of the Incarnation, when he united a human nature to his person. The second is made by his grace and by his love. . . . These two sorts of alliances are represented and signified by the marriage of a man and a woman."[8]

If marriage was a figuration of the true church, neither ecclesiastical

6. As Miriam Chrisman shows, both Martin Bucer and the Council of Trent drew on the passage from Ephesians ("Family and Religion in Two Noble Families: French Catholic and English Puritan," *Journal of Family History* 8, no. 2 [Summer 1983]: 190–210, see esp. 190–94). See also Wiesner, *Women and Gender*, 24.

7. Genesis 2:24. Charles B. Paris, *Marriage in XVIIth Century Catholicism, The Origins of a Religious Mentality: The Teaching of l'École française* (Tournai, 1975), 41–46. John's account of the wedding feast at Cana was also a key text in explaining marriage.

8. Charles Drelincourt, *Catéchisme ou instruction familière sur les principaux points de la religion chrétienne, fait par Monsieur Drelincourt en faveur de sa famille . . .*; and N. Turlot, *Thrésor de la doctrine chrestienne, descouvert en sorte qu'il n'est besoin d'aucune recherche pour l'enseigner ou pour l'apprendre . . .* (1651), quoted in Paris, *Marriage in XVIIth Century Catholicism*, 50, 55 (my translations).

institution could suffer, at least in principle, the peril of heterodoxy in households. No household could be properly ordered if the Catholic-Protestant boundary ran through it. A divided family would not be harmonious or well regulated, and thus social harmony was at risk. Indeed, the very fate of churches was at stake. For the leaders of the Reformed Church, the failure to maintain religious unity within its families threatened the survival of Protestantism in France. For the Catholic Church, the breakdown of family confessional uniformity undermined its campaign to regain France for the Roman faith. Each church had to ensure that the confessional boundary remained solid and did not intrude into the home. For these reasons, intermarriage between Catholics and Huguenots was a source of great anxiety.

Recent historians have seen it in a much more positive light. They recognize mixed marriages as a sign of the confessional border's permeability, and as "the most telling evidence of inter-confessional cooperation and association."[9] For them, more than any other social practice, intermarriage dissolved the boundary between the faiths. But the examination of religiously mixed households shows that this was not always the case. Mixed marriages do testify to the willingness of families to cross the confessional divide, but they did not necessarily lead to its disappearance. Instead, intermarriage could beget different constructions of the confessional boundary. If one spouse converted permanently to the other's faith, the boundary was pushed outside the home, just as church authorities wished. But if each spouse continued in his or her original faith, then different forms of the boundary could take shape in the household. When family members joined together in each other's religious observances (especially in the family rituals of baptisms, marriages, and funerals) the boundary could be blurred (as in boundary one).[10] Here family members defined themselves more by their kinship relations than by their confes-

9. Hanlon, *Confession and Community*, 102. Benedict sees intermarriage as "the acid test of social barriers between the different groups" ("Catholic-Reformed Co-existence," 87). In writing about Augsburg's Lutherans and Catholics, Etienne François describes intermarriage as a "permanent challenge to the dynamic of differentiation" by which each group maintained its separate identity in the city (*Protestants et catholiques en Allemagne*, 213).

10. On confessionally mixed families and the ceremonies of baptism, marriage, and death, see Eurich, "Speaking the King's Language," 133.

sion. Or both faiths might be maintained distinctly in the household, either through a cooperative arrangement (along the lines of boundary two) or through the unhappy incidence of household holy warfare (boundary three). Thus mixed marriages might illustrate the permeability of the confessional boundary, but they did not always create peaceful coexistence.

REGULATION OF MIXED MARRIAGE

In many respects, the Reformed Church's marriage rules accommodated the not always easily reconcilable goals of strengthening both parental and church supervision of weddings. Protestantism eliminated a vast array of the medieval Church's marriage regulations, and it radically pruned back the degrees of kinship within which people were forbidden to wed.[11] The *Discipline* also forbade clandestine unions and insisted that promises of marriage not made in the presence of parents, kin, and friends were unacceptable. Parents pursuing advantageous matches were not to force children into unions they did not want. But the family's interests were protected, and marriage's social, economic, and political purposes were implicitly acknowledged. Yet while disencumbering marriages and making them more like a civil contract than an ecclesiastical ritual, Protestant churches also sought to invest them with a greater spiritualization and moral discipline than reformers felt had been evident in traditional Catholic practice.[12] They made clear the Reformed Church's role in overseeing weddings by insisting on marriage's place as a religious institution in a godly life. Impending weddings had to be announced to the consistory, which would attest to their legitimacy and honorability (so that none

11. Davis, "Ghosts, Kin, and Progeny," 101–4.

12. As Lyndal Roper puts it in discussing Lutheran areas, "though reformers no longer considered marriage to be a sacrament, they greatly magnified the moral burden this institution now had to bear" ("Sexual Utopianism in the German Reformation," in *Oedipus and the Devil: Witchcraft, Sexuality and Religion in Early Modern Europe* [London, 1994], 79–103, see esp. 80). See also Roper, *The Holy Household: Women and Morals in Reformation Augsburg* (Oxford, U.K., 1989), chap. 4. On Luther's and Calvin's views, see Emile Stocquart, "Le mariage des protestants en France," in *Aperçu de l'évolution juridique du mariage* (Brussels, 1905–1907), 115–61, see esp. 118–19.

could follow from adulterous or premarital sexual relations). The announcements (banns) would be made in the temple over three weeks. All weddings would take place in the congregation's presence and would receive the minister's blessing.[13] In enforcing these rules, consistories would, in principle, be able to patrol the confessional boundary in weddings and thwart any desire families or individuals might have to pursue matches across the confessional divide.

Family objectives did not necessarily contradict church requirements, but in cross-confessional marriages the conflict was evident. The Reformed Church, as did the Catholic Church, recognized their validity. Genevan regulations, for instance, stated that the promises contracted in a mixed marriage could be nullified, but Calvin declared that a union with a Catholic was "matrimonium legitimum."[14] Still, the French *Discipline* tried to prevent such matches by stipulating that in cases in which one of the parties to a wedding was of the "contrary religion," the promises of marriage would not be received or publicized in the church, unless that party "is sufficiently instructed and has announced publicly in the church that in good conscience *she* renounces all idolatry and superstition, namely, the mass, and wishes by the grace of God to remain in His service for the rest of her days."[15] In other words, a Catholic marrying a Huguenot would first have to abjure her (or his) faith.

Authorities of the Reformed Church faced frequent requests, at least in the early years of the century, to bend the rules. In Poitou, the minister of Sainte-Hermine asked the 1601 provincial synod meeting at Couhé if he could accept a marriage between a Catholic and a Protestant even though the "papist" had not first been instructed in and made public profession of the Reformed faith. The synod stood by the *Discipline* and refused. But earlier that year the provincial synod itself had submitted a question to the national synod asking that if "two people of different religions want to contract marriage, can the pastor content himself with a profession

13. Méjan, *Discipline de l'église réformée de France*, 278–87.

14. Pierre Bels, *Le mariage des protestants français jusqu'en 1685: Fondements doctrinaux et pratique juridique* (Paris, 1968), 213–14.

15. Méjan, *Discipline de l'église réformée*, 283 (my emphasis); Stocquart, "Mariage des protestants," 142. The article (number 20) uses the female pronoun, suggesting that women were thought more likely to make marriage conversions than men. On this issue, see below, pp. 162–64.

made by one of them of the Reformed religion without demanding a renunciation of the mass and other Catholic observances." The national synod allowed no relaxation of the *Discipline's* rules. The 1609 synod of Saint-Maixent heard a proposal that would have allowed a nobleman to marry a Catholic woman before a minister without obliging her to make a profession of the Reformed faith. The synod rejected the proposition and ordered that the *Discipline's* marriage regulations be observed exactly and equally by all, no matter what "their quality or condition."[16] The Charenton meeting in 1623 insisted that those deserting the faith for marriage or their parents who had permitted the wedding (the latter is more likely, since the consistory had no control over a convert unless she or he asked forgiveness) would be publicly suspended from the Communion. The synod ordered strict compliance with the *Discipline* despite a plea from the Poitevin deputies that apostates be spared public embarrassment, so as to facilitate their later return.[17] Yet while remaining adamant that the rules on mixed marriages be enforced, synods did not attempt to make them more stringent. At the Vitré synod in 1617 Norman deputies proposed that a delay be established between an abjuration and a marriage so that a convert's sincerity and degree of instruction could be ascertained. The synod rejected the proposal, allowing each consistory to determine the length of the wait between a conversion and a wedding depending on its knowledge of the convert's piety and seriousness.[18]

16. For the 1601 request, see "Synode et assemblee des ministres et antiens deputtez des eglises refformees de la province de Poictou estant assemblez en la ville dy Nyort au lieu de Temple ou se presche la parolle de dieu commencant le . . . 14 avril 1601," AN TT 241, pp. 345–56. For the 1609 proposal, see Bertheau, "Consistoire . . . du Moyen-Poitou," 4:522–23.

17. Bertheau, "Consistoire . . . du Moyen-Poitou," 4:523. For a similar insistence in Gap, see Debon, "Religion et vie quotidienne à Gap," 141. On suspension from communion and excommunication, see Mentzer, "Marking the Taboo," 110, 122.

18. Méjan, *Discipline de l'église réformée*, 284. In 1631 the Charenton synod considered the controversial issue of permitting Huguenots to marry Lutherans without exacting abjurations. The synod declared that since those who followed the Confession of Augsburg were in agreement with the Reformed faith on most matters and since there was no idolatry or superstition in their faith, no abjuration was necessary. Catholics quickly decried what they considered the synod's hypocrisy, since the Lutheran and Reformed churches disagreed on essential issues, such as the meaning of Communion.

The Catholic response to intermarriage was more ambivalent. Ostensibly, if marriage was a sacrament, then no matches with heretics could be allowed, and diocesan regulations forbade them.[19] Protestants marrying Catholics would have to abjure. But canon law drew a distinction between marriage with an infidel, who had not received baptism, and marriage with a heretic or schismatic. Protestants, whose baptisms the Catholic Church considered legitimate, were deemed either heretics or schismatics.[20] Hence a marriage with a Huguenot, though prohibited, could be considered valid.[21] The state's recognition of mixed marriages further complicated the issue. The Catholic commentator Filleau posed the question of whether such unions were also valid sacraments. His acknowledgment of their civil legality made his reasoning rather tortuous. Under the Edict of Nantes, Huguenots had to respect Catholic rules on consanguinity (Article 23) in their weddings. And they were expected to observe other rules, such as the prohibition of weddings during Lent.[22] These regulations concerned matches joining Huguenots to each other, but Filleau suggests in his discussion of mixed marriage that

> these articles, which oblige those of the R.P.R. to observe the laws of the Catholic, Apostolic, and Roman Church concerning the degrees of consanguinity and affinity, are enough to show that such a marriage is esteemed valid and is elevated to the dignity of a sacrament. Because if it were only a simple civil contract, if it was not a sacrament, what would be the point of observing the degrees of consanguinity and affinity, which are considered impediments only in cases of true marriages?[23]

19. As, for example, the Council of Narbonne did in 1609 (Sauzet, *Contre-réforme et réforme catholique*, 165) and that of Bordeaux in 1624 (Hanlon, *Confession and Community*, 103).

20. Labrousse, *"Une foi, une loi, un roi,"* 99–101; Stocquart, "Mariage des protestants," 142.

21. The distinction was made between a marriage, whose impediments made it annullable (*dirimant*, in French), and one that was more simply prohibited. See A. Esmein, *Le mariage en droit canonique*, 2 vols. (Paris, 1929), 1:244–46.

22. Though they did not always do so. See Benedict, *Huguenot Population of France*, 80–86.

23. *Décisions catholiques*, 469–73, see esp. 473.

Furthermore, Filleau continues, Secret Article 41 gave ecclesiastical judges jurisdiction over cases in which the validity of a wedding between a Catholic and a Huguenot was in dispute. Such would not be the case if such a marriage were neither valid nor a sacrament. He thereby concludes: "although such marriages are valid, they are always illicit and prohibited."[24]

Mixed marriages thus were both forbidden and indisputably valid. Efforts by churches to regulate them suffered from the state's intervention into marriage regulation, from the laity's insistence on pursuing its own concerns in marriages, and, for the Catholic Church, from the complexity of its own marriage laws. Attempts to prevent mixed weddings also ran afoul of the political imperatives behind some of the most important ones. When Henri IV arranged for his sister, the Protestant Catherine de Bourbon, to marry the Catholic Duc de Bar, neither converted to the other's faith. And although the 1598 Montpellier synod declared the match illicit, certainly the Reformed Church was in no position to block the king.[25]

The rival clergies were not blind to the pressing reasons behind mixed marriages. Regardless of the injunctions in canon law and the Reformed Church's *Discipline*, those who married members of the other faith were not punished harshly. A Scottish student, John Lauder, who spent some months in Poitiers in the mid-1660s explained why: "It is not permitted for a [Protestant] man or woman to marry a papist. If they [*sic*] do they must come before the entire church and make a public confession of their fault and the scandal they have committed. But experience shows that such rigor is rarely or more lightly used. Because, if one enforced this rule, one would lose a member of the faithful, who would prefer to become a papist."[26] Lauder spoke here of his coreligionists, but his explanation would hold for Catholics as well. Besides, each church hoped that the spouse of

24. *Décisions catholiques*, 473. On Article 41, see Stocquart, "Mariage des protestants," 139.

25. Léonard, *Histoire générale du protestantisme*, 2:313–14; Wolfe, *Conversion of Henri IV*, 175; and Kate Curry, "Degrees of Toleration: The Conjuncture of the Edict of Nantes and Dynastic Relations between Lorraine and France, 1598–1610," in Cameron, Greengrass, and Roberts, eds., *Adventure of Religious Pluralism*, 231–44. On the private form of ceremony used in the wedding, over which the archbishop of Rouen presided, see Stocquart, "Mariage des protestants," 139–40.

26. J. Plattard, "Un étudiant ecossais en France en 1665–1666: Journal de voyage de Sir John Lauder," *Mémoires de la Société des Antiquaires de l'Ouest*, 3rd ser., 12 (1935):

its faith would bring his or her partner into the fold by a conversion that would be sincere and lasting.[27] Sometimes this happened. However, insisting on conversions prior to weddings did nothing to ensure the durability of such religious changes and thus left it possible for families to manipulate church regulations with a quick and temporary conversion of one spouse before the ceremony. What constituted mixed marriages thereby became difficult to define, and, as a result, they are difficult for us to count.

FREQUENCY OF MIXED MARRIAGES

Since both churches insisted on the conversion of spouses from the rival faith, marriages between people who were Catholics and Huguenots at the time of their weddings were rare. On occasion, political circumstances could dictate such matches, as was the case with that between Catherine de Bourbon and the Duc de Bar.[28] But evidence for truly mixed marriages at less exalted social levels is sparse.[29] More often one spouse converted. One might question whether the marriages following these conversions were really "mixed," since the term does not usually apply to unions between people of the same faith. But for purposes of thinking about coexistence, we can consider these matches to be mixed, since marriage was an alliance not just between two individuals but between two

1–129, see esp. 72. Elisabeth Labrousse found that women at Mauvezin returning to the consistory and expressing their regrets for having married Catholics were reintegrated into the community with little trouble. See "Conversion dans les deux sens," in Duchene, ed., *Conversion au XVIIe siècle*, 161–77, see esp. 166.

27. Dompnier, *Venin de l'hérésie*, 155–56; Diefendorf, "Houses Divided," 85; Labrousse, *"Une foi, une loi, un roi,"* 83.

28. Another involving a royal sister took place in 1625 between Henrietta Maria and Charles I. See Jacques Pannier, *L'église réformée de Paris sous Louis XIII*, 2 vols. (Paris, 1931), 1:250–55.

29. Although she does not provide a precise number, Labrousse found evidence of some at Mauvezin, all in the first half of the century; see "Conversion dans les deux sens," 165. And in his examination of Montpellier marriage contracts, Benedict found a small number from the years between 1605 and 1609 (10 out of 535) stipulating that each spouse could continue her or his own faith after the wedding—an acknowledgment that people of different faiths were marrying; see "Catholic-Reformed Co-existence," 89.

families that continued to be of different faiths. And some of these marriages resulted in biconfessional households when spouses who had converted returned to their original faith.

The speed with which marriages often followed upon conversions, and the quick return of some converts to their original religion, has led some historians to disparage such religious changes. Sauzet refers to them as a "comédie des abjurations pro matrimonio."[30] We would do better not to dismiss them, but rather to think of them as opening possibilities for families to pursue their interests while complying with their churches' marriage regulations. Abjurations eased the way for unions important to the families involved and to the community of which they were a part. And we cannot assume that the conversions for cross-confessional marriages were always short-lived.[31] Indeed, marriage converts might make a variety of choices: practicing the new faith, returning quickly to the original faith, returning to the original faith only years after the wedding, or practicing something in between the faiths such as choosing a Protestant burial while leaving testamentary bequests to the poor as would a Catholic.[32]

Given the rarity of truly mixed weddings, the general ambiguity about defining cross-confessional unions, and the sparseness of documentation, it is difficult to get a clear sense of just how common intermarriage was. The evidence we do possess suggests the number of cross-confessional alliances varied considerably from area to area. Much depended on the relative size of local Catholic and Huguenot populations (and, hence, of their marriage markets) as well as on the wealth and political power of each group.[33] In the southwestern town of Layrac, which Hanlon has studied, intermarriage was frequent; he identified 279 mixed weddings (in a population of some 3,000–4,000), most of which occurred in the first half of the century. Prior to 1620 the flow of marriage conversions favored the Huguenots, who dominated the town. After that year, Protestant power

30. *Contre-réforme et réforme catholique*, 269.

31. Hanlon found that in Layrac most of the women who abjured for marriage—and the converts were usually women—remained attached to their new faith (*Confession and Community*, 215–18).

32. Hanlon, *Confession and Community*, 218.

33. Benedict, *Huguenot Population*, 70.

declined, and the advantage in marriage conversions turned toward the Catholic Church.[34]

But local social and political dominance did necessarily ensure a favorable flow of marriage conversions. Protestants dominated Nîmes in the first half of the century, and thus not surprisingly Sauzet found frequent mention in the town's consistory registers of Catholic women abjuring their faith to marry Huguenots. However, his examination of the cathedral's registers shows considerable movement in the other direction as well. Between 1609 and 1621 the percentage of marriages in the church that involved a convert to Catholicism (almost always women) ranged from 13 to 40 percent annually.[35] In Layrac and Nîmes, people frequently crossed the confessional divide in both directions to marry. Elsewhere that was not the case. Labrousse found in the southwestern town of Mauvezin only thirteen cases between 1628 and 1656 of Protestants (eleven of them women) who married Catholics "à la messe."[36] In Luberon villages in Provence, where Catholics and Protestants lived in close proximity, confessional tensions ran high and mixed marriages were rare.[37] Thus while intermarriage existed in biconfessional areas, its incidence should not be exaggerated.

As is the case elsewhere, in Poitou the number of mixed marriages is difficult to pin down, though historians of local Protestantism have thought they were frequent. Certainly leaders of the Reformed Church

34. Hanlon, *Confession and Community*, 103–8; see the chart on 107. In another revealing measure of cross-confessional alliances, of eighty-eight women received by the consistory into the Protestant church between 1578 and 1609, fifty-five married soon after, "sometimes the same day" (104). See also Hanlon, *Univers des gens de bien*, 238–39.

35. He does not provide precise figures on the abjurations the consistory recorded. I calculated the percentages of Catholic conversions from the absolute figures in the table in *Contre-réforme et réforme catholique*, 166n.3; for the total population, see p. 49. As Benedict shows, the percentages of Protestant conversions to Catholicism for marriages seem high, but the city was 80 percent Protestant; had there not been a strong tendency toward Catholic confessional endogamy then four-fifths of all Catholic weddings would have been mixed. See "Catholic-Reformed Co-existence," 88.

36. "Conversion dans les deux sens," 164–65. Mauvezin was a town of about two thousand with a Catholic majority but in which Protestants were socially dominant. Labrousse does not have information on marriage conversions in the other direction.

37. Audisio, "Se marier en Luberon."

worried about them.[38] Niort's elders complained that such "scandals" happened "everyday." In Mougon, the consistory issued frequent injunctions against intermarriage, and was no doubt embarrassed when it had to depose one of its elders for allowing his son to marry a Catholic.[39] Despite problems of documentation, I can provide some support for the impression that mixed marriages were frequent, through soundings of consistory registers in two communities. This inquiry is in no way intended to be a complete examination of intermarriage in the province. Rather, it aims at giving a sense of the phenomenon from the perspective of the religious minority, an approach determined by the availability of sources but useful because the flow of marriage converts into the minority Reformed Church is a crucial test of the openness of the confessional border. In an atmosphere of hostility or one in which the minority felt particularly threatened, marriage conversions would have been rare, or they would have favored the majority faith. The soundings come from two different times. The first is from Loudun in the years around the Edict of Nantes's signing, when studies of other places suggest intermarriage was at its most frequent.[40] The second is from Melle in the 1660s and 1670s, years when the government was clamping down on intermarriage. At this time we might expect few mixed weddings favoring the Reformed Church, but in Melle they remained common and brought a steady stream of converts into the Huguenot community.

At the beginning of the seventeenth century, Huguenots were a little less than half of Loudun's population, but they dominated the town's politics. As we have seen in Chapter 1, there is evidence of tension between the groups in the 1610s, and Protestant political strength declined in the 1620s.[41] But around the turn of the century, to judge from the numbers of

38. Bertheau and Benoist have claimed that they were common in the Moyen-Poitou, but their evidence is mostly indirect, consisting of the criticisms consistories or Catholic authorities made about such unions. See Bertheau, "Consistoire . . . du Moyen-Poitou," 4:521–25; and Benoist, "Catholiques et protestants," 328, and "Populations rurales," 2:232. But Pérouas found only isolated cases in the diocese of La Rochelle, part of which was in Poitou; see *La Rochelle*, 175.

39. Bertheau, "Consistoire . . . du Moyen-Poitou," 4:521–25.

40. As, e.g., in Layrac and Nîmes. See Hanlon, *Confession and Community*, 107–11; and Sauzet, *Contre-réforme et réforme catholique*, 166.

41. See above, pp. 30–32.

mixed marriages noted in the Huguenot consistory register, the confessional border was still quite porous. Between the years 1598 and 1601, at least a third and as many as half the weddings the consistory approved each year were between Huguenots and converted Catholics.[42]

Sometimes these conversions appear to have been quickly arranged. On 31 May 1601 the consistory recorded that "Jacques Famerolle, oldest son of Nicolas Famerolle, écuyer, and Marthe Bourceau have, in the company's presence, ratified the promises of their marriage. And the said Jacques promises to live in the future in the Reformed religion and to make a good profession [of it]. He is admitted and the said marriage is blessed in the church."[43] Famerolle was among the few men to change religions for a wedding, at least to judge from the marriage conversions to the Reformed Church. In Loudun, as elsewhere, most marriage converts were women. Only one man joined the church for a wedding in each of the years 1599, 1600, and 1601; three joined in 1598.[44]

The consistory records say little about the numbers of Huguenots who left to wed Catholics. Only on those occasions when they returned do we get a sense of marriages across the confessional divide in the other direction. On 1 January 1598 Suzanne Judde and Judith Bonin appeared before the consistory and "recognized the great fault they [had] committed in having married their husbands by the hands of a priest." After giving evidence of their repentance, they were readmitted to the church. The register noted that it had been a long time since either had taken the Lord's Supper. It would seem that they had been married and lived as Catholics for some time. No mention is made of their current marital status, but it is at least possible that both were widows returning to their original faith only after the deaths of Catholic husbands.[45] If their husbands were still

42. Consistory Register of Loudun, 1594–1602, AN TT 250 (5). For 1598, eleven of thirty-three marriages; for 1599, three of eight; for 1600, eight of fifty-three; and for 1601, four of thirteen. The numbers must be judged approximations because of the document's difficult handwriting and the poor state of its preservation.

43. Entry of 31 May 1601, AN TT 250 (5), 538. For other examples, see the wedding of Charles Sabion and Suzanne Savary on 14 July 1594 (p. 319) and that of André Dumarais and Marie Bourreau on 3 June 1599 (p. 471).

44. Hanlon discerned the same gender imbalance in Layrac (*Confession and Community*, 215–19), as did Sauzet in Nîmes (*Contre-réforme et réforme catholique*, 165–66).

45. As Hanlon found to be the case with most women returning to Layrac's

alive, then their return to the Reformed Church meant that their households would now contain both faiths. That seems to have been the case with the unnamed daughter of a Madame Grazay. Both women came before the consistory on 14 September 1600 to ask forgiveness for the daughter's Catholic wedding. A young woman returning to the church accompanied by her mother was probably recently wed. Such examples are few in the consistorial records of these years, but then presumably others who converted in order to marry Catholics never returned to ask for forgiveness.

Early in the century marriage traffic across the confessional border was heavy in Loudun, and much of it was in the direction of the Reformed Church. One would expect later decades to reveal a very different picture.[46] After years of effort by the Catholic Church and the royal government to put Protestantism on the defensive, one might assume that either intermarriage would decline as each group closed in on itself or the flow of marriage conversions would be weakening the beleaguered minority. But in Melle that was not the case. Since Protestants dominated the town, it is not surprising that the flow of conversions favored the Reformed Church.[47] But what is unexpected is just how often Catholics came before Melle's consistory to abjure their faith in the years when French Protestantism was increasingly under attack.[48] A declaration of 1663 prohibited those who had converted from relapsing, and the legislation was rein-

---

Reformed Church after marriage conversions (*Confession and Community*, 216–21). Sauzet notes the return of some widows, but feels that most women converts who returned did so soon after the marriage (*Contre-réforme et réforme catholique*, 167).

46. Surviving Poitevin consistory records are very fragmentary for the following decades. They exist for Mougon in the strongly Protestant Moyen-Poitou for the period between 1610 and 1623. Despite the consistory's frequent injunctions against mixed marriages, in these years Mougon's elders considered only eight cases. The gender imbalance was the same as elsewhere; in six of the cases, Protestant women had made the marriage. However, in this strongly Protestant region, it is likely that more Catholics would have sought unions with Protestants and converted than the other way around. The consistory records are found in ADDS 1I (3) (unpaginated). Also see Bertheau, "Consistoire . . . du Moyen Poitou," 3:335n.16.

47. Bertheau, "Consistoire . . . du Moyen-Poitou," 3:335n.14; and Emilien Traver, *Histoire de Melle* (1938; reprint, Marseilles, 1980), 125–33.

48. I am relying on the typescript of the original consistory documents from 1660–1669 by Pierre Dez, contained in the Collection Dez of the Archives départmentales des Deux-Sèvres (ADDS 2J 35 [1]).

forced with stiffer penalties in 1665 and 1679.[49] The measures were aimed at Huguenots who converted to Catholicism and then returned to Protestantism, not the other way around. But clearly the government's and the Catholic clergy's surveillance of the whole issue of conversion and mixed marriages was increasing in the 1660s. They wanted to stop Catholics from converting too. Yet in that decade Melle's consistory received one hundred and six people (sixty-four of them women) who abjured Catholicism.[50] The lack of marriage records makes it difficult to know how many of these conversions were for the sake of a marriage. Still, if the gender imbalance in marriage conversions found in places like Nîmes, Layrac, and Loudun held true in Melle, then it is likely that a wedding lay behind most of the abjurations.[51]

More surprising yet is that as strictures on Protestantism grew in succeeding years, the frequency of converts appearing before Melle's consistory increased rather than decreased. Another series of registers covering the five years between October 1669 and October 1674 lists seventy-six, of which fifty-nine were women.[52] The traffic was heavy enough so that at eleven different meetings the consistory received two converts, and on one occasion it received three. Again, the overwhelming proportion of women among the converts suggests that many if not most were marriage conversions. And given Protestant dominance in the area, there is every reason to think that the men abjuring their Catholicism were about to marry Huguenots.

In only four of the conversions do the registers hint that other reasons may have been at work. In these cases, the records expand upon the usual-

49. Labrousse, *"Une foi, une loi, un roi,"* 143; Garrisson, *Édit de Nantes*, 135–36.

50. A majority of these people, sixty-four (of whom thirty-eight were women), appeared before the consistory after 1663, when the law against relapses went into effect. Bertheau counts one hundred and thirty-one Catholic abjurations between 1660 and 1668, but she may have included in this total former Protestants returning to their original religion ("Consistoire . . . du Moyen-Poitou," 4:525n.148).

51. See note 44.

52. Copies of the consistorial records from these years can be found in the Fonds Dez, Maillard, and Société des Antiquaires de l'Ouest in BFP Ms. 1500/6. There is a lacuna between 26 September and 19 December 1670. Three converts appeared in the last months of 1669, thirteen in 1670, twenty in 1671, eleven in 1672 and 1673 each, and eighteen in 1674. One man appeared at the end of 1669, two men in 1670, five in 1671, none in 1672, four in 1673, and five in 1674.

ly formulaic report of the converts' names, places of domicile, and, for men, occupation. Marie Mutot, who appeared before the consistory on 7 June 1671, was listed as a servant of a Huguenot family. While a marriage might well have been impending, it is also possible that she was joining her master's confession not a future husband's. Catholic polemicists complained often about Huguenot employers pressuring their servants into converting.[53] René Rabier and Louis Pinet both abjured on 23 June 1673, and the consistory made a point of adding that they had "frequented our holy" assemblies. Pinet, in particular, was noted as having "attended them assiduously for some time."[54] The more extensive comments suggest that these conversions did not result from marriage negotiations, but nothing in the statements precludes that possibility. Most striking was the declaration of Anne Groussard, who presented herself to the consistory on 4 May 1670. She stated that, although she had been born and baptized in the Roman Church, she had, up to the age of eight or nine, never taken Communion within it. Of course she would not have taken Catholic Communion before she was seven, but Groussard insisted that from the time she had reached the "age of reason," she had "frequented our holy assemblies desiring to live and die in our communion."[55] Groussard may also have been about to marry, but the unusual declaration suggests that it was not a wedding that motivated her religious change.

I have little evidence on Protestants who joined the Catholic Church for the sake of a marriage. However, not all conversions in Melle favored the Protestant group, as is evident in the consistory records of the 1660s, which indicate that a number of Huguenots returned asking to be readmitted into the Reformed community. The total is certainly not as large as

53. For instance, in 1681, Bishop Jules Mascaron of Agen worried about poor Catholics, who had "no religion," and as servants or workers would adopt the faith of their Huguenot masters, husbands, or neighbors in areas where Protestantism was the dominant religion (see Hanlon, *Univers des gens de bien*, 241). Daniel Hickey's work on Chef-Boutonne in Poitou indicates that a number of female converts were between the ages of twelve and sixteen and thus were women more likely entering service than marriage (personal communication, 30 May 2002). Labrousse discusses *dévot* Catholic women converting servants as an aspect of religious militancy more evident among women than men ("Conversion dans les deux sens," 63).

54. BPF Ms. 1500/6, p. 71 (Mutot), 85 (Rabier and Pinet).

55. BPF Ms. 1500/6, p. 60. Her age at the abjuration is unknown.

that of Catholic abjurations. But Protestant domination of the area did not prevent some from crossing the religious divide in the Catholic direction for marriages. In the 1660s, ten former Protestants (of whom seven were women) appeared before the consistory asking to be forgiven for having married Catholics.[56] It is possible that other Huguenots converted to marry but never returned to their original faith. In addition, the consistory reprimanded fifteen parents for allowing children to marry Catholics.[57] Ten of these appeared before the consistory after 1663, six in 1667 alone. And the frequency increased in the next decade, with one in 1671, six in 1672, five in 1673, and three in 1674.[58] The numbers suggest that the consistory, no longer able to impose a public recognition of fault on the individual who had deserted the faith, was that much more concerned with making an example of those who could be held responsible. The elders cited parents or relatives to appear before them and make a public apology for having permitted or been present at the wedding of a former Huguenot in the Roman Church. Were it not for the much larger number of Catholics converting to Protestantism in Melle, these numbers would seem substantial but not surprising in these years of increasing pressure on France's Protestants.

Thus despite Protestant domination of Melle and the consistory's surveillance of the Reformed community, a sizable group of Huguenots converted, at least temporarily, to marry Catholics. And a large number of Catholics converted to marry Huguenots. As late as the 1670s the confessional boundary in Melle remained very porous. This town's situation makes clear the importance of local factors in mixed marriages—in this case, the size and strength of the Huguenot community. The flow of conversions toward the Reformed Church might suggest that within Melle the third type of confessional boundary had taken shape. The minority group, feeling dominated and excluded, maintained its full membership in

56. In all cases they were received back into the Protestant community after having made public recognition of their fault.

57. One case involved a brother, who was his sister's guardian.

58. It is difficult to know just how many marriages these citations represent. Sometimes parents were cited for having permitted the weddings of their children, but the number of children was not specified. At other times, more than one individual was cited without it being clear whether it was for a single marriage or for more than one.

the community through marriage alliances with the dominant group, at the price of conversions. Only here the situation rapidly becoming established elsewhere in the country was reversed: those excluded by the harsh boundary would have been Catholics, not Huguenots. However, it seems more likely that a boundary of the first type, one that was fluid, was operating here. Mellois converted in both directions for marriages. To the dismay of the Catholic clergy and the consistory, the confessional boundary was not hard and fast. And therefore the confessional identity of mixed households could remain uncertain.

RELIGIOUS IDENTITY AND THE DANGERS OF INTERMARRIAGE

In at least one respect, intermarriage in Melle was typical of intermarriage elsewhere. A greater number of marriage converts were women than men. The reason for this gender imbalance appears obvious: the assumption of patriarchal early-modern society that women were the tokens of exchange in family alliance strategies, especially in aristocratic and bourgeois clans, even if it meant they crossed the religious boundary. However, we need to be careful in assuming that women were merely the pawns of families pursuing strategies of advancement—or seeking to mediate confessional tensions—through familial alliances. Both churches made clear the obligation of children to seek parental consent for weddings, but neither offered support for parents who wanted to force their children into unwanted marriages.[59] And recent work on early-modern France has shown that daughters exercised some autonomy in the choice of their future spouses, even if their weddings proceeded only after negotiations between the two families.[60]

59. On the reinforcement of parental authority in the French Reformed Church's regulation of this issue, see Bels, *Mariage des protestants français*, 63–173. On Catholic moralists' treatment of the matter, which made clear the children's obligations to their parents while also condemning the forcing of children into marriages for the sake of family honor or pride, see Paris, *Marriage in XVIIth Century Catholicism*, 153–56, 169–73.

60. For a recent discussion of this issue, see Hardwick, *Practice of Patriarchy*, 55–57. As Hanlon has shown, in the Agenais daughters exercised a considerable degree of autonomy in their choices of spouse, though this may have been truer for peasant

Nonetheless, more women than men converted for weddings; cultural and legal assumptions about women, their religious identities, and the roles they were expected to play in marriage alliances must account for the difference. Certainly seventeenth-century critics of intermarriage assumed that a mixed marriage would normally entail a woman's conversion rather than a man's, and, further, that a woman's religious identity was more dangerously malleable than a man's. The anonymous Catholic author of the 1618 report on the religious situation in Poitou complained that the young women of the province "attach themselves to neither one nor the other [religion] until they are married. And if one asks their mothers to what religion their daughters belong, they think about it civilly and respond that [their daughters] do not have [a religion] and what is more they will take that of their husbands."[61] The comment hardly seems credible, given what we know about the religious lives of early-modern women, but it had considerable staying power among Catholics.[62] The mid-seventeenth-century missionary Christophe Authier used almost identical words about the young women of the diocese of Die: "Parents allow their daughters not to declare for any religion before their marriage, and then they adopt the religion of their husbands."[63] Such comments, exaggerated though they were, reveal the widespread fear that women's confessional identities were more malleable than men's, and their inconstancy was a threat to properly ordered households and society as a whole. As we will see in Chapter 5, such statements contradict the equally widespread celebration by each side of the religious fortitude of its con-

daughters than for those from higher ranking families. See Hanlon, *Confession and Community*, 219, and *Univers des gens de bien*, 108–9.

61. The remark is part of a more general comment on the religious indifference of Catholics in the countryside; see "Estat de la religion en Poictou."

62. On Protestant women's religious lives, see the classic studies of Natalie Zemon Davis, "City Women and Religious Change," in *Society and Culture in Early Modern France* (Stanford, Calif., 1975), 65–95, and Nancy L. Roelker, "The Appeal of Calvinism to French Noblewomen in the Sixteenth Century," *Journal of Interdisciplinary History* 2 (1972): 391–418. On seventeenth-century Catholic women, see, e.g., Elizabeth Rapley, *The Dévotes: Women and Church in Seventeenth-Century France* (Montreal, 1990). Hanlon also mentions the 1618 "Estat's" view of women's religious indifference and remarks "this is certainly too strong, although the evidence of female conversion is compelling" (*Confession and Community*, 215).

63. Quoted in Dompnier, *Venin de l'hérésie*, 154.

fessional heroines. Ultimately, that women could be seen simultaneously as religiously malleable and as stalwarts of the faith suggests more about their use as weapons in the confessional conflict than it does about their actual religious piety and activities.

If a wife converted to her husband's faith, then her original church suffered the consequences of her inconstancy. If she returned to her first religion after the marriage, the rival church had gained nothing. And when she maintained her different beliefs and practices in the household, then the confessional boundary was imported into the family, a situation both clergies could only see as dangerous. Over the course of the century, the Reformed Church would have more to fear than the Catholic Church from women converting for marriage. Michel Le Faucheur, pastor at Montpellier and Charenton, denounced "horrible mixed marriages" as one of the prime dangers of coexistence, as threatening to Protestant girls as the debaucheries of "Roman" mascarades.[64] Pierre Dumoulin condemned mixed marriages because such alliances could not be a reflection of Christ's union with the Church. Nor could religiously divided households be centers of devotional life, as Calvinism envisaged: "Your families must be little churches and your homes little temples in which God is carefully served."[65] How could households serve God if Protestant men married Catholic women?

Dumoulin made the Protestant fears clear in his telling attack on intermarriage, the *Conseil fidele et salutaire sur les mariages entre personnes de contraire religion.*[66] As he explains, to contract a marriage with a Catholic was an extraordinary act of impiety. Catholics were idolaters, and Christ had nothing to do with idolaters (3–4). If a priest officiated over a wedding between a Protestant and a Catholic, then the "party of idolatry" would gain an advantage, since the Protestant would have had to make, at least, a tacit promise to join its religion. If the marriage was celebrated in the

64. Cited in Jacques Solé, *Le débat entre protestants et catholiques français de 1598 à 1685*, 2 vols. paginated consecutively (Lille, 1985), 2:1363. On Le Faucheur, see Léonard, *Histoire générale du protestantisme*, 2:320, 321.

65. Quoted in Michel-Edmond Richard, *La vie des protestants français de l'Édit de Nantes à la Revolution (1598–1789)* (Paris, 1994), 75.

66. (La Rochelle, 1620). Page references will follow in text. Arguments similar to Dumoulin's could be found frequently in Huguenot polemical works. See Labrousse, *"Une foi, une loi, un roi,"* 83.

temple, then the "party of the contrary religion would commit public perjury" because the formula of the marriage would ask "her" if she intended to live according to the Word of God (8). Apparently a papist's promise could never be trusted. Therefore, the minister would be engaged in suborning perjury and would be blessing a wedding that God condemned. If this image of breaking the spiritual union with God was not sufficiently convincing, Dumoulin reinforced it by referring to the concern of the French elite with familial reputation and the loss of honor that resulted from an unsuitable match. "The nobility esteem a misalliance to be a dishonor, and, as children of the king of heaven, so should you. Do you want to derogate your spiritual nobility in marrying yourselves outside the alliance with God?" (7). Proper marriages within the faith maintained the church and the divinely ordained natural order; *mésalliance* with idolaters threatened it. Children who sought a mixed marriage, despite their parents' wishes, were in revolt; a son who married a Catholic woman allied himself with his father's enemies. And their children will likely become idolaters in turn (6–7).

Dumoulin cites Deuteronomy 7, in which God forbids the Israelites to make marriages with the people of idolatrous nations for fear that they will come to serve other gods.[67] With religious attachments divided, discord within the household would be constant. If the spouses are attached to their religions, "it is impossible that a complete friendship could exist between them because there is no stronger tie of friendship than that of conscience" (8). Familial affection and respect would be threatened, and so too proper worship, a conclusion he illustrates by reference to Nehemiah (13:23–27), which repeats the proscription against marrying foreigners and refers to the language confusion such unions produced in families. Sons of the faithful had married the women of Ashdod, Ammon, and Moab and half their children spoke "the language of Ashdod, and they could not speak the language of Judah." Mixed families cannot speak the same language; normal social communication cannot be maintained.

67. He summarizes the passage (Deuteronomy 7:3–4) as saying that the Israelites should forbid their sons (but not daughters) from marrying idolaters. The implication is that the sexual attraction of infidel women will lead the faithful astray. He echoes here the Old Testament characterization of idolatry as a form of erotic temptation or as an illicit and adulterous sexual relation. See Moshe Halbertal and Avishai Margalit, *Idolatry*, translated by Naomi Goldblum (Cambridge, Mass., 1992), chap. 1.

Nothing but domestic trouble would ensue. What would a Protestant husband do if his "superstitious" wife dissipated the family's wealth paying for decorations in churches or furnishing a monastery (9)? A Catholic wife might also reveal family secrets during confession and then return home so filled with scruples that she believed she offended God merely by conversing with her spouse.[68] Furthermore (and here Dumoulin momentarily drops the assumption that the woman would necessarily be of the false faith), what would a Huguenot wife do if a synod ordered a fast day only to see her papist husband invite his friends home to dine? And if there were a persecution, should she flee the country, leaving her husband and children behind, or should she take the children with her, tearing them away from their father?

A mixed marriage, then, could not be a true marriage; crossing the confessional divide in a wedding could not produce social harmony or a godly home. Quite the contrary, if a mixed marriage succeeded at all, it was only because the Protestant spouse finally managed to "reduce the contrary party to the true religion" (13). And in that case it was God who achieved the success; those who contracted the marriage still committed evil. But as Dumoulin was well aware, Huguenots could expect far fewer such victories than Catholics. Conversion for marriage would favor the "contrary party" because it controlled "the country, the multitude, and the magistracy" (13). The only way to maintain the "piety of the domestic conversation" (7), the only way to preserve the body of the true faithful, the only way to ensure normal social bonds among them, was to construct an impermeable boundary between the confessions and avoid social contact with the other side, especially in marriage.

While Protestant polemicists could conceive only of danger in mixed marriages, their Catholic counterparts could imagine them as a possible way to reduce the heresy. A year after Dumoulin's text appeared, the Capuchin missionary Athanase Molé published a *Lettre envoyée aux ministres de Charenton*, which was cast as an account of one ex-Huguenot's reasons for leaving the Reformed Church.[69] The unnamed convert explains that he

68. Of course, a Calvinist theologian like Dumoulin would likely see confession as a pernicious Catholic practice.

69. P. Athanase Molé, *Lettre envoyée aux ministres de Charenton par un des leurs nouvellement converty, & receu la veille de la pentecoste en l'église catholique, apostolique, & ro-*

had been born and raised in the religion "that license allows in my country," but he had married a woman, who, though of the "contrary belief," was virtuous and feared God. When his daughters came of age, they had suitors "from honorable families, who were beyond reproach, of good morals, and of the religion appropriate for them" (4). In other words, the daughters had been raised in their mother's Catholicism rather than their father's Calvinism. After taking the advice of his relatives and friends, all Catholics, he agreed to one suitor for his oldest daughter. When the Charenton consistory heard of the decision, it summoned and reprimanded him "in an arrogant and ill-considered" way. The consistory could not object to a wedding between two Catholics, but it could oppose the Huguenot's participation in the ceremony. The elders demanded that he swear an oath to insert in his daughter's marriage contract the following words: "I will marry my daughter without adhering to papistic idolatries." The demand shocked him. Where, he asked, could you find a marriage contract that contained such a *belle clause*, what notary would ever write it? From that day, he "began to think deeply about my conscience." The notion "entered his soul" that it was "impossible the love and fear of God could be lodged in the hearts of those who pursue such quarrels."[70] He concluded that the Charenton elders "had more arrogance than religion and not much probity."

The incident also reminded him of how many times in the past the consistory had pressed him to "force his wife to embrace" Protestantism (5). This demand was an affront to her "liberty of conscience," an echo of the Edict of Nantes's term, which Catholic polemicists, who otherwise rejected it, resorted to when it suited their purposes. The Catholic wife was a virtuous woman and brought him into contact with a network of Catholic kin and friends he respected. His trouble was not with them but with those of his own faith. Soon after his daughter's marriage the Protestant

---

maine par le Reverend Père Athanase Molé, predicateur capuçin (Paris, 1621), 3–9. The text was likely the work of the Capuchin Molé, under whose name it appeared, rather than the unnamed ex-Huguenot. On the issue of conversion account authorship, see below, p. 249.

70. He also complains about the Protestant allowance of divorce, a frequent theme in the polemics over marriage. In addition, the convert was upset by the consistory's harsh reprimand for his having crossed the confessional divide to attend his Catholic mother-in-law's funeral.

was introduced to the Capuchin Athanase. Their discussions "planted within [him] the seeds of good doctrine" and led him to understand that the "other party was in no way reasonable" (7). At the next Easter the consistory refused him the Lord's Supper (8). The fulfillment of a family obligation had led to his being treated as a corrupted member of the church. He realized that the doctrines of those who condemned him were unacceptable, and he abjured.

The account might well have been fictional, but it illustrates why Catholics could be more open to mixed marriages than Protestants. The text suggests that it was the Huguenot's union with his virtuous Catholic wife, even before his meeting with the Capuchin friar, that allowed him to find the true faith. While each church counted on its spouse in a mixed marriage to bring the other to a true conversion, each likewise had to worry that it would be the loser. And despite what happened in a community like Melle, the Reformed Church suffered most of the losses. The account also highlighted another troubling issue, that of the religious indeterminacy that could result from having the religious boundary run through the home. The convert was well acquainted with Catholic ceremonies; he certainly would participate in his daughter's Catholic wedding, even if the consistory thought it was idolatrous. What is more, he saw nothing in such ceremonies contrary to religion. Of course, in a Capuchin text, no Catholic ceremony would be. But the account also describes, perhaps unwittingly, a situation of flexibility surrounding the family's religious observances. In mixed households family members of one faith attended the marriages and funerals of the other. Husbands of one religion often presented their newborns in the other church for baptism.[71] Baptisms, marriages, and funerals were family rituals, and in biconfessional households they could create a sense of cooperation across the religious divide or of mixture that blurred the boundary altogether.

Thus intermarriage could lead in households to the indistinct confessional boundary churches feared. But the guardians of orthodoxy were often forced to swallow the religious compromises mixed families made. If the parents a consistory cited for having consented to the marriage of their children "à la messe" gave evidence of their "extrême douleur" and

71. I provide examples below.

requested readmission to the "paix de l'église," the elders lectured them on the "enormité" of their fault and unfailingly accepted them back.[72] When the summons was not for having permitted the wedding but only for having been present at it, the delinquents (relatives or friends rather than parents) sought exculpation by claiming that they had attended only the signing of the marriage contract or the wedding banquet and not the church ceremony. For example, when a surgeon named Bourraut and a goldsmith named Palatre were hauled before the consistory of Melle on 22 April 1672 for having been at the wedding of a former Huguenot to a Catholic, they replied that they had participated only in the feast and not the ceremony. They did not believe they had done anything wrong. The elders found them at fault and told them that under no circumstances should they participate in a marriage in which "one of their brothers abandoned the true religion for the Roman one." However, those faced with charges of this sort knew well that a distinction could be made between the contract signing or the wedding's festivities and the "idolatry" a priest performed in a church ceremony.[73] Nonetheless, Huguenots attended these ceremonies as well, even if they then had to face the short-lived pain of an appearance before their elders.

The Catholic clergy too had to make concessions. In 1672 a Catholic attorney from Montmorillon named Demaillasson recorded in his journal that a Monsieur de Lérignat

> was married with Mademoiselle de la Coste after supper in the chapel of the château of Chasteaugarnier, by a rather peculiar priest [who performed the wedding] with the permission of the curé of the parish. [The curé] had wanted to marry them only in the morning and had wanted to say the mass. But because Mesdames de la Coste and de Monchandy—mother-in-law and sister-in-law of the damoiselle de la Coste—who were of the religion prétendue réformée—did not want to be present if the mass was said, matters happened in this manner.[74]

72. From the case of Nicolas Dampur in Melle on 27 March 1671 (BPF Ms. 1500/6, p. 70).

73. For the Bourraut and Palatre case, see BPF Ms. 1500/6, p. 76. See also the case of Daniel Boutet, who was criticized on 25 December 1673 for having attended both his brother-in-law's contract signing and wedding banquet (p. 89).

74. "Journal de M. Demaillasson, avocat du roi à Montmorillon (1643–1694)," in *Archives historiques du Poitou*, vols. 36 and 37 (Poitiers, 1907, 1908), 37:348.

Families were willing to bend church strictures to achieve their goals, and the clergy of both sides had to make compromises to satisfy them. A blurred household confessional boundary could result, but it was not the only possibility. In mixed households other forms of the boundary could also take shape along which family members could reach accommodations that allowed the peaceful practice of both faiths in the home. Or they could fall into bitter confessional strife.

THE CONFESSIONAL BOUNDARY IN THE HOUSEHOLD

The Capuchin Athanase Molé's convert eliminated the confessional boundary running through his home with an abjuration. Protestantism was excluded from the household. In other mixed marriages the Reformed Church gained the converts. But sometimes neither church won; each spouse continued in his or her original faith, and a persistent confessional boundary ran through the household. Much of what transpired in the daily religious activities of households went unrecorded and is therefore closed to our view. But we do have occasional glimpses of how mixed families negotiated the confessional boundary, and they allow us, at least, to sketch out the range of possibilities. At times, confessional rivalry was imported into the household, and the continuation of two religions provoked great tension between the spouses. In June 1615 Jeanne les Juliers appeared before the Chizé consistory to confess that several years earlier she had married "à la papauté." Despite the constraints her Catholic husband had imposed on her, she had persisted in attending the preaching of the Protestant pastor, and now she wanted to take Communion. Her wish to do so had angered her husband; he had taken "umbrage" at her intentions and restricted the "liberty that she had obtained only with much difficulty." Normally, the consistory, following the *Discipline*, would have exacted a public declaration before the congregation of the fault she had committed in her marriage. But advertising her readmission would only have aggravated the household situation and made it more difficult for her to return to the faith. Thus the consistory noted her "holy desire" and declared itself satisfied with her admission of error before the elders. They accepted her explanation of the conflicts within her home and agreed to receive her without a public display of repentance.[75]

Religious conflicts between spouses could escalate into household holy warfare. In 1613 Charlotte-Flandrine de Nassau, abbess of the Sainte-Croix convent in Poitiers, wrote a letter of complaint to her Protestant sister, Charlotte-Brabantine, duchesse de La Trémoille, criticizing a Huguenot client of the La Trémoilles, Laurent Chappeau, seigneur de La Bourdelière:

> I have enormous compassion for poor Mademoiselle [*sic*] de la Bourdelière, who is so afflicted by her husband. He wants her and her daughter to change religion. Ay my God, dear sister, I am assured that you are too good to want to see such great cruelty, because I have seen the mother and daughter so resolved to live and die in our religion that I believe it would cost them their lives to change. The daughter says since she was baptized [as a Catholic] and since her father had wished it so, she will resolutely continue as one. The mother says the same, and even more so since she was married as one [a Catholic]. Certainly, my heart, you know that we must patiently leave everyone in his own religion.

The abbess wanted the duchess to exert her influence and remind her client that it was contrary to the king's edicts to constrain anyone in the matter of religion. The duchess agreed to write to him, but matters turned yet more complicated. The duchess heard that the girl in question was well instructed in the Reformed religion. The abbess inquired of the mother and found this claim to be true. It seems that the Catholic mother had, herself, a Protestant mother. Apparently, her mother (the girl's grandmother) had threatened to curse and disinherit her if the granddaughter was not given Protestant instruction. The confessional boundary had run through this family for two generations at least. And, according to the abbess, the seigneur de La Bourdelière was determined that it would do so no longer. He wanted to force mother and daughter into Protestantism and even threatened to separate them and never let them see each other again if they did not comply. For her part, the daughter in-

75. Chizé, Registre du consistoire AN TT 241 (2), p. 131.

sisted that her father would have no success; she was of the age when he could not force her conscience.[76]

Of course, we have only the abbess's word for what was happening in this troubled family, and she was anything but unbiased. Charlotte-Flandrine de Nassau was an important member of the provincial Catholic elite and a campaigner for Protestant conversions, especially, though unsuccessfully, for her sister's. In their correspondence, she entreated the duchess to change religions and staged Forty Hours devotions in her convent to pray for her abjuration.[77] Still, it does seem that religious conflict beset the confessionally complex Bourdalière family. The abbess proclaimed her role and that of her sister to be one of maintaining space for both confessions in the home. She insisted that doing so would actually reduce tensions within it, and that by intervening the duchess could "bring peace and concord to this family." But, if the abbess's description of the family is accurate, that goal seems unlikely. La Bourdalière had wed a Catholic woman who remained a Catholic, though she probably was the product of a mixed household. He had permitted the Catholic upbringing of his daughter, and she identified with Catholicism perhaps thanks to her mother. But she had apparently also received Protestant instruction. Now her father had changed his mind, perhaps because he feared losing his mother-in-law's inheritance. The resolution of the conflict is unknown, but it is difficult to imagine a happy one. No evidence exists of the duchess bringing any pressure to bear on her client to relent, and if the abbess was at all correct in her account it seems unlikely that any pressure would have led him to accept religious difference in his home. Forced conversion of the daughter and mother would not have made the family happy either. The Bourdalière household, it seems, was doomed to confessional strife.

A more cooperative arrangement led to less tension and a household confessional boundary more akin to the second type, in which family members agreed on the continuation of both faiths in the home.[78] One

76. Letters of 26 February and 29 March 1613 in "Lettres de Flandrine de Nassau," 243–46. Copy of the letter in the Papiers Guitton of the BPF Ms. 870 (1).

77. The abbess was a convert from Protestantism and her religious change had created a different kind of mixed family, one of siblings. See the letter of 28 December 1627, in "Lettres de Flandrine de Nassau," 286–87. For further discussion of both women, see below, pp. 218–22, 231–32.

78. Dompnier suggests that spouses could respect each other's personal religious

household of this sort, about which we are well informed, is that of the La Trémoille family in its château in Thouars. The La Trémoilles occupied the pinnacle of Poitevin society. They had been Protestants since Duc Claude's adherence to the Reformed Church in 1585.[79] He married Charlotte-Brabantine de Nassau, and their son, Henri, wed the Huguenot Marie de La Tour d'Auvergne. According to mid-seventeenth-century intendant Charles Colbert de Croissy, Henri ranked as "chef" of Poitou's nobility because of his position as the province's "grand sénéchal," the illustriousness of his house, his great landed possessions, his large number of vassals, and the family's important alliances.[80] Henri converted to Catholicism during the siege of La Rochelle in 1628, and his abjuration was a major victory for the Catholic cause. Following his religious change, his wife and mother remained staunch Protestants.[81]

Admittedly, a ducal family can hardly be considered typical, but its situation is illustrative. The duke made his attachment to his new religion very public. During the 1640s Henri sponsored processions of relics in Thouars to petition saints for rain. In 1648 he took Communion with some sixteen hundred others during a Forty Hours devotion organized to combat "the debaucheries of Carnival."[82] In 1661 he requested diocesan permission for a general procession in Thouars to celebrate the opening of the jubilee. The duke issued a strict ordinance prohibiting cabaret openings, drinking, gambling, game playing, and so forth on Sundays or festivals during the jubilee.[83] And in 1664 he ordered public prayers for the queen's recovery from illness.[84]

---

choice and recognize each other's "expression of fidelity to a family and to a manner of affiliation that marriage did not interrupt" (*Venin de l'hérésie*, 156).

79. He became an important Huguenot military leader in the late stages of the Wars of Religion. See Imbert, *Thouars*, 257.

80. Colbert de Croissy, *Etat du Poitou*, 93–94.

81. *La conversion de Monsieur de la Trimoüille duc et pair de France faitte en l'armée du roy devant La Rochelle le 18 iour de juillet mil six cens vingt-huict* (Paris, 1628), 6. See also Parker, *La Rochelle and the French Monarchy*, 144. I will return to a discussion of the duchesses in Chapter 5 and to the conversions in this family in Chapter 6.

82. The phrase is from the curé François Guillé's registers of Thouars's St. Laon parish, quoted in Imbert, *Thouars*, 301.

83. Imbert, *Thouars*, 300, 308–10; Hugues Imbert, *Registre de correspondance et biographie du duc Henri de La Trémoille, 1649–1667* (Poitiers, 1867), 174–75, 231–32.

84. Imbert, *Registre*, 240.

Marie de La Tour was renowned among her coreligionists for her piety and her defense of the church. Ministers and later Protestant historians referred to her fondly as the "heroine of Thouars."[85] In the 1640s she helped meet the debts of the Protestant church in Thouars, and she arranged to pay the pastor's salary. She also provided money for the rebuilding of the temple in another La Trémoille possession, Vitré in Brittany (despite the obstacles the local bishop and Richelieu presented).[86] In 1664 the queen accused her of interfering with the work of Catholic missionaries in Poitou, despite her husband's support for them. Marie denied any hostile intentions against the missionaries, but took the occasion to defend liberty of conscience to her ruler.[87] At the 1659 national synod meeting in Loudun, she was received with the pomp befitting a magnate upon whom Huguenots depended, making an elaborate entry into the city where the entire *corps de ville* (the municipal officials) and a large retinue of horseman met her and accompanied her to her lodgings.[88]

One might imagine holy warfare between the duke and the duchess, each eager to demonstrate fidelity to his or her church. To be sure, it is difficult to assess their personal relationship. But evidence of conflict in the family is hard to find, despite an eighteenth-century history of Thouars that suggests that upon his return to the town after his abjuration in 1628 the duke prevented his wife from building a new temple near the chateau and that in their later years Marie "continually reproached" her husband for his conversion.[89] It is true that he hoped to convert her during her terminal illness in 1665; he arranged for a special exposition of the Blessed Sacrament in all local churches.[90] But he had not previously interfered

85. "Mémoire de Marie de La Tour d'Auvergne," edited by H. Imbert, in *Mémoires de la Société des Antiquaires de l'Ouest*, vol. 32 (1867), 89–129, see esp. 91.

86. Charles-Louis de La Trémoïlle, *Les La Trémoïlle pendant cinq siècles*, 5 vols. (Nantes, 1895), 4:72, 90, 91. See also Marie's own account of these activities in "Mémoire de Marie de La Tour d'Auvergne," 119.

87. Marie's comments are reported in a letter of her husband. See Imbert, *Registre*, 238–40.

88. "Synode du Loudun," ADV I2, 5v.

89. "Memoires de la ville de Thoüars, 1756," signed by Droyneau de Brie, avocat au Parlement de Paris, AN 1 AP 1050, pp. 55, 58 ("Factums, mémoires judiciaires et brochures relatifs à la famille de La Trémoille et à la ville de Thouars").

90. Imbert, *Registre*, 242.

with her practicing her faith. He allowed his wife to continue Reformed worship in the château chapel and the ringing of the chapel bell to call Huguenot servants to the service. Indeed, Louis XIV would write to the duke after the duchess's death complaining that he had been too complacent in allowing not only his wife but also his granddaughter to continue the practice of Protestantism in the château.[91]

A cooperative attitude was evident in the duke's important patronage role as a noble magnate and local seigneur. In the years following his conversion, he increasingly took on the commitments of a Catholic patron. He repaired churches and founded a college and hospital at Thouars. In the 1630s he brought the Ursulines to the town, and they in turn displayed his coat of arms on their church.[92] Catholics seeking posts—whether secular or clerical—now had a powerful benefactor. He employed Catholic clergy as almoners in his own household, and he proposed Lenten preachers for towns under his seigneurial jurisdiction.[93] His agents took pains to ensure that Catholics filled all seigneurial positions the family controlled.[94] The Visitandines at Poitiers sought his sponsorship in the campaign to canonize the cofounder of their order, François de Sales.[95]

However, the duke also continued to offer protection to Thouars's Huguenots, who comprised about half of the town's population.[96] In 1632 he took an active hand in recruiting a new pastor, Jean Chabrol, for the town.[97] In 1634 the court of the Grands Jours condemned the Thouars temple, along with many others in the province, for being too close to a

91. Imbert, *Registre*, 24, 256. Duc Henri's daughter-in-law was Amélie of Hesse-Cassel, his granddaughter Charlotte-Amélie of Aldenburg. The granddaughter worshipped in her mother's quarters, since after her grandmother's death the chapel was reserved for the mass.

92. Imbert, *Registre*, 15; *Thouars*, 290.

93. See the request in 1658 to the bishop of Bayeux for an almoner and letters concerning Lenten preachers for Mauléon (1661) and Thouars (1664) in Imbert, *Registre*, 58, 167, 219.

94. For examples, see Act of 1639 in AN 1AP 428 and Letter of 1651 in 1AP 429, 81.

95. Though the duke refused to write the pope on the matter; see letter of 16 June 1658, in Imbert, *Registre*, 42. The timing of this matter is unclear since the duke's letter is dated 1658, but De Sales's canonization was in 1655.

96. Imbert gives this approximation of the Protestant population in *Thouars*, 319.

97. See the 1632 letter from the Protestant church in Lyon in response to the duke's inquiries about Chabrol, in AN 1AP 353, 12.

church, thereby impeding Catholic worship. The Huguenot community delayed destruction of their temple for some years, but in 1640, after they had exhausted their legal options, they petitioned the duke for a site on which to build a new temple. He granted them a place near the wall of the city in what had been the Protestant cemetery. In doing so, he made clear his intent also to protect his fellow Catholics and prevent confessional conflict. He wanted to "treat favorably his Catholic dependents" since he had "embraced their" religion. And he wished to prevent "any pretexts of division" between the two groups and "maintain them in peace." The new temple would not be in the center of Thouars as had the old one. It was pushed to the town's edge, much in the same way Huguenot cemeteries were being moved in these same years, and with it the Huguenots were symbolically displaced as well. But the duke allowed their continued worship in Thouars, and he helped them mount a defense of the new temple against lawsuits seeking to prevent its construction.[98]

The duke and duchess worked together in matters concerning the national Reformed Church, for example, in the affair of Alexandre Morus. This charismatic preacher had a checkered career as a professor in the Genevan Academy and minister at Charenton. He was also associated with the Saumur theologian Moyse Amyrault, whose ideas on universal grace provoked great controversy.[99] The La Trémoilles offered Morus their patronage and corresponded frequently with him in the 1660s. He sent them his publications, and he served as an advisor to their agent in England.[100] In 1664 the duke and duchess invited Morus to Thouars. Henri reported to his son that Morus's stay had "set the Catholics murmuring

98. AN 1AP 428, 8–9; La Trémoïlle, *Les La Trémoïlles*, 4:88–90; Imbert, *Thouars*, 298–300.

99. Amyraut sought a middle way between Arminians and strict predestinarians by suggesting the idea of hypothetical universalism in which Christ's sacrifice served not just for the elect but for everybody, providing they believed. A second divine decree granted faith to the elect. Pierre Dumoulin, among others, criticized Amyraut's views. The national synod at Alençon (1637) did not condemn them, but they remained very controversial in the French Reformed Church. See Philip Benedict, *Christ's Churches Purely Reformed: A Social History of Calvinism* (New Haven, Conn., 2002), 316–17; Léonard, *Histoire générale du protestantisme*, 2:240–41, 345; and Brian G. Armstrong, *Calvinism and the Amyraut Heresy: Protestant Scholasticism and Humanism in Seventeenth-Century France* (Madison, Wis., 1969), 112–14.

100. For a selection of their letters, see Imbert, *Registre*, 94–113.

and had rendered him suspect," but the duke did not seem unduly concerned about the effect this display of benevolence toward the minister had on his fellow Catholics. The family's attention to Morus may have been part of a larger interest in Amyrauldianism. Certainly Amyrault was interested in the La Trémoilles. In 1663 he sent the duke and duchess works dedicated to their granddaughter, for which the duke responded with gratitude and the wish that these works might be employed in reducing doctrinal conflict among the Protestants.[101] The family's efforts in mediating such conflicts were long-standing. In 1649 the duke's son, Henri-Charles, had brought Amyrault and some of his Protestant opponents to a meeting in Thouars, which ironed out a temporary peace in the quarrel over universal grace.[102] So when, in 1664, the duke and duchess invited Morus to Thouars, they were continuing a family tradition of protecting moderate Calvinism.

In the 1660s, after a respite in the anti-Protestant campaign during the years of the Fronde and Louis XIV's minority, the government's attitude toward Huguenots turned more openly hostile. In that decade, as the king and his ministers put into place reforms restructuring royal administrative control over the country, the government also issued new laws and the courts issued new decisions against Protestantism.[103] The legislative and judicial attack continued to the Revocation of the Edict of Nantes in 1685. Louis appointed new commissioners of the edict to Poitou in 1665: Colbert's brother, Charles Colbert de Croissy, and the local Poitevin Huguenot Claude de La Noue. The commission outlawed temples in thirty-six communities, usually for infractions reflecting the strictest possible interpretation of the Edict of Nantes, such as for being located in places the edict did not permit or for standing too close to Catholic churches and in-

101. Imbert, *Registre*, 202–3.

102. Armstrong, *Calvinism and the Amyraut Heresy*, 114–15. As Susan Rosa has shown, a number of high-ranking converts in the 1650s and 1660s were concerned with doctrinal projects that might permit a reunion of Catholicism and Protestantism. Moderate Calvinism may have seemed likely to provide such a bridge. See "'Il était possible aussi que cette conversion fût sincère': Turenne's Conversion in Context," *French Historical Studies* 18, no. 3 (Spring 1994): 632–66.

103. On government changes in these years, see Collins, *State in Early Modern France*, 79–124. On anti-Protestant legislation, see Labrousse, *"Une foi, une loi, un roi,"* 125–47; and Garrisson, *Édit de Nantes*, 119–61.

terfering with Catholic worship.[104] As with other aspects of the royal program during these years, the anti-Protestant campaign proceeded through the combined efforts of central government authorities and local allies, in this case, Catholics like Jean Filleau. They agitated for harsher policies, investigated alleged Huguenot infractions, and filed lawsuits against Protestant congregations.

Duc Henri was, at first, not among these local allies, though he did not otherwise oppose royal authority. In response to the attack on Huguenot temples, he wrote a "discourse on the orders given for demolishing temples of the R.P.R."[105] The essay is as much an attack on the Jansenists as a plea for Protestants. The Jansenists are the true "criminals and rebels" whose disobedience of Church and king threatens the state. The Protestants are protected by the Edict of Nantes, which the duke refers to, adopting the terms common among Protestant apologists, as a "fundamental law of the state." Abolishing it would sap the foundations of that state. Protestantism is no longer a "newborn heresy" that can be "suffocated in its crib" but a considerable part of the state with families throughout all the provinces united by the "indissoluble bonds of religion and interest." So while waiting for God to "touch their hearts" and procure their conversion, the king should maintain peace by emulating the example of his "incomparable grandfather" and preserve the edicts that protect the Huguenots. The duke's discourse makes clear his political loyalty and his pious Catholic wish for the Huguenots' eventual conversion. It claims that attempting to eliminate the heresy is too dangerous an enterprise given the Huguenots' numbers and strength in the kingdom. But it insists that they should be recognized as a legitimate constituency in the state. They live in France by means of the legal privileges granted in the Edict of Nantes, which should not be overturned.

After the mid-1660s the duke's willingness to preside over a biconfessional household waned, and a discordant tone pervaded La Trémoille re-

104. Only thirteen were confirmed. Another eight were left undecided but placed in jeopardy. Six fief exercises were also condemned. For a discussion of this campaign, see Lièvre, *Histoire des protestants*, 2:71–80; Dez, *Histoire des protestants*, 325–41; and Krumenacker, *Protestants du Poitou*, 48–49.

105. The date of the discourse is uncertain, but Imbert includes it with the duke's correspondence from 1665 (*Registre*, 248–52).

ligious life. The king was complaining about Protestant worship in the château.[106] Anne of Austria was eager to send personally chosen missionaries to convert the duchess. The Catholic clergy, including the La Trémoilles' son Laval, frequently reminded the duke of his obligations to the Church.[107] But most importantly, Marie de La Tour died in 1665, and with her death disappeared a strong-willed defender of the faith in the family and the kingdom. It seems that without her presence and influence the duke's attitude turned more intolerant. For example, in 1666, he wrote to Laval approving efforts by the curé of Vitré to exclude Protestants from a deputation to the Breton estates.[108] And in the same year he rejected Protestant requests to hold a synod at Thouars, much to the satisfaction of the king's minister, Louvois, and Filleau, who had been corresponding with him on the issue.[109] Religious affairs in the household grew even tenser after the duke's son and heir, Henri-Charles, prince de Tarente, converted to Catholicism in 1670. The memoir of his Protestant daughter Charlotte-Amélie (the duke's granddaughter) gives a vivid picture of the now terrible relationship between her Protestant mother, Amélie of Hesse-Cassel, and her Catholic father; of her brothers being forced into Catholic conversions; and of embattled Huguenots in the château and town.[110] Charlotte and her mother eventually left for Copenhagen. This once biconfessional home—with members of two faiths and space for two religious observances—became a purely Catholic preserve.

For nearly four decades after Henri de La Trémoille's conversion, the family château at Thouars remained commodious enough for both religions and the family remained involved in the affairs of both churches. The accommodating confessional arrangement inside the household also promoted one in the community of Thouars, where new Catholic religious orders were established and a new temple built, albeit at a distance from the town's center. Two separate but connected trajectories brought

106. See the 1665 letters from Louis and Louvois to the duke and his responses in Imbert, *Registre*, 256–68.

107. Imbert, *Registre*, 245; also see the 1664 exchange of letters between the duke and the vicar-general of the Poitiers diocese, pp. 219–22, 231–36.

108. Imbert, *Registre*, 318–19.

109. Imbert, *Registre*, 284, 301.

110. Aldenburg, *Autobiography*, 66–72, 75–81. On Charlotte-Amélie, see below, pp. 225–29; on Tarente's conversion, see below, pp. 298–304.

this cooperation to an end, one the family's and the other the kingdom's. Government policy toward Huguenots turned increasingly harsh, and royal pressure on the family grew. The household's confessional composition also changed with the death of the Protestant duchess and the conversion of the heir.

We cannot presume that prior to this time family religious relations were always harmonious, only that they were subject to negotiations between the duke and the duchess. Clearly, one area of stress was the religion of their children and grandchildren, who were divided between the faiths (a matter to which I will return below). With mounting pressure on the minority from the 1660s on, the question Dumoulin had asked in his *Conseil fidele* a half a century earlier became particularly relevant: If there were a persecution, what should a Huguenot mother do? Should she flee the country, leaving her husband and children behind, or should she take the children with her, tearing them away from their father? Amélie of Hesse-Cassel and Charlotte, the future memoirist, provided one answer. The mother and daughter left the kingdom; the sons (and heirs) stayed with the father and converted to his faith. This family's status made these sorts of decisions important far beyond the château at Thouars, but the religious fate of children was always one of the most sensitive issues arising from mixed marriages, and one of the most heated in polemics against them. And it was an issue of far too great importance to the churches and the state to be left to families alone.

CHILDREN

Frustrated in their attempts to stop mixed marriages, the clergies sought, at the least, to prevent the baptism and raising of children in the rival faith. Each side recognized the validity of the other's baptism, but the rite still provoked disputes. Calvinists rejected the Catholic belief that baptism conferred grace essential for salvation, but it remained for them a sacrament and an important means of incorporating children into their church.[111] Baptizing the offspring of mixed marriages as Catholics repre-

111. Benedict, *Huguenot Population*, 22–27. The Catholic Church insisted on baptisms following birth as quickly as possible so as to minimize the possibility of infants dying without the sacrament. Calvinist consistories preferred delaying the rite until a

sented a serious loss to their side. Catholic bishops tried to insist on Catholic baptisms for children of mixed unions, not only to ensure for them sacramental grace, but also to help cement their affiliation with the Roman Church.[112] A Catholic baptism also provided an excuse for authorities to remove children from Protestant or mixed homes. Huguenots decried these ostensibly legal maneuvers as child abductions and complained particularly about Catholic midwives who surreptitiously baptized the children of Protestant parents (or of one Protestant parent) at birth so that they could be considered Catholic.[113] For example, in a case from Melle in 1667 the consistory criticized a father for not acting fast enough to stop a Catholic midwife who had baptized his infant quickly.[114]

Consistories had trouble preventing Catholic baptisms for children of mixed marriages. In Mougon, for instance, Jean Texier was called before the consistory several times from 1611 to 1613 for having baptized his children "à la messe." Isaac Chateraille was summoned in 1615 and again in 1616.[115] Different reasons could account for Protestants choosing Catholic baptisms. Some parents might have seen a Catholic rite as offering a more secure future for a child, especially given Protestantism's increasingly pre-

---

regular assembly of the congregation. Families often frustrated their consistories' intentions by seeking quick baptisms, as did their Catholic neighbors. Benedict's study indicates increasing delays in Protestant baptism as the seventeenth century progressed, suggesting a growing Huguenot sense of difference between their baptisms and those of Catholics. However, Catholics in southern areas with large Huguenot populations also delayed baptisms. See also Hanlon, *Confession and Community*, 145–49, 161–63.

112. E.g., the bishop of Strasbourg refrained from obstructing mixed marriages under the condition that their offspring were eventually baptized by parish priests (Louis Châtellier, *Tradition chrétienne et renouveau catholique dans le cadre de l'ancien diocèse de Strasbourg (1650–1770)* [Paris, 1981], 146–47).

113. Benoist's *Histoire de l'Edit de Nantes* presents numerous cases. The 1680 royal declaration prohibiting Huguenot women from serving as midwives effectively created a situation where Protestants had to rely on Catholic midwives and run the risk of Catholics baptizing their infants, who could thereby be considered, in Labrousse's words, "ipso facto a Catholic" (*"Une foi, une loi, un roi,"* 168). The law of the 1660s (to be discussed below) insisted on Catholic baptisms for children of Catholic fathers, thereby implying that baptism would determine definitively and legally the future religion of children.

114. ADDS 2J 35 (1), p. 28.

115. Mougon, Papiers des Consistoires 1593–1627, ADDS 1I 3. It is not clear from these records if these summonses are for the same offense or for separate infractions.

carious position in the 1660s and 1670s. And it is possible that the traditional protective or exorcistic nature of the Catholic rite seemed to some Huguenot parents more effective than a Calvinist baptism, shorn of any protective power.[116]

The baptismal choice could also reflect familial decisions about children's religious upbringing. The choice of religion in which children of mixed marriages were raised followed no single pattern. According to Labrousse, in Mauvezin the father's faith, or that of the godparents, decided the issue. Strasbourg's jurisprudence also dictated that children would follow their father's confession. But in much of Alsace the confession of the village in which a family resided often determined the religion of offspring. By contrast, in the Protestant-dominated areas of the diocese of Nîmes, Sauzet found cases of what he calls a "Huguenot matriarchy" in which Catholic fathers acquiesced in children following the faith of their Protestant mothers.[117]

But local custom was not the only factor. The family's internal religious dynamic could be decisive. Often the split between parents continued between the children: sons followed the religion of the father and daughters that of the mother. Clergymen on both sides denounced this practice. As Pierre Dumoulin complained, dividing children in this way was like making a deal with the Devil; it would condemn half of them to perdition.[118] But parents in many mixed households did not agree. Although it might seem important to continue a family's male line in the father's faith, the rival religion could be tolerated among women. Hanlon has found cases of mixed families in Layrac in which Catholic fathers presented daughters for baptism in the Protestant temple.[119] In Vanzay, in 1666, the Huguenot Pierre Michelet, who was married to the Catholic

116. Bertheau, "Consistoire . . . du Moyen-Poitou," 4:526; Sauzet, *Contre-réforme et réforme catholique*, 174; Dompnier, *Venin de l'hérésie*, 162. For examples of German Lutherans using Catholic baptisms, see C. Scott Dixon, *The Reformation and Rural Society: The Parishes of Brandenburg-Ansbach-Kulmbach, 1528–1603* (Cambridge, U.K., 1996), 166–67.

117. Châtellier, *Tradition chrétienne*, 146; Quéniart, *Révocation de l'Édit de Nantes*, 35, 79; Sauzet, *Contre-réforme et réforme catholique*, 269; Labrousse, *"Une foi, une loi, un roi,"* 84.

118. Pierre Dumoulin, *Conseil fidele*, 12.

119. *Confession and Community*, 218–19.

Joachine Quincarlet, brought his daughter Marie to the priest and three years later his daughter Françoise. These daughters would be of the same faith as their mother. But did the boys of this family follow their father's faith? That is not certain because in 1671 Michelet brought his son Pierre to the Catholic church to be buried. In Lusignan too Huguenot fathers with Catholic wives brought their daughters for Catholic baptism, as did Daniel Delagau in 1674. But they might also bring their sons, as did Pierre Barot in 1677.[120]

The consistory records of Melle for the 1660s reveal only five cases, four of them men, whom the elders criticized for allowing a child to receive a Catholic baptism.[121] The registers do not reveal the sex of the children, but they were probably daughters, since it does not seem likely that, in this heavily Protestant town, Huguenot fathers would have had much incentive for giving their family heirs Catholic baptisms. Still, five cases over the course of a decade in Melle do not seem like very many, especially given the number of mixed marriages there. It may simply be that with Protestantism dominant in the community and with most of the fathers in these mixed households being Huguenots, no strong reason existed to permit even daughters to follow their mother's Catholicism.

Some families reached no definitive solution, leading to an ongoing struggle over the children's religious fate. For an example, we can turn back to the La Trémoilles. Although, as we have seen, Duc Henri's conversion to Catholicism in 1628 did not set off a confessional conflict in the family, it did provoke a tug-of-war over the children's religion that lasted for decades. All of the La Trémoille offspring followed their father into Catholicism soon after his conversion. But according to the memoir of the oldest son, Henri-Charles, prince de Tarente, his Huguenot mother, Marie de La Tour d'Auvergne, applied a good deal of maternal pressure to encourage his return to Calvinism, including sending him to Holland, where he stayed with his Protestant great-uncle, Frederick Henry, prince of Orange.[122] He reconverted to Protestantism in 1640, much to his fa-

120. Vanzay, Extraits des Registres Catholiques, BPF Ms. 1500/6/1; Lusignan, Extraits des Registres Catholiques, BPF Ms. 1500/6/i.

121. ADDS 2J 35 (1).

122. "Motifs de la Conversion de feu Monseigneur le Prince de Tarente: Ecrits par luy-même vers l'année 1671," AN 1AP. *441; and *Mémoires de Henri-Charles de La Trémoille, Prince de Tarente* (Liege, 1767).

ther's displeasure.[123] Henri's other son, Louis-Maurice, comte de Laval, remained a Catholic and would eventually give up a military for an ecclesiastical career.[124] But the religion of the family heirs was of more importance to the duke than that of his female children. I have found no record of his objecting to his daughter Elisabeth's return to Protestantism in 1640. Her sister, Marie, was also a Protestant and made a prominent Protestant marriage with Bernard de Saxe, duke of Jena.[125] The tussle over the religious affiliation of the La Trémoille children continued into the next generation. After Tarente returned to Catholicism in 1670, he forced his sons to follow him. Less willing than his father to allow religious division in the family, he also pressured his daughter, Charlotte-Amélie, to convert, but without success.[126] Certainly not all mixed families could carry out their struggles over children on a national, even international, stage, as did the La Trémoilles, and not all such contests possessed the political importance of the one in this magnate clan. But this case can remind us that in mixed marriages the decision about the children's religion was not always made cooperatively, even when confessional difference was accommodated in the home. Furthermore, children's religious attachments were not always fixed. The need to make marriages or, as was the case with the La Trémoille's, the need to reassert political fidelity to the monarch could lead children to convert, sometimes more than once.[127] But as the French state applied increasing pressure on the minority, these changes of religious identity more and more often favored the king's faith.

STATE INTERVENTION

The persistence of religiously divided households and concerns over their children provided the royal government with increasing opportuni-

123. To judge from his complaints about the conversion in letters to Tarente and the Duc de Bouillon. See AN 1AP 397, 106–7.

124. Also, initially, much to his father's chagrin. Eventually the duke did help him obtain the bishopric of St. Malo. See Imbert, *Registre*, 38–39.

125. After the rejection of the Duc de Meilleraye. See above, p. 145. Also see La Trémoïlle, *Les La Trémoïlles*, viii.

126. Aldenburg, *Autobiography*, 76–77. See below, pp. 226–29.

127. As we will see with the case of Henri-Charles in below, pp. 298–304.

ties for intervening into families during the legislative campaign against French Protestantism that began in the 1660s. Mixed families became a major target of that campaign. And the government's efforts against them, and Huguenot families more generally, created a contradiction with the policies it promoted through the "family-state compact." In tightening the reins on Protestantism and then in seeking to suppress it entirely, the state worked against the patriarchal regime it otherwise sought to promote.

A royal declaration of 1663 prohibited those who had converted to Catholicism from relapsing.[128] Protestants who abjured to marry Catholics would no longer be able to return legally to their original faith. And to further ensure the durability of conversions made for marriage, a 1664 order instructed clergy of both faiths to delay the weddings of converts for six months.[129] The royal declaration of 1666 that enacted a major reregulation of French Protestantism made it possible for anyone who objected to a mixed marriage to bring the matter before a judge and thereby delay the wedding.[130] Such ordinances sought to prevent the quick conversions and relapses that allowed the establishment of mixed families. Offenders were liable to harsh punishment, as was Catherine Collineau of Lusignan. The local curé informed judicial authorities in 1678 that although she had converted to Catholicism four years earlier to marry Michel Duchiron, she had relapsed and "shamelessly attended" Reformed worship. Collineau declared to the court that "she knew nothing of the *religion catholique apostolique et romaine*." She was ordered to pay a fine and was banished from the kingdom.[131] The government's measures provoked resistance. In 1674 the Poitou provincial synod meeting in Civray voted to pay the fines of any minister convicted of marrying converts to Protes-

128. The legislation was reinforced with stiffer penalties in 1665 and 1679. See Labrousse, *"Une foi, une loi, un roi,"* 143; and Daniel Ligou, *Le protestantisme en France de 1598 à 1715* (Paris, 1968), 119–20.

129. Dompnier, *Venin de l'hérésie*, 157; Garrisson, *Édit de Nantes*, 135.

130. "Déclaration du roi du 2 avril 1666 qui règle les choses que doivent observer ceux de la R.P.R.," in Bergeal and Durrleman, eds., *Protestantisme et libertés*, 88–99, see Article 11, p. 90.

131. J. Rivierre, "Six cents procédures et arrêts anti-protestants en Poitou, 1678–1730," BPF Ms. 1956, No. 3 bis. Ministers who received relapses in these years were also liable to banishment and their temples could be closed.

tantism before their six-month waiting period was up. The provincial intendant René de Marillac was outraged at this affront to royal authority.[132] But the royal orders did not necessarily end mixed marriages—as we have seen in Melle. And so the king dealt with the whole matter more directly in 1680 by outlawing mixed marriages entirely.[133] In the same year he also outlawed conversions to Protestantism.

The monarchy thus tried to impose the strictest form of confessional boundary between families of different faiths. With the numbers of their coreligionists falling, Huguenots seeking marriage partners would be increasingly isolated, unless they abjured. But in obstructing intermarriage, the royal government undermined the ability of families to use marriage arrangements for their social and economic advancement, an essential aspect of the "family-state compact." One of the reasons, and perhaps the major reason, for intermarriage was that it allowed families to cross the confessional divide in the pursuit of advantageous matches. Insofar as French families complied with royal legislation, the prospects for making suitable matches in biconfessional areas were henceforth restricted. Certainly this change hurt Huguenots more than Catholics, who had more potential partners for their children.

The government also interfered in parents' decisions about the religion of their offspring, though these interventions were not new in the 1660s. Hostile courts had often rendered decisions in cases about children that the Protestant community found outrageous. Take two examples from 1621, which Benoist recorded in his *Histoire de l'Edit de Nantes*. The first concerned the children of a Parisian Catholic who had been condemned for murdering his Protestant wife. His Catholic relatives brought suit before the Parlement to have the children raised as Catholics, despite their deceased mother's wishes. The court decided that because of the father's crime, the right to determine the children's education had passed to the king, who decided they would be raised as Catholics. In the other case, a Huguenot father had put two of his sons (one thirteen and the other eleven) in a Jesuit college in Paris.[134] Deciding that their "liberty of con-

132. Letter from Marillac to Le Tellier of 20 January 1674, in AN TT 241, pp. 206–8.

133. A prohibition reiterated in 1683. See Benedict, "Catholic-Reformed Co-existence," 82; and Krumenacker, *Protestants du Poitou*, 56.

134. Huguenot families sometimes sent their sons to Jesuit schools, though they

science" was restricted there, he withdrew the boys and sent them to the Protestant academy at Sedan. While they were on their way, a relative who was a priest kidnapped the youngsters and sent them to a Jesuit school in Pont à Mousson. The father pursued the matter in the courts, where he had to face the curious legal argument by his Catholic opponents that by putting the boys in a Jesuit school, he had forfeited his rights to govern their education. The judges did not find the argument convincing, but his sons were produced in court, where (under what Benoist assumed was careful coaching) they asked to be raised as Catholics. The father lost his case, and he was ordered to pay for the boys' maintenance at the College de Navarre in Paris. "Never did a court decision," Benoist concluded, "so violate the Edict of Nantes as this one." Catholics "try to make child kidnapping legitimate by saying that children have become Catholics by their own choice and that there is a very old law that makes them masters of their own choice at the age of fifteen" (though neither boy in this case had reached even that age).[135]

State interference increased in the 1660s, when, as part of the anti-Protestant campaign, royal legislation increasingly took over the determination of children's religion. In 1663 the royal council ordered that all children with Catholic fathers and Protestant mothers would be raised as Catholics. The royal declaration of 1666 made this order part of its new regulations for the French Reformed community. Those children whose Catholic fathers had died would also be raised as Catholics. To ensure that this was done, the declaration ordered that they be put "into the hands of Catholic tutors or relatives." And it expressly prohibited "bringing these children to temples or to schools of . . . the R.P.R." Another declaration of 1669 added that even those whose Catholic fathers had relapsed into Protestantism (prior to 1663 presumably) and who had Protestant mothers would now be raised as Catholics.[136] These regulations might be seen

---

might well have occasion to regret the decision when the boys converted. Perhaps the most famous example was Pierre Bayle.

135. Benoist, *Histoire de l'Edit de Nantes*, 2:364–66.

136. "Déclaration du roi du 2 avril 1666" and "Déclaration du roi du 1er février 1669 portant règlement des choses qui doivent être gardées et observées par ceux qui font profession de la religion prétendue réformée," in Bergeal and Durrleman, eds., *Protestantisme et libertés en France*, 88–109; see Article 45 (1666), p. 96, and Article 39 (1669), p. 107. See also Garrisson, *Édit de Nantes*, 141. The declarations responded on

as reinforcing patriarchal order in that the father's religion would now determine the children's, assuming that the father was, or at least had once been, a Catholic. But when it came to increasing the legal stranglehold on the Huguenot community, maintaining paternal authority over offspring was not on the monarchy's agenda so much as expanding its powers over families, at least Huguenot families. Protestant widows had less and less legal control over their children, but so did Protestant fathers.

The assault on Protestant family authority was nowhere more evident than in the issue of child conversion. The state permitted minors to convert to Catholicism without parental permission and protected them from their families' wrath when they did so by allowing their removal from the home. In 1664 the royal council ordered that Huguenot boys of fourteen and girls of twelve could convert legally without their parents' permission, and a declaration of the next year stipulated that their parents would be legally responsible for maintaining them, even if that involved payments to Catholic orphanages, convents, schools, or other religious establishments in which the young converts would be installed.[137] Protestants argued that children of such an age could not possibly make reasoned decisions about conversion, and hence they would only choose to leave the true faith and challenge parental authority under the malign influence of Catholics who bore ill will against Protestant families.

This situation grew more shocking, even to Catholics, when a 1681 declaration lowered the age at which children of either sex could convert to seven, the traditional "age of reason."[138] Royal officials engaged in the anti-Protestant campaign, like René de Marillac, intendant in Poitou, were quite ready to make use of the law to further conversions. Demaillasson, the attorney from Montmorillon, recorded in his journal the abjuration in October 1681 of one René-Jessé de Gollier, who was about nine or ten years old. Like children in similar cases, he was caught between the two faiths. Up to the age of seven, a Catholic woman, whose relationship to

---

this point and many others to the wishes of the Assemblies of the Clergy, especially that of 1665. See Blet, *Le clergé de France et la monarchie*, 2:386.

137. The 1669 "Déclaration" confirmed these orders. See Bergeal and Durrleman, eds., *Protestantisme et libertés en France*, Article 39, p. 107.

138. Déclaration du roi du 18 juin 1681 portant que les enfants de la R.P.R. pourront se convertir à l'âge de sept ans, in Bergeal and Durrleman, eds., *Protestantisme et libertés en France*, 126–28.

the boy the journal does not make clear, had raised him. His Huguenot father took him from her and sent him to a Protestant relative. When Marillac was informed, he ordered a local official to ask the boy if he wanted to be a Catholic and to arrange for his official abjuration before the local curé. The new convert was then brought to the intendant, and he was removed from his father's supervision. The Catholic writer approved of what had happened and had served as a witness to the act of abjuration.[139] But for many, of both faiths, such incidents were akin to child abduction. Of all the restrictions placed on Huguenots, none seemed, to people at the time or to posterity, as odious as the laws that undermined parental control over their offspring and gave children, who were otherwise too young to exercise any legal independence, the right to leave their families.[140] And no regulations were so at odds with the other laws governing family life or went as far in challenging parental authority, one of the pillars of the early-modern social order.

The state chose to pursue religious uniformity over its other goal of promoting social and political stability through the "family-state compact," which encouraged patriarchal control over families. We must not exaggerate here; the monarchy did not seek to overturn family control of property transmission across generations or the authority of parents in deciding their children's futures. And the contradiction between the royal government's religious policies and its family policies obviously affected the religious minority far more than Catholics. But whereas previously religious difference did not impede the pursuit of family aims, now it would. For as long as the state sought to enforce vigorously its legal persecution of Protestantism, other goals would be secondary to that of confessional conformity.

St. Paul said: "a man shall leave his father and mother and be joined to his wife, and the two shall become one" (Ephesians 5:31). Given that both churches shared the heritage of Paul's words, it is hardly surprising that they found mixed marriages deeply troubling. For if husband and wife

139. "Journal de M. Demaillasson," 37:8–9.

140. Labrousse, *"Une foi, une loi, un roi,"* 172. Garrisson quotes the compiler of royal laws François Isambert as writing in 1829: "It is difficult to find a means of conversion more odious and more contrary to public morality" (*Édit de Nantes*, 141–42).

were to be one, then presumably their religion would have to be one as well. For seventeenth-century polemicists, it was difficult to conceive of a household divided between the confessions as being well ordered. The tradition Paul's instructions shaped has given modern historians a different view of intermarriage; they have stressed its capacity for establishing cross-confessional alliances and harmony between spouses and families of the rival faiths. Mixed weddings allowed other social imperatives and other means of familial identification—with social status groups, communities, or local traditions—to override confessional allegiance.

This examination of mixed marriage has shown that seventeenth-century polemicists were not always wrong, and historians are not always right. Establishing the confessional boundary within households had a variety of consequences. It could create the first form of confessional boundary, where the line between the religious groups was overshadowed by common beliefs or the pursuit of shared aims. Confessional difference could be blurred as each spouse participated in the other's religious observances. We might even hypothesize the existence of an irenic household religion built around family religious observances, such as baptisms, marriages, and funerals. Admittedly, evidence for such a mixed religious practice is not plentiful. More apparent are situations in which the confessional boundary was not eliminated but ran right through the family. Religious division was maintained out of respect for the beliefs of individuals and the familial traditions in which they were raised. This situation is more akin to the second form of confessional boundary. A cooperative but carefully delineated arrangement allowed the separate continuing existence of both faiths within the home. The examples of parents who agreed to raise some children as Catholics and others as Protestants suggest such a cooperative tolerance of religious division. In aristocratic châteaux with domestic chapels, this cooperation might extend literally to the existence of two forms of practice in the household, as in that of the La Trémoilles, which had room for both Catholic and Reformed worship. Furthermore, family life was not static. As families changed over time—from the celebration of a wedding, to the birth of children, to the death of one of the spouses—the nature of the confessional situation in the home could change.

However, tolerance did not always triumph in biconfessional families;

at times, religious conflict was imported into the home. We should not assume that confessional difference was the only cause of tension. Families had other matters to fight over besides religion.[141] But religious difference could place an imposing psychological burden on some households, disrupting long-standing connections between family members and their lineage's religious traditions as well as with the practices that tied the kinship group together and associated it with local temples, churches, religious houses, cemeteries, and so forth. Family confessional conflict characteristic of the third form of boundary was the result. Individuals and families would then have to choose between the religious affiliation of their spouses and that of their original families.

If a marriage conversion proved durable, as was often the case, if the converted spouse remained committed to his or, more often, her partner's faith, then religious unity in the home was secured at the expense of that spouse's original confession. In such families, the third type of boundary was constructed but pushed outside the house altogether. This situation, of course, is what the Reformed Church had the most reason to fear. But neither the Catholic Church nor the monarchy felt confident that such a boundary would be constructed often or quickly enough to bring about the disappearance of the minority group. Thus, together with the Catholic Church, the state sought to eliminate intermarriage and, whenever possible, impose Catholic confessional uniformity in homes, even if doing so undercut patriarchal authority and the "family-state compact." The monarchy chose religious uniformity over what it otherwise promoted: the patriarch's (and the lineage's) control over marriage alliances to further strategies of social, economic, and political advancement. Insofar as this royal policy succeeded—and the evidence from Melle suggests it did not achieve total success—Huguenots would be forced to choose.[142] Either they would marry only within their increasingly shrinking religious

141. As Diefendorf reminds us in "Houses Divided," 92.

142. Elisabeth Labrousse's work on Mauvezin in the eighteenth century indicates that mixed marriages continued even after the Revocation, when old Catholics married *nouveaux convertis*, who were still attached to the practice of Protestantism ("Les mariages bigarrés: Unions mixtes en France au XVIIIe siècle," in *Le couple interdit, entretien sur le racisme: La dialectique de l'altérité socio-culturelle et la sexualité. Actes du colloque tenu en mai 1977 au Centre Culturel International de Cerisay-la-Salle*, edited by Léon Poliakov [Paris, 1980], 159–76).

group and forgo whatever rewards matches with Catholics could bring or they would convert to the majority faith and continue to seek advantageous unions.

Either result contributed to the hardening of the confessional boundary and of individual religious identity. Most often intermarriage entailed at least a temporary confessional realignment through marriage conversions. Most of the converts were women. The often back-and-forth movement of women across the divide through marriage conversions would now stop; their families and they would be more decisively identified with either the Reformed or the Catholic Church. Polemicists on both sides promoted this end. They decried women's lack of commitment or easy confessional changeability by complaining that women had no religion until they married and adopted that of their husbands. The critics were wrong; women did have religions—those of their families. But women may not have always shared the strictest form of confessional identity as defined by a hard-and-fast boundary between the faiths. The sense that women's religious attachments were flexible was useful for families seeking to make cross-confessional matches. For opponents of intermarriage, such flexibility was dangerous because it permitted an indistinct boundary between the faiths to continue. And yet, as the next chapter suggests, the issue of women's confessional identity was far more complicated. For, if women's religious lives provided a way to break down the confessional barrier, they also were seen as one of the most useful means of constructing it.

MARKERS OF DIFFERENCE

Heroines, Amazons, and the Confessional Boundary

CATHOLICS AND PROTESTANTS dissolved the confessional boundary or cooperated across it to establish families and religious coexistence. Those in both churches who wanted to stop such boundary crossing sought to construct the strictest form of division between the faiths to keep each religion distinct, concretize the confessional identity of church members, and limit interactions between Catholics and Protestants. The guardians of orthodoxy in both churches had to combat religious indeterminacy and pliable confessional identities, which, as in mixed marriages, made boundary crossing possible. Since early-modern gender attitudes often figured malleability and inconstancy as feminine characteristics, the nature of women and of their religious experience became crucial in debates between the churches. And it was so for reasons that went beyond the issue of intermarriage. As has been frequently the case in other times and other places, this culture's perceptions of gender differences provided it with a means of thinking about other sorts of differences; they constituted a "system for remarking difference."[1] The vocabulary of gendered categories offered polemicists terms for drawing distinctions between the churches and for attacking their rivals.

1. Frances E. Dolan, *Whores of Babylon: Catholicism, Gender and Seventeenth-Century Print Culture* (Ithaca, N.Y., 1999), 23. The literature on employing gender categories to create social distinctions is enormous, but Dolan's study examines their use specifically in the construction of religious difference. The polemical battle between the English Protestant majority and the Catholic minority in many ways mirrored that in France.

In their crudest form, gendered characterizations gave each side a ready means for denigrating the other as a religion of women or, at least, as a religion that "inappropriately empower[ed] women."[2] But the debates over women were complex, and therefore so were the means by which these debates were put to use in the arguments between churches. Those who criticized the rival church for being dominated by women were not referring to the supposedly natural tendency of women to be inconstant or changeable. Instead, they were complaining about the tendency of women to be obstinate in their religious wrong-headedness—another trait assumed to be naturally feminine. Women of the rival confession had too much prominence or had gained too much power, in public life and within their families. Characterizing the other religion as women-dominated immediately threatened to invest it with an array of negative traits. Women's presumed position in the rival confession was both a cause and a sign of its tendency to overturn the world's proper order. It was irrational and deceptive as a result of women's supposedly essential irrationality and deceptiveness. For both Catholics and Protestants, the disorder evident in the opposite faith paralleled the disorder evident in the female sex; indeed, it was directly due to disorder in the female sex. And the obvious fact that both churches were male-dominated institutions did nothing to undermine this commonplace.

Yet the defenders of churches could also look to women for a rhetorical advantage over their foes, and it is for this reason that women took on great "symbolic visibility" in the conflict between the churches.[3] For at the same time women were characterized as disorderly in religious life, they were also championed as the "devout sex." They could surpass men in piety. The notion of women as the devout sex was encountered frequently in the sixteenth and seventeenth centuries in part because of the interest confessional polemicists had in promoting the female exemplars of their faiths. While criticizing the public prominence and excessive religiosity of women from the other side, defenders of Protestantism or Catholicism were quick to honor their own women if they exceeded gender ex-

2. "Each [side] could claim that what was wrong with the other was that it inverted the hierarchy in sexual and familial relations" (Dolan, *Whores of Babylon*, 53; see also 8, 85). See also Davis, "City Women and Religious Change," 65.

3. I take the term "symbolic visibility" from Dolan, *Whores of Babylon*, 30.

pectations by protecting their church or by displaying a "virile" spirituality through their extraordinary devotion.

Polemicists celebrated the virile piety of their heroines because it suggested that the church being defended provided a proper outlet for female spirituality while keeping women in their socially acceptable place. Those women reputed for their virile piety were not more manlike than other women. Rather, according to their defenders, if not their detractors from the other side, they had developed a feminine virtue or quality beyond the norm of their sex.[4] The characterization of women as protectors of their churches was much more problematic. Powerful women were important to both churches as public figures, polemicists, proselytizers, and financiers. Women who engaged in these activities attracted praise from coreligionists for defending the faith and criticism from their rivals as a source of disorder.

The argument had great resonance in seventeenth-century religious polemics because it coincided with two other debates over women in French political and cultural life. One stemmed from the political power women held in regencies: specifically, Catherine de Medici's in the sixteenth century, Marie de Medici's and Anne of Austria's in the first half of the seventeenth century. By French law and tradition, women could not formally exercise rulership. The authority these women wielded was controversial. Political upheavals, such as the Wars of Religion and the Fronde, were easily blamed on women's presumed incapacity to wield power well.

The other controversy was the ongoing debate known as the "querelle des femmes."[5] This dispute pitted women's detractors, who drew on age-

4. According to Constance Jordan, the virile woman was a model for Renaissance feminists; she could attain heroic proportions that made her the equal of man, but she was endowed with feminine, not masculine, virtues (*Renaissance Feminism: Literary Texts and Political Models* [Ithaca, N.Y., 1990], 8, 11n.1).

5. The "querelle des femmes" may have involved more Catholic than Protestant writers, but in confessional polemics both sides used its terms to promote their own or to criticize their opponents' heroines. Wiesner outlines the history of the debate in *Women and Gender*, 20–26, and Carolyn C. Lougee discusses its seventeenth-century French manifestation in *Le Paradis des Femmes: Women, Salons, and Social Stratification in Seventeenth Century France* (Princeton, N.J., 1976). See also Jordan, *Renaissance Feminism*, 86–104, and the magisterial work of Linda Timmermans, *L'accès des femmes à la culture (1598–1715): Un débat d'idées de Saint François de Sales à la Marquise de Lambert*

old ideas about women's supposedly natural shortcomings and the social danger they represented, against defenders of their intellectual capacity, ability to lead exemplary lives, and important cultural contributions. The debate offered categorizations that religious disputants could use to argue over women and distinguish between the faiths. But there was an inherent slipperiness in using the vocabulary the "querelle des femmes" provided because the terms for describing the "good" women of one side and the "bad" ones of the other were largely the same. Women who acted beyond the norms of their sex might be known as "amazons" or *femmes fortes* (powerful women), but the labels could be either positive or negative. Writers criticized the amazons and femmes fortes of the opposing religion but celebrated their own precisely because they defended the faith. One side's "champions" were the other's "viragos." As was the case with women of virile piety, amazons and femmes fortes had not simply become "men"; they were exceptional women. Nonetheless, they fit into recognizable characterizations of women, though amazons pushed such characterizations to the limit.[6]

The rhetoric on women in religious life, positive or negative, derived from a discourse deeply embedded in European culture and from the need for gender-based distinctions that the confessional rivalry generated. This rhetoric helped polemicists draw a clearer distinction between the churches, which was necessary for establishing concrete confessional identities and the third, strictest form of boundary. Despite similarity in the terms used to champion and castigate controversial women, they became markers of difference. Their examples also countered the presumed indeterminate nature of female religious identity apparent in intermarriage, which promoted either the blurred confessional situation of the first form of boundary or the negotiated accommodations of the second form.

(Paris, 1993), to which I am much indebted for the discussion that follows. Ian Maclean's *Woman Triumphant: Feminism in French Literature, 1610–1652* (Oxford, U.K., 1977) argues that the formal "querelle des femmes" ended by 1630, after which debates between feminists and their opponents took other forms, for example, debates over *femmes fortes* (see 25–63). The religious debate, however, made use of many of the "querelle's" ideas.

6. On the politics and cultural discourse about women's exceptionality, see Mary D. Sheriff, *The Exceptional Woman: Elisabeth Vigée-Lebrun and the Cultural Politics of Art* (Chicago, 1996).

But the rhetoric also reflected on women's actual activities because of the controversy such activities provoked. Disagreement focused on the ways women pursued endeavors that were supposedly beyond their sex, such as the reading of Scripture, the study of theology, proselytizing, preaching, and offering political or financial support to their churches. In short, at dispute were women's roles in, and sometimes their leadership of, their churches. The women examined in this chapter achieved great prominence in Poitou and beyond because of their piety, their religious endeavors, and their public positions in their churches. However, they were chosen as case studies because, as Huguenot amazons or femmes fortes, or as Catholic nuns battling demonic possession, they were both heroines to their coreligionists and targets for their confessional rivals. They allow us to see at work both sides of the rhetoric on women religious figures, that which celebrated them and that which denigrated them. Thus this chapter is not a history of women's religious lives, important as that subject is. Rather, it concerns the rhetorical use of women in the process of distinguishing between the faiths. We must therefore look first at how this rhetoric grew out of the general discourse on women's learning and piety. The case studies that follow demonstrate how the rhetoric was put to use in the churches' polemical battle.

WOMEN'S LEARNING AND PIETY

In distinguishing themselves from each other, Catholic and Protestant polemicists used essentially the same arguments about female piety, women's access to religious learning, their engagement in public debates or proselytizing, and their propensity for superstition and heresy. The rivals also shared the same contradictory assumptions about women's religiosity. If Catholic and Protestant writers agreed on women's natural lack of reason and their susceptibility to the Devil's entreaties, they also believed in the notion of women as the "devout sex." They differed on where women could best demonstrate their devotion. For Protestants, the only truly pious life for a woman was in the household as a wife and mother. For centuries, Catholics had seen the convent as the locale most suitable for the highest forms of feminine spirituality. But they too began to entertain the belief that women could lead truly pious lives outside convents.[7] Catholics and Protestants shared with equal fervor the notion that women were to submit to the clergy and to their husbands.[8] In both religions, the husband's tutoring of his wife was essential for ensuring her proper moral behavior and the repression of her natural, dangerous, and impious tendencies.

Catholic and Protestant writers believed that women could play a vital (though not public) role in disseminating true belief and in encouraging proper moral behavior. Their situation within the home positioned them perfectly for domestic proselytizing. Although the clergies of both churches worried about this possibility when the women in question were of the wrong faith (i.e., in mixed marriages), they encouraged it among their female coreligionists.[9] Women's proselytizing efforts among their female relatives, friends, and acquaintances were welcomed. Clergymen also expected women of their faith in mixed families to work for their husbands' conversions. As providers of religious instruction for their children, mothers could help keep their offspring in the true faith or turn them to it if their husbands took them in the other direction. And women could pressure servants of the opposite confession to convert—at least, they were often accused of doing so.[10] But women were usually allowed to pursue proselytizing efforts only in a domestic setting or among members of their own sex. Moving into the public, male-dominated realm of religious controversy was not acceptable.

Women's religious learning and public prominence as well as their purported tendency to manifest excessive piety were at issue because of the assumption that women had a natural propensity for religious heterodoxy. For Catholic writers, women were the very cause of heresies or at least were responsible for their spread. According to the ex-Calvinist Florimond de Raemond, they had been responsible for heresies going back to

7. As, e.g., did François de Sales who argued in his *Introduction to the Devout Life* (1609) in favor of a woman's capacity for leading a pious life in the world, not in the convent.

8. Timmermans, *Accès des femmes*, 457, 743–45.

9. According to Wiesner, Catholic writers were more open than Protestants to women working as "domestic missionaries." However, English Puritans encouraged women to do so (*Women and Gender*, 190, 202).

10. Each faith accused mistresses of households of pressuring servants. See Chapter 4, note 53; and Timmermans, *Accès des femmes*, 400, 469.

Arianism, and the current one only confirmed the fact, as its history of female Bible readers and psalm singers illustrated.[11] Nicolas Le Maire took the same line later in the century and even more straightforwardly blamed women for heretical sects: "they give birth to heresies or allow them to grow; it is in the *ruelles* that these great quarrels that trouble the Church have begun."[12]

Huguenot writers could not very well hold women responsible for Catholicism, but they could certainly criticize the prominent Catholic women mystics whom the Church celebrated. Protestants saw female mystics as pseudo-devout women; for example, they denounced the spirituality of a Teresa of Avila as outlandish, nurtured by fallacious Catholic religious texts and a false piety.[13] Teresa's followers in France, the mystics grouped around Madame Acarie, were targeted for the same sort of criticism. Huguenot author David Blondel referred to them as false prophets and energumens (those suffering from demonic possession).[14] Protestants also used other feminine figures to embarrass their rivals. They accused Catholics of supplanting the devotion due only to God with that to the Virgin Mary and female saints. And Huguenot polemicists frequently dredged up the legend of the medieval "Pope Joan" to demonstrate further the Roman Church's shortcomings.[15]

The Protestant clergy was suspicious of women whose intellectual curiosity exceeded strict limits. André Rivet, onetime chaplain of the La Tré-

11. *L'histoire de la naissance, progrez et decadence de l'hérésie de ce siècle* (Rouen, ed. 1622), quoted in Solé, *Débat*, 1:295–96; Davis, "City Women and Religious Change," 65.

12. From Nicolas Le Maire, *Le sanctuaire fermé aux profanes, ou la Bible deffendue au vulgaire* (1651), quoted in Timmermans, *Accès des femmes*, 746. "Ruelles" refers to the bedside of women around which salons gathered or to the literary or intellectual coteries over which prominent women intellectuals presided. Hence, Le Maire makes an association here between women's learning and heresy.

13. I am following here Solé's description of Pierre Dumoulin's ideas from his *Le juge des controverses, Traité auquel est défendue l'autorité et la perfection de la Sainte Ecriture, contre les usurpations et accusations de l'église romaine* (1630). See *Débat*, 1:297.

14. Solé, *Débat*, 3:1560.

15. Solé, *Débat*, 2:662–70. Dolan's work shows how Protestants in England saw women as being both the sign of Catholicism's error (e.g., devotion to Mary) and the means of its survival in the Protestant country (e.g., Queen Henrietta Maria) (see *Whores of Babylon*, 95–156).

moille family in Poitou and later a professor in Leiden, wrote to the eminent and controversial theologian, linguist, and spiritual autobiographer Anna-Maria van Schurman that "it suffices in my opinion that there are some [women] who, feeling pushed by a particular inclination and animated by a noble desire to understand beautiful things, raise themselves above others of their sex and render themselves capable of the highest learning." But they should not read the Bible in its "holy languages" because they do not have "strong enough minds" or "minds capable of *bonnes lettres*."[16] Van Schurman's later association with the Labadist sect would give ample proof to Protestants and Catholics of the dangers of women meddling in theology.[17]

Yet, as a means of criticizing their confessional rivals, Protestants also celebrated women who exceeded gender expectations. These heroines were exemplars of the "devout sex"; they displayed a virile spirituality and a legitimate desire for religious learning. Protestants had maintained the necessity of women reading and studying the Bible, though only under the careful guidance of their husbands and pastors. And they frequently praised Huguenot women for their religious knowledge. Some even argued that women should be allowed access to, at least, a limited religious education so that they could serve as proselytizers. The noted minister and ardent anti-Catholic polemicist Pierre Dumoulin played to women's devotional concerns and desire for learning as a means of criticizing his Catholic opponents. In a sermon to his congregants in Sedan, delivered in the presence of Capuchin friars, he criticized the Catholic clergy for forbidding women any role in religious life. Priests would rather see their female parishioners reading novels than Holy Scripture. "If the least woman among you went to the greatest doctor of the Roman Church and asked him 'Monsieur, please write down for me the scriptural passage in which Jesus Christ instituted in his church the sacrifice of his body [the Eu-

16. On the Rivet-van Schurman correspondence, see Timmermans, *Accès des femmes*, 303–8; and for Rivet's words, see p. 458n.154. See also Anna Maria van Schurman, *Whether a Christian Woman Should Be Educated and Other Writings from Her Intellectual Circle*, edited and translated by Joyce L. Irwin (Chicago, 1998); and Natalie Zemon Davis, *Women on the Margins*, 161–62, 231n.57.

17. Timmermans, *Accès des femmes*, 736. However, Pierre Bayle defended van Schurman; see p. 779.

charist],' you would see that he would be rendered mute or he would say that a woman should not have so much curiosity."[18]

Catholic writers, especially those like De Sales who were sympathetic to women's religious aspirations, were also willing to grant them access to Scripture providing they had special permission from the clergy.[19] Theology was more problematic. Throughout the century, most would consider it beyond women's natural capacity and detrimental to the proper feminine spiritual values of humility, simplicity, and submissiveness. And yet some writers suggested that theological reading was possible for "honorable girls," if only to improve their moral lives. In 1640 François de Grenaille (reflecting perhaps a certain courtly civility) argued that theology could not be bad for the "most perfect of [God's] creatures."[20] Writing late in the century, the ex-nun Gabrielle Suchon claimed that the full range of scriptural, patristic, and theological texts should be open to women. Through "education, study, and work, they would be capable of the greatest accomplishments."[21] Bossuet granted the women who joined his Filles de la Propagation (founded in Metz in 1658) permission to read the New Testament and receive theological instruction so that they could

18. Pierre Dumoulin, *Trois sermons faits en presence des pères Capucins qui les [nous] ont honorez de leur presence* (Paris, 1641), 37–38 (Second sermon on the sacrifice of the mass, delivered 27 November 1640).

19. I simplify here a complex series of prescriptions. Certain biblical books, such as the Apocalypse, were to be off limits to Catholic women; they were not to make Scripture the sole focus of their spiritual reading like Protestants; they were to approach their reading with a proper disposition and not seek after novelty (see Timmermans, *Accès des femmes*, 703–26). According to Timmermans, attitudes toward women's religious learning grew harsher across the seventeenth century, though the reason was the Church's struggle against Jansenism and Quietism more than its conflict with Protestantism.

20. François de Grenaille, *L'honneste fille* (1640), quoted in Timmermans, *Accès des femmes*, 769.

21. Gabrielle Suchon, *Traité de la morale et de la politique* . . . (1693), quoted in Timmermans, *Accès des femmes*, 777–79. No one went so far in arguing in favor of women's learning as did François Poullain de la Barre, whose notion that the mind has no sex led him to argue that women should not only be allowed to *study* theology but also to *teach* it. They should be able to take degrees, including "doctor and master of theology." They should be allowed to preach and take on all other ecclesiastical functions. See François Poullain de la Barre, *De l'égalité des deux sexes* (1673), quoted in Timmermans, *Accès des femmes*, 775–76.

undertake the task of working for the conversion of Protestant women.[22]

However, in the context of Catholic-Protestant polemics, women's scriptural and theological learning was quickly condemned, especially by Catholic authors. For the Jesuit Louis Richeome, the schism of the Reformation derived from women's unquenchable desire for knowledge (an echo of Eve's sin) and for public approbation. Addressing his Protestant rivals, he wrote:

> You threw the first seeds of your heresy into the world by women whom you claim to be very capable. . . . It is the customary ruse of the old Abuser to suborn women so as to deceive men. . . . [Women are] haughty in their hearts, curious for knowledge, ambitious for [public] esteem, audacious in their weakness, arrogant in their ignorance, fickle in their beliefs. . . . As soon as they have gone two or three times to your worship, [and] paged through the Bible, . . . they are more learned and capable than you. . . . It is not at doctrine that they should excel but at silence and managing the household. . . . Your women are as worthy of contempt for being learned as you are for being ignorant ministers.

Catholic women, and thus their church, were completely different.

> In the Catholic Church one has seen and sees now women well informed and instructed in God's law and even in good letters, but their knowledge has not led them to abandon modesty, as yours have, to throw themselves into disputes. . . . They remember very well the teaching of St. Paul, which prohibits women from speaking in public and permits them only to pose questions to their husbands at home.[23]

Catholic women are not ignorant; they are not to be denied an understanding of their faith. But Protestant women are condemned. The question for Richeome is how women's religious knowledge is used. It is only proper if exercised privately or domestically. Where Protestant women go wrong is in seeking to usurp a public role that is not properly theirs. Of course, the cause of their error is not simply in themselves; it is in their church. All women would act this way if they were not kept within prop-

22. Jacques-Bénigne Bossuet, *Catéchisme*, quoted in Timmermans, *Accès des femmes*, 455–56, 712.

23. Richeome, *Idolatrie huguenote*, 573–77.

er boundaries, which is what the Catholic Church does. Catholic women are mindful of Scripture, especially of Paul's admonitions. It is a sign of Protestantism's falsity that its women are not similarly constrained.

Catholic writers ridiculed Protestant *doctoresses*, and thereby condemned the Reformed Church.[24] Nicolas Le Maire claimed that "it is an old custom among the heretics to corrupt Scripture and adulterate . . . the word of God. And after having corrupted it, they sow it among the vulgar, principally among women, and give everyone the right to read and interpret it."[25] The Jesuit Jean Gontery criticized the Reformed Church for admitting women to pastoral functions, which, of course, it did not do.[26] Huguenot women's liberty to read Scripture resulted in an insatiable desire that was both intellectual and sexual. The Jesuit François Garasse charged that the daughters of Protestant ministers have filled their fathers' homes with scandal for having read Scripture "too licentiously."[27] And some Catholic writers felt anxious about just what Protestant women might do with their learning. For Léonard de Marandé, it was unacceptable that Huguenots "took such care in the instruction of their women and children, thereby rendering them capable (through the deceitful ruses of their false doctrine) . . . of embarrassing in debates those among us who are of the highest dignities."[28]

Huguenot writers similarly dismissed the intellectual and theological interests of Catholic women. In April 1609, Dumoulin met the Jesuit Gontery in a debate in Paris.[29] The details of the contest were disputed in each side's subsequent publications, but as in many such encounters the occasion for the debate was a Huguenot woman's ostensible interest in conversion.[30] Unlike other debates, however, the audience appears to have

24. Timmermans, *Accès des femmes*, 726–806.

25. Le Maire, *Sanctuaire fermé aux profanes*, quoted in Timmermans, *Accès des femmes*, 716.

26. *Pierre de Touche* (1614), cited in Solé, *Débat*, 2:296.

27. Garasse, *Doctrine curieuse*, quoted in Timmermans, *Accès des femmes*, 718.

28. Léonard de Marandé, *Le théologien françois* (1641), quoted in Timmermans, *Accès des femmes*, 455–56. This comment might be taken as a backhanded compliment of Protestant women's learning, though certainly it was not intended as such.

29. On the debate and the various publications by both sides that emerged from it, see Kappler, "Conférences théologiques," 2:93–98.

30. I follow here Kappler's discussion of Pierre Dumoulin's *Veritable narré de la conference entre les Sieurs Du Moulin et Gontier secondé par Madame la Baronne de Salignac, le*

consisted primarily of women, and, what is more striking, initially they appear to have been Dumoulin's chief interlocutors. Before the Jesuit's tardy arrival, one of the women began posing questions to the minister on Article 31 of the French Reformed Church's *Confession of Faith* concerning the vocation of pastors. He tried to evade the issue by saying that he needed to return to his lodgings to prepare for such an interrogation. Another woman retorted by saying that one should always be ready to give the reasons for one's faith; Dumoulin should not refuse to instruct those who requested it. Again, by his own account, the minister responded that he well knew that they were not interested in instruction and that to debate religion with women, who all wanted to speak at the same time and then go off and publish whatever pleased them, would be to do wrong to religious truth. The topic then changed to the issue of the Real Presence, and Gontery, who had appeared, took over for the Catholic side. But at least one woman, a Madame de Salignac, continued to intervene by adding citations from Church Fathers to the Jesuit's from Scripture, though Dumoulin dismissed her knowledge of patristic texts.[31] It might seem to us that the minister's own account puts him in a bad light. He comes across as patronizing and petulant. But his description of the encounter may have made a different point to his coreligionists. Here was a debate scene that women dominated, an affront to religious truth and to decorum. And his retelling of the encounter reflected badly on his Jesuit rivals; they appear to need the help of women. Ultimately, of course, it is the Catholic Church that is at fault: it allowed women too prominent a role. How could such a church claim to be the true faith?

Thus early-modern women faced deeply embedded contradictions in attitudes toward their religiosity. Writers invested their religious lives with exemplary worth, while simultaneously disparaging female spirituality. The male clergy castigated women for seeking or exercising authority, but

samedy 11 avril, 1609 (1609). The woman in question was a Madame Mazencourt, wife of a Catholic. According to Kappler, in another publication, Dumoulin presented a different version of what happened, in which the target for conversion was not Mazencourt but a relative (see "Conférences théologiques," 2:95–96).

31. Some details from this second part of the debate come from Kappler's discussion of another Protestant account by Louis de Corbozon de Montgommery, *Refutation du faux discours de la conference entre le Reverend Pere Gonthery de la Compagnie de Jesus, et le Sieur du Moulin . . .* (Rouen, 1609). See "Conférences théologiques," 2:95–96.

at the same time celebrated them for their religious accomplishments and sought them out because of those accomplishments, thereby endowing them with authority. The contradictions in these attitudes made the discourse on women, both real women and, as we will see below, imagined ones, a potent means of attacking and a redoubtable means of defending churches. But more than that, in creating a "complex dynamic that both recognized [women's] importance and repudiated the value of their influence," the opposing views of women made them an ideal way of thinking about religious difference and for constructing the strictest form of boundary between the churches.[32]

THE "MINISTRESSE NICOLE": A POETIC CHARIVARI

The contentious discourse on women's religious lives did not appear just in the debates among the clergy. It could also be found in literature intended for a less professional audience, as was evident in the account of a Poitevin woman named Nicole. She was a *ministresse*, in other words, a female minister. Of course, no such thing as a ministresse existed; no women became ministers in the French Reformed Church. Instead, the ministresse Nicole appeared in an anonymous mid-seventeenth-century poem, written in the local Poitevin language.[33] The poem recounts the "true" adventures of a Protestant servant to the minister of Fontenay-le-Comte, Isaac Du Soul, who served from 1663 to 1685.[34] The Catholic au-

32. I borrow this formulation from S. Annette Finley-Crosswhite, who makes it concerning women's roles in the Wars of Religion ("Engendering the Wars of Religion: Female Agency during the Catholic League in Dijon," *French Historical Studies* 20, no. 2 [Spring 1997]: 127–54, see esp. 154).

33. "La ministresse Nicole. Dialogue poictevin de Josué et de Jacot, ou l'histoire ou vray de ce qui arriva chez le ministre Dusou et dans le temple des huguenots de Fontenay le premier jour de may 1665" (Niort, 1882). Page citations will follow in the text.

34. Dez, *Histoire des protestants*, 446. It is worth remarking on the "truth" of what the poem describes. Its title claims the story's validity and the editor of the nineteenth-century edition I have used agreed. I have, however, found no other trace of Nicole. The Fontenay historian B. Fillon suggests that the poem emerged from a period of heightened confessional tension in Fontenay after the court decision of 1665 that ordered the closure of Huguenot temples in numerous Poitevin communities, though not in Fontenay (*Recueil de notes sur les origins de l'église réformée de Fontenay-le-Comte et sur ses pasteurs* [Niort, 1888], 101). He does not, however, mention a real Nicole. Since my concern here is the poem's use in religious polemics and boundary construction,

thor poked fun at Huguenots by using Nicole's carnivalesque deeds to demonstrate what happens when a woman gains religious knowledge and attempts to use it in public. She turns things upside down. The poem targets the church in which a servant woman could carry on in such a manner and get away with it. Nicole was not the only Huguenot ministresse to show up in Catholic polemical writing, though it more often criticized Protestant doctoresses than ministresses. The Jesuit Jacques Gaulthier pilloried the Huguenots of his native Vivarais for their ministresses and made even more explicit than the Poitevin poet the connection between their authority and immorality. According to him, the influence women had among Protestants derived from sexual depravity, of which Catholics had accused Protestants since Luther. It was what had led to their break with and criticism of the Catholic clergy's practice of celibacy.[35]

"La Ministresse Nicole" was written in the provincial patois, which is significant for its purpose as a confessional polemic. Poitevin became a literary language in the late sixteenth century. Writers who attended the Poitiers salon of the poets Madeleine and Catherine des Roches turned to the patois for literary amusement, after undertaking their more serious endeavors in Latin or French.[36] Poitevin was used primarily for comic poems, which recounted the events of the day through the characters of "simple" locals, added a picturesque element to literary gamesmanship, and—perhaps—also testified to a certain local chauvinism. In the seventeenth century, Poitevin poems were still used to comment on local events, but the language was no longer the preserve of Poitiers humanists. The authors now included a small-town apothecary, Jean Drouhet, and a parish priest, Jean Babu. The subjects of their poems were the confession-

the existence of an actual Nicole hardly matters. However, other anti-Protestant Poitevin poems of the seventeenth century did retell real events.

35. Solé, *Débat*, 3:1420.

36. Local elites produced a patois literature as did their counterparts in other provinces—Normandy, Burgundy, Flanders, and so forth—just as French was becoming established as a national language. See J. Pignon, *La gente poitevinrie: Recueil des texts en patois poitevin du XVIe siècle* (Paris, 1960), 6–15; Pierre Gachignard, *Dictionnaire du patois du marais poitevin: Particulièrement celui du canton de Maillezais et des communes voisines de Vendée, Charente-Maritime, et Deux-Sèvres* (Marseilles, 1983); and Pierre Rézeau, *Le "Vocabulaire poitevin" (1803–1825) de Lubin Mauduyt: Édition critique d'après Poitiers, Bibl. Mun., ms. 837* (Tübingen, 1994).

al debates of the day and the destruction of Protestant temples.[37] The use of Poitevin in these poems raises the possibility that the language itself was seen as a weapon in the confessional battle. I know of no local Huguenot literature in the patois; the literary language of Protestants was resolutely French. Was, therefore, this use of Poitevin to recount the misfortunes of Poitou's Huguenots a means of suggesting they had no right to the local language and no rightful place in local communities?

The poem is a dialogue in which "Josué," a Huguenot of Fontenay, relates the scandal of Nicole to his fellow Huguenot, "Jacot." "I have to tell you what is weighing heavily on my chest," Josué says to his friend, "you know the servant Nicole who has long served Monsieur Dusou [Du Soul], a minister . . . with as worried a look as you can find in this country and perhaps in all of France . . . but who preaches with great eloquence . . . in the marketplace . . . to every priest, monk, Jesuit, and Capuchin." His servant Nicole "has learned to read." Indeed, she has learned so well that she "has surpassed many of our elders" (14).

What happens when a woman, and a servant at that, learns to read is what one might expect. She apes her master, the pastor "Dusou." "One fine day I saw her," Josué reports, "dispute a learned papist in the street"—much as her minister might have debated Jesuits or Capuchins—"even though she had only just learned her ABC's."[38] She "took courage" from her encounter with the papist and threw herself into her studies. She offers to help her master write his sermons, which she can accomplish in such "a good fashion, that no *proposant* [a minister in training] would do better." She becomes so eager to learn that "she neither sews nor spins;

37. Jean Drouhet, *Les oeuvres de Jean Drouhet, maître apothicaire à Saint-Maixent*, edited by A. Richard (Poiters, 1878); see in particular "Les deloirements d'in Oncien des Huguenots de Chondené apré la rouine do Préche: surtout ce qui s'est fait & passé pendant la demolition du temple le 13 sept. 1663" (Poitiers, 1663). Also see Jean Babu, *Églogues poitevines sur différentes matières de controverse, pour le vulgaire du Poitou* (Niort, 1875), and *Poésies de Jean Babu, curé de Soudan, sur les ruines des temples protestants de Champdeniers, d'Exoudun, de La Mothe-Saint-Hérayе (1663–1682)*, edited by A. Richard (Poitiers, 1896).

38. In doing so Nicole had a real sixteenth-century predecessor, the Poitevin servant Marie Becaudelle, who appears in Jean Crespin's martyrology. Having learned Scripture thanks to her master, she used her knowledge to debate a Cordelier. See Evelyne Berriot-Salvadore, *Les femmes dans la société française de la renaissance* (Geneva, 1990), 66; and Davis, "City Women and Religious Change," 79.

night and day at her work she just sings [hymns] . . . and irritates her master" (15). Her arrogance grows day by day; she is like a "cock of the walk." But "she speaks so well and with such good grace that I [Josué] have never seen a doctor who could everyone so enlace."

The servant woman with a minister's learning assumed the minister's duties. A number of inebriated friends arrive, unmarried men and women, ready to be paired off. They want a group wedding, but no pastor would ever agree to such a thing. So "they cast their eyes on Nicole . . . she is well educated, and even if she is only a servant, her master has trained her well." They go to the temple and plant themselves before the pulpit, which Nicole mounts dressed in the robe and hat of her master. An element of cross-dressing has been added to the carnivalesque fun. But the clothing is significant because what she is wearing—the robe and hat—are a pastor's insignia. She performs the wedding by reading to "her small flock what a minister reads for a marriage." She leads them in singing the 51st Psalm, which "they butcher right up to the last line." She then teaches them another, the 110th: "'He is the all-powerful,'" a "ravishing air," to which she adds the phrase "kiss me my dear" (18). Nicole also wants to marry one Jacques Pinet, and so she turns her pulpit and robe over to one of the company. He sets himself furiously to reading the New Testament, like "the school ass," and then says outloud: "You, Pinet and Nicole, do you want each other? Then take each other." This is a disgraceful wedding to be sure, and another member of the group says so: "My faith! Don't you know anything, my son? Lend me that robe; I'll have to marry them, and I'll do better than you. . . . Gather around everyone and see if I have what it takes to be a minister" (19).

With everyone now married, the group returns reveling to "Dusou's" house. News of the scandal spreads and Nicole is called before the consistory. She is anything but repentant and vaunts her learning to defend what she has done. "She has seen in Luther and the savant Saumaise that women and men and all who are alive, as long as they are faithful and learned, can be ministers and perform the exercises [of the church]" (22).[39] The reference here is not simply to Nicole's presumption but also

39. Claude de Saumaise (1588–1653), Huguenot scholar and professor at the University of Leiden, noted for writings against the papacy's authority and claim to apostolic succession. See Léonard, *Histoire générale du protestantisme*, 2:334, 353.

to Luther's notion of the priesthood of all believers. Of course, it pushes Protestant doctrine to the point of absurdity; Luther did not envision ministresses. But Nicole thus argues that she has done nothing against her conscience and should not be blamed for what the great doctors allow. She believes with complete confidence that "[the Lord] gives to each of the elect a particular spirit" that enables each to go "here and there doing the divine will" (perhaps a caricature of Calvin's notion of the "calling"). What she has done is not wrong; it is well founded in doctrine as prescribed in the "articles of faith." The consistory does not frighten her, and if they call her before the regional colloque, she "will rent a hundred horses to take her there." And if the colloque does not judge her "according to her style," she will appeal to the provincial synod. As far as she is concerned the elders are "as dumb as a stump" (lit., "a rug"). They cannot read, and if one of them is challenged, it becomes quickly apparent that he "knows nothing other than how to eat his bread." "She knows the truth better than those young scoundrels [the proposants] who climb into the pulpit as soon as they return from school." She has had lessons for ten years while working in the kitchen. And "if Mr. Dusou or Mr. Pin [Daniel Pain, second minister at Fontenay from 1665 to 1685] happened to be absent on a Sunday, she could mount the pulpit to give the sermon and marry people without anyone preventing it" (23).

What are the men of the consistory to do with such a woman? She has turned the tables on them with her "learning"; she has claimed religious authority no woman should have. And her challenge suggests a certain social tension as well as gender difference. For she is a servant, and as she says of the elders, we know "who are the best mounted when returning from the fair." The use of a servant girl to mock and outwit her superiors is a common literary motif; one need only think of another nearly contemporary Nicole, that in Molière's *The Bourgeois Gentleman*, who outmaneuvers her master, Monsieur Jourdain, at every turn. Here too the servant is more than a match for the men she is supposed to obey. Nicole's challenge to them, or that of the poet, is shrewd. By the second half of the century, when the state's legal campaign against Protestantism was escalating, real consistories often hesitated to treat offenders harshly for fear they would desert to the other side.[40] So too the poem's consistory. The

40. Hanlon, *Confession and Community*, 204–6.

astonished elders, faced with Nicole, agree to say nothing, for "fear that she would undertake . . . to render herself a papist and do in our church" (23). Poor Josué—the story has weighed on him heavily—and his friend Jacot is also worried: "This tale is vexing, I cannot say less. But my greatest torment is that it will make all the papists of the town and those from far away laugh. It could run through the rest of Poitou" (24).

I like to think of "La Ministresse Nicole" as a poetic charivari. Townspeople and villagers often employed charivaris to maintain communal norms by ritually humiliating spouses who made what were deemed inappropriate weddings—for example, matches in which the couple differed widely in age. They were also used in situations in which women assumed too much authority, and thereby criticized husbands who allowed their wives to rule or beat them.[41] "La Ministresse Nicole" picks up both themes but with twists. The poem's marriages are certainly irregular, but it is the church, which allows such a state of affairs, that is targeted. These matches turn Protestant marriage regulations upside-down, but what else is to be expected from a religion based on error? And the church and its minister cannot control Nicole. She has become a burlesque man. Her master and pastor, "Dusou," has taught her to read, a mistake for a woman and a servant. She should have no need for and not be exposed to such an education, but because she is a woman she pursues more learning until she is preaching, teaching, performing marriages, defending herself through her half-baked knowledge of doctrine, and successfully defying the dim-witted elders. Only in a false church could a woman and a servant learn and make public use of what only a clergyman is supposed to know. No wonder this scandal so worries poor Josué and Jacot; they and their coreligionists will be laughingstocks, rejected by all who adhere to the true faith and who know how to keep women in their place.

HUGUENOT AMAZONS

Nicole was a comic invention intended to provoke laughter among Catholics and embarrassment among Huguenots. Real Protestant wom-

41. Natalie Zemon Davis, "The Reasons of Misrule" and "Women on Top," in *Society and Culture in Early Modern France* (Stanford, Calif., 1975), 97–123, 124–51. See also Jacques Le Goff and Jean-Claude Schmitt, eds., *Le charivari* (Paris, 1981).

en, especially those from aristocratic families, were more frightening to Catholicism's defenders. In the Catholic imagination, such women became protectors of the false religion through their power, stubbornness, and immodest entry into public affairs. The efforts of these women were important to the existence of Protestantism in France, but because they could be accused of transgressing the acceptable limits on womanly behavior, their actions appeared remarkable and outrageous. The most shocking were Protestant "amazons," whose engagement in military action on behalf of their faith singled them out for special opprobrium and punishment. The figure of the amazon occupied a prominent and troubling place in early-modern culture, appearing in dramatic works, in novels, and in the reports of explorers who described amazons they encountered in the Americas. As Joan DeJean has pointed out, real amazons seemed to share a great deal with literary representations of amazons, and the general proliferation of amazons was all the more disturbing when it was coupled with religious heterodoxy and political disorder.[42]

The Duchesse de Rohan

Poitou produced a number of Huguenot amazons, but the most notable was Catherine de Parthenay, duchesse de Rohan. She provoked all sorts of anxieties. Rohan came from one of French Protestantism's most illustrious families. She was the daughter of Jean de Parthenay-l'Archévêque, a sixteenth-century Huguenot military leader, and the granddaughter of Michelle de Saubonne (Madame de Soubise), one of the first aristocratic women who openly joined the Reformed Church.[43] Her sons, Henri, duc de Rohan, and Benjamin, duc de Soubise, were the last great Huguenot military leaders and opponents of royal authority. She served as a guardian of Protestant worship in her seigneurial domains, such as in Blain (Brittany) and Parthenay (Poitou). As we have seen, the Capuchin mission in Poitou made a special target of her estates at Mouchamps and Vendrennes, where Huguenots worshipped in the duchess's château. According to the mission chronicle, the mass was not celebrated there because the curé was under the power of this "sworn en-

42. Joan DeJean, *Tender Geographies: Women and the Origins of the Novel in France* (New York, 1991), 24–26.

43. Roelker, "Appeal of Calvinism," 399.

emy of the Catholic Church."[44] Huguenot leaders, like Duplessis-Mornay, conferred with her frequently on political matters and respected her opinions. She provided, along with him, leadership for the moderate Huguenot party during the 1610s. She tried directly, though not very successfully, to exert maternal influence over her dangerously ambitious sons by reminding them of the loyalty they owed their monarch.[45]

During the wars of the 1620s, however, she seemed less interested in displaying "feminine" moderation. On Christmas Eve 1623 in her seigneurie of Mouchamps, where Catholic worship had only recently been reestablished, Huguenots resorted to violence to prevent Catholics from going to mass. The duchess may not have encouraged the attack, but she did turn a blind eye to it. And over the next two years she pointedly ignored royal orders that the churches at Mouchamps and Vendrennes be turned over to Catholics.[46]

The duchess and her daughters, Henriette and Anne, also confounded the prejudices against women's intellectual activities. All were learned humanists and poets, well versed in religious issues; Anne read the Old Testament in Hebrew.[47] As we have seen, women's learning could be a controversial matter. Nonetheless, Huguenots commended the Rohan women for their achievements, albeit with the sort of condescending gallantry common in male writers' comments about their female counterparts. Agrippa d'Aubigné wrote of them: "We have seen shine in France, that excellent mirror, the Duchesse de Rohan . . . and her daughter Anne. The writings of these two have more than once made us hide our pens! In these two, intellectual and moral virtues engage in gentle combat to see which one will triumph."[48]

44. On Blain, see Nicole Vray, *Catherine de Parthenay, duchesse de Rohan: Protestante insoumise (1554–1631)* (Paris, 1998), 133–34. On Parthenay, see above, pp. 23–26 and BMP Collection Fonteneau, vol. 79, 303–6 (other copy in BPF Ms. 869 [1]). On the mission, see above, p. 98. The Catholic version of what happened at Mouchamps can be followed in the "Recueils" and in *Saincte messe restablie a Mouchamp*.

45. Vray, *Catherine de Parthenay*, 136–37. Duplessis-Mornay sought the duchess's help in reining in her troublesome sons during the political disputes of the 1610s.

46. Vray, *Catherine de Parthenay*, 152.

47. Timmermans, *Accès des femmes*, 65, 66n.20; Papiers Maillard: Notes on the Huguenot prisoners of the donjon of Niort, BPF Ms. 868 (5). See also Vray, *Catherine de Parthenay*, 176–77.

48. Quoted in Vray, *Catherine de Parthenay*, 176. The catty Tallement des Réaux was

But it is not for her learning and literary accomplishments that the duchess was celebrated and condemned as a Huguenot amazon; rather, it was because of her role in the defense of La Rochelle in 1627–1628. Although she was in her seventies at the time, she and her daughter Anne remained in the city throughout the long siege, which won them great popularity among the Rochelais. Sylvie Steinberg has described how helping to defend besieged cities was one military role that writers found acceptable, if still exceptional, for women. D'Aubigné and François de la Noue, both former Huguenot military leaders and contemporaries of Rohan, recalled the Protestant women who had helped defend Poitiers in 1569 and La Rochelle in 1572.[49] Catherine and Anne de Rohan thus fit into a model, even a local model, of Protestant amazons.

Their role in rallying Huguenot military resistance earned them Richelieu's enmity, and he imprisoned them in Niort after La Rochelle's fall. The cardinal described the duchess as "malign to the end." And when she offered to intercede with her son Henri, who was still campaigning in the south, if Richelieu would grant her release from prison, he refused her request for fear that she would instead work "right up to the end to strengthen her son and his party in rebellion."[50]

Catherine de Parthenay was celebrated as a Protestant heroine and condemned as a "sworn enemy" of Catholics precisely because she exceeded the usual gender expectations. She fulfilled a heroic role in protecting Huguenot churches, in defying royal military might, and in pursuing learning and literary accomplishment. But we must recognize that aristocratic status, family political ambitions, and seigneurial obligations shaped Rohan's activities as much as did her religious convictions. Con-

---

less impressed. In commenting on Anne's poems, he wrote: "to tell the truth, the poems weren't the best in the world" (*Les Historiettes de Tallemant des Réaux*, 3rd ed., 10 vols. [Paris, 1840–1861], 3:98).

49. Sylvie Steinberg, "Le mythe des amazons et son utilization politique de la renaissance à la Fronde," in *Royaume de fémynie: Pouvoirs, contraintes, espaces de liberté des femmes de la renaissance à la Fronde*, edited by Kathleen Wilson-Chevalier and Eliane Viennot (Paris, 1999), 261–73, see esp. 263–64. On women's military activities in the Wars of Religion, see Finley-Crosswhite, "Engendering the Wars of Religion."

50. Quoted from Richelieu's *Mémoires* in Vray, *Catherine de Parthenay*, 173. See Parker, *La Rochelle and the French Monarchy*, 99, 105. She was released in a general amnesty in 1629 and died in 1631.

temporaries and later commentators found her an exceptional woman, but in many respects she was not unusual. Her literary and intellectual endeavors were part of a tradition of aristocratic women humanists. Her management of the Rohan family interests and her protection of those living on her family's estates were customary obligations of noblewomen, especially widows like Catherine. Her protection of local Huguenot congregations was part of a tradition extending back to the beginnings of the Reformed faith in France and forward beyond the Revocation.[51]

If Catherine de Parthenay was perceived as more heroic or more frightening than a typical aristocratic woman, it was because she was very useful to both sides in the confessional conflict. She fit both the positive and the negative images of the amazon drawn from contemporary literature. Steinberg has shown how the literary amazon combined the masculine aristocratic value of magnanimity with the feminine value of chastity. In this way, amazons proved their leadership qualifications. The duchess lived up to both sides of the image. Courage and self-sacrifice she displayed at La Rochelle. Chastity she demonstrated by never remarrying after she was widowed in 1586 (her daughter Anne never married). On her own she raised her children, managed family affairs, and took on a leading role in the Reformed Church. Furthermore, fictional amazons often served as defenders of last resort for the places they protected; God chose them to act when men had lost their courage.[52] During the siege of La Rochelle, she was the figure with the highest social rank in the city, rallying its defense of God's beleaguered "petit troupeau." Her sons, who would have seemed the more "natural" leaders of Huguenot armed resistance, did much less to help the city. She thus was well suited to be-

51. For discussions of earlier Protestant heroines and their place within French Protestantism, see Roelker, "Appeal of Calvinism" and "The Role of Noblewomen in the French Reformation," *Archive for Reformation History* 63 (1972): 168–95. See also Davis, "City Women and Religious Change"; Charmarie Jenkins Blaisdell, "Renée de France between Reform and Counter-Reform," *Archive for Reformation History* 63 (1972): 196–225; and Blaisdell, "Calvin's Letters to Women: The Courting of Ladies in High Places," *Sixteenth Century Journal* 13, no. 3 (1982): 67–84. As Wiesner points out, the ability of "a woman to act out her religious convictions" was always greater for noblewomen than for their social inferiors (*Women and Gender*, 189).

52. Steinberg, "Mythe des amazons," 261–73. On the amazons of the Fronde and literary models, see Danielle Haase-Dubosc, *Ravie et enlevée: De l'enlèvement des femmes comme stratégie matrimoniale au XVIIe siècle* (Paris, 1999), 41.

come a symbol for both sides: to Huguenots, of conviction and courage in the face of defeat; to Catholics, of stubbornness and female aristocratic power used to maintain heresy. Both groups would have found her amazonian because she was a woman who took on male roles. For Catholics, such unnaturalness was exactly what happened when a woman of the rival faith went beyond the bounds of her sex. Protestants celebrated her precisely for that reason.

The Amazons of Exoudun

The fall of La Rochelle in 1628 and Henri de Rohan's submission the next year marked the end of Protestant military power in France. But the efforts of Huguenot amazons in defending their faith did not come to an end. They continued to protect their increasingly beleaguered coreligionists—for example, by resisting government attempts to close down Reformed worship. Among the numerous temples condemned during intendant Colbert de Croissy's 1665 campaign against Protestantism in the province was that of Exoudun in Moyen-Poitou.[53] Condemning temples, however, was easier than actually destroying them. Huguenots themselves were responsible for the demolition, and when they dragged their feet, it fell to the syndic of the province's Catholic clergy and local judicial officials to undertake the job.

In Exoudun, Catholic authorities ran into trouble. By late 1666 local Protestants had done nothing to carry out the demolition orders. At that point, the Poitiers diocese's syndic, Hubert de Bret, took matters in hand. He advanced a sizeable sum to hire workers, but when they arrived in the vicinity of Exoudun, they found that two Huguenot noblewomen—Marguerite de Saint-Georges, widow of Bonaventure Forain, seigneur d'Exoudun, and her daughter, Louise Forain, widow of Pierre Vasselot, seigneur de Regny—had organized large-scale resistance.[54] They had gathered some two to three thousand men (the numbers vary in different accounts of the confrontation), armed them, and stationed them in the tem-

53. On the temple condemnations, see above, pp. 177–78.

54. On the two women, see the comments of Alfred Richard in Babu, *Poésies de Jean Babu*, 78–79. Marguerite de Saint-Georges was from a powerful aristocratic Protestant family of Couhé. According to Richard, some considered Louise Forain the prime instigator of the incident.

ple, the château, and around the town's perimeter. Provincial officials and the royal government were well aware of strong opposition in the area to the destruction of temples. Pastors reportedly had urged resistance in their sermons. The provincial synod that met at Lusignan in 1666 included ministers from interdicted communities, despite orders not to do so. The synod urged them to continue preaching in the ruins of temples already destroyed or in nearby fields, thereby frustrating attempts to shut down Protestant worship. But authorities were clearly shocked by the "seditious assembly" in Exoudun and by the role of the two women. When Colbert de Croissy's successor as intendant, Jacques-Honoré Barentin, investigated the armed resistance, the women greeted him with "seditious and assertive discourses."[55] The response was swift. A royal *lettre de cachet* (extrajudicial warrant) ordered their arrest and imprisonment. Marguerite de Saint-Georges's fate is not clear; she may have died in prison or perhaps she was released because of her age. Louise Forain spent three years in the Bastille and was released only upon promising not to return to Poitou.[56] Louis's order referred to the women as "unsubmissive"; their activities were "prejudicial to my authority" and a "dangerous example."[57]

Not surprisingly, the Protestant historian Elie Benoist had a more positive view. He suggested that the syndic and the Catholic intendant thought they would have an easy time destroying Exoudun's temple precisely because the town was under the authority of women. "However, the [Catholics] did not find the docility they expected." "It was hardly worthy of a great king to expend so much of his authority and so many troops to stop two women." But "such was the fear [royal officials] had of a bold and enterprising woman [Forain], who, by her example, could have raised the courage of the Protestants in a province where they were still capable of defending themselves."[58] Ironically, the removal from Exoudun

55. According to Benoist, *Histoire de l'Edit de Nantes*, 4:90–91.

56. "Requestes presentée au roy . . . par le sindic du clergé du diocèse de Poitiers," (no date), AN TT 262, pp. 204–7.

57. Filleau, *Décisions catholiques*, 851–54, see esp. 852. On the Exoudun resistance, see also Lièvre, *Histoire des protestants*, 2:77–79; and Dez, *Histoire des protestants*, 337–40.

58. Benoist, *Histoire de l'Edit de Nantes*, 4:90–92. In the wake of the Exoudun incident, Barentin took no chances in closing the temple in nearby Couhé, which also had

of the two Huguenot amazons left another woman in authority, Saint-Georges's granddaughter, the Marquise de La Barre. But she offered no further obstruction to the temple's destruction.

The resistance of Huguenot women at Exoudun was ultimately unsuccessful, but it did contribute further to the reputation of Poitevin Protestant women as amazons, stubborn and tenacious defenders of their faith, who offered hope to beleaguered Huguenots. These women have not commanded as much attention as Catherine de Parthenay, but, like her, they fit the literary image of amazons as brave, magnanimous, and chaste. They displayed their courage in a last-ditch defense of their local congregations, and they acted without the protection or guidance of men. Although reports suggested that local ministers helped whip up enthusiasm for resistance, political and military leadership came from these women, who were widows.[59] The government's reaction to them shows how little it was willing in the 1660s to suffer any open resistance to its religious policies, and indeed any resistance at all in potentially restive provinces. But it also betrays a particular anxiety about amazons. Louis and his officials may have been especially sensitized to the issue of women-led rebellion by humiliating memories of armies led by notable and notorious aristocratic amazons during the Fronde.[60] They were not Protestants, and the danger they had presented was far greater than that of the women in Exoudun. But the Poitou amazons compounded their threat with heresy, an association further confirming Catholics in their belief that both were unnatural and both would have to be defeated together.

---

a woman defender, Marguerite de la Muce, dowager marquise de Vérac. She filed a legal protest with the intendant to stop destruction of the temple, which was located in the courtyard of her château. He ignored her and sent two cavalry companies to carry out the demolition. The Huguenot commissioner La Noue complained that Barentin had resorted to force unnecessarily; his coreligionists had offered no other resistance than that of the marquise's legal plea. See "Procez-verbal au sujet de la demolition du temple de Coué, 12 janvier 1667," AN TT 241 (2), pp. 398–410.

59. See Filleau's comments on Minister Cuville of Couhé, *Décisions catholiques*, 853.

60. DeJean, *Tender Geographies*, 24–42; Haase-Dubosc, *Ravie et enlevée*, 88–89.

THE HUGUENOT 'FEMMES FORTES'

Not all controversial Protestant women participated in the military defense of their faith. Thus they were not all seen literally as amazons, an increasingly problematic characterization of women in the years after the Fronde. They might better be thought of as femmes fortes, another depiction of provocative women and one which, like the amazon, was used both to denigrate and to celebrate powerful women. The two stereotypes shared much. In both, women could be praised for demonstrating virtues deemed masculine: courage, magnanimity, and continence. Or they could be described, as Joan DeJean has pointed out, with the terms used for aristocratic literary or historical heroes, usually of the distant past, such as strong, heroic, illustrious, and of a noble soul ("forte," "héroïque," "illustre," "généreuse"). Indeed, as we have seen with the amazons, the accounts of these women often depicted them in language borrowed from literature.[61] Yet, in contrast to the femmes fortes DeJean describes, who were part of a community of women (a characterization that works well for figures from literature or the world of literary production in salons, which is DeJean's concern), Huguenot femmes fortes, and amazons, acted as part of a confessional community. They were celebrated or vilified for doing just precisely that. Still, as was the case for literary femmes fortes, these heroines, both Protestant, and as we will see, Catholic, operated within a tradition or cultural pattern of extraordinary women's behavior. As a result, they were subject to the same praise from their coreligionists and disparagement from their religious rivals as were the amazons. In pursuing activities beyond the strictest acceptable gender boundary, they provided a means to establish a different boundary, that between the faiths.

The La Trémoilles

Aside from the Duchesse de Rohan, the most significant of the Poitou Protestant heroines were the women of the La Trémoille family. As we have seen in the previous chapter, the duchesses, Charlotte-Brabantine de Nassau and Marie de La Tour d'Auvergne, remained Protestants despite

61. DeJean, *Tender Geographies*, 17–42.

Duc Henri de La Trémoille's abjuration in 1628.[62] Even before Henri's conversion, the aristocratic patronage the duchesses could offer Huguenots was of enormous importance to the Reformed Church. Their influence was considerable throughout France and beyond. In July 1617 the pastor and elders of the Béarn churches asked Charlotte to support a commission they were sending to Paris. She urged André Rivet in 1619 to undertake a publication refuting a Catholic polemicist. Rivet wrote to her in the same year to keep her informed of the Huguenot assembly at Loudun, and, a year later, to seek her protection for a young proposant with Catholic parents.[63] In 1620 the church of Leiden wrote asking the duchess to intercede with her son and the church of Thouars so that Rivet might resign his post there and take up one it was offering him.[64] In 1625 the minister of Charenton, Charles Drelincourt, wrote praising the duchess for her encouragement of his publications and seeking a post for a Huguenot supplicant.[65]

But it was in the region of the family's seigneurial possessions that the duchess had the largest role to play. In Poitou, Saintonge, and Brittany, she provided financial support for ministers and congregations, obtained posts for Protestant clergy, and appointed coreligionists to local offices. Protestant synods and political assemblies deferred to her. In 1606 the Huguenot church at the ducal seat of Thouars asked for Charlotte's intervention when Catholics tried to obstruct their use of the church bell. The Huguenots of Saint-Savinien wrote in 1609 concerning land for a new temple that the deceased Duc Claude had granted them but which they had yet received. In 1611 she helped the Huguenots in her seigneury of Vitré (Brittany) to gain a favorable court decision, which permitted them to build a temple.[66] And in 1622 the Protestants of Thouars asked her to

62. See above, p. 173.

63. AN 1AP 353, letters 160 (concerning the publication), 165 and 169 (concerning Loudun), 173 (concerning the proposant). Charlotte-Brabantine's role as protector of Huguenot churches expanded after her husband's death in 1604, when her son was not yet six. On the duchess, and especially on her relations with her young children, see Berriot-Salvadore, *Femmes dans la société française*, 139–55, 481–502.

64. AN 1AP 353, letters 1, 8. Other letters in this dossier arrived from Pau (Béarn), Lyons, and Blois.

65. AN 1AP 652, letter of 6 September 1625.

66. AN 1AP 642, letter of 12 January 1609 (Saint-Savinien); 1AP 345, letter 15 (Thouars); 1AP 665, letters of 27 June 1611 and 12 July 1611 (Vitré).

block a local Catholic magistrate from sanctifying a chapel. The letter insisted that the mass had not been celebrated in the chapel for two hundred years; the present plan was nothing more than a scheme by their "adversary . . . to decrease the reign of God."[67]

As with the Duchesse de Rohan, social rank as much as religion obliged Charlotte to take on these responsibilities, and Catholic dependents too sought her aid. In an aristocratic clan, religious matters were part of the household's concerns but did not circumscribe them. However, Protestants felt that they had a special claim on the duchess and did not hesitate to remind her of their expectations. In 1619 the pastor of Montaigu, Nicolas de Marbais, wrote urging her not to appoint any Catholics to the offices over which she had control. To choose papists for these posts, he said, was an offense against God. Catholics were proud and intolerably presumptuous and would never serve her as well and as faithfully as her fellow Huguenots. Their rivals were convinced that "those of the religion are infallibly damned and therefore [Catholics] have no scruples against doing wrong" to Protestant employers. It was the duchess's responsibility to look out for her fellow Huguenots and thereby serve her family's interests as well. The Word of God enjoined her expressly to take care of her "domestiques" of the faith, to do well by them, and to preserve them from all others. Furthermore, by choosing Huguenots for the posts at her disposal in all her lands, she would acquit herself "of what she owed God and her own soul for the increase of this church, which is so small."[68]

Nevertheless, the duchess did not respond as her Huguenot supplicants wished if their requests conflicted with family interests. Or, at least, she sometimes found it better to mediate between the confessions rather than simply favor her own. When Louis XIII's forces were campaigning against Huguenot strongholds in 1622, the attorney of the Protestants of Vitré sought her help in preventing violence between the religious groups. He complained that a Catholic judicial officer had been conspiring against local Protestants for over a year. First, he had spread rumors that Vitré's Huguenots had filled the temple with weapons and had tried to tunnel under

67. AN 1AP 665, letter of 28 January 1622.

68. AN 1AP 668, letter of 11 April 1619 from Nicolas de Marbais (alternate spelling "Marais"). The reason for the letter was the need to choose a fiscal procurator for Montaigu. The chief candidate was a Catholic.

the château from a nearby house. He had hoped "by this fabrication to raise the Catholics against those of the religion." Having seen his first plan fail, the Catholic conceived another in which he would place ladders against the city's walls and then sound the alarm and accuse the Huguenots of trying to attack the city, a falsehood that he hoped would lead to a massacre of Vitré's Protestant inhabitants. The writer appealed to Charlotte to help Vitré's citizens "to live together in peace and good understanding . . . under the king's edicts and your authority." The duchess, having also heard from the other side in the case, responded cautiously by saying that she could take no action until she came to Vitré herself to investigate the matter. With rumors of peace circulating and "the causes of our disunity passing" it seemed better to her to urge the people of Vitré to live together "without distinction of religion in the service of his Majesty."[69] It is not surprising that conflicts such as this one, over the chapel in Thouars, or over the seigneurial posts in Montaigu, appeared in the late 1610s and 1620s, a time of heightened confessional tensions between Protestants and the royal government. However, Charlotte sought accommodation rather than confrontation by pursuing a role as an advocate strictly for her coreligionists.[70]

Still Huguenots saw Charlotte as a heroine, a femme forte. They celebrated both her activities on their behalf and her heroic piety. Drelincourt wrote in 1625, "I know how useful you are Madame to the public and to your illustrious family."[71] In 1628 the minister of Isle-Bouchard (a La Trémoille domain) pronounced her the "principal member and protectress" of his church; he counted on her "spirit, which is strong" and her "boldness, which is known to all."[72] Her coreligionists sounded this theme especially after her son's conversion in that year. She had worked hard to secure her children in the Protestant faith, directing their religious educa-

69. AN 1AP 664, letter of 31 August 1622, with duchess's note attached. The rumors of peace mentioned in this note presumably concern an end to the royal campaign against Huguenot rebels in 1622. Peace was not agreed to, however, until October. See Parker, *La Rochelle and the French Monarchy*, 13.

70. Both before and after he converted, her son followed the same policy of accommodating each side while maintaining the family's seigneurial authority over both. See above, pp. 175–77.

71. AN 1 AP 652, letter of 6 September 1625.

72. AN 1AP 650, letter of 2 September 1628, from M. Cottière.

tion and sending them to spend time in Holland during their childhood. In 1609 she sent the young Duc Henri a copy of James I's *Admonitio regis magnae brittaniae ad principes christianos*, telling him that she wanted him to read this book written "against the pope in Latin" so that he "could explain it to her in French."[73] She did not succeed in keeping him within the faith, and given the duke's rank, authority, and military power in the west, the loss to the Reformed community was a serious blow. More than ever, Protestants had to depend now on Charlotte's influence and dedication to the faith. After Henri's conversion, Pierre Dumoulin wrote that all recognized Charlotte's "zeal and ardor for God's service" and knew how she "lamented" her son's abjuration "as a wound to the Church and as idolatry planted within [her] family." She could console herself by realizing that she had done "all she could do for her son as a virtuous mother, more careful for the benefit of her children than for her own."[74] Another correspondent praised her example of "firmness, constancy, and also holy perseverance in the profession of the truth."[75] He took his terms from the discourse on women as the devout sex rather than from the negative characterization of them as weak and irresolute. In other words, Huguenots seeking her help exploited the standard descriptions of the femme forte, the devout woman, and the good mother both to encourage her continued support and, one suspects, to raise their own spirits in the face of the serious losses they faced in 1628.

Charlotte's daughter-in-law, Marie de La Tour d'Auvergne, inherited these expectations. When Henri converted in 1628, letters from prominent ministers poured in to Charlotte conveying their sorrow at the "strange and unexpected downfall" but also expressing, as did André Rivet, their confidence that the duchess and (even more importantly) her daughter-in-law would remain firm in their faith.[76] Pierre Dumoulin suggested that God, "who had given her [Marie] such wisdom, prudence, and zeal, would make use of" her.[77] She did develop the reputation of being a

73. Letter to Henri of 30 July 1609, reproduced in Berriot-Salvadore, *Femmes dans la société française*, 494.

74. AN 1AP 653, letter of 15 August 1628.

75. AN 1AP 660, letter of 24 September 1628. The writer, G. de Kinschot, was a La Trémoille family agent in the Hague.

76. AN 1AP 353, 207, letter of 21 October 1628. For similar letters, see 1AP 650 (Cottière), 653 (Dumoulin), and 660 (Kinschot).

77. AN 1AP 653, letter of 15 August 1628 to Charlotte de Nassau.

determined defender of the faith. Her prominence made her the target of Catholic attacks and Protestant defenses, which allow us to see how the churches deployed the same discourse on the religious femme forte to confront each other.

Catholics recognized the authority and influence Marie wielded and were critical not only of her but also of her husband for not exercising proper patriarchal authority over his wife. In a 1642 note on political troubles in Poitou, Cardinal Mazarin, Louis XIII's chief minister, commented that the Duc de La Trémoille "allows himself to be dominated by his wife, who is a Huguenot and sister of one of the malcontents, the Duc de Bouillon. She is a woman of spirit, who is attached to the house of the Prince de Condé. . . . [And] Poitou is a country very susceptible to sedition; the Huguenots there are powerful."[78] The connection the minister made between the potential seditiousness of the province, the strength of Protestants there, and the power and the influence of the duchess is clear. She was a Huguenot, who dominated her husband, overturning the accepted gender order in the family and, because of this family's prominence, thereby threatening political authority. The political problems to which Mazarin referred did not stem from religious conflict, but heresy and gender disorder were easily associated with them. In the 1660s the intendant Colbert de Croissy saw her as "very attached to her religion," and hence as an obstacle to Catholicism's advance. She had an "elevated spirit," but she knew "how to make herself obeyed throughout her lands; . . . she makes everyone tremble under her authority." She allowed her grandchildren only Huguenot servants, and because her husband was too complaisant, she ensured that ministers in their household instructed these children in the "so-called reformed religion." She inspired in them an extreme aversion to the word "Catholic."[79]

Her coreligionists, of course, saw her differently. Huguenots, such as those of Vitré, knew they could count on her "piety and the particular affection she has always had for those of the religion."[80] For the Charenton pastor Jean Daillé, she was the "heroine of Thouars."[81] The provincial syn-

78. L. Favre, *Histoire de la ville de Niort*, 311.

79. Colbert de Croissy, *Etat du Poitou*, 94–95.

80. La Trémoïlle, *Les La Trémoïlles*, 4:72, 90, 91–93. See also Marie's own account of her religious activities in "Mémoire de Marie de La Tour d'Auvergne," 119.

81. In a 1660 letter to Alexandre Morus, in Imbert, *Registre*, 102–3.

od at Châtellerault made a point of praising her zeal and piety because of the help she provided the church of Thouars in its search for a new minister.[82] Writing in the 1690s, Elie Benoist would remember the duchess as very "worthy . . . zealous for the religion, which she loved to the bottom of her heart," but also as an aristocrat "aspiring only to the glory of the house" into which she had married. He knew that Catholics held the contrary opinion, and they criticized the duke for not exercising his proper authority: "In truth, the Duc de La Trémoille was of a passive and unambitious spirit, but [Catholics] feared the cleverness of his wife, [who was] ambitious, full of courage, and who was in ascendance over her husband. He had no will other than hers."[83] Benoist, in other words, does not so much disagree with the Catholic characterization of the duchess as a femme forte as he accepts it and turns it around to a positive assessment.

But the most interesting accounts of her from contrary Catholic and Protestant points of view are in memoirs that emerged from her own household, one by her son, the Prince de Tarente and the other by her granddaughter (Tarente's daughter), Charlotte-Amélie, gräfin von Aldenburg. Tarente wrote after his definitive conversion to Catholicism in 1670; Charlotte wrote in Germany after having witnessed from abroad the Revocation and the end of her religion's legal existence in France. We cannot say that their appraisals of Marie de La Tour are truer or more realistic than others simply because of their proximity to her. But the duchess looms large in their accounts. The views of her in both memoirs are shaped by the important role she played in the authors' lives and by the faiths they sought to defend.

After Duc Henri's conversion in 1628, all of Marie's and his children followed him into Catholicism. However, the oldest son, Henri-Charles, future prince de Tarente, returned to Protestantism in 1640 and then reconverted to Catholicism two years before he died in 1672.[84] Charlotte-

82. Synode de Châtellerault 1663 in BPF Ms. 579 (1) Collection Auzière: Synodes et Colloques du Poitou.

83. Benoist, *Histoire de l'Edit de Nantes*, 3:56. As Benoist suggests, her activities on behalf of the Reformed Church were inextricable from aristocratic prerogative. For instance, when she authorized funds for the construction of Thouars's new temple in 1645, she instructed the family's treasurer to see that the La Trémoille arms were affixed to the main door. See AN 1AP, 1056, letter of 14 January 1645.

84. I discuss these conversions below, see pp. 299–304. His sister Marie-Charlotte

Amélie, daughter of Tarente and the German Protestant Amélie de Hesse-Cassel, was raised as a Protestant and remained one throughout her life. Tarente wrote his memoir, at least in part, to explain how it was that he had strayed from Catholicism after his first conversion to it following that of his father in 1628. He absolved himself of his relapse by blaming his mother. His father's abjuration "greatly affected" her. He returned to Protestantism because he "preserved in [his] heart the first instructions she had given [him] since [his] birth." These first impressions from his mother left him with "disgust for the Catholic religion." The duchess had sent the young Catholic boy to stay in Holland with his grand-uncle the Prince of Orange because she was "pushed by the *passion* she had to see me in the religion she professed." The Prince of Orange's good treatment "reinforced his mother's intentions" (268). His relapse finally came during a serious illness. He had received news of his much-loved sister Elisabeth's death (in 1640). His mother let him know that she was extremely sad and further that he was "on the point of losing her if [he] did not give her the consolation of embracing her belief."[85] Thus his leaving the true path was due to his mother's influence on him from his early years. The final shove came from what we could only call the guilt his mother, so passionate for her faith, inflicted on him.

Women were criticized often for their "passion," whether for religion, learning, politics, or any matter thought to be beyond their sex. Their passion was contrasted with the reason of men or at least with that of men and women who did not presume to stray beyond accepted gender boundaries. In Catholic criticism of Protestant women, "passion" was a code word for a stubborn and unreasonable attachment to heresy. Marie de La Tour's Huguenot granddaughter Charlotte-Amélie presented a picture of her grandmother's piety, seriousness, and reasonability that contrasted directly with her father's account of the duchess as driven by passion. For example, the duchess took on primary responsibility for her granddaughter's religious education, and her approach was careful and methodical. "Her goodness to me was not wasted in trifles, for she took

---

would also become a Protestant, but the second son, Louis-Maurice, comte de Laval, remained a Catholic and gave up a military for an ecclesiastical career. On Marie-Charlotte, see La Trémoïlle, *Les La Trémoïlles*, 4:viii. On Laval, see Imbert, *Registre*, 38–39.

85. "Motifs de la Conversion," 3, 267–68; emphasis added.

great trouble to teach me, especially religion, for which she had an excellent system, making me acquire everything by *reason* rather than routine. She never allowed me to learn a catechism by heart, but asked me questions about what I had learned in the Bible or in a catechism, wishing me to answer out of my head, to see if I understood what I had read."[86] The duchess also examined young Charlotte to see if she remembered sermons. Charlotte thus defended her grandmother's reason, intellectual endeavors, and religious learning.[87]

Such training served Charlotte well when she lived with her parents for several years in Bois-le-Duc after the duchess's death in 1665. "My intellect receded by six years during those three and my disposition grew worse instead of improving. . . . However, what I had learned from my grandmother was not quite effaced from my heart, and I sometimes stopped and thought. But the torrent of my passions usually carried me away. I believe that my early teachings were the reason (with God's grace, without which earthly means cannot work) that I chose the right path" (56). Charlotte did not escape the passions that infect women, but her grandmother's teaching and example saved her.

In Charlotte's autobiography this meticulous instruction is important because it prepares her to respond tenaciously and with rational argumentation to her father's attempts to compel her abjuration after his own. "I think that a certain foreboding of what was to happen to me urged her [the duchess] to instruct me so carefully. . . . It was as if she knew that great temptations awaited me." Indeed, it required no clairvoyance on Marie de La Tour's part to anticipate such "temptations." Her husband had converted, and the court, particularly Anne of Austria, was exerting considerable pressure on her in the 1660s to follow suit.[88] Perhaps she

86. Aldenburg, *Autobiography*, 31, 35–36; emphasis added. Further page references will follow in text. She also mentions her education in a variety of other subjects besides religion, such as writing, dancing, German, geography, astronomy, morals, and music; see p. 55. See also Mark Motley, *Becoming a French Aristocrat: The Education of the Court Nobility, 1580–1715* (Princeton, N.J., 1990), 80–81.

87. It is possible that this passage was also a critique of a presumed Catholic approach to the catechism that stressed memorization over reasoned analysis, or perhaps a critique of Catholic fideism as opposed to a rational approach to religious understanding.

88. See the letters of Anne of Austria of 1663 and Henri de La Trémoille of 1663 and 1664, in Imbert, *Registre*, 206–8, 210, 213, 215.

could not have foreseen that her son, Tarente, would reconvert to Catholicism, but the drift to the king's faith among the high Protestant nobility was clear. And royal as well as Church authorities strongly pushed Catholic fathers of religiously mixed aristocratic households to raise their offspring as Catholics. Hence Colbert de Croissy's report on the duchess's machinations to ensure a Protestant education for her grandchildren. After the duchess's death, Louis XIV complained to the duke about still allowing his grandchildren to worship as Huguenots.[89] Charlotte would try to fill her grandmother's shoes. After her father's conversion, as Charlotte reports it, her distraught mother retreated to her chambers.[90] And, although Charlotte's efforts would ultimately be in vain, she became Protestantism's chief defender in the household and at Thouars. While local Catholics celebrated Tarente's conversion by receiving him back into town with a torchlight procession, the Huguenots were clearly watching the events in the château with great apprehension. Their ability to continue Reformed worship in the community depended on its continuation in the La Trémoille family. And here Charlotte quickly ran up against the gender limits on her ability to defend the faith: she could never inherit the ducal title. One of her brothers would become duke and, if Catholic, would marry a Catholic who would become duchess. There would be no further Huguenot heroines in the Thouars château.

The Prince de Tarente wanted to see his children follow him into Catholicism. But the pressure he exerted on his son and heir was, not sur-

89. Louis also wanted the duke to obstruct the plan of his daughter-in-law and, at that point, still Protestant son to take their children to Holland where they could be raised as Protestants. See the exchange of letters between Louis XIV, Louvois, and the duke, 21 June, 28 June, 3 July, 24 July, and 7 August 1665, in Imbert, *Registre*, 256–61.

90. While Charlotte emphasizes her grandmother's role in her life, she diminishes that of her mother, Amélie de Hesse-Cassel. Perhaps Amélie's foreign birth, the checkered political career of her husband, Tarente, and his frequent absences from France prevented her from playing as influential a role in the life of the French Reformed Church as the two preceding duchesses. But despite Tarente's abjuration, she remained a Protestant. Charlotte reports that she was in the habit of reading the Bible with her mother, who defended doing so when her husband expressed reservations about female Bible reading. And Tarente gave a rather offhanded recognition of his wife's Protestant learning. When he announced to her his intention to convert, he added, "You wrote me letters like a minister" (p. 65). Amélie arranged Charlotte's departure from France after Tarente's abjuration in 1672, and she was allowed to leave France after the Revocation. See Aldenburg, *Autobiography*, 64–68, 82.

prisingly, greater than that on his daughter. When she protested his plans for her brother, her father replied: "Gently, gently, mademoiselle. Do not let us annoy each other on the subject of your brother. . . . I intend him to follow me, and I will see that he does so. . . . Though I should be very glad if you too followed my example, I will nevertheless promise to love you as much in the future as in the past, and will treat you like my other children" (67).

Charlotte, the Huguenot heroine-in-training, supplied her younger brother theological arguments with which to defend himself from the Catholic clergy just as she had told him stories of children martyrs in years past to firm up his faith. But her brother found himself threatened by his father, deprived of his Huguenot servants, removed from the household, and placed in priests' hands. He succumbed after six weeks of intense pressure. She also worked hard to preserve the second son, Talmont. But despite his promise to her to "die making profession of the truth," he quickly succumbed and "even had the cowardice to say in [their] mother's presence that when they elevated the Host he believed it was Jesus Christ just as he saw Him in flesh and blood" (77–78). His "inconstancy" infuriated Charlotte. She reproached "him for his falseness and his wicked compliance," and she "could not restrain herself from giving him a good blow" (73–79).

If she resisted pressure more successfully, it was due not only to her father's indulgence but also to her early preparation. Well before her father's abjuration, Charlotte was already, by her own account, an experienced controversialist. She had defended her faith against the arguments of her Catholic uncle Laval. He had debated religion with her and sent other Catholic clerics to do so as well. "But God strengthened me against these attacks . . . and enabled me to reply often and to the point. When they said things I could not reply to, I got Monsieur Chabrolle [*sic*], pastor of Thouars, to come and see me in secret and asked him to instruct me."

After her father renounced Protestantism, he asked about her intentions. She "replied very firmly that I hoped God would never so far abandon me as to permit me to abandon Him, and that I would employ my time in praying God to pardon [her father's] sins." She referred to the masses that he ordered to be said daily at Thouars as "idolatrous farce[s]" (76). When she discussed religion with him during frequent carriage rides, she "spoke with much boldness and frankness; for, besides the fact that I was and always had been in his good graces, I was also well instructed and absolutely convinced of the merits of my religion." During one such drive they passed a Capuchin house near which stood a large cross. As they passed it her father put his hand on her back and pushed her forward, thus making her bow before the cross. He asked her why she would not willingly do this "honour to Jesus Christ," and she replied, "we might as well salute an ass, for Jesus Christ had been mounted on one." She defied her aged grandfather, Duc Henri, just as well. After he urged her to "follow her father's example." She "replied very shortly that I hoped God would preserve me from such foolishness and stupidity" (67, 76–77, 79). When her grandfather and uncle took her on long walks, she resisted their efforts to convert her, just as had generations of Huguenot heroines, by singing psalms (44–45).

By the 1670s and 1680s Protestant children of Catholic fathers, especially in aristocratic families, were in a difficult position. They faced both paternal and state pressure to convert.[91] In such a situation, the only appeal was one, customary among Huguenots, to the inviolability of personal conscience, even against the God-given authority of fathers: "Though I was defending the cause of God, I ought to recollect that I was doing so against a father to whom I owed respect, though no false complaisance, of which my conscience would disapprove" (81).

Charlotte's account of her religious instruction at her grandmother's hands and of her defense of the faith in the household place her directly in the line of La Trémoille Huguenot heroines extending through her grandmother back to her great-grandmother, Charlotte-Brabantine de Nassau. She would be the last. Elie Benoist recognized her as a femme forte but was willing to pay her what he presumably saw as an even greater compliment. In commenting on her resistance to her father's pressure, he said that Charlotte had acted "with a firmness beyond her age." And since the death of her German husband, "she has lived a pious life worthy of Duc Claude, her great-grandfather and all the other *heroes* of her house."[92] In her courage and piety, Charlotte too had transcended her sex.

91. See above, pp. 186–89.

92. Benoist, *Histoire de l'Edit de Nantes*, 3:129; emphasis added.

CATHOLIC HEROINES: NUNS CONVERTED AND POSSESSED

Heroic Huguenot women had their counterparts across the confessional divide. But fewer Catholic than Protestant amazons or femmes fortes appear in confessional polemics, which says less about the religious activities of Catholic women than about the relative positions of the two religious groups. Given the increasing difficulty Protestants had across the century in publishing polemics, they were less able to make an issue of Catholic heroines as a means of attacking the rival confession. As the dominant faith, Catholicism was also less in need of heroines, and less likely to celebrate women acting beyond the bounds of their sex. A controversial "apostolic amazon," such as Mary Ward, an Englishwoman and would-be founder of a Jesuit-like order for women, provoked dismay among many within the Church.[93] Nonetheless, French Catholicism recognized heroic female piety and religious accomplishments, for example, among the abbesses who reformed convents and in mystics like Barbe Acarie, who did so much to shape Catholic piety in the early seventeenth century.[94] And because of the public attention these heroines attracted as well as the image confessional polemicists constructed of them, they did enter into the effort to create a clear confessional boundary between Catholics and their rivals.

Poitou, and western France more generally, were home to some of these reformers and mystics. Not all of them were well known or of high rank, such as Marie Baron, a merchant's wife from Marennes (Aunis), noted for her mystical piety and for serving as a spiritual counselor.[95] But as

93. Though she did have her supporters as well. On Ward as an "apostolic amazon," see Davis, "Women on Top," 145.

94. Later in the century, pious heroines became much more controversial because of their prominent roles in Jansenism or the Quietist movement. On female mysticism, see Henri Brémond, *Histoire littéraire du sentiment religieux en France depuis la fin des guerres de religion jusqu'à nos jours*, 11 vols. (Paris, 1921), 2:36–74, 193–262, 282–314, 323–62; Michel de Certeau, *The Mystic Fable*, Vol. 1: *The Sixteenth and Seventeenth Centuries*, translated by Michael B. Smith (Chicago, 1992); and Timmermans, *Accès de femmes*, 501–659, 663–700.

95. Timmermans, *Accès des femmes*, 552, 555–56. On women spiritual counselors in the early seventeenth century, see Barbara B. Diefendorf, "Discerning Spirits: Women and Spiritual Authority in Counter-Reformation France," in *Culture and Change: Attend-*

was the case with Protestants, the Catholic heroines about whom we are best informed were aristocrats, for example, Antoinette d'Orléans-Longueville. She was the founder of the Filles du Calvaire, which she established first at Lencloître in 1612 and then moved to Poitiers in 1617. An associate of Père Joseph de Paris, she shared both his interest in reform and his austere mystical piety.[96] The Capuchins, who appreciated female mysticism, acknowledged her "masculine" qualities. Benoît de Canfeld and Père Joseph thought of her as possessing a "more than feminine courage" and a "virile spirit."[97] And her convent played its part in Père Joseph's anti-Protestant struggle, as it did in other of his endeavors. In urging the pope to accept the new order, Joseph said that the Calvairians' primary task would be to pray for the expulsion of "infidels" from the Holy Land and for the conversion of heretics. He put them to work praying specifically for the fall of La Rochelle and the success of Capuchin missionary enterprises.[98]

Other abbesses demonstrated their worth to the anti-Protestant cause as much by their personal example as by their convents' activities: they were ex-Huguenots. They demonstrated their "heroinism" (to borrow a term from DeJean) through their conversions as well as through their virile piety and religious activism.[99] They thereby offered proof of their adopted faith's truth. They had crossed the confessional boundary, but their piety and accomplishments as convent reformers proved that boundary's rigidity, not its flexibility. Charlotte-Flandrine de Nassau, daughter of William of Orange and Charlotte de Bourbon—and sister of Charlotte-Brabantine, duchesse de La Trémoille—was raised, after her mother's

ing to Women, edited by Margaret Mikesell and Adele Seeff (Newark, Del., 2003), 241–65.

96. Formon, "Évêque de la Contre-Réforme," 171–74. See also Raoul de Sceaux, *Histoire des capucins*, 165–66, 173–74, 299–300, 303, 333, 369; and Mauzaize, *Rôle et l'action des capucins*, 2:723–24.

97. Quoted in Nicole Pellegrin, "L'androgyne au XVIe siècle: Pour une relecture des savoirs," in *Femmes et pouvoirs sous l'ancien régime*, edited by Danielle Haase-Dubosc and Eliane Vienot (Paris, 1991), 11–48, see esp. 47n.59. On the Filles du Calvaire, see Marcadé and Fracard, "Un triomphe difficile," 140.

98. Mauzaize, "Rôle et l'action des capucins," 1:381, 2:897; Michel Carmona, *Les diables de Loudun: Sorcellerie et politique sous Richelieu* (Paris, 1988), 118; and Dedouvres, *Politique et apôtre*, 2:140.

99. DeJean, *Tender Geographies*, 26.

death in 1582, by a Catholic aunt, the abbess of Poitiers's Sainte-Croix convent. She converted and eventually succeeded to her aunt's position in the convent, which she rebuilt and in which she installed a strictly cloistered regime.[100] Another former Protestant, Jeanne Guichard de Bourbon-Lavedan, was also raised in the care of a Catholic aunt, the abbess of Poitiers's Convent of the Trinity. She converted to Catholicism in 1595 and became abbess in 1601. She too installed a regime of strict cloistering, against considerable resistance from the other nuns. Guichard had the support of Bishop La Rocheposay and was also closely associated with Père Joseph, whose mystical ideas influenced the piety and deep religious learning for which she was renowned. The Jesuit François Garasse claimed "to have learned more in his interviews with her than on the benches of the Sorbonne."[101] Finally, Bishop La Rocheposay's own sister, Gabrielle Chasteigner, who was raised as a Protestant by her mother but who converted at eighteen years of age, became the founder of Poitiers's Visitandine house in 1633. However, she did not take orders and lived in the convent as a lay sister.[102] All these women were salutary examples for the anti-Huguenot campaign.

For Protestants, such figures could easily have been examples of women's religious inconstancy and "natural" affinity for falsehood. But there is little evidence that they attracted polemical attacks. Perhaps their high rank, connections with the Catholic elite, and obviously austere but in no way outlandish piety put them beyond their former coreligionists' reproach. Much more obvious targets could be found in Poitou. Indeed, in seventeenth-century France, no more notable or notorious case exists of extraordinary Catholic women used in the confessional struggle than that of the demonically possessed Ursuline nuns of Loudun. They served not just as markers of religious difference; their bodies literally became weapons in the effort, of both Catholics and Protestants, to establish the

100. Formon, "Évêque de la Contre-Réforme," 149–51. As we have seen in Chapters 2 and 4, Charlotte-Flandrine de Nassau also participated directly in the effort to convert her sister, the Duchesse de La Trémoille, by debating theology with her and staging Forty Hours devotions in her convent to pray for her abjuration.

101. Formon, "Évêque de la Contre-Réforme," 151, 164–65; Marcadé and Fracard, "Un triomphe difficile," 140; Wendy Gibson, *Women in Seventeenth-Century France* (London, 1989), 219.

102. Formon, "Évêque de la Contre-Réforme," 174–76.

third, most solid, form of confessional boundary. To be sure, the label of "Catholic heroine" fits these women uncomfortably. They were controversial even among those of their own faith. And they were not necessarily acting beyond the bounds of their sex, since women were thought to be all too susceptible to the Devil's machinations. Nonetheless, they achieved considerable fame and their prioress, Jeanne des Anges, was promoted to great stature because of her role in the Loudun affair. Historians have retold the Loudun story many times, as have novelists, playwrights, filmmakers, and opera composers.[103] The case's political, intellectual, psychological, sexual, and religious histories are well mapped out. This account will focus on how the nuns and their demons became objects of contention in religious conflict and how they were used in the construction of the confessional boundary.[104]

Recall that in the century's early decades Loudun was a surety town, that is, a town in which the Huguenot elite and governor assured the Protestants' local dominance.[105] The town had been a center of Huguenot political organizing and hosted the 1619 national synod.[106] By the late 1620s the city's politico-confessional situation was shifting. The governor, Jean d'Armagnac, had converted to Catholicism.[107] New Catholic religious orders were established in the city: the Jesuits in 1606, the Capuchins in 1616, the Filles du Calvaire in 1624, and the Ursulines in 1626.[108] In the wake of La Rochelle's fall, the Protestant group lost some

103. Moshe Sluhovsky, "The Devil in the Convent," *American Historical Review* 107, no. 5 (December 2002): 1379–1411, see esp. 1380.

104. I will be relying primarily on the following works: Carmona, *Les diables de Loudun;* Michel de Certeau, *The Possession at Loudun*, translated by Michael B. Smith (Chicago, 2000); Robert Mandrou, *Magistrats et sorciers en France au XVIIe siècle: Une analyse de psychologie historique* (Paris, 1980); Marc Venard, "Le démon controversiste," in *La controverse religieuse: XVIe–XIXe siècles: Actes du 1er colloque Jean Boisset*, edited by Michel Péronnet (Montpellier, 1980), 45–60; and Robert Rapley, *A Case of Witchcraft: The Trial of Urbain Grandier* (Montreal, 1998). See also Aldous Huxley, *The Devils of Loudun* (Harmondsworth, U.K., 1971).

105. See above, pp. 30–32.

106. The synod undertook the rebellious act of ordering troops to be raised. It opposed Louis XIII's changes in regulations concerning the Reformed Church's deputy general, its official representative. See Certeau, *Possession at Loudun*, 11, 20, 25–26; and Carmona, *Diables de Loudun*, 55, 84, 146.

107. Rapley, *Case of Witchcraft*, 10.

108. Certeau, *Possession at Loudun*, 25.

of its notable members to conversion.[109] Richelieu, eager to weaken both Protestant resistance and the city's autonomy, targeted Loudun; he ordered the citadel demolished as part of his château-razing campaign.[110]

When demons first made their appearance among the Ursuline nuns in October 1632, they brought to public view various rivalries in the city, not merely the one between the confessional groups. Those members of Loudun's elite who took opposing views on the possessions did not divide simply along religious lines.[111] The chief victim of the nuns' accusations of bewitchment was the priest Urbain Grandier, the subject of rumors about sexual misbehavior. Grandier maintained good relations with Loudun's Huguenots and with those who supported local autonomy against Richelieu.[112] The demons speaking through the nuns would serve well the purposes of the cardinal minister's agent Jean Martin de Laubardemont, who sent Grandier to the stake in August 1634. The execution was a serious blow to Richelieu's political and religious opponents.

Nevertheless, heresy was always on the minds of the exorcists, the nuns, and their demons. The association of Protestantism with demonism was automatic for Catholic polemicists and was reinforced frequently in possession cases.[113] Under the power of exorcists, demons frequently maintained that Protestants were their servants and disciples.[114] The Ursu-

109. Including in 1628 the gazetteer Théophraste Renaudot and the judge Paul Grouard as well as, in 1629, the royal attorney Pierre Menuau, who would play a significant role in the Ursuline affair.

110. Carmona, *Diables de Loudun*, 203.

111. One of the bitterest conflicts was between two Catholic parties, one led by the Trincant family and the other by the local bailiff, Guillaume de Cerisay. See Rapley, *Case of Witchcraft*, 37.

112. For a recent retelling of Grandier's story, see Rapley, *Case of Witchcraft*. On his relations with Loudun's Huguenots, see pp. 15, 63.

113. Mandrou, *Magistrats et sorciers*, 125; Venard, "Démon controversiste," 55; and Rapley, *Case of Witchcraft*, 101–2, 118. Demonologists such as Pierre de Lancre thought of heresy as a form of possession. Protestants associated witchcraft with idolatry. See Solé, *Débat*, 2:714–15.

114. Marthe Brossier, whose 1599 case gained great notoriety, claimed her demon went daily to La Rochelle to seek new souls for his cauldron. See Mandrou, *Magistrats et sorciers*, 166, 171; Venard, "Démon controversiste," 49; and Denis Crouzet, "A Woman and the Devil: Possession and Exorcism in Sixteenth-Century France," in *Changing Identities in Early Modern France*, edited by Michael Wolfe (Durham, N.C., 1997), 191–215.

line convent's chaplain, Jean Mignon, reported to local judicial officials that the possessions' purpose was to confound the heretics, who infested the city.[115] The Capuchin Tranquille de Saint-Rémi, sent to exorcise the nuns, pointed out that it was no accident that the provincial Huguenot stronghold had become the scene of a demonic struggle:

> Having perceived itself to be reduced to despair in that place [La Rochelle] by the fall of heresy and unable to prevent the Catholic truth from triumphing over error, hell wanted to make a second effort . . . and vomit its rage against heaven with more liberty. . . . That city [Loudun] is baleful and fatal because it is the place where the evil spirit conceived of his pernicious designs for heresy and magic. . . . For who does not know that the assembly of Loudun [1619] was the egg from which has sprung the latest rebellions . . . that sought to seat heresy on the throne. Is it not in this same city that devils have assembled to make war on God by magic and to prevail by charms and spells over those who are the most precious to him?[116]

Demonic power flowed like an underground magma, which, blocked at La Rochelle, found its outlet in a nearby center of heresy. And, tellingly, the Capuchin exorcist connected heresy not only to Satanism but also to political rebellion in an area that had recently endured the wars of the 1620s and where Richelieu was hard at work imposing royal authority.

Skeptics saw the possessions as a theatrical fraud or a manifestation of mental illness. They pointed out that demons, reputedly masters of lies, would not willingly expose their disciples and servants. The Church's answer was that the exorcists had the power to constrain the demons inhabiting the women's bodies to tell the truth, Catholic truth. Thus the demons supported the true faith against the satanically inspired heresy, and they reinforced the power and authority of the Catholic clergy and rites.[117] For Père Tranquille, the demons were useful because the exor-

115. Carmona, *Diables de Loudun*, 173.

116. Quoted in Carmona, *Diables de Loudun*, 327–28; see also Venard, "Démon controversiste," 49. Certeau, in *Possession at Loudun*, provides a slightly different version (158–59).

117. As Rapley points out, many in the Church were also skeptical of whether demons would ever tell the truth. But the Capuchin order strongly supported the idea, and its exorcists in Loudun maintained it in sermons they preached during the affair. See Rapley, *Case of Witchcraft*, 148–49. See also Venard, "Démon controversiste," 46;

cisms could make them "confess the virtue of the Blessed Sacrament and other things, which could promote the edification of the Catholics and the conversion of the heretics."[118]

Under the exorcists' control, demons identified Protestants in the audiences at exorcisms, just as they did at Thonon (Savoy) during Chérubin de Maurienne's missions in the 1590s, where those people demons possessed could "discern the heretics hidden among the Catholic [spectators] and pointing them out . . . cried in loud voices, 'There is one of ours.'"[119] In the 1611 possession case of Ursuline nuns in Aix, which preceded and set the pattern for that at Loudun, one demon, Verrine, tried to engage a Huguenot present in the room in a debate on issues such as the Eucharist and the intercession of saints. When the Huguenot refused to participate, another demon, Leviathan, inhabiting a different nun, took up the Protestant side. Under the exorcist's guidance, the "Catholic" champion Verrine defeated his opponent.[120] In Loudun, Jeanne des Anges also identified Huguenots during her exorcisms.[121] And the demons speaking through her proclaimed their revulsion toward those who were deserting them to join the Roman faith. Behemoth announced that "I have a continual aversion to God; I have no greater object of hate than his goodness and the facility with which he pardons those who want to convert."[122]

In addition to pursuing Grandier and his allies, Laubardemont made every effort to use the possessions against Loudun's Huguenots. When the demons Leviathan, Asmodeus, Aman, and Gresil promised to leave

---

Carmona, *Diables de Loudun*, 269; Solé, *Débat*, 2:715–16; and Lyndal Roper, "Exorcism and the Theology of the Body," in *Oedipus and the Devil: Witchcraft, Sexuality, and Religion in Early Modern Europe* (London, 1994), 171–98, esp. 181.

118. Quoted in Venard, "Démon controversiste," 53. In writing about the 1566 possession of Nicole Obry of Vervins, Jean Boulaese claimed that certain "notable gentlemen . . . said 'I believe because I have seen; I will no longer be a Huguenot. Cursed be those who have deceived us'" (quoted in Venard, "Démon controversiste," 48; see also Crouzet, "Woman and the Devil").

119. Charles de Genève, *Trophées sacrés*, 1st part, p. 323.

120. Venard, "Démon controversiste," 49–50.

121. Though apparently not to the satisfaction of doubters. During one session when the prioress claimed that there were two Protestants present, the Catholic bailiff who remained skeptical of the possessions recorded that he counted nine (Carmona, *Diables de Loudun*, 185).

122. Quoted in Carmona, *Diables de Loudun*, 196.

Jeanne des Anges's body on 20 May 1634, the occasion promised to be so spectacular that Laubardemont was determined to make Huguenots attend. He threatened to force them, but they refused, citing in their defense the Edict of Nantes's guarantee of liberty of conscience.[123] In the same year, he decided to build the nuns a new convent but failed to procure the necessary funds. Instead, in March 1635, he fixed on the Protestant school as a suitable lodging for them and ordered occupants out within forty-eight hours. The response was a riot of Huguenot women (another case of Protestant amazons?), which Laubardemont suppressed with the help of eight hundred archers he called in from Poitiers.[124]

The exorcists and their supporters in Loudun made conversions a central strategy of their public sessions, both because they were a blow against the heresy and because conversions supported the truth of the possession against the criticisms of skeptics, Protestant and Catholic. Certain conversions at Loudun, both of Huguenots and of morally lax Catholics, gained wide publicity. The Breton Catholic Monsieur de Kériolet witnessed exorcisms in 1636 that led him to give up a life of notorious degeneracy and become a celebrated priest and evangelizer.[125] The Englishman Lord Montagu attested to the miraculous nature of the name of St. Joseph inscribed on Jeanne des Anges's hand as a sort of stigmata. The experience pushed him to abjure his Protestant faith and accept Catholicism, after which he made a pilgrimage to Rome, where he took holy orders.[126]

In a letter to Richelieu on 20 August 1634 (two days after Grandier's execution), Laubardemont proudly reported that the "occasion already produced the conversion of ten people of different qualities and sexes. We will not rest there. . . . By the force of your courage and very generous conduct, God has entirely extinguished the Huguenot faction. He will give you the resolution to convert them to him by the authority of his

123. Carmona, *Diables de Loudun*, 219–20; Rapley, *Case of Witchcraft*, 157.

124. Carmona, *Diables de Loudun*, 279–80. Recall here also Laubardemont's role in these years in depriving Loudun's Protestants of their cemetery. See above, p. 133.

125. Also spelled "Queriolet." See Mandrou, *Magistrats et sorciers*, 276–77; and Carmona, *Diables de Loudun*, 293–94.

126. Carmona, *Diables de Loudun*, 289–90. The names that appeared miraculously inscribed on Jeanne's hand in 1637 included Joseph, Mary, Jesus, and François de Sales. They provoked a good deal of pious wonderment on the part of Catholics, including the king and queen, and also a good deal of skeptical speculation about fraud.

miracles and the power he has given his church." Laubardemont linked here the Loudun case with the fall of La Rochelle, which was the defeat of the "Huguenot faction." And he further connected the hoped-for success of the Loudun exorcisms with the issue of political obedience and the exercise of political power. "I have promised myself as the end of this task the [conversion] of all the heretics in the kingdom; all that will be necessary is the sovereign's command, which will return them to the bosom of their mother who always has her arms open to receive them."[127] Not all of Laubardemont's fellow Catholics were so certain that the possessions would bring that result. Loudun's Catholic bailiff Guillaume de Cerisay, who was suspicious of the possessions from the first, told Bishop La Rocheposay that such a manifestly false phenomenon would never encourage Protestants to convert. More likely it would provoke their scorn. The possession would be a "counter-miracle."[128]

Indeed, the Loudun possession did not lead many Huguenots to convert. Although early-modern Protestants believed in the Devil's workings as much as did Catholics, they reacted with skepticism to possessions and with suspicion of how Catholic authorities would use such cases against them. They saw the Loudun possessions as a fraud, which Laubardemont and the exorcists were perpetrating. They refused to succumb to Laubardemont's threats and stayed away from the exorcisms. Or they attended and "shrugged their shoulders" on leaving the public sessions.[129] Even after the possessions had ceased, Loudun and other cases would continue to provide Protestant polemicists with examples of Catholic superstition and deceit, or, at least, of the Catholic clergy's exploitation of poor sick women. Charles Drelincourt ridiculed the use of hysterical nuns as a means of provoking conversions. The involvement of priests in these affairs proved to him that Catholicism was suitable only for infantile imaginations. Those who incited these extravagances belonged in the hospitals where the insane were shut up.[130] According to Elie Benoist, Loudun's

127. Quoted in Carmona, *Diables de Loudun*, 267–68; there is a slightly different translation in Certeau, *Possession at Loudun*, 192–93.

128. Carmona, *Diables de Loudun*, 191.

129. According to Loudun's royal prosecutor Louis Trincant (quoted in Carmona, *Diables de Loudun*, 218–19).

130. Solé draws this summary of Drelincourt's views from various works; see *Débat*, 3:1501, 1549, 1550.

Protestants railed in secret against this "farce" or "comedy that played for several years at the Ursulines of Loudun." Many Catholics had been "praying for an affair of religion," and the possessions gave it to them.[131]

The criticisms of the Huguenot theologian and historian echo those of medical doctors, who found the possessions dubious. They were by no means only Protestants. The medical community split along professional, not confessional, lines. Some local practitioners, often surgeons and apothecaries, were willing to attest to the validity of the demonic possession. University-trained physicians, both Protestants and Catholics, who often came from outside Loudun, believed that illness or fraud were at work rather than the Devil.[132] The individual who played the largest role among the medical skeptics was Marc Duncan, a distinguished physician from the Protestant academy in Saumur. He did not merely consider the possessions a fraud. Instead, he thought them the result of psychological disorders brought on by convent life and women's susceptibility to the influence of male authorities. These women were not possessed; they suffered from melancholy because they could not endure a cloistered life. According to him, it was a frequent problem in women's communities and could take dangerous forms.

> Let us assume there is no trickery or fabrication in this affair. Does it necessarily follow that these girls are possessed? Can it not be that, through folly and error of the imagination, the women believe themselves to be possessed without being so? This happens frequently to minds that are predisposed to folly, if they are closed up in a convent. . . . It may occur after fasts, vigils, and deep meditations upon hell's punishments and devils and their trickery. . . . It would be preferable that such minds not give themselves over to solitary religious life, for ordinary contact with other people might serve to shield them from such ills. . . . A word from their confessor, well said but ill interpreted, might give rise to it. For if he told them that certain evil desires, such as that of leaving the convent and getting married, desires that they might

131. Benoist, *Histoire de l'Edit de Nantes*, 2:538, 547.

132. Certeau comments on the divisions among the medical specialists according to their origins in or outside of Loudun and their different attitudes toward the possessions (*Possession at Loudun*, 109–12). The Loudun Huguenot physician Gaspard Joubert reported after examining the nuns that the drugs they were being given, such as antimony, were the cause of their illness (see Rapley, *Case of Witchcraft*, 112).

> have had and to which they may have confessed, come from the Devil's temptations and suggestions, then, they, feeling these desires arise within them time after time, might come to believe themselves possessed. . . . A confessor, seeing and hearing them say and do strange things, might, by ignorance and simplicity, believe them to be possessed or bewitched and then persuade them of it, through the power he had over their spirits. . . . If such thoughts dominate the spirits of one or two of them, they rapidly spread to all the others. For the poor girls have a lot of faith in what their companions say, and daren't doubt the word of their mother superior. Whereupon they become frightened, and by dint of thinking of it day and night, they take their dreams for visions and their apprehensions for visitations.[133]

For the Parisian physician and "libertine" Guy Patin, matters were simpler. The Loudun case might have been a fraud perpetrated by the "cardinal tyrant." Otherwise, "in all these modern possessions, there is never anything but women or girls, bigots or nuns, and priests or monks afterwards. It is not at all a question of a devil of hell but a devil of the flesh that holy and sacred celibacy has engendered. . . . You see [in these affairs] only priests and monks mixing themselves in under the pretext of the Gospel, but they do so because of the *fillette* who is at the bottom of it all and who enrages them."[134] The Parisian Gabriel Naudé was even blunter in reflecting on the opinions of his correspondent, the Chinon physician Claude Quillet, who had examined the nuns: "it would be better to speak of hysteromania or erotomania. . . . Those poor she-devil nuns, finding themselves shut up between four walls go crazy, fall into a melancholic delirium, tortured by urges of the flesh, and in reality what they need is a carnal remedy in order to be perfectly cured."[135]

Thus there is nothing uniquely Protestant about the skeptical view of possession cases. Nonetheless, it is interesting to note how much Duncan's medical analysis corresponds to the general Protestant critique of

133. Quoted in Certeau, *Possession at Loudun*, 135–36. See also Mandrou, *Magistrats et sorciers*, 280–81. And on Duncan, see Rapley, *Case of Witchcraft*, 156.

134. Quoted in Mandrou, *Magistrats et sorciers*, 290–91. Venard also points out the skepticism of papal authorities about possessions ("Démon controversiste," 54).

135. Quoted in Certeau, *Possession at Loudun*, 135; and Mandrou, *Magistrat et sorciers*, 281. According to Certeau, this is Quillet's opinion as reported in a letter of Naudé to Guy Patin. See also Sluhovsky, "Devil in the Convent," 1397.

monastic life. Monastic vows were harmful. Celibacy was unscriptural and unnatural; few were capable of it, and most who tried to follow celibate lives were bound to fail. The nuns' desires for marriage were entirely natural and proper to women. Worthless Catholic rites and practices—fasts, vigils, meditations—weakened their psychological condition. The visions the nuns thought they saw were false. The priestly claim to authority in confession is unfounded. Here it led to a tragic end as nuns were led astray because they were susceptible to the suggestions their confessors made and because, like all women, they were highly impressionable and had only weak powers of reasoning. For Duncan, the events in Loudun's Ursuline convent were the symptoms of a mental pathology; for his coreligionists, they were the signs of a false religion.

It is worth noting that the Catholic-Protestant dispute over these women centered around a perception of them as sexualized bodies, which made the nuns perfect markers of difference between the faiths. Skeptics, Protestant or not, saw the problem as one of fraud or frustrated female sexuality. The nuns' natural destiny was marriage. Or, as Naudé put it, they needed a "carnal remedy." Women's inherent weaknesses made them susceptible to the false belief in demons and the craziness bred in convent life or it made them susceptible to the frauds of unscrupulous priests. Either way, their tormented bodies could not possibly be a locus of truth about demons or Protestantism. Catholics appear more sympathetic; the exorcists—for example, the Capuchin Tranquille de Saint-Rémi and especially the Jesuit Jean-Joseph Surin—had deep compassion for the women and deep respect for their travails and for their status as holy figures.[136] Catholics believed that the nuns' bodies could convey truth, though to be sure, it was a truth that demons, not nuns, spoke, and only when under the careful guidance of male exorcists. The Catholic view may seem more positive, but it was no less gendered. It did not see the nuns as sexually frustrated, but possession was linked inextricably to their sex. Women were more susceptible to the Devil than men. Almost all of the sixteenth- and seventeenth-century cases of group possession con-

136. Sluhovsky describes the spiritual understanding both nuns and theologians had of possession and demonstrates how early-modern conceptions of possession's sexual nature differed from that of the nineteenth and twentieth centuries, which frequently attributed cases to "female hysteria" ("Devil in the Convent").

cerned women in convents.[137] Demons could torture men and women alike, but when members of male religious communities exhibited behavior similar to that of nuns, they were more likely to be described as "obsessed" rather than "possessed."[138] The Catholic writer Jean Le Breton described the difference. Men could be "obsessed" by the Devil wherein the Devil acted "in an extraordinary manner, such as by appearing to them visibly and often, or by troubling them, or by provoking in them passions and strange movements." But in "possession the demon actually disposes of the faculties and the organs of the possessed person to produce, not only in her but by her, actions which that person could never have produced herself." The writer's choice of pronouns makes clear his gendered assumption.[139]

The nuns were problematic figures, even for Catholics, but the career of their prioress subsequent to the possession case suggests that, because of their notoriety, the potential existed to turn them into Catholic heroines. Jeanne des Anges became a celebrated mystic. The names of Jesus, Joseph, Mary, and François de Sales mysteriously inscribed on her hand

137. Roper, "Exorcism and the Theology of the Body," 190–91. She points out that possessions involved a gender reversal. The demons were a hypermasculine caricature; exorcism was successful when it returned a woman to a feminine persona.

138. Sluhovsky has uncovered two cases of male religious who appear to have been suffering from possession, one from the early thirteenth century and the other from 1671. In both cases, the men were described as obsessed rather than possessed. See "Devil in the Convent," 1405–7.

139. From Jean Le Breton, *La deffense de la vérité touchant la possession des religieuses de Louviers* (Evreux, 1643), quoted in Certeau, *Possession at Loudun*, 38. See also Joseph Klaits, *Servants of Satan: The Age of the Witch Hunts* (Bloomington, Ind., 1985), 108. Hence the confusion over the fate of the exorcist Jean-Joseph Surin, whose own psychological state deteriorated when he started to work with the nuns. His description of his condition sounds much like possession: "The devil passes from the body of the possessed person and, coming into mine, assaults me, . . . possessing me for several hours like an energumen." "Great disputes are arising about it . . . and I become a great question: whether there is possession; whether such mishaps can befall ministers of the Church?" The scholar Nicolas-Claude Fabri de Peiresc, who heard about the Surin's situation, was puzzled: "If the possession or obsession of this good exorcising father has progress, it will be more notable than all other things of that nature, which commonly befall the very weak spirits of little womenfolk." The Capuchin Tranquille de Saint-Rémi also suffered psychologically from his contact with the nuns and died in 1638, the victim of what Laubardemont called "obsession." See Certeau, *Possession at Loudun*, 194, 207–9.

made her a miraculous figure. In 1637 St. Joseph appeared to her in a vision and spread a balm on her that saved her from a grave illness. Pieces of her chemise infused with the balm worked subsequent miracles, including the saving of Laubardemont's wife during a dangerous childbirth.[140] In 1638 she undertook a triumphal tour of the country, which led her eventually to De Sales's gravesite in Annecy. At Saint-Germain-en-Laye she had interviews with the king and queen. Anne of Austria was moved by seeing the famous hand and had Jeanne recount to her the entire story of the possession. Louis examined the hand and reportedly exclaimed that "he had never doubted the truth of this marvel . . . but now his faith was fortified." She met with Richelieu at his château in Rueil, and in her memoirs she recalled the cardinal telling her that she was "greatly obliged to God for having chosen her in these unfortunate times to serve his glory and the honor of his Church by the conversion of many souls and the confusion of evildoers." Throughout her tour she attracted great crowds and worked miracles of healing with the balm, including the curing of another possessed woman. Upon returning to Saint-Germain-en-Laye, she assisted the queen with the miraculous chemise during the birth of the future Louis XIV. And the connection between Jeanne's miraculous nature and the confessional conflict was never forgotten. Upon seeing her hand, the papal nuncio wrote that "he was astonished the Huguenots remained so blind after such an evident proof of the truths against which they fight."[141]

The nuns proved themselves to be very useful for the construction of the religious boundary. Even if their affair did not convert many Huguenots, it succeeded in raising the level of confessional tension in Loudun, in Poitou, and throughout the country. For Catholics who found the possessions and the miraculous events associated with Jeanne des Anges credible, they confirmed that Huguenots were allied with the Devil and opposed to royal authority. They also revealed the undeniable truth of Catholic belief. For Protestants, fraud or illness accounted for the possessions, but they were also the mark of religious falsehood. Some might mock the nuns, but their case was a sensitive enough issue that, even

140. Carmona, *Diables de Loudun*, 300–302.

141. Carmona, *Diables de Loudun*, 309–15.

decades later, Elie Benoist felt it necessary to dismiss the affair as a farce and comedy.

Furthermore, despite the controversy and potential embarrassment they caused the defenders of Catholicism, the Ursuline nuns played their part in a way that was comprehensible to men worried about the public roles of amazons and femmes fortes. Michel de Certeau has suggested that they belonged to the larger tribe of amazons, women who commanded public attention as regents, religious reformers, mystic saints, and writers.[142] It is true that at the origin of their order, the Ursulines' public charitable and educational work marked them out as women who were, at least potentially, provocative. But by the late 1620s, French Ursulines had accepted strict cloistering; they did not appear in public, except, in the case of the Loudun nuns, when they were being exorcised. And while their behavior during the exorcisms was frequently aggressive, we must remember that they did not speak with their own voices; demons and exorcists spoke through their bodies. The nuns did not preach; they were not noted for their intellectual ambitions; they did not raise military forces to protect themselves from persecutors. Ultimately, then, they seemed perfect tools for those who sought to use them in the confessional struggle. The combination made them heroines, even if controversial ones.

The confessional boundary was imported directly into the nuns' bodies, where "Protestant" demons battled with Catholic women and exorcists. The exorcists' polemical task was to make this boundary clear: on one side Catholicism, religious truth, and the sexual purity of nuns; on the other side demons, heresy, and the nuns' violated bodies. Eventually the expulsion of the demons and the reconversion of the nuns into holy bodies would dissolve the boundary. The process could stand as a figuration of the Catholic campaign against Protestantism. The first step was to make the confessional boundary absolutely clear. The second was to eliminate it and the heresy through the conversion of Huguenots, or, in other words, to get the Protestants out of the body of France just as the demons were expelled from the nuns' bodies.

142. Certeau, *Possession at Loudun*, 104–5.

CONCLUSION

Public life in seventeenth-century France presented women with extraordinary opportunities and provoked extraordinary controversy. The regencies of Marie de Medici and Anne of Austria raised the issue of women's political leadership. Women writers were more prominent than ever, but they provoked disputes about women's capacity for learning and the propriety of their ideas appearing in print. Religious leaders acknowledged the importance of women for their respective churches, either as reformers and spiritual exemplars within Catholicism or as defenders and leaders of beleaguered Protestantism. Such prominence and controversy about what women did, when coupled with age-old and often contradictory assumptions about their natural incapacities or their natural devotion, made women particularly salient in debates between the confessions. They were "good to think with" about the religious boundary, even if, in many cases, their religious lives actually crossed the boundary, as in mixed marriages. Religious upheaval continued to open opportunities for women to play important public roles—or forced them to do so. Late in the century, new women religious leaders in the Jansenist and Quietist movements would push the Catholic Church in controversial directions. Huguenot amazons and femmes fortes reappeared in sufficient numbers during the 1680s and after the Revocation of the Edict of Nantes to once again provide important leadership for the Reformed Church and to prompt royal authorities to target them especially for repression. As always, such women challenged accepted gender distinctions and boundaries, which raised questions about other sorts of boundaries and made them signs of difference between the sexes and in religious life.

MATTERS OF CONSCIENCE

Conversion, Relapse, and the Confessional Boundary

THIS STUDY HAS EXPLORED the confessional frontier between Catholics and Protestants in the arrangement of communal space, in the establishment of religiously mixed families, and in the gendered characterizations of religious identity. These sites of boundary construction reveal how the confessional barrier could be more or less porous in the everyday relations of Catholics and Protestants. However, for those determined to make the barrier impermeable and to end religious mixing, constructing the boundary in these locations was not enough. It also had to be established in a place that was simultaneously the most inaccessible to the power of church and state and yet their most important target, namely, personal conscience. Both faiths understood the conscience as the ultimate sanctuary of religious truth, and so it was the ultimate battleground for differentiating the religions as well as for constructing a firm confessional boundary. The Edict of Nantes granted members of the Reformed Church "liberty of conscience," and they appealed to this privilege repeatedly during the seventeenth century as a refuge from persecution. Catholics were more suspicious of the notion of liberty of conscience; they saw it as a danger to proper piety and social order. Nonetheless, they also appealed to it in situations where they felt local Huguenot power was preventing the full exercise of Catholic worship. Yet, in the end, individual conscience was not a refuge from but the definitive arena of the confessional struggle. It was the locus of religious truth, the place where God's will finally had to be acknowledged. With each church convinced of its own monopoly on truth, neither could allow for complete freedom of the conscience, and neither thought of the conscience as really free. It was too important to be left to individuals.

In the battle over consciences, conversions signaled victories. Christian tradition understood conversion as an individual matter, a change arrived at in a convert's conscience once he or she had received the illumination of God's grace. Hence the way each seventeenth-century French church explained the conversion process had to allow for a degree of individualized pursuit of religious truth. At the same time, however, each had to set up strict limits around the independence of personal conscience to ensure that converts adhered to the teachings of the church they joined. In addition, given the potential tensions in biconfessional communities, conversion was also an issue in communal religious relations and in the construction of local social identity. As this chapter will suggest, contrary to what churches taught, conversion could actually permit a fluid rather than a fixed confessional identity. And since the Catholic Church had a powerful ally in the state, which pressured Huguenots to abjure their faith, conversion and conscience were also deeply politicized issues. Thus personal conscience, social identity, doctrines, confessional polemics, family and communal relations, and state policy all shaped the meaning of conversions and their use for constructing the confessional boundary.

Examining seventeenth-century conversions in the context of the confessional conflict requires an approach different from that often found in modern scholarship on conversion. Scholars of religion, historians, literary critics, and social scientists have devoted enormous efforts to the subject. And, certainly, while they are aware that the meaning of conversion depends on its broad cultural context, they nonetheless focus on the question of the convert's inner experience, his or her personal psychological transformation.[1] The sources on which they rely—primarily interviews

1. Sociologists working on contemporary notions of conversion have demonstrated how it responds to certain dominant cultural codes and symbols, whose meanings can be studied as historically specific. The religious groups converts join shape conversion's meaning to their own particular ideas and needs. See, e.g., James A. Beckford's study of the Jehovah's Witnesses in the 1970s, "Accounting for Conversion," *British Journal of Sociology* 29 (1978): 249–62; Robert W. Hefner, "Introduction: World Building and the Rationality of Conversion," in *Conversion to Christianity: Historical and*

with contemporary converts or personal conversion narratives—foster that approach, which we might call "interiorist." The stories converts tell about their religious changes are taken as giving insight into their authentic interior experiences. The classic example of this interiorist approach, the one that has done so much to shape later inquiries, is that of William James, in which conversion is described as a transformation, regardless of time or place, by which the self regains wholeness or unification through the interior emotional drama of the conversion experience.[2] However, it is worth remembering the warning of the historical anthropologists Jean and John Comaroff not to treat "conversion" as a transhistorical analytical category. Its meaning changes in different cultural contexts and as part of other historical transformations.[3]

My approach to conversion is different in that I examine not the *individual experience* of conversion but the *model* of conversion that churches constructed. My focus, in other words, is "exteriorist" rather than "interiorist." My goal is not and cannot be to explain what the conversion meant to individual converts, but instead to explore what it meant to and in the cultural context of confessional interaction and boundary construction in seventeenth-century France. This approach is more appropriate to the questions with which this book is concerned and to the sources available. The materials to be used here include records of abjurations, professions of faith the churches promulgated for converts, and, especially, published conversion accounts (*récits*). These accounts were important weapons in the polemical battle between the churches.

Conversion accounts, from those of St. Paul and St. Augustine to those

Anthropological Perspectives on a Great Transformation, edited by Robert W. Hefner (Berkeley and Los Angeles, 1993), 3–44, see esp. 4; and Lewis R. Rambo, *Understanding Religious Conversion* (New Haven, Conn., 1993). Karl F. Morrison too argues that notions of conversion are historical artifacts; they take on meaning in specific historical contexts. See his *Conversion and Text: The Cases of Augustine of Hippo, Herman-Judah, and Constantine Tsatsos* (Charlottesville, Va., 1992), xi, and *Understanding Conversion* (Charlottesville, Va., 1992), chap. 1.

2. William James, *The Varieties of Religious Experience*, in *The Works of William James*, vol. 15 (Cambridge, Mass., 1985), 140, 143–44, 146, 156, 157. Robert W. Hefner has criticized James's psychological account of conversion by pointing out that it "project[s] an interiorist bias onto a phenomenon that comes in a wide array of psychocultural forms" (Hefner, "Introduction," 17).

3. Comaroff and Comaroff, *Of Revelation and Revolution*, 1:243, 249–51.

of modern American evangelicals, have long provided scholars with their main access to the phenomenon of Christian conversion. Few if any would hold that they provide us simply with an unmediated view of what was really going on inside converts' minds. Yet they do make the individual the focus of attention, and therefore are crucial for the interiorist approach. The accounts are seen as an expression of individual experience, even if it is acknowledged that they are, more accurately, an indication of how a convert felt capable of describing the conversion experience within the framework of a specific religious institution's teachings. The seventeenth-century French texts to be examined here were usually cast as individual accounts, but we cannot assume that they give us direct access to the personal experience of conversion. Their characteristic form raises questions about their authorship and their status as narratives of authentic individual thoughts and feelings.

The authorship of the accounts is rarely certain even when they are written in the first person (and they are sometimes written in the third). The polemical value of the accounts to each side, and the fact that they were published at all, ensured that the rival ecclesiastical institutions played a large part in either composing or vetting them. In some cases, it seems entirely possible that the convert "wrote" his or her own narrative, either because the result seems very personal or because the convert would likely have had sufficient education to construct the discussions of doctrine these accounts contain. Yet other récits are so stuffed with citations from Scripture, patristic authorities, and church history that it is unlikely that converts, presuming they were not clergymen, could have written them. At the very least, a convert's new clerical mentors likely played a crucial editorial role.[4] Converts probably wrote some of these texts, their clerical amanuenses others, and collaborations between the two produced still others.

However, uncertain authorship is only a problem if we are concerned with uncovering the authentic individual experience behind the text. If, in-

4. Elisabeth Labrousse has shown how one convert to Catholicism, Jean Gesse, a member of the local elite in the southwestern town of Mauvezin and a man of some education, submitted the explanation of his conversion to his local priest and bishop, and then revised it according to their requirements. See "Conversion d'un huguenot au catholicisme."

stead, we turn the question around to ask not what the convert experienced but how such texts were used to shape what converts would experience or what they would attest to—to ask, in other words, how the récits shaped a model of the "authentic" conversion—then the question of who really wrote them is no longer important. The issue becomes not whether there is a real person behind the text whose authentic experience can be discerned but rather what model of conversion do the texts construct and why.[5]

As a result, we need not concern ourselves with the matter of the converts' "sincerity" or the question of whether their conversions were "true." To be sure, the question of sincerity is by no means anachronistic. It was of great concern to both churches precisely because of the polemical value of the récits. Each had a stake in defending the sincerity of its own conversions; those favoring the opposite side would be castigated as insincere. But converts' sincerity was not measured in the accounts by the baring of their souls in deep spiritual struggle. Rather, their adherence to a church's teachings revealed the validity of their religious change. True conversion, as testified to in récits, had to prove the truth of the church that the converts joined. They did not follow the promptings of their unique, inner selves; they attached themselves to an established institution that defined the truth and shaped the discourse in which their experiences were reported. Thus French accounts are not individualized spiritual explorations; their value does not lie in self-revelation, in the manner of English Puritan spiritual autobiographies or John Bunyan's *Grace Abounding*.[6] Instead, they present the figure of an individual convert who

5. Indeed, it is questionable to what extent we can even apply the concept of individual identity to the seventeenth-century conversion *récits*. The modern notion of the self that would form the intellectual basis for "individualism" and the self-contained individual personality was only starting to emerge in this period in the work of philosophers like Descartes or Locke. See Charles Taylor, *Sources of the Self: The Making of Modern Identity* (Cambridge, Mass., 1989), 143–98; and Natalie Zemon Davis, "Boundaries and the Sense of Self in Sixteenth-Century France," in *Reconstructing Individualism: Autonomy, Individuality, and the Self in Western Thought*, edited by Thomas C. Heller, Morton Sosna, and David E. Wellbery (Stanford, Calif., 1986), 53–63.

6. By contrast, Susan Rosa has argued that official conversion accounts could reflect the authentic individual spiritual development; see her "Turenne's Conversion," 650; "The Conversion to Catholicism of the Prince de Tarente, 1670," *Historical Reflec-*

has adhered to a predetermined religious truth. Or to put the matter differently, the issue here is less what the récits reveal about the converts' true selves than what they contribute to the construction of identities that are concretized as "Catholic" or "Protestant." The polemical purpose of the conversion narratives is to make this difference clear. An account established a convert's sincerity by following a certain pattern that included the subject's reception of God's grace in a troubled conscience, the often-lengthy examination of doctrine, and a rejection of all worldly matters. Each church's model of conversion fixed the individual experience of religious change within normative conceptions, and put it to work for the polemical purpose of setting up the clear confessional boundary.

Of course, conversion also implied the eventual disappearance of the confessional boundary. Therefore the process that the conversion models served was of two parts. The first furthered the construction of the barrier; accounts made evident which side was true and which false. Proclaiming the converts' discovery of truth would attract new converts across the frontier. Success in doing so would lead to the second part: the eventual elimination of the boundary altogether. A triumphant conversion campaign would end religious difference and unify everyone within one church. Certainly, for the Catholic majority, this end was far more realistic than for the Protestant minority. Still, the goal was implicit in each church's polemical use of conversion accounts. There could be only one true church, and successfully proclaiming it would inevitably lead to its triumph.

However, an examination of the phenomenon of conversion reveals that the models conversion accounts constructed did not always work. Conversion did not always mean what the models said it should mean. For instance, people often changed religion to marry spouses of the opposite faith, and their conversions did not necessarily follow their wrestling with doctrinal issues and spiritual dilemmas in the depths of their consciences. Marriage conversions were made for other reasons, which does not mean that they were "false," though churches frequently criticized them as such. Rather, these religious changes suggest that conversion was

tions/Reflexions Historiques 21, no. 1 (1995): 57–75; and "Seventeenth-Century Catholic Polemic and the Rise of Cultural Rationalism: An Example from the Empire," *Journal of the History of Ideas* 57, no. 1 (January 1996): 87–107.

essential to the construction of social identity and to other social purposes beyond what conversion models recognized, such as forming families and maintaining membership in communities. Even more revealing of the failure of conversion models were relapses. Religious changes were not irrevocable. A certain number of those who abjured their original faith later returned to it. Models that stipulated conversion was always to the true faith had no room for inconstancy, which smacked of opportunism and insincerity. But converts' motives were complex, which does not mean they should be dismissed as insincere. What I will suggest here instead is that relapses signal the continuing instability of the confessional boundary and the continuing flexibility of confessional identity.

THE CONVERSION MODELS

Despite each church's determination to use conversion to distinguish itself from its rival, the Catholic and Protestant models of conversion shared a great deal: they were variations on the traditional Christian understanding of conversion as a turning away from sin and toward God. But leaving the false faith for the true one was not the only form such a turn could take. Another prominent sense of *conversion*, as dictionaries of the period suggest, stressed not a change of religions but a spiritual renovation or renewal. Richelet's 1680 *Dictionnaire françois* described *convertir* as "to quit libertinage and search out the ways of salvation." Conversion was "to change one's life for the better by the pure grace of God."[7] However, heresy and immorality stood only as different points on the same spectrum of evil, which converts had to repudiate. The 1694 *Dictionnaire de l'Académie française* offered a definition of *conversion* as operating "in matters of religion and of morality and signifying a change of belief, sentiments, and of morals from bad into good"; attached to the description is the notion of changing religions: "Preaching the gospel has converted all the earth; convert pagans, idolaters; convert heretics; convert sinners."[8]

7. Quoted in Pierre Dumonceaux, "Conversion, convertir, étude comparative d'après les lexicographes du XVIIe siècle," in Duchene, ed., *Conversion au XVIIe siècle*, 7–17, see esp. 13, 14.

8. I have consulted the *Dictionnaire de l'Académie française* (1694) through the ARTFL online database of the University of Chicago.

These dictionaries fix the terms for us at a point late in the century, but they highlight elements in the understanding of conversion that were long-standing and that both churches shared. And they reflect the confessional competition. The term frequently used to mark a change of religion—"abjuration"—emphasized renunciation in the sense of a public not an interior act of religious change. The Academy's dictionary described *abjuration* as "public, solemn; he made his abjuration between the hands of the bishop." In its verb form, *abjurer* meant "to renounce a bad religion or false doctrine by oath and public act; abjure an error; abjure heresy." Adopting the true faith involved more than the reception of God's grace and the renunciation of evil; it also entailed the rejection of what were now declared to be false beliefs along with the acceptance of correct doctrine and the institution that embodied and protected it. The emphasis, in other words, is less on personal transformation than on the polemical uses of religious change.

The conversion models' similarities also appear in their reliance on the most enduring elements in the Christian conversion tradition: the experiences of St. Paul on the road to Damascus and St. Augustine in the garden in Milan. Their examples have shaped understandings of Christian conversion to this day, but the meaning of those examples has changed according to the preoccupations of particular periods.[9] Conversion models must refer to them to remain true to the sources of the Christian concept of conversion but can interpret and combine in different ways their lessons concerning human sin and merit, the infusion of divine grace, and the commitment to long-term discipline. Paula Fredriksen has shown how Paul likely understood his experience in the terms his religious tradition offered: God summoned him to work for the redemption of his people as an Old Testament–style prophet. Augustine interpreted Paul's change in the light of Christian doctrinal combats at the time he wrote the *Confessions*. He saw Paul's conversion as a "drama of human will and divine grace" in which Paul, a sinner, was redeemed by the inexplicable and un-

9. As can be seen, for example, in the history of conversions in America. See Susan Juster, "In a Different Voice: Male and Female Narratives of Religious Conversion in Post-Revolutionary America," *American Quarterly* 41 (1989): 34–62; and Virginia Lieson Brereton, *From Sin to Salvation: Stories of Women's Conversions, 1800 to the Present* (Bloomington, Ind., 1991), 14–27.

merited gift of God's grace.[10] In the *Confessions* Augustine interpreted his conversion experience similarly, stressing his sinful nature and the role of unmerited grace, which God granted him in the Milanese garden.

Medieval monks drew a different lesson from Paul's and Augustine's examples, which focused less on the dramatic moment of change that God works in converts and more on a long and gradual "process of adoption, or transformation . . . [in which] all of life, rightly lived was conversion." Monastic life, with its renunciation of the world and lifelong obedience to an institutional regime, thereby became the truest form of conversion.[11]

The seventeenth-century conversion models again reinterpreted these prototypes to suit their immediate needs. The medieval notion of a monastic life as the highest form of conversion became far less evident. Calvinists, of course, rejected monasticism but emphasized justification by faith. Thus they had far less reason than medieval monks to see conversion as a lifelong process and much more reason to stress God's role in predestination and election. But among Catholics too the idea, associated with the humanism of François de Sales, that holiness was possible in secular life undermined the primacy of a monastic understanding of conversion. As the *Introduction to the Devout Life* put it, "All are called to holiness. . . . Daily meditation can create a new heart in all of us." The creation of a new heart could stand as a metaphor for conversion, one brought about by disciplined daily effort, not by the sudden infusion of grace, but one that anybody, not just monks, could achieve.[12]

Augustine, and even more so Paul, remained the exemplars of true

10. Paula Fredriksen, "Paul and Augustine: Conversion Narratives, Orthodox Traditions, and the Retrospective Self," *Journal of Theological Studies*, n.s., 37, no. 1 (April 1986): 3–34. For Augustine, Paul became the great example of a redeemed sinner, and the impetus for Augustine's religious turn is his reading of Paul's letter to the Romans (Romans 13:13–14).

11. Morrison, *Understanding Conversion*, xii; see also *Conversion and Text*, 45–46. He is concerned specifically with the twelfth-century understanding of conversion. Marilyn J. Harran shows that the idea of conversion as a lifelong process was dominant at certain points in the Middle Ages, while at other moments the notion of a sudden, initial interior change dominated. Nonetheless, she agrees that true conversion was seen as pertaining to the monastic life (*Luther on Conversion: The Early Years* [Ithaca, N.Y., 1983], chap. 1).

12. Quoted in Dumonceaux, "Conversion, convertir," 9.

conversion. Anne de Fromentières, baronne de Courville, a convert to Catholicism, compared her interior struggle to that of the apostle: "I saw myself almost at the point of imitating Saint Paul and of surrendering myself to the celestial voice that struck . . . my heart. . . . At that moment I felt I had at the tip of my tongue even the words of Saint Paul: 'Lord what would you have me do.'"[13] It is also significant that when the former Carmelite Michel Le Camus described his conversion to the Reformed Church, he pointed out that previously he had achieved great renown as a preacher *against* Protestantism. In other words, he placed himself in the position of Saul before his conversion as a persecutor of the true church. But Le Camus went further. He started his récit with the claim that, although the comparison seemed presumptuous, his experience was much like Paul's. He had been on the road to Brittany to preach against the Huguenots, just as Saul had been on the road to Damascus. God's call came to him suddenly while on route. He was not struck blind, but God's grace did awaken in him a desire for instruction in the new faith. Paul found Ananias; Le Camus found Protestant pastors meeting in an assembly in Blois.[14]

The constructors of conversion models could also emphasize the differences between the churches by drawing on Paul and Augustine and using them polemically. In his effort to encourage Henri IV's Huguenot sister, Catherine de Bourbon, to convert, the royal confessor René Benoist referred to the two examples extensively. They were particularly pertinent because they were given "divine illumination and drawn out of their errors by salutary conversions during a time [like his own] troubled by a diversity of opinions in the matter of religion." As their experiences showed, God offers sinners his grace in His own time and "according to His own good pleasure." But it is necessary that the "reasonable creature

13. *Les justes motifs de l'heureuse conversion à la religion catholique de Madame la Baronne de Courville faite en une conference tenue en la maison de Monsieur du Moulin ministre de Charenton, qui plus que tres-ignominieusement prist la fuite . . .* (Rouen, 1618), 10.

14. *Declaration du Sr. Michel Le Camus cy-devant appellé Pere Eusebe de S. Michel de l'ordre des Carmes Reformez predicateur & prestre en l'Eglise Romaine: Contenant les moyens de sa conversion à la religion reformée addressee a Messieurs de l'eglise romaine avec les paroles de son abjuration & profession prononcée par luy, en l'Eglise Reformée de Bloys, sur le poinct de la Sainte Communion* (Charenton, 1640), 4–5.

who is a free man [in other words, a person of free will] possesses a disposition to receive [God's] gifts and divine graces." His aim here was to dispute Calvinist notions of justification by faith and predestination. "God only accepts those who imitate" Paul and Augustine in certain ways. Converts must "frequent and adhere to worthy priests, edifying and official pastors, by whom the divinely sent Holy Spirit operates efficaciously to provide knowledge of the truth to those who follow them faithfully, listening to them, receiving it from them, and obeying them."[15] For Benoist, the examples of Paul's and Augustine's conversions reinforced the validity and authority of the Church's clergy, a central issue in Catholic polemics against Protestants and one that appears frequently in Catholic conversion discourse. They taught that sincere religious change brought converts into accord with the institution that defined truth.

Benoist used Paul and Augustine to draw a distinction between the churches. But references to these most important of Christian converts tied both sides' conversion models to long-standing Christian tradition. And, as the examination of conversion accounts shows, the models' similarities are more striking than their differences. Certainly each church's récits defended its particular beliefs and attacked those of its rival. But the issues both churches' accounts addressed—the sincerity of converts, the importance of proper religious instruction, the acceptance of correct doctrine, the problem of worldly interests and obligations, and the role of God's grace as the means of overcoming all obstacles to true conversion—are often discussed in common terms. On only one issue does a major difference appear: the concern for obedience to the Catholic monarch. Catholics, who shared the king's faith, could make a stronger claim to loyalty than Huguenots, whose refusal to do so always left them politically suspect.

Sincerity and Struggle

Churches tried to ensure converts' sincerity by a thorough investigation of their lives and their reasons for changing churches. Any scandals

15. René Benoist, *Briefve proposition des admirables conversions à la vraye foy, eglise & religion catholique de S. Paul & de S. Augustin . . . envoyée & dediée à l'Altesse de très sage, très verteueuse & magnanime princesse, Madame la duchesse de Bar, soeur unique du roy très chrestien* (Paris, 1601), 7–10.

converts had committed or any hint of opportunistic motives would only serve as grist for the opponents' public attacks. The Reformed Church's national synod of 1565, which composed the *Discipline's* essential instructions for the reception of converts, ordered that "those who wish to be introduced into the Church . . . will make their intention known to the elder of their quarter, who will inform himself about their lives and make a report to the consistory of the evidence he has gathered." A 1572 Catholic "form of abjuration" insisted that a heretic intent on converting first present "himself" to the local curé or vicar and then to the bishop, vicar-general, or other diocesan official before abjuration.[16] The reception of converts then usually required their public oath to renounce former errors and accept the authority of the new church and its teachings. The publicity of the act was deemed essential both for guaranteeing the convert's sincerity and for achieving the greatest possible polemical punch.

But the conversion models insisted that true evidence of sincerity came from within each convert as a result of great personal struggle. No true conversion was easy. Human weakness, self-interest, worldly obligations, and rewards held them captive in the error of false belief. A former Huguenot minister by the name of La Mothe described how he had been held in "chains that tied him to the profession of error." The "baleful impressions of birth, preoccupations, study, interests, and engagement in a party customarily impose[d]" such chains "on . . . the *religionnaires*."[17] Those leaving Catholicism had also been held in shackles. Charles Roy, a Loudun notary, wrote of how he had been "imprisoned in darkness

16. Quoted in Paul de Félice, "Les abjurations de catholiques dans les temples Huguenots," *Bulletin de la société d'histoire du protestantisme français* 45 (1896): 561–72, see esp. 562–63. For the Catholic document, see Benoist Rigaud, *Forme d'abiuration d'heresie & confession de foy qui doivent faire les desvoyez de la foy pretandans estre recevez en l'Eglise* (Paris, 1572), n.p. Neither church required converts to be baptized. Each recognized the validity of the other's baptism. For Catholics, in particular, to have required another baptism would have called into question the sacrament's efficacy. See Rev. Joseph G. Goodwine, *The Reception of Converts: Commentary with Historical Notes*, The Catholic University of America Canon Law Studies 198 (Washington, D.C., 1944), 3–4, 116–63. For the Protestant attitude, see Labrousse, "Mariages bigarrés," 159.

17. *Les motifs de la conversion du Sieur de La Mothe, ministre, envoyez à Messieurs de la Religion pretenduë reformée* (Paris, 1665), 6.

by papal chains."[18] And the former Cordelier friar Charles Andrieu explained:

> I had been . . . at an early age nourished in superstition and what is more I was put in a place that one could properly call a sewer [a monastery] with all the stench and abomination with which the world is today infected. . . . I followed for a long time not the royal way that leads us to heaven but the dark paths, the disastrous detours, in which stray those who unfortunately lose themselves in the labyrinth of the world. I was so sick with error and heresy that my vital parts could subsist no longer; I had lost all sense . . . [I was like] a madman who refused to see the doctor.[19]

Growing recognition of their captivity would lead future converts to suspect the falseness of their faith, but their change required contact with people from the rival faith, who nourished their initial misgivings. Such contacts, of course, were just what the confessional boundary builders on either side feared. In many accounts an individual's disenchantment with his or her church started when he or she encountered clerics from its rival. They disabused the potential convert of falsehoods about their faith that their opponents propagated. For example, the ex-minister of Poitiers, Samuel Cottiby, had heard a Catholic preacher at Saint-Maixent two years before seeking him out to make his conversion. He had found the preacher's "conversation gentle and obliging."[20]

Initial doubts about the truth of their religion prompted two responses from potential converts. One was great emotional turmoil and the other

18. *La declaration que fait M. Charles Roy notaire royal, à Loudun contenant les raisons qui l'ont induict à se retirer de l'Eglise Romaine moderne pour se rejoindre & unir aux Eglises Reformées* (Saumur, 1603), 4.

19. *Declaration chrestienne du pere Charles Andrieu Iadis cordelier de l'ordre pretendu de S. François natif de la ville de Murat en Auvergne & reduit en la ville de Figeac en Quercy le 27 mars 1602* (Pontorson, 1602), n.p. See the very similar language in *La verification de Vincent du Jordain natif de Bourges en Berry cy-devant Predicateur Cordelier . . . suivant la protestation qu'il en a publiquement faicte en l'Eglise reformée de Soubize . . .* (Pontorson, 1602), n.p.

20. *La conversion du Sieur Cotiby ministre de Poictiers, faite entre les mains de Monseigneur l'Evesque de Poictiers . . .* (Paris, 1660), 1. Cottiby's father was also a prominent pastor. The convert's brother, Jacques, had briefly converted to Catholicism in 1637, and then relapsed to Protestantism. See below, pp. 286–87.

the reasoned search for doctrinal truth. Converts endured great inner turbulence, as did Catholic convert Madame de Frontenac, who experienced a fierce "interior combat," or Madame de Fontrailles, wife of the royal governor of Lectoure, who suffered horrible "interior agitations."[21] Early inclinations toward the true faith, followed by periods of growing doubt and numerous meetings with clerics, all suggest that conversions took a long time. Indeed, a quick religious change might not seem sincere. An ex-Capuchin convert to Protestantism named Du Tertre had to endure "five or six entire years since that first ray of light had illuminated in his soul and heart the desire and affection for the truth."[22] The emotional struggle was fought, as Du Tertre suggests, in the convert's conscience and heart.

Clerics who converted were "men of erudition" well trained for the rational examination of doctrine, but they too grappled with the emotional turmoil of conversion. François Cupif, previously a parish priest, converted only after a long contest between his spirit and his flesh: "[my] spirit wanted to [convert], [but because of my] flesh I did not do what I wanted to do."[23] François Clouet (the former Capuchin Basile de Rouen) had "combated for a long time the difficulties and prickings of his conscience, which tormented his heart and pressed [him] to leave the Roman Church."[24] Those moving in the opposite direction experienced the same

21. *La verité de la conversion de Madame de Frontenac, de Dimanche 27 may 1618* (Paris, 1618), 12; *Manifeste de l'abiuration publique de la religion pretendue reformée faicte en la Ste Chapelle de Nostre Dame de Garaison par Madame & Mademoiselle de Fontrailles le jour de la nativité de Sainct Jean Baptiste 24 juin 1618* (Toulouse, 1618), 21, 23. Mademoiselle de Fontrailles was her sister-in-law. According to a seventeenth-century history of Toulouse's blue penitents confraternity, Fontrailles's husband converted in 1621 after he had witnessed one of their processions. See Lisa Silverman, *Tortured Subjects: Pain, Truth, and the Body in Early Modern France* (Chicago, 2001), 124.

22. *Declaration et manifeste des principaux suiets et motifs qui ont poussé & induit Maistre M. du Tertre Sr. de la Mothe Luyne, autrefois predicateur en l'ordre des capucins sous le nom de P. Firmin, à s'en retirer de l'Eglise Romaine pour se ranger joindre & unir aux Reformées de ce Royaume & en icelles professer la pureté de l'Evangile* (Saumur, 1616), 12.

23. *Declaration de Maistre François Cupif cy-devant curé de Contigné diocese d'Angers, docteur en theologie de la faculté de Paris, ou il deduict les raisons qui l'ont meu à se separer de l'Eglise romaine pour embrasser la reforme, addressee a Monsieur l'Evesque d'Angers* (Charenton, 1637), 38–39.

24. François Clouet, *Declaration du Sr François Clouet cy-devant appellé Pere Basile de*

trouble. The former minister of Parthenay, Jean Guillemard, felt "violent interior reproaches that prick[ed] at the depths of the heart."[25] Olivier Enguerrand, once a Catholic who had converted, become a Huguenot minister in Chef-Boutonne, and then returned to Catholicism, endured "great combats in himself."[26]

Accounts made much of the converts' struggle before their "tribunal of conscience," which they often described with judicial imagery. The young Sieur Parabère, son of the Huguenot governor of Niort, explained in his conversion account that "the most certain proofs of our good and bad actions are those which derive from our consciences. It is an interior judge that puts [us] on trial; it is a commissioner of divine justice, which accuses and excuses [us] before the tribunal of the Eternal. . . . It is the strongest power with which I have had extreme combats [and] assaults perilous for my soul."[27]

Emotional combat was troublesome for a learned culture (and for churches) suspicious of the passions' effect on personal self-control and social order. As we have seen, the dangers passions posed were particularly projected onto women. Male converts, however, endured conflict in their hearts and consciences just as much as their female counterparts. In these struggles the heart played a double role. Its passions could obstruct conversion: ex-minister La Mothe admitted that his "heart for some time held truth captive against the lights and the conviction of [his] mind."[28]

Rouën, Predicateur Capucin & Missionaire du Pape, où il déduit les raisons qu'il a euës de se separer de l'Eglise Romaine pour se ranger à la Reformée . . . (Sedan, 1639), 119. Clouet would eventually reconvert to Catholicism and publish an account of that change as well. See below, pp. 289–91.

25. Jacques Mestayer describes Guillemard's conversion as well as his own in *Conversions signalées*, 13–16.

26. *Declaration de Maistre Olivier Enguerrand de Mante sur Seine, cy-devant ministre en l'Eglise pretendue reformée de Chef-Boutonne en Poictou contenant l'abiuration de l'heresie Lutherienne & Calvinique & la protestation de vivre & mourir en la doctrine de l'Eglise Catholique Apostolique & Romaine, qu'il a faict & prononcée publiquement dans l'Eglise de Mairé l'Eveschaut* . . . (Bordeaux, 1607), 5, 6.

27. *La conversion du Sieur de Parabere faicte à Rome le premier Janvier 1617, addressée a Monsieur de Parabere, Gouverneur pour le Roy en la ville & chasteau de Niort, son Pere* (Paris, 1617), 3.

28. *Motifs . . . La Mothe*, 5. The "heart" was metaphorically rich and not always seen in negative terms. For François de Sales, it was the source of feelings of charity; for Pascal, it was the location open to God's grace. See A. H. T. Levi, "La psychologie de la

But a change of heart was the sign of victory, of a true conversion. The Catholic convert and physician Samuel Paul Mugod explained in his conversion account how, when he had made his abjuration before the pope in Rome, he vowed that "all roots of the heresy and schism in which he had been born and raised have been totally torn out of my mind and heart."[29] The Protestant pastors the former Carmelite Le Camus met after he had received God's call told him that to "make a true change of religion that glorified God and [brought him] salvation, he had to believe with all his heart and confess with his mouth the truth of the Gospel they professed."[30]

Instruction in the New Faith

The troublesome emotional turmoil and conflict the passions provoked could only be included in the conversion récits because their outcome was certain. Inner struggle led to a predetermined end: adherence to a church, which insisted that a neophyte fully recognized and publicly stated the errors of the faith he or she was leaving and the truth of that he or she was joining. By the early seventeenth century, synods had added to the Reformed Church's profession of faith an explicit stipulation that converts reject the errors of Catholicism. They were expected to denounce publicly "all the idolatries and all the superstitions of the Roman Church, particularly the mass."[31] When Jacques David appeared before the Niort consistory in 1662, he swore "that he wanted to embrace the [Reformed] religion and do so publicly" and that he wanted "to live and die in the profession of Christian truth and to renounce all doctrines contrary to it, namely, the so-called sacrifice of the mass, the invocation of saints, and the cult of images."[32] When Jean Guillemard, the minister of Parthenay, abjured Protestantism during the Capuchin mission in Poitou, he ac-

conversion au XVIIe siècle: De François de Sales à Nicole," in Duchene, ed., *Conversion au XVIIe siècle*, 19–28.

29. *Exomologese de Samuel Paul de Mugod, Docteur en Medicin, retiré par la grace de Dieu de l'heresie de Calv. à la foy catholique Faicte au pieds du souverain pontife Paul V en l'an 1608* . . . (Paris, 1611), 21–22.

30. *Declaration . . . Le Camus*, 6.

31. Félice, "Abjurations des catholiques," 563. The national synods of Gergeau (1601) and Gap (1603) added this wording.

32. Bertheau, "Consistoire . . . du Moyen-Poitou," 4:525n.149.

knowledged "all his errors." He had been too "opinionated" (a common characterization of heretics), but now he recognized the fallacies in his previous beliefs.[33]

In principle, a valid profession of faith could only follow a period of instruction long enough to imbue converts with the knowledge of and respect for correct doctrine. Such preparation was essential for conversion models that insisted on a rational process of recognizing errors and accepting truth. Many accounts stressed the careful preparation neophytes underwent through reading, and they emphasized the role of clergymen who guided those making a religious change. Converts to Protestantism sought their instruction from Huguenot pastors and Scripture, to which the Protestant church gave them direct access. Jacques David told Niort's consistory that he had "for some time been frequenting the pious exercises of our religion, and had read Holy Scripture along with some books of controversy." The elders had "examined him on the principal points of religion and were satisfied by his responses that he was instructed in God's truth."[34] Catholic converts consulted works of theology but also turned to priests and missionaries to resolve their doubts about which faith was true. Ex-minister La Mothe read "ancient doctors" of the Church but then consulted "living ones" including Jesuits, an Oratorian, and a Feuillant, a man of divine eloquence "who could be called the Chrysostom of these times."[35] Unsurprisingly, Jesuits and Capuchins, the best known of the anti-Protestant campaigners, figure most frequently in the Catholic récits as those responsible for winning Catholic conversions. The *Lettre de conversion d'une Damoiselle de Poictou* recounting the conversion of the widow of a Poitou minister, celebrated the Jesuits for traveling the world—including "China, Japan, and Tartary"—to win conversions, and it proclaimed Capuchins to be "miracles of our times."[36]

Each side scored polemical points against the other by accusing rival clergymen of failing in their instructional responsibilities. Charles Roy of

33. *Recueils*, 58.

34. Bertheau, "Consistoire . . . du Moyen-Poitou," 4:525n.149.

35. *Motifs . . . La Mothe*, 6–7, 10. He only converted, however, after years of study with the Jesuits.

36. *Lettre de conversion d'une Damoiselle de Poictou, vefve d'un des plus anciens ministres pretendus* (Lyon, 1600), 11–12. Neither the widow nor her husband the minister is named.

Loudun recounted how in his search for truth he had sought out "doctors of the Roman Church" and had spent years diligently listening to them preach, conferring with them, and reading their writings. But he "could find no resolution or easing of his conscience." He resolved to read Holy Scripture "despite that he had been strictly prohibited from doing so." The refusal of the Catholic clergy to let him read Scripture raised his suspicions. One priest insisted that it was not for him to undertake such study and that he should stick to matters of his own "estate." But he did read Scripture, and he compared the Catholic sermons he heard to what he read and found them wanting. He left the Church because within it he had no means of "inquiring into that upon which his salvation depended, and it was not possible to find any resolution" to his doubts.[37] In an account of his mother's conversion, a Catholic prior named Villevielle tells how she, in seeking religious instruction, was "astonished to see herself forsaken by her pastors." She asked a Jesuit to undertake a debate with a minister as a means to "enlighten" her. A pastor named Chauve, a man of great reputation, was summoned, but he completely refused to participate. Villevielle's consistory sent her a text "as long as Lent," but it was full of errors. She saw herself abandoned by "mercenary pastors"; very dissatisfied, she sought her instruction from Catholics and abjured Calvinism.[38]

Interestingly, the role of instruction is often most stressed in accounts of women converting to Catholicism, such as that of Villevielle. Women dwelled on their desire for instruction and their search for clergy to obtain it. Madame de Fontrailles completed her return to Catholicism by means of careful tutoring received from the Jesuit preacher Alexandre Rigourd. She met with him five or six times. She attended his debates with Ministers Isaac Sylvius of Layrac and Jean Alba of Tonneins. She read the published accounts of his debates with others, most notably the Huguenot luminary Daniel Chamier of Montauban. Her participation in these "private and public instructions" and her reading of the acts of debates resolved her to abjure.[39]

37. *Declaration . . . Roy*, 4–12.

38. *Lettre escrite a Monseigneur l'Evesque de Nismes par Monsieur le Prieur Villevielle, sur l'heureuse reduction de Mademoiselle sa mere à la religion Catholique* (n.p., 1625), 2–7.

39. *Manifeste . . . Fontrailles*, 9, 11, 13–14, 20. Fontrailles had been born a Catholic, but her account suggests she had converted when she married her Huguenot husband.

The search for religious instruction is also the basis of Anne de Fromentières's conversion récit.[40] Like other Catholic women converts, Fromentières found that ministers could not justify their beliefs by Scripture, which increased her desire for instruction that would "clear up [her] doubts" (7). She sought out the eminent Pierre Dumoulin but was astonished when he refused to defend his beliefs to her (8–9). Disappointed by the Huguenot clergy, she conferred with the Capuchin preacher Ange de Raconis and tried to arrange a debate between Dumoulin and him on the issue of the Real Presence. The minister closed himself up in his room and would not participate, leaving a colleague to take his place (29–33). The debate was complicated, and Fromentières acknowledged that she did not really understand all the terms being used. But she recognized that the Huguenot did not understand them either. That "began to give me the courage to attack him myself and gave me reason to believe the contest would not be as unequal as I might have imagined because he was not as strong in reason as he was in words" (57–58). She argued with him in her "simple and vulgar" language about the controversial passage "This is my body" (62). As in the other cases, the minister's failure to convince her led Fromentières to leave her religion for Catholicism.

Framing these accounts of women's conversions to Catholicism around the issue of instruction, despite the Catholic clergy's misgivings about religious education for women, was no doubt intended to challenge Protestant claims of providing a suitable religious education for women. In the récits ministers refuse to respond or fail to answer the doubts that raise "apprehensions" in the women's souls; they deny the intellectual and spiritual satisfaction these women desire.[41] But the accounts were also a riposte to the much-criticized Huguenot "ministresses" and "doctoresses," who, Catholics charged, shamefully pursued a religious education on their own. These women were not Nicoles. They were, first of all, aristocrats; their intellectual ambitions were appropriate to their social station. And they properly sought instruction submissively from the clergy, though it is notable that Fromentières is presented as going beyond a normally acceptable role by engaging in her own debate with a Huguenot minister. By presenting their conversions as the result of often-long quests

40. *Justes motifs . . . de Courville* (pages cited in text).
41. *Justes motifs . . . de Courville*, 5.

for certainty, these women converts deflected the charge that they had acted frivolously.

The concern was not unique to women. Men too worried that they would be accused of *légèreté* (lightmindedness or flightiness). The former Jesuit Pierre Jarrige argued that one could not accuse him of having left the Roman Church "for any frivolity since he was no longer at an age where such a shortcoming could be imputed to him."[42] The ex-Capuchin Du Tertre declared to his erstwhile coreligionists, "God only knows the sinister opinions I have encountered among many of you. You take my plan for frivolity, inconstancy, and thoughtlessness."[43] But women appear particularly concerned about accusations of a lack of seriousness. Fromentières wrote her account to "shut the mouths of those who would slander her and impose silence on those who would too easily accuse her of lightness in this change." She "had done nothing lightly but only with full knowledge of the facts."[44] Marguerite de Terride wrote her récit because she knew that people "would accuse her of frivolity and inconstancy." And she turned the gender-based accusation around against Protestants. She had come to recognize that it was they who were "prejudiced and whose consistories judged matters only by passion or made laws only according to their humors."[45] These women were not lightweights, and the careful instruction they received before their abjurations proved it.

It seems likely, however, that in many cases converts received little instruction prior to their abjurations. In winning conversions, too much was at stake for churches always to demand long periods of study. Indeed, despite the churches' formal requirement of careful preparation prior to acceptance, they allowed for a different sequence. The Reformed *Discipline* ordered pastors to "exhort [would-be converts] to be present regularly at worship and at catechisms to be instructed in the faith until they are found capable of participating in the Holy Communion."[46] Yet it drew a distinc-

42. *La conversion de Monsieur Jarrige cy-devant Jesuite confesseur et pere spirituel de la maison des Jesuistes à la Rochelle admoniteur du recteur & predicateur ordinaire* (Charenton, 1648), 12. I return to Jarrige's case below.

43. *Declaration . . . du Tertre*, 5.

44. *Justes motifs . . . Courville*, 3, 67.

45. *La conversion de damoiselle Marguerite de Terride, vefve de feu Monsieur de Belle-assize, cy-devant de la Religion pretendu reformée, & maintenant tres-bonne catholique, Avec deux siens fils & aussi deux siennes filles* (Paris, 1605), 10, 11.

46. Félice, "Abjurations de catholiques," 562–63.

tion between recognition of the conversion and admission to Communion, which was the sign of complete membership. Full admission depended on the convert attending worship for some months, listening to sermons, undertaking study of the catechism, and achieving a "knowledge of the Word of God" at least sufficient for understanding Catholicism's errors. Eventually the convert would have to give proof to the consistory of his or her understanding of doctrine. The elders wanted to know not only that the convert believed in the Lord and Savior Jesus Christ as the sole and unique advocate and mediator between God and humans (in other words, not the institution of the Church), but also that the convert "detested" the abuses of the Roman religion.[47] Perhaps we might consider this point, reached only after a long process, the true conversion. But the récits stressed the earlier moment of abjuration; it was more dramatic and served greater polemical purpose.

The Catholic Church might require, as it did in the 1572 "form of abjuration," that a convert believe that the "holy mass is a sacrifice of the body and blood of Jesus Christ," as well as believe in the seven sacraments, the intercession of saints, purgatory, relics, and so forth.[48] But it too insisted more on the abjuration, the rejection of the other side's errors, than on an immediate positive understanding of Catholic doctrine. And thus instruction might follow the religious change. Nonetheless, the lack of instruction did not necessarily prevent full participation in the rituals of the Church, as became especially apparent after the Revocation of the Edict of Nantes. Proponents of forced conversions argued (against their Catholic critics) that faith followed performance. The sacraments conferred grace, and participation in the Church's rituals made people into good Catholics even if they did not have a full understanding of the doctrines behind the practices.[49]

47. Félice, "Abjurations de catholiques," 563–65. Félice's information comes not from the *Discipline* but from his examination of various seventeenth-century consistory registers.

48. *Forme d'abiuration d'heresie.* The French Catholic Church did not have a single prescribed profession of faith. Pius IV issued one in 1564 in his Constitution *Iniunctum nobis*, which the Council of Trent promulgated. Trent's decisions did not have legal status in France, but it does not seem likely that French forms would have differed greatly. See Goodwine, *The Reception of Converts*, 120–21, and note 31.

49. Catholic bishops were divided on the issue. The most acute point of contention was whether new converts should be forced to take the Eucharist, which some regard-

Reason and Doctrinal Polemic

Proper instruction under the clergy's tutelage was one safeguard against emotions leading converts astray. The other was the neophytes' reasoned examinations of doctrine, which brought them to a well-considered submission to the true church. Reason combated passion; it was the antidote to sin and error. In speaking of the "extreme combats and assaults perilous for [his] soul" that he endured prior to his Catholic conversion, Parabère admitted that he deserved God's "chastisements and punishments for not having accepted the good and favorable instincts of his mind, which reason and truth freely offered him."[50] In trying to persuade Henri IV's sister Catherine to abjure her Protestantism, René Benoist explained that sin and error came from human pride, but to make penance and convert was the result of "praiseworthy reason and faith." He encouraged her to exercise her "good and subtle mind" to think about such an urgent matter. Her reason, something that male writers were not always willing to recognize in a woman, would lead her in the right direction.[51]

In the accounts, discussions of doctrine were usually formulaic and rather dry or emotionally unengaged. In this respect, the French texts differ from the conversion narratives English Puritans and Dissenters were writing in these same years. They focused on the converts' feelings of sin and unworthiness. But the presence in the French texts of these often-long doctrinal deliberations served the purpose of shifting attention away from the individual making the abjuration toward confessional polemics. They affirmed the church the converts were joining.[52]

The topics considered were essentially those Catholics and Protestants had debated since the time of Luther; they have, as Susan Rosa aptly put

---

ed as sacrilegious. Forcing them to attend mass was less controversial, though some clergy were, in general, critical of constraint. See Orcibal, *Louis XIV et les protestants*, 114–15, 130–39, 157–58; Pérouas, *La Rochelle*, 327–30; and Quéniart, *Révocation de l'Édit de Nantes*, 129–30.

50. *Conversion . . . Parabere*, 3–4.

51. Benoist, *Briefve proposition*, 7–8.

52. And they confirm the *récits*' kinship with other sorts of polemical works, such as formal doctrinal treatises and the published debates between ministers and missionaries. On this polemical literature, see Desgraves, *Répertoire des ouvrages de controverse*, 1:ii.

it, "the definite air of boilerplate."[53] Converts (or their clerical amanuenses) wrote at length of their personal examinations of good works versus faith in salvation; the authority of Scripture versus that of the Church; the sacraments, especially the Eucharist; the vocation of pastors; purgatory; the veneration of saints, relics, and images; clerical celibacy; and so forth. While the issues had remained largely the same over the long decades of Catholic-Protestant conflict, new approaches to the debate were developing, and the texts reflected the changes. As Rosa has shown, in the seventeenth century the debate over the authenticity of doctrines seemed to reach a dead end. With neither side able to convince the other, Catholic polemicists turned to arguments based on the *notae*, or marks, of the true Church so as to emphasize the validity of the institution that manifested their doctrine. The Church was true because of its marks: it was one, holy, catholic, and apostolic. Its beliefs were universal, were supported by miracles, and had existed unchanged since the Church's origins. Its clergy's vocation was valid because of the unbroken succession of its leaders since St. Peter.[54] Arguments based on the *notae* emphasized the role of reason in religious change. They required a reasoned assent on the convert's part, not just an emotional response.[55]

The account of the former minister Arnoul Martin incorporated the notion of the marks into its defense of Catholic doctrine. "There are as many religions as there are nations in the world, and each esteems itself to be true. . . . But there is only one . . . holy and catholic . . . and it is known by certain proper marks . . . its antiquity, its continuous existence, the perpetual succession of its legitimate pastors, and its continuous agreement on all the points of faith. Where these items are not found, there is no church." Protestants, he claimed, tried to propose the written word of God as the true mark, but Arians and Anabaptists had made the same claim and thus the written word alone could not distinguish the true church from the false. Parabère provided a similar list of marks but added the glory of the Church's victories over all its enemies and its miracles (frequently found on such lists).[56] Miracles proved Catholicism's holiness.

53. Rosa, "Turenne's Conversion," 646.

54. Rosa, "Turenne's Conversion," 638–39, "Conversion to Catholicism of . . . Tarente," and "Seventeenth-Century Catholic Polemic."

55. Rosa, "Conversion to Catholicism of . . . Tarente," 69n.25.

56. Arnoul Martin, *Declaration des causes qui ont meu Arnoul Martin jadis ministre en-*

Protestant churches claimed no miracles. Protestant ministers worked no exorcisms and delivered no one from demonic possession. Thus they could not have a true vocation.[57]

The Church insisted on its unity as another mark of its validity; this assertion provided a powerful incentive for many who abjured Protestantism. Martin insisted that the Church had enjoyed permanent accord, whereas there were only disputes among the different Protestant churches.[58] Madame de Fontrailles had been troubled by the frequent "discord she experienced among those of her party." Protestantism's tendency to sectarianism proved that all Protestant beliefs were false.[59] The widow of the Poitou minister argued that the Huguenot claim to liberty of conscience was itself "contrary to religion." Religion required the renunciation of one's own will and submission to a rule that ensured unity.[60] Catholicism was orderly, properly hierarchical, and authoritarian, qualities that paralleled the social and political outlooks of, especially, elite converts to the Roman faith, and which they emphasized in their conversion récits.[61]

Hence the truth of the institution would guarantee the truth of its beliefs rather than the other way around. This argument was presented as an infallible means of attaining certainty and, as Rosa has pointed out, paralleled the efforts of philosophers, such as Descartes and Grotius, to combat seventeenth-century skepticism.[62] It also made use of new conceptions of historical argumentation. The increasing sophistication of sixteenth-century historiography provided both sides in the confessional struggle with church history as a polemical weapon, epitomized for Catholics by Cardinal Caesar Baronius's *Ecclesiastical Annals* and for Protestants by the work of German Lutheran historians, the *Magdeburg Centuries*. The conversion récits were not works of history, but they sometimes used his-

tre les calvinistes, d'embrasser la foy catholique (Paris, 1601), 11–12; *Conversion . . . Parabere*, 6.

57. *Declaration . . . Martin*, 25, 31.

58. *Declaration . . . Martin*, 25.

59. *Manifeste . . . Fontrailles*, 10.

60. *Conversion d'une Damoiselle de Poictou*, 6, 12.

61. Rosa, "Turenne's Conversion," 658–59.

62. Rosa, "Turenne's Conversion," 638–39; Richard H. Popkin, *The History of Skepticism from Erasmus to Descartes* (New York, 1964), 175–96.

torical evidence and often incorporated conclusions from polemical historiography. For Catholics, the point was to show that Protestantism had no historical roots other than earlier heresies. Antiquity was a sign of truth; since it was new, Protestantism could not be true. The Catholic Church was stable; it had not changed over time, and the uniformity of its doctrines over the centuries demonstrated their truth. In returning to Catholicism, René de Cumont, sieur de Fiefbrun, a magistrate of Civray and Saint-Maixent, wrote of how, after conferring with Catholic clergymen, he read the Church Fathers and compared their "maxims with the authority of Scripture and the Church's doctrine." He found little difference between the ceremonies and beliefs of the Catholic Church of his day and those of the first centuries. The "invocation of saints had been in usage; the Savior of the world was adored in the sacrament; . . . the Church's hierarchy was in place and honored."[63]

In Protestant conversion accounts discussions of doctrine and ecclesiology were as prominent as they were in their Catholic counterparts. And their reasoning was based not only on Scripture, as they frequently claimed, but also on logical, even Scholastic-style, argumentation. The former Franciscan Daniel Dusert promised to show that "the doctrine preached in the Roman Church is as far from the doctrine of the evangels as earth is from heaven." He would demonstrate that contention by means of "antithesis and opposition."[64] Protestants could not make use of the *notae* for support. Instead, they suggested that in relying on them, the Catholic Church failed, as Le Camus argued, to provide an authority on which "conscience could repose." Defenders of the Church played a double game, "on the one hand basing the authority of Scripture on that of

63. *Les raisons qui ont meu monsieur de Fiebrun chevalier, Conseiller du Roy . . . et son Seneschal en Poictou, Civray, & Sainct Maixant, lequel a esté instruict & absou avec Madame sa femme, Mademoiselle leur fille . . . par le Reverend Père Athanase Molé, Predicateur Capucin* . . . (Paris, 1622), 13–14 (Fiefbrun identified in Desgraves, *Répertoire des ouvrages de controverse*, 2:470). See also the letter of 8 March 1622 from Flandrine de Nassau to her sister, the Duchesse de la Trémoille, defending Fiefbrun's conversion in "Lettres de Flandrine de Nassau," 274.

64. *Declaration de Maistre Daniel Dusert, natif de Cinte-gavelle prés Thoulouse, cy-devant Religieux de la Reforme selon la reigle de S. Francoys, contenant l'abiuration de la doctrine de l'Eglise Romaine & la protestation de vivre & mourir en celle de l'Eglise Reformee, qu'il a faite publiquement en l'Eglise de Melle* . . . (La Rochelle, 1603), 3–17.

the Church, and on the other basing the authority of the Church on that of Scripture."[65]

Huguenot authors also resorted to historical evidence specifically to support four assertions: that the pope was the Antichrist, as the 1603 national synod in Gap had declared in a controversial article added to the *Confession of Faith*; that the Protestant reform was linked with earlier opponents of the papacy, such as Wyclif, Hus, and the Waldensians; that Protestantism closely followed the form and beliefs of the primitive church; and, especially, that the Catholic Church had betrayed its pure origins and become increasingly corrupt.[66] The historical record, for instance, showed that the early Church did not hold doctrines such as those of the Real Presence and purgatory.[67] Nor did the Catholic Church really enjoy the unity its defenders claimed. The ex-Capuchin François Clouet claimed that as a friar he had witnessed "the hierarchs and privileged devouring each other a thousand times."[68] Subjection to a false authority had led Catholicism astray. Rather than looking to the Word of God, the Church followed human leadership. Le Camus came to "reject [the] yoke of sovereign authority over us that the Roman Church attributed to itself and to abhor the pretensions of the pope over consciences."[69] Thus Charles Roy echoed a common Protestant refrain: Catholicism's beliefs were not divine, but merely "human inventions." By contrast, in the Reformed Church, the Word of God was "preached in its purest form and the holy sacraments were administered the way Jesus Christ had instituted them, as they had been in the primitive church."[70]

65. *Protestation chrestienne de Francoys Goupil cy-devant Cordelier au Couvent de Chasteau-roux, prononcée publiquement en l'Eglise Reformée de Thouars . . .* (Niort, 1601), 6; *Declaration . . . Le Camus*, 7, 29.

66. Bernard Dompnier, "L'histoire religieuse chez les controversistes réformés du début du XVIIe siècle: L'apport de Du Plessis Mornay et Rivet," in *Historiographie de la Réforme*, edited by Philippe Joutard (Paris, 1977), 16–36; Jacques Solé, "Le débat confessionel français entre 1598 et 1685: Esquisse de bilan," in Péronnet, ed., *Controverse religieuse*, 17–23.

67. Although not new in Protestant polemics, this contention reflected the increased interest in a historical critique of Catholicism and reinforced the traditional Protestant argument that Catholic doctrines could not be found in Scripture.

68. *Declaration . . . Clouet*, 119.

69. *Declaration . . . Le Camus*, 22.

70. *Declaration . . . Roy*, 12, 27.

Catholic and Protestant conversion accounts arrived at conclusions that are entirely unsurprising. Converts never had anything new to say about disputed issues, nor were they supposed to. Huguenots may have championed *"libre examen,"* but they did not allow, and neither did Catholics, for the convert's intellect to pursue truth independently of prescribed church teachings. Conscience was not the place in which the individual followed the inclinations of an independent self. Or, rather, if an individual did, he or she fell into sin. As Elie Benoist put it, "[T]he most precious and natural liberty is that of serving God according to the rule that one is persuaded he has given."[71] Converts did not follow the promptings of their unique inner selves; they followed either the doctrinal teachings of the Catholic Church or the Reformed Church's *Confession of Faith*. They thereby attached themselves to an ecclesiastically and politically established institution that defined truth and shaped the discourse in which converts reported their experiences and beliefs. Only then could the turmoil of the conscience find resolution and the unreasonable passions of the heart be projected onto the rivals.

The Obstacle of Worldly Interests

Former coreligionists could not accept the idea that converts had abjured for truly spiritual reasons. Their desertions must have had other motives and hence were false. The most common criticism of converts was that they had acted from worldly interests or "human considerations." Money, positions, sexual temptation, the patronage of powerful people—these were the real motives for changing churches. Catholics claimed that converts to the Reformed Church hoped to receive preference from Huguenot employers or patrons. And former members of the Catholic clergy were accused of having switched to escape the obligation of celibacy. Protestants charged converts to Catholicism of being motivated by royal favor or simply by the offer of financial support.[72]

71. He was not necessarily speaking here of conversion, but the notion of being persuaded (an act of reason) to submit to God's will is one that fit well with both faiths' conversion models (*Histoire de l'Edit de Nantes*, 1:4).

72. Especially when, as former ministers, they received pensions from the Assembly of the Clergy or from the "caisse des économats," a fund the convert Paul Pellisson-Fontanier started to pay pensions to converts. Huguenots referred to it as the "caisse des conversions." See Labrousse, *"Une foi, une loi, un roi,"* 159–63.

Conversion accounts anticipated such accusations. As the former Cordelier Charles Andrieu wrote, "those who are troubled by passion will give my act a sinister interpretation; the vulgar and ignorant will amuse themselves with false rumors. But having the evidence of my conscience for the sincerity of my actions, why should I be affected?"[73] The récits turned worldly advantages from a motivation for religious change into an obstacle to it. The ex-priest François Cupif had hesitated to convert because of his respect for his parents, his possessions and his hope of gaining more, the reputation he had thanks to his doctoral degree from "the most celebrated faculty in Christianity," and his desire for even greater dignities.[74] All of these concerns had hindered his search for the truth, and they all had to be overcome. It was not enough, however, merely to reject worldly concerns. The convert's sincerity was established by showing how attractive or tempting they had been. True conversion did not bring rewards; it required sacrifices. François Clouet asserted that he had reached an elevated rank in the Capuchin order, but joining the Reformed Church had now "reduced him to certain poverty" (and this from a former friar sworn to a life of poverty!).[75] Converts to Catholicism said the same. Fiefbrun did not seek any gain; he had already enjoyed important positions as a Protestant. He "protested before God . . . that neither fear, nor honors, nor riches had been the object of his conversion."[76] When Henri de Clermont d'Amboise, the eighteen-year-old son of the Reformed Church's deputy general, converted in 1638, he described how, in preparing for conversion, he had gained the protection of powerful political figures. But he denied doing so for any advantage: "My only motive was to search for my salvation; worldly interests contributed nothing."[77]

73. *Declaration . . . Andrieu*, n.p.

74. *Declaration . . . Cupif*, 38–39.

75. *Declaration . . . Clouet*, 103. Clouet had to deny specifically that when he had left the Capuchins, he had made off with twenty thousand livres intended for pious works.

76. *Raisons qui ont meu . . . Fiebrun*, 6, 7.

77. *Les motifs qui ont obligé M. de Clermont d'Amboise Marquis de Garlande de faire abiuration de la Rpr & profession de la foy Cath., Ap. & Rom. entre les mains du reverend Pere Hyacinthe de Paris Predicateur Capucin* (Paris, 1638), 75. On Deputy General Clermont and his son's conversion, see Jacques Pannier, *Église réformée de Paris sous Louis XIII*, 1:329–30.

Converts also had to assure their readers that no worldly disappointments or frustrations drove them to abjure. In the introductory letter to ex-minister Cottiby's account, an anonymous Catholic writer raises the issue directly. "You will see," he addresses the reader, "that he [Cottiby] proves here that he was not motivated by any displeasure; he had no discontents with his flock; the national synod of Loudun did nothing to disadvantage him." Instead, "he proceeded from pure and disinterested reasons . . .; his only motive was the knowledge he had of the truth."[78]

To further the accounts' polemical purpose, the accusation of worldly interests had to be turned around so that fault lay with the convert's previous religion. In joining the Reformed Church, Le Camus contended that Catholics, not Protestants, offered converts worldly rewards such as honor, prosperity, and the favor of high-ranking people. Cupif's "conscience gave him evidence that in the change [he] had made . . . [he] had had no other goal than the glory of God and the salvation of [his] soul. The interests of the world and my flesh . . . today are found completely on the side of the Roman Church."[79] In addressing his former coreligionists, a one-time minister of Loudun named Durand contrasted his religious change to that of Catholic clergymen converting in the other direction by stressing their sexual motivations. "We know how easy it is to discard the habit and the cloister to come among us [Protestants] to marry women and enjoy the pleasures of the world. . . . You Messieurs . . . have debauched many religious by this appetite for women. . . . But to leave the ministry to enter the monastery seems very unusual."[80]

Family ties were a particularly prominent worldly problem with which converts had to contend. The potential for family conflict was presented as a powerful disincentive for conversion. Young Clermont had delayed his conversion "for fear of doing something contrary to the sentiments of his relatives blinded by the heresy."[81] Prior to his abjuration, François Cupif's parents, "zealous for the Catholic belief[,] had come to see him to try

78. *Conversion du Sieur Cottiby*, 1–2.

79. *Declaration . . . Le Camus*, 5–6; *Declaration . . . Cupif*, 3.

80. *La nouvelle conversion du Sieur Durand ministre de Loudun à la religion catholique* (Bordeaux, 1601), 2, 3, 6. Pierre Dez's list of Loudun's ministers does not include a Durand, but it may not be complete for the late sixteenth century (*Histoire des protestants*, 447–48).

81. *Motifs qui ont obligé . . . Clermont*, 79.

to . . . harden [his heart] to God's voice." But "God had called him by his efficacious grace and broken [this] impediment."[82] Worry over conflicts with parents troubled converts deeply. Anne de Fromentières knew that because of her conversion her mother's soul would be "dominated by two violent passions—the first, the love she had . . . for a religion that she continued unjustly and falsely to think of as a holy reform, and the second, the tender affection she had always shown for her [daughter]." But Fromentières continued to recognize the "natural . . . honor [she] owed [her mother]." Indeed, the "Catholic Church taught her powerfully . . . the honor, respect, and obedience owed to the one who had given her life."[83] Parabère took refuge from his father's anger in the dictates of his conscience. He had long been prevented from converting by filial obedience, but God gave him the resolution to "vanquish all human considerations." "You know," he addressed his father, "there is nothing as sensitive as that which involves our conscience, and we have no greater self-interest than in its condition."[84]

As with any worldly concern in the accounts, the family obstacle was always surmounted. Charles Andrieu found support in Scripture to overcome his parent's objections. He echoed Matthew: "Whoever loves his parents more than Christ is not worthy of him."[85] In a letter to his father Clermont stressed that he meant no disrespect to him by leaving the Reformed Church, but he insisted on the religious liberty heretofore denied him. He hoped his father would offer no barrier to the "interior impulse" that God had given him to embrace Catholicism. "The particular affection I know you always have had for me makes me believe that you will not oppose the change of religion I have made for the sole motive of searching for my salvation."[86]

The family problem was particularly acute for those converts whose kin were split between the faiths. Madame de Frontenac was caught between her Catholic husband, who pushed her to convert, and her Hugue-

82. *Declaration . . . Cupif*, 39.

83. And she added that "no human or temporal considerations" had led to her religious change; see *Justes motifs . . . de Courville*, 1–2, 10–11, 68.

84. *Conversion . . . Parabere*, 3, 4, 44.

85. *Declaration . . . Andrieu;* Matthew 10:37.

86. *Motifs qui ont obligé . . . Clermont*, 56, 75, 76.

not brother, who urged her to reject the solicitations of the Jesuit who was trying to win her for Catholicism. Respect for her brother had long delayed her change, and when she did decide to convert to Catholicism he retired from her room with tears in his eyes.[87] However, a mixed family could also encourage a conversion, since it led to close contact with those of the other faith. Anne de Fromentières, for example, had married a Catholic, apparently without converting. But the mixed marriage led to attendance at Catholic family rituals, which prompted her first doubts about Calvinism.[88]

The conversions of those from mixed families are often presented as both the discovery of the true faith and the rediscovery of a family tradition, though this claim worked better for Catholics than for Protestants, especially among aristocrats. Madame de Fontrailles had been raised a Catholic but then married a Huguenot. The account places the blame for this misstep on her otherwise pious Catholic mother, who sought an advantageous match for her daughter. But the mother came to recognize her wrongdoing and on her deathbed begged Fontrailles to return to the true faith. The conversion reversed what worldly family interest had, at one time, required and reunited her with her mother's religion.[89] Church polemicists made the point repeatedly to Huguenot nobles that their ancestors had at one time been Catholics. Heresy sullied their families' heritage, and only conversion could restore their lineages to proper honor and respect. After Duc Henri de La Trémoille converted in 1628, Catholic writers declared that his religion had been the only matter in which he differed from his glorious ancestors. Now that he had rejoined Catholicism, he could truly say that he was descended from the likes of the "chevalier sans peur" (Louis II de La Trémoille).[90] In cases such as these, family concerns were not a worldly interest at all; instead, they helped bring the con-

87. *Verité de la conversion . . . Frontenac*, 12–15.

88. Her eyes first opened to Catholicism's truth when her son was baptized a Catholic. Her account does not state that she was married to a Catholic, but that seems the most likely explanation for the child's Catholic baptism (*Justes motifs . . . de Courville*, 4–5). For a discussion of family rituals in mixed families, see above, pp. 147, 168.

89. *Manifeste de l'abiuration . . . Fontrailles*, 7–8.

90. Renowned for his exploits in the Italian wars, he was killed at the battle of Pavia in 1525. See *Conversion de Monsieur de la Trimoüille*, 8; and Boissonnade, *Histoire de Poitou*, 169.

vert into alignment with not only a spiritual but also a social and political Catholic order.

The Politics of Conversion

In the récits worldly interests had to be specified, rejected, and projected onto the other side to serve the boundary-constructing purpose of the conversion models. However, it was difficult to criticize one particular worldly interest that appeared frequently in Catholic accounts, that of loyalty to the king. Huguenots belittled deserters who received positions from the king once they had joined his religion; it was easy to disparage as insincere any conversion made apparently for political motives. According to François Cupif, some Catholics believed that it did not matter which religion one practiced if one led a moral life. Therefore, they said, one might as well accommodate to the times and the prince's beliefs.[91] But Protestants and Catholics shared an equally fervent royalism, and thus Huguenots could not characterize fidelity to the monarch as a matter of mere opportunism.

Catholic polemicists denied that Protestants were loyal and condemned them as inevitably opposed to the monarchy. The widow of the Poitou minister asked in her account: "[D]id [Calvin] not say that monarchy is the worst form of government?"[92] The association of Protestantism with disloyalty prompted many to leave the Reformed Church. Huguenot rebellion was brewing in 1617, when the pastor of Lusignan, Jacques Mestayer, abjured. He demonstrated his sense of political duty in his account by deriding his former colleagues for provoking war against the king. He wanted no part of a ministry of anger, of condemnation, and of death. The Protestant Church was no longer "reformed" but "deformed by seditious troubles and movements that would lead only to confusion and anarchy." "I detest," he wrote, "the rebellions against the king and his state by ministers who have the direction of their churches' public affairs."[93]

The Poitevin seneschal Fiefbrun converted in 1622 because "God had opened his eyes, and he submitted to reasons stronger than his own" (7). The reasons he offered first, however, had nothing to do with doctrine or

91. *Declaration . . . Cupif*, 4, 5.

92. *Conversion d'une Damoiselle de Poictou*, 14.

93. *Conversion du Sieur Mestayer*, 3, 7–9, 18. See above, pp. 62–63.

belief (though he returns to them in his account). Foremost in his mind was the Huguenots' resistance to royal authority. Openly disobeying the king's commands, their unlawful political assembly was meeting in nearby La Rochelle. These were "seditious people" (11); their ministers meddled in affairs of state and sowed anarchy (18). They were guilty of executions, assassinations, and murders. "God's spirit cannot reside amidst such crimes and disorders" (11–12). He admired the "paternal clemency, merciful justice, and incomparable piety of our king" (12). Scripture "instructs us to render unto Caesar that which is Caesar's. It commands us to honor superior powers, and recognize and obey magistrates even in matters of conscience" (8).[94]

Like Fiefbrun, numerous Huguenot nobles succumbed to the royal campaign of the 1620s to bring them into the Catholic fold by stressing the issue of political loyalty.[95] Madame de Fontrailles's account made the connection explicit: "The nobility, which was detached from the bosom of the Church by the misfortune of civil conflicts, is now returning."[96] But the connection between political fidelity and conversion to Catholicism continued beyond this troubled decade and beyond the reign of Louis XIII. His successor also capitalized on it. Charles I's execution and the Interregnum in England provoked great suspicion of Protestants in France, despite their declarations of fidelity. After the failure of aristocratic (though not Protestant) revolt in the Fronde, and with Louis XIV's charismatic appeal growing among aristocrats, the desire to demonstrate obedience proved a powerful incentive to convert. It played an important role in the abjurations of prominent Huguenot nobles like Henri de La Tour d'Auvergne, vicomte de Turenne, in 1668, and Henri-Charles de La Trémoille, prince de Tarente, in 1670.[97] But nonnobles shared the desire. When Poitiers's minister Cottiby converted in 1660, he also pointed to Catholic suspicions about Huguenot politics. Because of a "religious motive, [they] have interests separate from those of their natural prince and their dear country." He charged that his former coreligionists' claims of political loyalty were "mockeries."[98]

94. *Raisons qui ont meu . . . Fiebrun.*

95. Parker, *La Rochelle and the French Monarchy*, 122.

96. *Manifeste de l'abiuration . . . de Fontrailles*, 6.

97. On Turenne, see Rosa, "Turenne's Conversion." On Tarente, see below, pp. 298–304.

98. Samuel Cottiby, *Lettre de M. Cottiby, envoyée le XXV Mars au Pasteurs et Anciens de*

For Catholic converts, spiritual and political motives were impossible to separate. So eager were royal authorities to win the young Henri de Clermont that Chancellor Pierre Séguier offered his patronage, and Cardinal Richelieu sent his agent Laubardemont (fresh from the affair of the Loudun Ursulines), to spirit the would-be convert out of the academy in which his father had installed him. Clermont wrote that he owed his conversion to "the grace of God and the protection of the king" (44), with whom he met. And he made his abjuration in a royal chapel surrounded by members of the court nobility.[99]

Converts were flattered by royal consideration. The ex-minister La Mothe dedicated his 1665 conversion account to the king by declaring, "Sire . . . after having thrown myself at the feet of altars, I now come to throw myself at the feet of your throne. After having paid homage to Jesus Christ in [my] heart, . . . I now come to pay homage to Your Majesty . . . and to reenter the church honored by having you as its eldest son. . . . Your Majesty has had the goodness to grant me and my family the marks of your benevolence."[100] The accounts insisted that the rewards the king offered were not to be considered materialistic inducements. Clermont, for instance, was at pains to make clear that he had not sought royal favor; that would be a mere worldly interest. But now "he had no greater passion . . . than to serve the king" (77).[101] Still, royal generosity was linked directly to conversion. The most famous example concerned the Huguenot military leader François de Bonne, duc de Lesdiguières, who received the post of constable after his abjuration in 1621. Protestants saw the king's offer as a payoff. Not so, one conversion account insisted: "The resolution of this great man [to convert] so touched the king's heart that he wished to honor [Lesdiguières] with the charge." The convert had wanted to refuse it, but the king insisted.[102]

---

l'Eglise Reformée de Poictiers (published with Jean Daillé, *Lettre escrite a Monsieur Le Coq Sieur de la Talonnière sur le changement de religion de M. Cottiby*) (Charenton, 1660), 5. As Mary D. Sheriff has suggested to me, it is also possible, that the emphasis on political loyalty in Catholic discourse might have been a means for them to lobby the king for a revocation of the Edict of Nantes.

99. *Motifs qui ont obligé . . . Clermont.*

100. *Motifs . . . La Mothe*, 3.

101. *Motifs qui ont obligé . . . Clermont.* Note here the positive use of "passion."

102. *La conversion de Monseigneur le duc D'esdiguières à la Religion Catholique, Apos-*

In Catholic conversion discourse the faithfulness of the heart and conscience was both religious and political, and it was linked with the corporal imagery found frequently in royal political propaganda. Associating conversion rhetoric with political loyalty ensured the conjoining of sincere religious change, Catholicism, and obedience to the monarchy, thereby guarding the political element in Catholic conversion accounts from the charge of opportunism. According to Fontrailles, the "royal heart, which is the . . . prime mover of the whole body of the state, inspires all its other parts. It takes its life from the spirit of God so well that the king's heart is in God's hands, as the prophet says, and all hearts are united with the king's heart, which conceives only of the hope of seeing soon the hearts of all the French, even those the most lost, return to God's hands."[103] No one whose heart was not faithful to the king and his religion could ever be a true part of the kingdom's body.

The inextricability of religious and political conversion was made explicit in accounts of the conversion to Catholicism of a Protestant grandee, Duc Henri de La Trémoille. It was one of the major successes of the 1620s campaign to lure Huguenot aristocrats to the king's faith. He abjured in Louis XIII's presence during the siege of La Rochelle in 1628.[104] The duke did not write a conversion account of his own, but Catholic polemicists quickly produced justifications and celebrations of his abjuration.[105] They acclaimed the duke's political loyalty as a sign of his sincere conversion. Writers stressed his moderate character, which had made him open to instruction in the true faith. That teaching had allowed his real self to emerge; he found it easy "to follow the instincts that the hand of God had touched. . . . God had permitted him to be born and to live for some time in error so that, by his example, the pride and insolence [of the heretics] could better be repressed."[106] The movements of the duke's soul,

tolique & Romaine ensemble le Brevet de l'Estat de Connestable de France à luy envoyé par sa Majesté . . . (Paris, 1622), 6.

103. *Manifeste de l'abiuration . . . Fontrailles*, 5–6.

104. Imbert, *Registre*, 9.

105. *Conversion de Monsieur de la Trimoüille; Dicours* [sic] *theologique sur la conversion de Monsieur le duc de la Trimoüille, à la Religion Catholique, Apostolique & Romaine, contenant une sommaire narration des raisons & motifs qui l'ont porté à ce changement* (Paris, 1628).

106. *Conversion de Monsieur de la Trimoüille*, 2, 8; La Trémoïlle, *Les La Trémoïlle*, 4:86–87.

however, brought him back not just to God but also to the king waging war against his former coreligionists. And "to show how interested he was in the salvation of his subjects," Louis honored the duke by making him a cavalry commander.[107] Protestants seized on the king's favor as a payoff for La Trémoille's change of religion. But for Catholic writers, the duke's return to the faith reversed his father, Claude's, desertion of it. It reestablished the duke in his rightful place in the monarchical order and restored to its proper political standing the renowned La Trémoille lineage, which had formerly served the Church and the monarchy so well.[108] This demonstration of political loyalty reflected deep interior change. As he presented himself to Louis, La Trémoille "offered [the monarch] as proof of his fidelity, a new conscience with a desire to serve him without exception."[109] Henceforth, his conscience belonged not just to God, but also to his sovereign.

Protestants, of course, rejected the charge that they were unfaithful to the monarchy. Instead, they insisted that their opponents, especially among the Catholic regular clergy, were disloyal. Members of orders such as the Capuchins and the Recollets were guilty of sowing dissension and promoting violence wherever they went.[110] Jesuits with their heritage of regicidal theories were especially dangerous.[111] Charenton pastor Jean Daillé claimed, as did many of his colleagues, that Jesuits could not be loyal because of their obedience to the pope.[112] The Huguenots' loyalty, by contrast, was not divided, and they lived peacefully under the king's edicts. Protestants believed firmly in obedience to superior authorities and were as aware as Catholics of the scriptural injunction to render unto Caesar. The ex-Carmelite Le Camus insisted that it was papal power that threatened states.[113] He "abhorred the pretensions of the pope over . . .

107. La Trémoïlle, *Les La Trémoïlle*, 4:87.

108. *Conversion de Monsieur de la Trimoüille*, 8; *Dicours*, 3.

109. *Conversion de Monsieur de la Trimoüille*, 6–7.

110. Drelincourt, *Avertissement*, 18; Garrisson, *Édit de Nantes*, 111–14.

111. The writings of the Jesuits Emmanuel de Sâ and Juan de Mariana provided the fuel for such claims. They were much on the minds of polemicists after Henri IV's assassination. See Mousnier, *Assassination*, 100–103.

112. Jean Daillé, *Replique aux deux livres que Messieurs Adam et Cottiby ont publiez contre luy*, 2nd ed. (Geneva, 1669), cited in Rosa, "Turenne's Conversion," 653, 657.

113. *Declaration . . . Le Camus*, 40.

[the estates] of kings, republics, and peoples" (22). "We revere the superior powers God has established over the state; we hold the king to be the first after God. . . . We teach and profess that all souls should be subject to princes, even if they are . . . enemies and persecutors of the Gospel." Nonetheless, for Le Camus, political loyalty did have a limit: should any man, of whatever quality, prohibit serving God according to the Gospel, "'then it is better to obey God rather than men' [Acts 5:29] and suffer disgrace for His cause rather than betray it by complaisance or timidity" (23). Such an argument allowed for the possibility of resistance to secular authority, though not armed rebellion. Other Huguenots would not leave open even this small window for political disobedience. Charles Drelincourt, writing after the Fronde, insisted that "we let pass no occasion to preach the inviolable fidelity and sincere obedience that we owe to superior powers and to teach that we are subjected to them [not only outwardly] but also by our consciences."[114] Even Protestant consciences could be aligned with the necessity of political fidelity to the Catholic monarch.

As opponents of the king's religion, Huguenots were, nevertheless, always at a disadvantage. Those who abjured Protestantism could always describe their change as an adherence not only to the Catholic Church but also to the king's faith. The appearance of such ideas in the récits can make the conversions they describe appear to us as insincere or inauthentic. But what might look like mere political opportunism was, on the contrary, central to the conversion discourse of French Catholics. In their accounts the seemingly worldly issue of politics was actually essential to the construction of sincerity and, indeed, to the type of personal identity the accounts offered. In the Catholic conversion model, a return to the Church restored the convert's proper place in the divinely prescribed political and social order, and therefore necessarily included the political dimension. Protestants also insisted on their loyalty to the king and were as politically and socially conservative as their rivals, but their conversion model and thus their converts could not escape the problem that their faith was not the king's faith.

114. Drelincourt, *Avertissement*, 39.

Grace and Tranquility

Converts endured turmoil in their hearts; they wrestled with their consciences; they reasoned long and hard over matters of doctrine. But none of these struggles was sufficient to bring about their conversions. None of them could be. No Christian conversion model allowed authentic religious change to result only from human effort. True conversion was God's work, not that of humans. Emotional distress could not be assuaged without God's help. Consciences could not reach assurance. And the intellect could not, by itself, understand God's truth. In converting to Protestantism, François Cupif knew that his "judgment is not infallible, my senses can mislead me, but I do not rely on their judgment to discern light from shadows." After his conversion to Catholicism, Arnoul Martin warned "we should not follow human reason, but have the spirit of God for our guide."[115]

God communicated his spirit through grace. It was grace that allowed converts to discern truth from error. The new Catholic Fiefbrun explained that "it pleased God to take [him] by the hand. He opened his eyes and submitted to reasons stronger than his own. And after having prayed so many times that the gifts of the Holy Spirit would be given to him, he felt . . . the efficacy of his vocation." Grace enlightened the ex-minister Martin, pulling "him from the shadows of error, and took him to the kingdom of light and truth." It had shown the new Protestant François Goupil how "mistaken he was in works and doctrine." And for Charles Andrieu, the former Cordelier, it was the "eye of [God's] grace that had wished to change [his] heart of stone . . . open his mouth, untie his tongue, so that [he would] publish the praises due [God] by the work of his conversion."[116]

Catholic and Protestant conversion models differed over the precise relation between grace and the convert's intellect and will.[117] For Catholics,

115. *Declaration de . . . Cupif,* 11; *Declaration . . . Martin,* 7.

116. *Raisons qui ont meu . . . Fiebrun,* 7; *Declaration . . . Martin,* 4; *Protestation chrestienne de Francoys Goupil,* 4; *Declaration . . . Andrieu,* n.p.

117. W. M. Spellman provides a useful overview of medieval and early-modern ideas on grace in *The Latitudinarians and the Church of England, 1660–1700* (Athens, Ga., 1993), 88–96.

intellect operating through reason discovered truth and prompted the will to adhere to it. Faith was the result. God's infusion of grace worked the initial transformation within the sinner, which allowed the intellect to pursue truth and a righteous life.[118] As Benoît Berault, a city official in La Rochelle, put it in his conversion account, "God sends his illumination to all by an antecedent will; He wants . . . all souls to be saved." But "God leaves us free to refuse or receive the grace which carries with it justification. If in a state of sin the soul resists grace, it will be forever abandoned by God who rejects rebellious consciences."[119]

For Calvinists, human will and intellect could not be so transformed; grace, predestined and unmerited by human action or intention, converted and saved. Le Camus summed up the classic Calvinist view: "All of Scripture makes clear that man is a humble sinner, defiant and despairing of himself and his strength, assured in his conscience only by the Savior's grace."[120] But, in the seventeenth century, Calvinist theologians (not just Arminians but also orthodox Calvinists) eager to shape their flock's moral behavior were willing to allow a somewhat greater role for human action, will, and reason, and hence for instruction and discipline.[121] During the first half of the century Philippe Duplessis-Mornay and Pierre Dumoulin elaborated the notion of "*preambula fidei* [the steps toward faith]," which created a "disposition" for the reception of faith and in which human reason could play a role. It was only in the later part of the century and in the thought of eighteenth-century German pietists or John Wesley that the infusion of grace took on a more dominant role as the crucial moment in conversion.[122]

118. This summary simplifies the different tendencies within Catholic thought due to Scholastic theology's separation of intellect and will. For Dominicans, the act of faith was primarily an act of the intellect; for Jesuits, it was an act of the will. See Levi, "Psychologie de la conversion," 20.

119. *L'heureuse conversion de noble homme Benoist Berault, Escuyer Sieur de Fraisne, premier pair de La Rochelle & premier tresorier des deniers de laditte ville . . .* (Paris, 1623), 5–6.

120. *Declaration . . . Le Camus*, 37.

121. Rosa, "Conversion to Catholicism of . . . Tarente," 69n.25. Spellman's description of the increased emphasis on discipline and instruction as preparation before saving grace became effectual (though still dependent on prevenient grace) concerns English Puritans but could also characterize Calvinist developments elsewhere (*Latitudinarians*, 89–96).

122. Jean-Robert Armogathe, "De l'art de penser comme art de persuader," in

Nonetheless, the seventeenth-century French conversion récits did not dwell on the rival theologies of grace. In them the matter seems clear: grace—God's illumination of the mind, heart, and soul—resolved all conflicts and brought the convert to the truth that the conscience then recognized without fail. The struggle ceased; the assaults of worldly interests and religious rivals were no longer an obstacle. Tranquility was achieved. Indeed, serenity was a sign of God's favor. God had wanted Michel Le Camus to find "that repose and peace of mind that surpasses all feeling," and therefore granted the ex-friar His grace.[123] In returning to the Church, Olivier Enguerrand found a tranquility and repose of conscience that he "prized much more than . . . a great number of friends and other comforts, since there is nothing more dangerous than . . . spiritual torments, which are sharper and more vehement than physical afflictions."[124] The prior Villevielle described his mother, after her Catholic conversion, "as feeling in her soul a consolation so perfect that it appeared on her face and in all her actions similar to the contentment of those who have survived a shipwreck."[125]

The seventeenth-century French conversion accounts thus constructed models of sincere conversion by incorporating from the Paulinian-Augustinian tradition the necessity of God's grace at work in the sinner's conscience and the emotional experience of personal transformation. They added the extensive rational examinations of doctrinal differences between the churches and (though more for Catholics than for Protestants) a declaration of political loyalty and integration into the monarchical order. Both models described and shaped the individual experience of religious change, fixed it within institutionally established norms, and put it to work serving the polemical purposes of churches in setting up a clear confessional boundary. Despite their important differences, the relative similarity in form of the Catholic and Protestant texts in itself suggests their fiercely competitive purpose. They were trying to claim the same contested ground. A true and sincere convert, following the models the

---

Duchene, ed., *Conversion au XVIIe siècle*, 29–43. See also his comments on Levi, "Psychologie de la conversion," 27.

123. *Declaration . . . Le Camus*, 5.

124. *Declaration . . . Enguerrand*, 6.

125. *Lettre . . . Villevielle*, 7.

récits established, created a firm boundary between truth and falsehood, political loyalty and disloyalty, God's grace and worldly interests, and between him- or herself and the rejected church. No such change could ever be reversed.

RELAPSES

However, converts did not always live their lives according to the prescribed models; some reconverted or relapsed, leaving their new religion to return to their old one. Churches, which stipulated that conversion to the true faith was necessarily irrevocable and that had accepted a convert as inspired by the truest of spiritual reasons, could not explain inconstancy except to denounce it as hypocritical, opportunistic, and as resulting from only the basest of motives. Perhaps that is why scholars have not paid much attention to reconversions either.[126] But examining the accounts of relapses and the practice of reconversion reveals the complexity of converts' motives. Relapses are important to study because they indicate the continuing openness of the confessional boundary and the social purposes for which conversion and reconversion were essential. When matters of family, kinship, community, or even political allegiances and intellectual certainties were involved, individual religious and social identities were not necessarily confined within the confessional boundaries ecclesiastical institutions established.

Relapses were a bitter pill for either church to swallow, and they posed a serious problem for the polemical value of each side's conversion model. The acclaim that greeted a convert could quickly turn sour, as happened in the case of Jacques Cottiby, son of a Poitiers minister and brother of Samuel, whose abjuration was discussed above. The journal of Antoine Denesde, a Catholic merchant of Poitiers, recorded Cottiby's religious itinerary. In an entry for 8 March 1637, Denesde reports:

> Monseigneur of Poitiers led by the hand to the sermon at St. Pierre's church, the one named Cotiby [*sic*], around 19 years of age, oldest son of Sieur Cotiby, minister of the religion of Calvin at Poitiers. . . . The

126. For an exception, see Michael C. Questier, *Conversion, Politics and Religion in England, 1580–1625* (Cambridge, U.K., 1996), 77–79.

son received absolution of the heresy in public the next day. . . . [He] was on the point of preparing for the ministry with a pension from the Huguenots, but he frustrated their expectations. God give him the grace to persevere and die a true child of the Roman Church.

The Catholics seemingly had triumphed. The son of a minister, an aspiring minister himself, and the object of great expectations among local Huguenots had abjured. But the convert did not persevere, and Denesde later had to add a laconic comment: "Three weeks later, Cottiby reverted to his errors."[127] For churches backsliders provoked only repugnance. But to other converts seeking to recross the confessional divide, cases like Cottiby's taught a different lesson: the confessional boundary was not closed.

When those who relapsed wrote accounts of their reconversions, they had to add an element not found in other conversion récits. They needed to explain why they had made the "wrong" decision in their previous religious change. François Clouet, a Capuchin who had abjured Catholicism in 1639, returned to it and rejoined his order in 1648. He echoed the standard Catholic charge that members of the clergy left the Church only so they could pursue unbridled sexual desires. He made clear that his first conversion had resulted from the "Devil's instigation" as well as his own "depraved concupiscence."[128] Others who reconverted blamed psychological weaknesses—furor and melancholy—for their first abjurations, or they attributed their change to worldly disappointments. Their original churches had not given them due recognition or the positions they deserved. And so mistakenly they had abjured.[129] Thus their first conversions had never been sincere.

To combat the suspicion relapses provoked and to convince readers of the sincerity of their second religious changes, those who reconverted had to rely on the language the conversion models provided.[130] They

127. Antoine Denesde, "Journal d'Antoine Denesde et de Marie Barré, sa femme (1628–1687)," edited by E. Bricaud, in *Archives historiques du Poitou* (Poitiers, 1885), 78.

128. Basile de Rouen, *Le retour au giron de l'eglise du Pere Basile cy-devant apostat & maintenant capucin contenant 25 articles de ses protestations & dernieres volontez faites par luy estant en son lict malade* (La Rochelle, 1648), 9.

129. See, e.g., *Retraction du Pere Pierre Jarrige de la Compagnie de Jesus retiré de sa double apostasie par le misericorde de Dieu* (Antwerp, 1650). I return below to Jarrige's case.

130. I focus here on those who were returning to Catholicism after an initial

dwelled on the role of the heart, conscience, and intellect; they combined the reasoned examination of doctrine with the outpouring of emotions; they struggled for long periods before arriving at the truth; they overcame worldly temptations and obstacles. And they gave due credit to the illumination of God's grace as the essential element in ensuring the genuineness of their change. Olivier Enguerrand, a Cordelier monk, initially converted to Protestantism around 1601 or 1602, and in 1603 he became a minister in Chef-Boutonne. But in 1607 he returned to the Catholic Church.[131] To assure readers that this second religious change was true, he deployed in his *Declaration* the terms of the Catholic conversion model, though accented by the Protestant language he now repudiated. He described how for five years he had been a zealous Calvinist because his "heart was veiled and his understanding hardened." He had preached against the Catholic Church, calling it "abominable, dissolute, a mother of fornication, a seedbed of all impiety, and so forth." He had declared the pope to be the Antichrist. He had denounced Catholics as superstitious idolaters and abusers who were damned.[132] In other words, in his protestation of Catholic faith, Enguerrand used exactly the sort of harsh language against the Church one could find in Protestant conversion accounts. Here, however, such words indicated just how wrong he had been, though one wonders if Catholic readers would have been pleased to see such odious terms trotted out once again.

As was the case with other converts, Enguerrand claimed that, while a Protestant, he had harbored doubts about his religious beliefs. For two years prior to his reconversion, he had felt a "worm in [his] conscience, which gave him no rest either night or day, evening or morning, in the

---

Protestant conversion because of the examples available to me, primarily Catholic ones. It also reflects the overall trend in conversions, which favored the Catholic Church. After royal declarations in 1663 and 1665 made relapses to Protestantism illegal, they obviously could no longer be advertised in publications.

131. *Declaration . . . Enguerrand.* On Enguerrand's account, see Louis Desgraves, "Un aspect des controverses entre catholiques et protestants, les récits de conversion (1598–1628)," in Duchene, ed., *Conversion au XVIIe siècle,* 89–110, esp. 94, 103. Daniel Hickey's forthcoming study will discuss Enguerrand as minister in Chef-Boutonne ("Living in France under the Edict of Nantes: Confessional Conflict and Coexistence in Poitou and Aunis, 1598–1685"). I thank Professor Hickey for sharing his work with me.

132. *Declaration . . . Enguerrand,* 4–5.

fields or in the home." His conscience was "an alarm that never slept." This troubled man, who "prized tranquility of spirit and repose of conscience more than friends and conveniences," was faced with "interior illness and spiritual torment." Enguerrand's consternation sprung from two sources. One was a letter he had received from his Catholic brother after his reception as a minister, which told him how obvious it was that he did not have a tranquil mind. The letter touched his heart and provoked a great combat within his soul.[133] Even more importantly, God, "who wants not the death of a sinner but his conversion," made it known that He would not allow Enguerrand "to be lost along with the other heretics but would save him by calling him to [the] Church." God's grace brought him "out of darkness and led him into the light."[134] Repose of conscience also required intellectual certainty; he denounced Calvinism as a "pestilential and damnable sect" and provided a list of beliefs on which he had previously "spat," including the blessed sacrifice of the mass, purgatory, the invocation of saints, good works, fasting, abstinence, penance, and celibacy. He now recognized that he was in error about them all, and admitted that the Catholic faith is "universal [and] its teachings . . . have never varied."[135]

That a second conversion could be construed as a direct about-face of a first was even more evident when a convert published accounts of both changes, as did François Clouet (also known as Basile de Rouen). The former Capuchin's account of his first conversion (1639) had all the elements of the Protestant model. Clouet spoke of how, as a Catholic preacher, he had persecuted the true church by speaking vehemently against the Huguenots. But God had struck at the "door of his conscience and given him no rest." He fought a long time against what his conscience urged him to do, and he had great turmoil in his heart. God eventually "illuminated his understanding." He recognized the errors of the Catholic faith and demonstrated that in a long discussion of doctrine.[136] No worldly interests

133. *Declaration . . . Enguerrand*, 6.

134. *Declaration . . . Enguerrand*, 4, 5. Enguerrand here paraphrases Ezekiel: "As I live, says the Lord God, I have no pleasure in the death of the wicked, but that the wicked turn back from his way and live" (Ezekiel 33:11; 18:23, 32). The passage was repeated often in conversion discourse.

135. In other words, he refers to the concept of the Church's true marks. See *Declaration . . . Enguerrand*, 5, 8.

136. *Declaration . . . Clouet*, 7–73.

guided his decision. He had not sought wealth in leaving the Capuchins. Nor was he pursuing sexual satisfaction; monks, not Protestant ministers, chased after women. He rejected the calumnies that Catholics would launch against him, but he took them as a mark of honor because he suffered them for God's cause. His conversion resulted only from a recognition of the truth and from God's work within him.

Clouet reconverted while he was on his sickbed in 1648. He issued a récit, including twenty-five articles professing his refound Catholic faith and apologizing for his previous errors. Indeed, he felt he had much for which to be sorry. Not only was he an apostate, but, while a Protestant, he had become a minister because no other "honest condition" was open to him. He had published harsh condemnations of the Church in general and especially of his former order, the Capuchins. He now renounced all his Calvinist beliefs and writings. As we have seen, he blamed his mistakes, in part, on the Devil and his own "depraved concupiscence."[137] But he also excused his guilt by pointing the finger at his Huguenot patron, Pierre Dumoulin. He had written his attacks on the Capuchin order at Dumoulin's behest. And he insisted that Dumoulin was the true author of his first conversion account. The apostate now declared that it had been published "only to ensure the continued benevolence of Huguenots . . . who had sent money to support him."[138]

The second account is clearly constructed to reverse the assertions of the first. He now admitted what he previously denied; worldly, not spiritual, reasons prompted his previous conversion. "I lined myself up on the side of the heretic Calvinists only because I was absolutely persuaded that I would thereby enjoy more freely the unbridled desires of my perverse covetousness." He had contacted other apostate priests in Sedan and Holland (including François Cupif), all of whom had since admitted that it was their "carnality" that led them to leave the Catholic Church.[139] As was the case with any true conversion, his return had not been easy. He had

137. *Retour au giron de . . . Basile de Rouen*, 9, 16.

138. *Retour au giron de . . . Basile de Rouen*, 9, 10, 13. As we have seen, the authorship of many conversion *récits* is unclear; and it is entirely possible that Dumoulin wrote or had a large role in writing Clouet's account.

139. *Retour au giron de . . . Basile de Rouen*, 10, 13, 23. Unlike Clouet, however, Cupif did not return to Catholicism.

wrestled with it for two years, during which he had ceased attending Reformed worship or having any contact with the heretics. He now insisted that "no human motive had brought him to his holy resolution . . . but only his conscience and the desire for the salvation of his soul." His heart, which had once led him into Protestantism, was now sincere, "contrite, and humbled by God's mercy."[140]

As with all converts, God's grace operating in his conscience had led him to the truth. But in the account of this relapse, conscience operated somewhat differently than it did in other conversion narratives. Here it was the locus not of a profound change but of a surprising continuity. For, the apostate claimed, his conscience had always been true to Catholicism, even when he was acting like "the most detestable of all miserable sinners." The evidence for the claim is that when he spoke against the Church and the Capuchins, he was aware that he did so "against his conscience for human and carnal reasons." His first conversion account was published "against [his] conscience." He now revoked the beliefs he had maintained "against [his] conscience . . . in public debates during two years at the [Protestant] Academy in Sedan and for five years of preaching in the heretics' temples." And he requested forgiveness for having professed "against [his] conscience that [he] would live [his] life in the beliefs of the so-called reformed religion." Furthermore, "even when [he] was most engulfed in sin, [he] continued to pray every day to the Virgin so as not to leave this world impenitent."[141] Therefore the apostate's return to the Church was not just a reversal of his earlier departure. It was also a recognition that in the depths of his conscience he had never really changed. Now he was bringing his actions and beliefs into line with what his conscience had always taught him. Conscience, where conversion was supposed to work its most profound transformation, had remained untouched, and thus it provided a way back. In other words, the returning convert had to maintain that the boundary conversion was supposed to construct in the conscience between the true and the false faiths had never really been closed.

Such a possibility, however, created a dilemma; it called into question

140. *Retour au giron de . . . Basile de Rouen*, 9, 21.
141. *Retour au giron de . . . Basile de Rouen*, 5, 13, 16, 22.

the effectiveness of the conversion model and its construction of the true, sincere, and irrevocable religious change originating in a profound personal transformation. Relapses indicated a continuing fluidity across the confessional divide and were therefore deeply problematic for both churches, even as they had to welcome back those who returned. Since most reconversions favored the Catholic Church, the case of Pierre Jarrige can exemplify the difficulty relapses posed. His conversion and relapse were among the best publicized and most notorious in seventeenth-century France.

Jarrige was a Jesuit who converted to Protestantism in 1647 and returned to Catholicism in 1650. The accounts of Jarrige's first religious change present a classic example of the Protestant conversion model.[142] As we would expect, the convert describes how he arrived at his decision to leave the Church only after enduring a long struggle, this one lasting sixteen years.[143] "God [had] put into his heart the first inkling" of his change while he was a student in a Jesuit college. He was assigned the task of accompanying a Jesuit who visited Huguenot temples to debate ministers. He thereby came into contact with Protestant worship and ideas, and he was impressed with the Protestants' simple and straightforward manner of speaking about Scripture. In contrast, the Jesuits acted in bad faith; they were inconsistent and theatrical (i.e., false). He found himself more "attached to profane letters" than to Scripture and spent more time "reading Cicero than Saint Paul's Epistles." Eventually he became head of the Jesuit house in La Rochelle and thus was on the front lines of the battle against Protestantism. As he began his own preaching career, he had more

142. I rely here primarily on the *Declaration du Sieur Pierre Jarrige cy-devant Jesuite Profez du Quatrième Voeu & Predicateur, Prononcé dans le Temple de l'Eglise Française de Leide, le 25 mars 1648* (Leiden, 1648). I also make use of *Conversion de . . . Jarrige.* The latter consists of a series of letters, the most important of which are either by Jarrige or Philippe Vincent, pastor at La Rochelle, where Jarrige made his abjuration. The "Registre contenant les noms de tous ceux qui ont abjure la RPR dans les diverses églises et couvents de La Rochelle entre la reduction de La Rochelle et la Révocation de l'Edit de Nantes. 1628–1662 [*sic*]" (Archives départementales de la Charente-Maritime C. 134) contains an account of Jarrige's appearance before the consistory that has been inserted into a register that otherwise contains records of conversions to Catholicism.

143. The accounts are not consistent on this point; the *Declaration . . . Jarrige* (p. 1) states sixteen years, while *Conversion . . . Jarrige* (p. 8) says fourteen.

need to study Scripture. It "tormented his mind," but "he could not extinguish by his stubbornness the light of the Holy Spirit."[144] He also had to study Calvinist doctrine, which, he increasingly felt, corresponded to the Word of God more than his own Catholic faith. While disputing pastors in marketplaces, his "conscience fought all [his] refutations [of Calvinism] and accused [him] before God of combating the truth." He was assaulted by "the world, the Devil, and the flesh."[145] He was troubled by educated priests kissing images and relics like superstitious peasants, while insisting cynically that such practices were necessary to keep peasants on the Catholic side. He began to complain to his fellow Jesuits "about the abuse of relics, the vanity [of the doctrine] of purgatory, and the roman pontiff's usurpation" of power.[146]

As with all converts, Jarrige had to make an effort of intellect and will to separate himself from the false faith. He studied closely Church doctors and Calvinist writings on them. He presented the results in a long list of Catholic beliefs he now found wrong, including transubstantiation, the invocation of saints, use of images, purgatory, indulgences, papal authority, relics, and miracles. Like all converts, he resisted and did not immediately abjure the false faith. He was hard-hearted and worldly interests held him back, including his importance and rising rank in the Jesuit order. God's grace finally "broke the chains of his obstinacy." Everything—reason, Scripture, the inspiration of the Holy Spirit—"spoke to [his] heart in favor of the religion" he now "embraced."[147] In letters to the rector of La Rochelle's Jesuit college and the Jesuit provincial for Guyenne, the convert explained that it was not frustration with nor any lack of success in the Jesuit order that moved him. Nor did he desire any gain. Worldliness was Catholicism's failing, and that was particularly true of the order he had repudiated. He denounced Jesuit hypocrisy, false poverty, error, and secrecy. Through the "marvelous secret of predestination, God [had] called him to

144. *Declaration . . . Jarrige*, 2–3; *Conversion . . . Jarrige*, 8. His comment about Cicero was a criticism of Jesuit education, since such reading was to prepare him to teach "eloquence" when, he implies, he should have been learning how to talk about Scripture in a simple manner.

145. *Declaration . . . Jarrige*, 3–4.

146. *Declaration . . . Jarrige*, 3; Hanlon, *Confession and Community*, 206.

147. *Declaration . . . Jarrige*, 4–32.

the realization that he had lived in the darkness of error." "The motive behind the change I make today," he claimed, "is not hope for some benefit. . . . It is not ambition or the desire for honor that attracts me. For what could I expect among a people, who for the love of Jesus Christ, live in France as if rejected by the world. . . . My conscience tells me that [my change] comes from heaven."[148]

The convert explained to the elders of La Rochelle's consistory that he sought no publicity about his change. The claim is disingenuous in a published conversion account, but it was intended to set up a rhetorical contrast with the Jesuits. As La Rochelle's minister Philippe Vincent explained, Protestants did not want to imitate the "triumphant boasts and uproar" their Catholic opponents made every time they converted the least "cobbler or woman dealing in secondhand goods." But Huguenots did celebrate Jarrige's conversion, which they saw as a true movement of conscience in which "God's grace had opened [Jarrige's] eyes and made him recognize . . . the errors and superstitions in the Roman Church and . . . the true and pure beliefs of the Reformed Churches." As Vincent added, it would be a sin not to publicize Jarrige's conversion and provide the world with an illustrative example. No mere cobbler or secondhand dealer, Jarrige was a former Jesuit and therefore a great prize.[149]

Thus the boundary between the true and the false faith was clear. The convert was an edifying example of one who had crossed the boundary, despite everything he had to relinquish, and who had testified in favor of the truth. His change should have been secure and so too the boundary he had helped construct. But neither was. Three years after his initial conversion, Jarrige returned to Catholicism and announced his relapse in a new publication.[150] As with others who relapsed, Jarrige had to offer explanations for his grievous error that deprived his first conversion of any validity. He did so by accepting the accusations that Jesuits had made against him after his desertion. They alleged that only the basest motives had prompted his desertion of the Church. Jarrige now agreed. "Furor and melancholy brought me to leave the house of God and adhere to the

148. *Declaration . . . Jarrige*, 33–34, 38.

149. "Lettre de Monsieur Vincent à Monsieur Drelincourt sur la conversion de Monsieur Jarrige," in *Conversion . . . Jarrige*, 2–11.

150. *Retraction du . . . Jarrige*.

heretics and to abandon an order so devout, religious, and flourishing to live among the Church's enemies" (4). He had left the order disgruntled by its treatment of him (a charge he had previously and vociferously denied). "Anger toward my provincial envenomed my heart. . . . I envisaged vengeance against him I believed . . . to be the author of my disgraces" (16). It is interesting, however, that he does not admit to what the Jesuits saw as his most serious crime: the sacrilege of continuing to celebrate the mass after he had secretly left the faith.[151] On this charge, they brought a criminal case against Jarrige in a La Rochelle court, which led to his flight to Holland.[152]

As with others who reconverted, God's continuing influence over his heart, conscience, and reason enabled his eventual return to the Church. Deep as his anger may have been, he now claimed that it had not ultimately altered his conscience, his inner core. He struggled with it, but it remained true. When he arrived in Holland, he went to see the Leiden professor and pastor Friedrich Spanheim. "I was," he wrote, "stung by an interior remorse so sudden that tears came to my eyes." Spanheim recognized his feelings and said that "there was much dissimulation in what I had done, and little truth" (7). "I tried to veil my apostasy under the specious designation of divine inspiration, but that imposture was always diametrically opposed to my judgment" (18). When he appeared before Protestant congregations in Holland, "my heart did not agree with my words and condemned my dissimulation" (11). He spoke "against the dictates of my reason and the light of my conscience" (10). "God had armed my conscience against me. It prosecuted me like a redoubtable attorney; it condemned me like a judge" (86). He "lived for two years among the heretics like a demon deprived of God's grace" (21); he suffered from a perpetual "reflux of inquietude like a sick man in his bed tossing and turning to find some repose" (83–84).

Jarrige thought about returning to the Church, but his anger and desire for revenge stopped him (8). Also the Estates of Holland had given him a

151. Filleau, *Décisions catholiques*, 715–16; Eugène and Emile Haag, *La France protestante*, 10 vols. (Paris, 1846–1859), 6:41–42.

152. He does not acknowledge the crime, though he does allow that fear of the suit delayed his return to Catholicism (8). The court found him guilty and sentenced him to death for committing sacrilege.

pension and the liberty to do what he wanted (83). In such a context, liberty could have only the negative meaning of immorality or impiety and thus joined the list of other worldly rewards he had gained through his apostasy. For such advantages, he tried to "stifle the light of the Holy Spirit that shined in his heart" (9). He sought out meetings with members of the Catholic clergy, who helped him resolve his difficulties. An unnamed Augustinian reassured him as he cried bitter tears about the horrible difficulties that prevented his return (88). The general of the Society of Jesus, Francis Piccolomini, promised him that he would be welcomed back (3–4). And the Jesuit Jean Ponthelier, the "principal instrument God used to bring [him] out of the abyss," also managed to bring him out of Holland (5). More than fifteen months passed as Jarrige, "step by step" disentangled himself from the connections he had made there, but God's grace eventually resolved the conflicts and led him back to the Church.

Jarrige now recognized the heresy for what it was, "a sewer" (12), which lured religious like him to leave their orders purely for reasons of the flesh (15). He renounced his anti-Jesuit writings, particularly the notorious *Les Jésuites mis sur l'eschafaut*. He claimed he had been completely deprived of reason and seized by a spirit of vengeance when he wrote it (60–61). He also repudiated his earlier conversion accounts and reversed what he had said in them. The debates with ministers he had attended as a young Jesuit had not revealed to him Calvinism's truth (22–23). The sixteen years he claimed to have spent wrestling with his conscience before his first abjuration are now reduced to a mere two months. And he reproduced the list of disputed doctrines from his Protestant accounts, so as to reverse what he had previously said.[153]

Within the text of the *Retraction*, the apostate was welcomed back to the Church with open arms. Outside of it, his reception was far less certain, and his fate remains unclear. The title of the account suggests that he rejoined the Jesuit order, but other reports indicate that he became a canon in his native city of Tulle.[154] His reputation made him of little use

153. Indeed, he resorts to quoting his earlier statements directly and at length so as to denounce specifically what he had professed a few years before.

154. According to Benoist, Jarrige disappeared, presumably shut up inside a Jesuit house, though he suggests that the apostate met a more sinister fate at the hands of the order he had rejoined (*Histoire de l'Edit de Nantes*, 3:93–94). Hanlon also suggests he rejoined the Jesuits (*Confession and Community*, 206). But according to the Haags, Jar-

to either church. The Huguenot historian Elie Benoist wrote that the relapsed Jesuit was turbulent, violent, vindictive, and ambitious. He had left the order because he was insulted at not having been promoted as high or as fast as he had expected. His diatribe, *Les Jésuites mis sur l'eschafaut*, reflected only his personal interests and animus.[155] Jesuits had said precisely the same after his first conversion. And Catholic opinion did not change much after his relapse. Certainly Jean Filleau had nothing good to say about Jarrige when he discussed the case in his *Décisions catholiques*: "Libertinage has often opened the door of cloisters to bad religious, which the purity of the faith has tossed up like dead bodies that the ocean of graces could not suffer. We have many examples but in our days one has appeared who seems to surpass all the others, Pierre Jarrige, formerly of the Jesuit order and then apostate."[156]

Relapses were an embarrassment to all concerned. Even if Catholicism claimed most of them, inconstancy served no one's cause very well. Cases such as those of Jarrige or Clouet seem to suggest that relapses, if anything, hardened the confessional boundary. Tensions between the rivals were heightened, while those who switched back and forth just became odious to all. Relapses smelled particularly of worldly inducements. As Huguenot minister Charles Drelincourt remarked, "[T]he comings and goings of certain people who play at changes of religion are very lucrative."[157]

But reconversions might signify something quite different. They could indicate the essential failure of the boundary the conversion models tried to construct. On one level, they did so by example. The easy return of one convert could encourage others. On another level, the language of a relapse account, though presumably patrolled by the church publishing it, suggested that conversion might mean something other than what the conversion models intended. The difference is evident in the accounts' description of the role of conscience in reconversion. According to the models, in a true conversion, conscience was the location of a profound

rige did not rejoin the Jesuits; he became a secular canon at Tulle and died there in 1670 (*France protestante*, 6:41–42).

155. *Histoire de l'Edit de Nantes*, 3:93–94.

156. Filleau, *Décisions catholiques*, 715–19.

157. Drelincourt, *Avertissement*, 7.

rupture. With God's grace, it was transformed, rejected falsehood, recognized truth, and held fast to it despite all the obstacles to the religious change. Relapse accounts stress the role of conscience even more than other conversion récits. But they present the conscience as remaining unaltered through the previous conversion. The conscience was constant; it had never forsaken truth. It remained a source of continuity, which led the apostate on a journey, difficult though it might have been, back across the divide. Thus, at least within the conscience, the convert had never really changed. The true self, the interior self, had not converted, even if individual stubbornness or rebelliousness and worldly interests prevented the apostate from acknowledging it. The language of relapses then implies that the essential reconstruction of personal identity that conversion was supposed to produce did not really happen, or at least did not happen in the way that the conversion models suggested it should.

Of course, those who relapsed had to use this rhetoric to explain away their earlier conversions and win acceptance in the church they were rejoining. But the language of conscience opened the possibility that conversion could be conceived as something other than a profound interior change. Instead, it could be the result of a search for truth by an essentially unchanging self, despite the confessional divide. And although the discourse of conversion accounts did not allow for it, relapses can also illustrate the role of conversion in the pursuit of aims apart from that of confessional boundary building. When we look beyond the notorious cases of wayward clerics to other relapses, we can see that conversion and reconversion were closely bound up with the complex construction of social identities without clear-cut confessional allegiance. These conversions concerned families, communities, and politics and did not easily fit within confessional definitions. Two examples, one concerning an individual and one a community, can illustrate these other meanings and uses of conversion. The first is the case of Henri-Charles de La Trémoille, prince de Tarente, whose multiple religious changes suggest how an individual's life, and even his conversion narrative, could belie the strict confessional categorization of the conversion models. The second example, from the town of Melle, can help us understand how conversions and relapses for the sake of marriage contributed to coexistence between the confessional groups. Taken together, these examples demonstrate that neither conversion nor the confessional identity it conferred were strictly matters of doctrinal adherence. They also resulted from the interplay of belief with family bonds, membership in communities, and the politics of the Catholic monarchy.

In 1670 Tarente converted to Catholicism in what was his third religious change. He was born a Protestant, had previously become a Catholic in the late 1620s, and had returned to his original faith while living in the Netherlands in the 1640s. He was thus a double relapse. In the year after his final conversion, he wrote a memoir on the "motives" that had led to his religious changes.[158] Given his Protestant upbringing and that he passed much of his adult life as a Protestant, it might seem unwarranted to think of Tarente as writing a Catholic account. But the memoir is written to defend his final conversion to Catholicism and to explain away his earlier ones. In its discussion of doctrinal issues, it hews very closely to the standard seventeenth-century French Catholic conversion narrative. Thereby the récit validates his new faith and criticizes his old one.

It is, of course, not possible to determine the true "author" of the narrative. It likely had to meet the approval of Tarente's Catholic clerical mentors, but he certainly had the education and doctrinal knowledge to compose it himself and to explain how he came to draw a strict boundary between Catholic truth and Protestant falsehood. In the first section of the memoir Tarente describes the reasons that originally "threw him into error." He essentially recasts his wayward life into a series of steps from heresy and religious inconstancy to orthodoxy, but also from political rebelliousness to loyal subject of the monarch. The second section, by far the longest, relates the "means by which God drew him out" of error. It details his lengthy study of doctrinal issues separating the churches, which eventually brought him to his recognition of Catholic truth. The third part recounts his resistance to following that truth. As always conversion was a struggle: no easy change could be considered truly sincere. But in

158. "Motifs de la Conversion." A briefer version of his conversion story appears at the end of his published memoir. That text places the conversion within the context of his entire life, including importantly his political and military careers *(Mémoires de Henri-Charles de la Trémoille)*. I will draw on both versions. References to the "Motifs" will contain the page number and those to the memoir will be listed as *Mémoires* and page number.

1670 he claimed to have crossed the confessional boundary for good. Indeed he had, if for no other reason than he died two years later.

Tarente dismisses his earlier religious changes as not to be taken seriously. "I had been at first a Protestant, then a Catholic in obedience to my father; I became a Protestant again by the advice and insinuations of my mother. But it was by the freest choice and the one upon which I reflected most carefully at a much more advanced age that I embraced forever the Catholic religion" (*Mémoires*, 306). However, if we read the narrative against Tarente's mixed religious family background as well as his checkered political career, those earlier changes can suggest to us the complex reasons behind his conversions and relapses.

Tarente first converted at seven years of age, after his father, Duc Henri de La Trémoille, abjured his Protestantism during the siege of La Rochelle (1628).[159] The duke obliged all his children to follow him into Catholicism. As we have seen in Chapter 5, Tarente placed much of the blame for his eventual apostasy from Catholicism on his Protestant mother, Marie de La Tour d'Auvergne. The first conversion "was made at an age when I did not know what I was doing and the second could not properly be called a true religious change because my mother had preserved in my heart the first instructions she had given me since my birth." Recall that his mother's lessons left him with "disgust for the Catholic religion" (268). She sent him to Holland to live with his Protestant granduncle, the Prince of Orange. There he "tasted with pleasure the liberty of depending only on himself . . . and lived in disorder" (267). The influence of the Dutch Protestant milieu and family connections combined with his mother's pressure to lead him to renounce Catholicism. She made clear to him that he was "on the point of losing her if [he] did not give her the consolation of embracing her belief" (267–68). Thus his leaving Catholicism was due to his mother's power over him from his early years.

It was only retrospectively and much later that Tarente could characterize the reasons for these early religious changes as insincere and worldly. They might be understood instead as the result of his confessionally

159. In addition to Tarente's accounts, see *Nouvelle Biographie Générale* (Paris, 1859), 25:864–65; La Trémoïlle, *Les La Trémoïlle*, 4:viii–ix; and Winifred Stephens, *From the Crusades to the French Revolution: A History of the La Trémoille Family* (London, 1914), 175–97.

mixed household and kinship network with its competing family pressures and religious traditions. The La Trémoille family was Catholic until the late sixteenth century, when Tarente's grandfather, Claude, became a Protestant and an important leader of the French Reformed Church during the Wars of Religion. Tarente's grandmother came from the Dutch Protestant House of Orange. A Protestant family tradition continued among his, especially female, kin, including his mother, wife, and daughter. But after 1628, his father was a Catholic, and the filial obedience of the family heir was a powerful obligation.[160] Given the religious divide in his own family, we might well wonder to what degree his movements back and forth were really the consequence of the sort of profound changes in personal religious identity and belief upon which the conversion models insisted.

Tarente's beliefs are difficult to ascertain. In its lengthy discussion of doctrine, the conversion narrative presents him as having finally recognized and accepted Catholicism's truth in all matters in which it differed from Protestantism: the Real Presence, Communion in one kind, the authority of Church tradition versus that of Scripture alone, clerical celibacy, auricular confession, fasts, festivals, images, cults of the Virgin and saints, the vocation of priests versus ministers, the Church's antiquity, and the uniformity of doctrines over time. Like other noble converts, Tarente found Catholicism's claim to uniformity appealing; divisions among the Protestant churches troubled him. And he admired the Church's hierarchical organization; it corresponded well to an aristocratic concern with social hierarchy.[161]

However, Tarente may have long been seeking a theological accommodation between the churches. In the years before his final religious change, Tarente, like many leading Huguenot aristocrats, and even some of the clergy, was attracted to the ideas of Moyse Amyraut, which he may have seen as a way of reconciling the faiths.[162] Once Tarente had joined the other side, he argued that the two faiths had grown closer together. In his memoir he overcame any lingering doubts about his conversion by re-

160. For a discussion of the pressure Tarente put on his own children to convert, see above, pp. 226–29.

161. Rosa, "Conversion to Catholicism of . . . Tarente."

162. On this issue, see Rosa, "Turenne's Conversion," 643, above, p. 176.

sorting to the Catholic argument that the Church had accommodated itself to Protestant complaints. He wrote: "Those of the so-called reformed religion who are of good faith cannot deny that in recent years purity has been reestablished in the Church's discipline. The pretext for any issues they have raised—about praying in vernacular languages, or reading Scripture, or that priests were rudely ignorant and disorderly, or that [Catholics] practiced a merely exterior devotion—has been removed. We have entered into [the Protestants] sentiments in such matters" (274). Certainly this line of reasoning was a useful Catholic polemical ploy, but it is at least possible that it carried real weight for Tarente, who had been seeking a middle way. A church that had corrected its shortcomings left no cause for further separation. For Tarente, then, conversion could have meant less a radical change than an alignment with an institution that now he could see represented his long-standing beliefs.[163]

Nonetheless, even if Catholicism's truth was finally evident to him, his narrative, to fit the conversion model, had to demonstrate how he had long resisted it. Obstacles had stood in his way, obstacles identified with the worldly concerns of reputation and family. It had been a point of honor not to quit the religion he had professed for a long time; he feared his social credit would suffer. He also knew a conversion would sadden his wife, who remained a Protestant.[164] What would break such impediments to following the truth and securing his salvation? In Christian conversion, there was, of course, only one answer: God's grace. "The world was too present in . . . my heart. I had strange agitations. . . . I was continually distracted by the opposed thoughts occupying my mind. . . . I did not have the strength to accomplish what God had put in my heart" (286). But God

163. Labrousse has argued that many who abjured the Reformed faith referred to the Protestant idea of "libre examen" and described their conversions more as the result of a search for the "better" church rather than a rejection of a "false" church for a "true" one (see "Conversion dans les deux sens," 168–69, and "Conversion d'un huguenot au catholicisme," 63). But such a search was predicated on the unorthodox idea that there was validity in both churches. Tarente's final conversion may also have been the result of such a realignment rather than a radical transformation of beliefs, but his conversion account definitely rejected Protestantism as false.

164. According to the memoir of his daughter, Charlotte-Amélie, Tarente's conversion did create a great split between her parents (Aldenburg, *Autobiography*, 31, 35–36).

"fortified [my] faith and gave [me] through his grace the [spirit of] submission of which I had need" (283). Grace gave him victory over his worldly obstacles, "his *amour-propre* [self-respect], tenderness for his loved ones, and temporal advantages" (286–87).

Like other Catholic accounts, Tarente's memoir raised the issue of political loyalty to the French monarch and presented it not as another worldly interest but as the antidote to such problems. When he first went north, the good treatment he received led him to see the Dutch Republic "as my patrie and France as a foreign country" (267). It was thus "easy to make me understand that my [then Catholic] religion stood in the way of advantages for which I might hope" (267). His relapse to the "false" faith led him into misguided political activities. He returned to France in 1647 and entered the Fronde because of his attachment to Condé. "I was living in such a great forgetfulness of God . . . that I threw myself into revolt against the king, since I thought my interests were opposed to his service and my duty." Tarente's personal independence brought confusion and rebellion, just as the independence of new sects provoked disorder in souls (272). After the Fronde, he returned to a military post in the Netherlands and only returned to France definitively in 1669.[165]

Political and religious revolt were linked, as were submission to the king and submission to the true Church: "My revolt against God preceded that against the king" but "my return to the king preceded that to God" (268). Political rebelliousness and religious heterodoxy had put him at odds with his monarch. Yet the account presented Louis XIV as always generous in response. The convert wrote that "I could not but regret keeping posts in a state [the Dutch Republic] that suffered with intolerance the closeness and prosperity of France . . . [but] I was so little determined to reenter the Church that when the king spoke to me with much kindness and charity, I responded only with silence" (286). How insulting was this to a monarch who had always given evidence of "his desire for his subjects' salvation" (285)? When Tarente finally decided to convert, it was the monarch he informed first. "I went to Saint-Germain, where I declared to the king my resolution to change religions, which brought his

165. He claimed that during this period, Cromwell tried to entice him into leading a rising of French Protestants, but the conspiracy came to nothing (*Mémoires*, 170–71).

majesty much surprise and joy" (*Mémoires*, 303). His conversion was both a return to Catholicism and the last step in his return to political favor.

Prior to his abjuration, Louis had told Tarente "religion was the only obstacle that stood in the way of [his] advancement" (*Mémoires*, 296). But unlike the advantages Protestantism had brought him, the king's offer was no worldly matter. Rather, it was true faithfulness that led him back to the Catholic monarchy, and that is what brought the conversion narrative to its conclusion. Theological ideas, material concerns, family interests and pressures all contributed to an almost lifelong confessional flexibility and kept the religious boundary open for Tarente. But, in his account, joining the king's religion was the only way to bring to a good conclusion a lifetime of political waywardness and religious indeterminacy.

As recounted in conversion accounts, relapses show the way the confessional boundary failed in individual cases. But to understand how this back-and-forth across the religious divide helped foster confessional coexistence, we must look at the practice of conversion and reconversion within a biconfessional community, where available evidence suggests that intermarriage provided the occasion for most abjurations and relapses. In Chapter 4 I discussed the practice of intermarriage and its effect on the construction of confessional boundaries. Here I want only to return briefly to the relapses that often followed mixed marriages with the example of Melle, where consistorial records for the 1660s and 1670s allow us a glimpse, at least from the Protestant side, of how marriage conversion and reconversion kept the confessional boundary open.

Recall that since Catholic priests and Huguenot consistories rarely allowed a wedding between people of the opposing faiths, one or the other spouse had to convert. However, these converts did at times revert to their original faiths. Former Huguenots, who asked their consistories for forgiveness, quickly received it once they had endured a stern lecture and made a public acknowledgment of their repentance.[166] The return of former Catholics to their Church was no more difficult.[167] The degree of re-

166. Though earlier in the century, especially in strongly Huguenot areas, consistories might have felt freer to act more harshly.

167. Dompnier, *Venin de l'hérésie*, 155.

lapsing after marriage conversions is difficult to determine, but Melle's consistorial records suggest that it remained a readily available option for former Huguenots, even at a time when the government was beginning to exercise greater surveillance over marriage conversions.

As we have seen in Chapter 4, Melle's consistory in the 1660s accepted over a hundred Catholics asking to be received in the Reformed Church.[168] It is not possible to say how many of these later returned to their original faith. It does not seem likely that anywhere near as many Huguenots converted in the other direction in this town that Protestants dominated. But some did and later returned. In the same decade, ten former Protestants (of whom seven were women) appeared before the consistory asking to be forgiven for having married Catholics.[169] To these ten cases of relapses we might be able to add another twenty (of whom nine were women) in which former Protestants returned to the faith without stating a reason for their original departure, though marriage seems a likely possibility. Thus a sizable group of Huguenots converted and then returned to the Reformed Church. Or at least they did so before 1663, the year in which the royal government forbade those who had converted to Catholicism from relapsing. Of the ten cases in which a former Huguenot admitted marrying a Catholic, only one occurred after 1663. Of the other twenty cases, all but one of these instances occurred before or during 1663. As other consistory records show, between 1669 and 1674 no one returned asking for readmission. This silence is hard to interpret. It is possible that some converts did reappear and were accepted back into the faith without the elders taking the risk of recording the names of those involved in its official register. But it might also mean that those who converted to Catholicism were not relapsing and not contravening the law.

The state may have succeeded in creating a stricter confessional boundary in marriages and marriage conversions, but the churches had not. Clearly, their conversion models had not worked in Melle. Conversion here was not irrevocable, which does not suggest its lack of meaningfulness but rather the opposite. The models construed conversion as a

168. See above, pp. 158–61.

169. ADDS 2J 35 (1) Collection Dez. In all cases they were reintegrated into the Protestant community after having made public recognition of their fault.

deeply significant act that resulted in a strong personal identification with a particular church; conversion concretized personal identity as either Catholic or Protestant and thus drew a sharp line between the two. But within a community such as Melle, personal identity was a more complicated matter that was centered not only on adherence to a church but on membership in families and in a biconfessional community.[170] Identity depended not only on religious attachment (though that was part of it), but also on social position, neighborliness, kinship networks, and family interests. Conversion served these other elements of personal identity as much as it served that of religious affiliation. Abjurations for interconfessional marriages were required, but relapses permitted the flexibility necessary so that family interests could be served, family religious traditions continued, and space maintained in the community for both confessional groups.

Marriage conversions and relapses do not imply that the local frontier between the faiths was indistinct in the manner of what I have called the first type of confessional boundary formation. The return of a spouse to the consistory suggests that she or he identified clearly with the Reformed faith and that in the future the confessional boundary would run through the household. This situation created the second form of boundary. The confessional divide was clear, but interactions across it allowed for each group to maintain a recognized and accepted place within the community. As long as the possibility for relapse existed, it could prevent the border from closing behind marriage converts and allowed both religious groups to pursue a communal coexistence together. Once the state shut down that possibility, families of the minority had to watch their children convert definitively to the Roman Church or choose spouses for their offspring from within the shrinking membership of the Reformed faith. And the Revocation of the Edict of Nantes eliminated that possibility. Or did it?

Once all were, at least nominally, Catholics, then conversions and relapses were no longer an issue. But Huguenots did often practice a de facto relapse, by making a declaration of Catholic belief just before a marriage and then refusing ever to return to the parish church again.[171] And

170. Labrousse, "Conversion dans les deux sens," 170.

171. Krumenacker, *Protestants du Poitou*, 226.

many continued to marry "within the faith" by choosing other "new converts" as spouses and then establishing their marriage by means of a contract before a notary. They did not seek a blessing by the priest, who would, in any case, likely have refused it if he deemed them deficient in meeting Catholic religious obligations.[172] But in her study of Mauvezin, Elisabeth Labrousse also found "mixed marriages" of "old Catholics" with "new converts," who were clearly still committed to Protestantism. When the local curé informed on these couples and they were hauled before a local judge, those who were "new converts" insisted that in the future they would "do as the others of the RPR [religion prétendue réformée] and not otherwise," while their "old Catholic" spouses promised only to "act according to the inspirations the Lord gave" them. Both replies suggest that the minority religion dominated these households. As Labrousse concluded, "[I]t was as if the 'Roman Catholic' spouse had submitted to the demands of 'Protestant spouse' or, otherwise said, had *virtually converted to Protestantism.*"[173] These "conversions" were, of course, only "virtual," but they suggest how the state, in preventing the back-and-forth across the confessional divide that conversion and relapse permitted, had achieved precisely the opposite of that for which it had hoped.

172. Labrousse, "Mariages bigarrés." Or they might simply find a complaisant priest, who did not demand a confession and communion of the future spouses (see Krumenacker, *Protestants du Poitou*, 225–30).

173. "Mariages bigarrés," 168, 171 (my emphasis). The cases date from 1737–1740, and were few in number but are offered here as an example of the sort of marriage arrangements that the outlawing of Protestantism could produce.

CONCLUSION

ACCORDING TO THE CHURCHES' conversion models, truth resided in the individual conscience. Once a convert accepted the truth, conscience would secure his or her religious affiliation and prevent any recrossing of the confessional boundary. Relapses, however, described conscience as a bridge back across the divide, thereby raising doubts about the boundary's impermeability and the converts' true confessional identity. The boundary also remained open because Catholics and Protestants had to live together, govern their communities, carry on their business and professional affairs, marry each other, and bury their dead. French Catholics and Protestants shared these concerns, crossed the confessional border to deal with them, and hence left religious identities blurred. For the churches, the problem was not new in the years when the monarchy was trying to force Protestant consciences into conformity with the majority faith. It had vexed them from the beginning of religious conflict in the sixteenth century. How were they to make clear to people who shared so much the differences between the faiths and the dangers their rivals represented? The power of conscience was their ultimate recourse.

Nearly a century before the relapses at Melle, the religious tergiversations of Pierre Jarrige, and Tarente's final return to the king and the Catholic Church, Michel de Montaigne turned his always perceptive eye on the issue and found out how troublesome it could be. In his essay "Of Conscience," Montaigne tells a story of how, one day during "our civil wars," a companion and he "met a gentleman of good appearance," who was "of the opposing party" (i.e., a Huguenot). "I knew nothing of it," the essayist reports, "for he pretended otherwise; and the worst of these wars is that the cards are so shuffled that your enemy is distinguished from yourself by no apparent mark either of language or of bearing, and has been brought up in the same laws and customs and the same atmosphere, so it is hard to avoid confusion and disorder."[1] For Montaigne, writing in the wake of the Saint Bartholomew's Day massacres and during or immediately after the fourth civil war, such confusion posed a dilemma: How could you tell friend from foe when all spoke the same language, followed the same laws and customs, and breathed the same air?[2]

Montaigne was certain he knew; he was confident that conscience made the truth of one's confessional affiliation evident. He continues his story by describing how the gentleman in question seemed so fearful and constantly on guard "that I finally guessed that his alarms were caused by his conscience. . . . So marvelous is the power of conscience! It makes us betray, accuse, and fight ourselves, and, in the absence of an outside witness, it brings us forward against ourselves. . . ." Those who do not hold to the true faith, like the unnamed gentleman, reveal their internal disorder in their outward demeanor and behavior. Those who are true believers are not at war with themselves. "As conscience fills us with fear, so also it fills us with assurance and confidence."[3] In the sanctum of the conscience, truth was clear, and, as a result, people of the rival faiths could be clearly distinguished from each other.

Montaigne's language foreshadows the rhetoric of the conversion models with their descriptions of conscience as an alarm that never sleeps or as an internal tribunal that puts converts on trial until grace helps them overcome all obstacles on the path to truth. But, as we have seen, the conversion models did not succeed in securing individual confessional identity or in building the third form of boundary. Nor did the other discourses of differentiation that issued from the opponents of coexistence, targeting shared civic and religious space, religiously mixed families, and women's roles in their churches. They did not succeed in creating an impermeable barrier between the groups that would isolate Protestants completely and

1. "Of Conscience," in *Complete Essays,* 264–66, see esp. 264. Frame's edition dates the essay to 1573–1574.

2. Recall the Huguenots' 1597 complaint about being denied access to cemeteries: "our fathers had rights to [parish cemeteries] . . . that were public and common. Have we not inherited their rights just as much as this French air we breathe, the cities we frequent, and the homes we inhabit?" See "Plaintes des églises réformées," in Read, "Cimetières et inhumations" (1862), 142. Also see above, p. 111.

3. "Of Conscience," 264, 265.

pressure them to convert as the only means of reintegrating themselves into their communities and the kingdom.

As Louis XIV became determined not to suffer the regime of coexistence his grandfather had established, he sought to establish the third boundary through a legislative campaign against the Reformed Church. He attacked many of the sites of religious mixing or cooperation this book has described and mobilized many of the strategies that had been deployed over the decades to undermine coexistence. One example here will suffice, an example that reprises some of the major issues this study has examined. It concerns the city of Niort, where the Huguenot and Catholic inhabitants had devoted so much effort to constructing coexistence over the course of the century.

On 19 April 1684, in the early afternoon, a crowd of Catholics numbering around ten thousand gathered in front of Niort's Protestant temple. Among them were about one hundred and twenty Catholic priests and monks and the children of the poor hospital, who had marched there in procession. The city's magistrates opened the temple's doors, and six or seven thousand people rushed in. The clergymen set themselves up on the side of the building that faced the nearby hospital chapel. They opened the window and doors on that side and began to chant as loudly as they could ("in voices screaming like thunder," according to the Huguenot complaint). They blew horns and trumpets to accompany their chanting. The rest of the crowd sacked the temple. They destroyed New Testaments and psalters, broke benches, tore up seat cushions, and defecated in the pulpit.[4]

This extraordinary act of aggression, reminiscent of popular violence during the Wars of Religion, was actually a legal procedure. For years Catholic and royal authorities had been seeking ways to close down Huguenot temples and Protestant worship in Poitou and throughout France. One means at their disposal was to prove that the sound of Protestant worship disturbed the celebration of the mass in a Catholic church,

4. I draw this account from the complaint Niort's Huguenots sent to the king's minister Louvois, a copy of which was inserted into their consistory record. See "Consistoire de Niort," BMP Fonds Fonteneau, vol. 37, 261–63. See also Lièvre, *Histoire des protestants,* 2:141–43; and Krumenacker, *Protestants du Poitou,* 88–89. A very similar attack on the temple of Cherveux occurred the next day.

chapel, or religious house. Interference with Catholic worship was grounds for closing or moving a temple. On that day in Niort the province's intendant, Nicolas Lamoignon de Basville, positioned himself in the nearby hospital chapel along with the city's Catholic mayor and échevins; the Protestant commissioner of the edict in Poitou, the Marquis de Villarnoux, had absented himself from the proceedings. The officials had no trouble confirming that they could hear chanting from the temple. Niort's Huguenots complained bitterly about the procedure: they certainly did not scream at the top of their voices when singing psalms; they did not open all the windows; they did not blow horns and trumpets. Even the chapel's priest had recently testified that Protestant worship did not hinder his performance of the mass. Of course, none of this was to any avail. The intendant was satisfied that the temple's proximity to the chapel was a problem, but apparently it was only enough of a problem to obtain the relocation of the temple, not the complete cessation of Protestant worship in Niort.

To accomplish that goal Catholics resorted to another legal maneuver, which was based on the 1663 law against relapses. If a convert to Catholicism was found returning to a temple, not only could he or she be prosecuted, but so too could the minister and the congregation. The minister could be removed from his post and Protestant worship in the community outlawed. Consistories zealously guarded the doors of their temples to make certain no apostate slipped in, thereby providing Catholic authorities with the necessary excuse for shutting the temple. But their vigilance was for naught. Of the thirty-four Poitevin temples prohibited in the early 1680s, at least twenty-two were targeted because of new converts who had reentered.[5] Niort joined the list on 30 April 1684. After the service on that day, the mayor accosted Minister Pierre Bossatran and produced a young man, a convert to Catholicism, whom he claimed to have found in the temple.[6] Huguenots protested that the mayor's declaration was false, but Reformed worship in the city was forbidden. On 19 October the intendant gave the final command for the temple's demolition.

5. Krumenacker, *Protestants du Poitou,* 87. He refers to the law against relapses as a "veritable war machine" against Protestant temples.

6. "Consistoire de Niort," BMP Fonds Fonteneau, vol. 37, 134–35; Lièvre, *Histoire des protestants,* 2:144.

The order put an end to decades of negotiation between Niort's Huguenots and Catholics. We have seen how they, with the participation of the state's agents, partitioned communal sacred space and reached accommodations on their respective observances in the temple, churches, cemeteries, and city streets. The result had been the construction of the second form of confessional boundary in the town, which minimized conflict and allowed both groups to practice their religion and maintain membership in the community. The destruction of the temple and the outlawing of Reformed worship would eliminate the Protestants' public presence in Niort. It looked as if the third form of boundary had triumphed. Through legislation and the intendant's activities, the role of the state here was essential. But local people and the local dynamic of religious relations were also crucial for constructing this boundary. Huguenots complained that the Catholic mayor had stated, "I will do all that is possible and search for any occasion to ensure you lose [your temple]"; and he threatened Huguenots by declaring "say good-bye to your temple."[7] If such were his feelings, little room was left in Niort for interconfessional negotiations and accommodations.

Under these circumstances, there was not much Huguenots could do, but in their reaction we can see other themes this study has raised. Minister Bossatran's last sermon to his coreligionists was a lament filled with the sort of Old Testament references that often infused Huguenot rhetoric and gave voice to their sufferings.[8] He had heard the "sad news" that their temple was to be demolished and that they would "lose the liberty they had to assemble in this place." Their city of Niort was covered in darkness; it had become a second Egypt. But the minister reminded them of the Israelites, whose city had been destroyed and who had been taken into captivity. They eventually returned to rebuild the walls of Zion and repair the ruins of their temple.

God's anger at their sins had brought this disaster upon Niort's Huguenots, and they had to submit. He reminded his flock: "Do not follow Job's example and contest God's will." Humility and repentance were the prop-

7. "Consistoire de Niort," BMP Fonds Fonteneau, vol. 37, 264–65.

8. "Sermon sur ces paroles: 'Je cognoist Ô Eternel que tes jugements ne sont que justice,'" BPF Ms. 869 (1) (Niort). The manuscript is not paginated.

er response.[9] Nonetheless, his coreligionists did not bear all responsibility. The minister did not point the finger at the king and his officials, but he certainly directed his fury at the rival church. And he did so in the gendered terms that had long characterized Protestant-Catholic polemics. He consoled his flock by comparing the true church to Rachel, "that grieving mother who cried for her children." He thereby associated Protestants with an Old Testament heroine. In the years to come new heroines would appear among the Huguenots, noblewomen who hid Protestant refugees in their châteaux, women who refused to convert and were imprisoned in Catholic religious establishments, and prophetesses who inspired Huguenot resistance in the Cevennes. When Bossatran turned to the oppressor, he did not depict the Catholic Church as dominated by amazons who transgressed gender boundaries. But neither did he mince words. The Catholic Church was a "*paillarde*," a whore, and the "mother of abominations." "Do not be turned by such a woman," he warned his listeners.

As was frequently the case among Protestant polemicists, Bossatran singled out Catholic missionaries for inflaming tensions. They "disguise the errors of Rome in a thousand ways" and depict the true religion in "horrible terms." It is not likely that the minister was thinking of the Capuchins who had worked in Poitou some sixty years earlier. However, he was well acquainted with their legacy and successors. Missionaries had been active in the province since 1681, preceding or accompanying the first dragonnade, during which troops terrorized Huguenots into conversion.[10] Capuchins were among them, such as a Père Alexis, who preached at Couhé in December 1681, but other Catholic clergy were also seeking converts. Bossatran debated an Abbé de Chalusset in June 1682, despite his consistory's refusal to countenance his participation.[11] Missionaries certainly did not win as many abjurations as the dragoons. But since the days of Père Joseph's mission in the province, Huguenots had understood the close association between military and evangelization campaigns.

As the anti-Protestant program gained ground, the third form of confessional boundary became increasingly apparent in biconfessional com-

9. For examples of others who wrote of Huguenots receiving just punishment for their sins, see Garrisson, *Édit de Nantes*, 135–36.

10. Krumenacker, *Protestants du Poitou*, 63.

11. Krumenacker, *Protestants du Poitou*, 97–98.

munities. However, in one sense, the boundary failed insofar as it succeeded. As various historians have suggested, the religious groups became increasingly closed in on themselves. For at least a core of the Protestant movement, the response to persecution was more commitment than ever to their faith and to their separation from Catholics.[12] These Huguenots might have been increasingly isolated, but they did not convert. It was this failure of a program to eliminate Protestantism by ostracizing Huguenots that prompted the state to undertake a more brutal policy. Nonetheless, force also failed. Many Huguenots fled the country.[13] Others were compelled to abjure the Reformed faith. But as became apparent in the years after the Revocation, many of the converts never observed Catholicism, and a large number continued the clandestine practice of Protestantism.

Available evidence also suggests, however, that the third boundary never succeeded because of continuing good local relations between Catholics and Huguenots. We can see examples in the memoir Jean Migault, a Protestant schoolmaster from Mougon in Poitou, wrote of his escape from France. He described how Catholics frequently helped him and his family. For example, during the 1681 dragonnade, a local abbé rescued Migault's wife from soldiers by promising to convert her. She later made her escape. Of course the priest might well have been serious about converting her, but, according to Migault, when he heard of her flight, he said, "God wish her well." Even more instrumental in the Migaults' escape were two Catholic sisters, longtime neighbors of theirs, who hid Jean and then spirited his wife out from under the noses of soldiers.[14] In the journal, these examples contrast with the inhumanity of the king's persecution of Protestants. And they show that Catholics and Protestants could still live together peacefully. Admittedly one cannot make too much of a single family's experiences. But many Huguenots succeeded in fleeing France, and among them were others who received Catholic help. Migault's experience illustrates the persistence in localities of the first form

12. As Raymond A. Mentzer Jr. puts it, "Persecution, far from destroying the Protestant community in France, reinvigorated it" (*Blood and Belief,* 191).

13. Approximately one-fifth of the Huguenots emigrated. See Hanlon, *Confession and Community,* 255.

14. Migault, *Journal de Jean Migault,* 71–95. He also presents other examples of Catholic aid.

of confessional boundary based on personal relations of neighborliness and friendship. We cannot say that the individuals involved in the Migaults' escape blurred their confessional identity, but they were still willing to consider their neighbors of the minority faith as people with whom they shared common bonds and obligations, even at the considerable risk of disobeying their ruler.

Thus, by the 1680s in France, the state and the Catholic Church were making the third type of confessional boundary stronger than ever before, though it never completely separated people of the two faiths. It could not do so because at least certain features of the first boundary still contributed to local Catholic-Protestant relations. What had disappeared was the second form of boundary, one in which Catholics and Protestants reached accommodations within the institutional framework of their communities and the legal structure the state provided in the Edict of Nantes. Individuals on either side of the divide might still get along, but no longer would the two groups be able collectively to negotiate peaceful coexistence. In a country with a history of religious rivalry and bloodshed, and with continuing suspicions and tensions between the two sides, it was this second form of boundary, more than the first, that offered the best chance for avoiding conflict and finding a way the rival religions could live together. The second boundary had concretized confessional identities because negotiations required the careful definition of religious spaces and practices in biconfessional communities. It had drawn a clear line between the groups, but it had accommodated both. And, in the early decades of the century, the monarchy had promoted the process of accommodation. It was when the policy changed that the presence of a clear boundary left the Protestants exposed to persecution.

It is in examining the process of confessional boundary building, especially of the first and second forms of boundary, that this study has significance for thinking about religious coexistence in other times and places. Indeed, it is what lends the study of Catholic-Huguenot relations urgency beyond the realm of early-modern French history. For while the French experience cannot simply be transposed to other places, it does share much with other situations of religious conflict, including rival faiths, a long history of violence, and continuing tensions between the two sides.

But, as is the case elsewhere, French Catholics and Protestants shared a common culture underlying religious difference that was evident in, for example, a shared language, political ideas, and views on civic and family life. And they possessed means of social identification not necessarily defined strictly along religious lines. In places with these conditions, establishing coexistence—though not perhaps true tolerance—requires finding a way to emphasize the positive elements over the negative ones, and that in turn depends on a weariness with violence and a desire for peace and order along with the presence of a political entity that can exercise authority over both groups or, at least, can act as a referee between them.

No doubt the ideal circumstances for coexistence are those in which people's willingness to get along is based on means of individual self-definition that cut across religious affiliation. Confessional difference is less salient than other ways people have of identifying with each other, such as through kinship, neighborliness, professional connections, economic interests, civic ties, and political allegiances—in short, everything that people have in common apart from religion. In such circumstances, the first form of confessional boundary, the most permeable one, is evident in the arena of daily life. Although this boundary undermines confessional difference, it may well have a foundation in religious belief. Those Catholics and Huguenots who told their clergymen that people could be saved in either faith as long as they were good people understood their neighbors as Christians regardless of their church affiliation. They could well have been fortified in this belief when they participated in religious observances of the other faith, for example, in family rituals. Insofar as cross-cutting social identifications and the recognition of religious commonality can be emphasized, the tensions that result in religious conflict decrease and the possibilities for coexistence expand.

But where there is deep-seated religious antagonism, such a situation has no institutional anchor to secure it. With the second form of boundary, which a political entity standing outside rival churches (e.g., the monarchy in France) promotes and local people negotiate, religious division is not blurred. Indeed, it is recognized, but accommodations can be reached. Ideally, in such a situation, the political entity would be religiously neutral. The French state was never neutral; the monarchy was committed to Catholic unity, as even the Edict of Nantes made clear. That commitment led eventually to the dismantling of coexistence and the persecution of Protestants. But in the early decades under the edict, the monarchy interpreted its religious and political mission as ensuring peace and order until such time as God reunited the churches. No doubt this view could appear an excuse for the monarchy's inability to enforce religious unity. Or, as Montaigne put it, French kings, "having been unable to do what they would, . . . have pretended to will what they could."[15] But we need not take so skeptical a view. For the state's willingness to encourage coexistence reestablished order in the country and provided the all-important political support and legal framework for building coexistence. The support and the framework were necessary precisely because Catholics and Huguenots were not always able to get along. With the state's active intervention, they could reach agreements that defused sources of potential conflict.

Where peace between religious groups hangs in the balance, we might hope for the first confessional boundary, a situation in which people set aside religious difference to coexist amicably. But in many cases that is simply too much to expect. Certainly, that was the case in early-modern France, where confessional tensions never disappeared. Here the second type of boundary proved to be the most feasible way to resolve conflict. Constructing this boundary does not require a presumption of good relations between confessional groups; instead, it builds them. It does not displace confessional identity, but it brings people together to negotiate how they will get along. The settlements they reach, but also the act of reaching settlements, construct coexistence. The very process of negotiating how they will live together can create a setting in which people of rival faiths will peacefully find their place.

15. "Of Freedom of Conscience," in *Complete Essays,* 506–9, see esp. 509.

BIBLIOGRAPHY

MANUSCRIPT SOURCES

Archives départementales de la Charente-Maritime

C. 134. "Registre contenant les noms de tous ceux qui ont abjure la RPR dans les diverses églises et couvents de La Rochelle entre la reduction de La Rochelle et la Révocation de l'Edit de Nantes. 1628–1662 [*sic*]."

Archives départementales des Deux-Sèvres

Unclassified. Siège royal de Saint-Maixent Civil Divers 1631–1666 [*sic*].

1I 1. Dossier 20: La Mothe-Saint-Héray; Dossier 21: La Mothe-Saint-Héray.

1I (3). Mougon.

2J 35 (1). Collection Dez. Melle consistory.

Archives départementales de la Vienne

C 49 "Sommaire des raisons que ceux qui font profession de la religion refformée ont de se plaindre de l'arrest du seiziesme septembre 1634 donné par nos seigneurs du parlement tenants les grands jours en la ville de Poictiers. . . ."

Papers Concerning Cemetery Division. Chenay (10 June 1684).

F 183. Fonds du legs Alfred Richard. Saint-Maixent.

F 184. Fonds du legs Alfred Richard. La Mothe-Saint-Héray.

Archives nationales

1AP. *Papers of the La Trémoille family.*

*441. "Motifs de la Conversion de feu Monseigneur le Prince de Tarente: Ecrits par luy-même vers l'année 1671."

TT. *Affaires et biens des protestants:*

232 (7). Argenton in Issoudun.

241. "Synode et assemblee des ministres et antiens deputtez des eglises refformees de la province de Poictou estant assemblez en la ville dy Nyort . . . 14 avril 1601."

241. Letter from Marillac to Le Tellier of 20 January 1674.

241 (2). Chizé.

241 (4). "Synodes, Exercices de la RPR 1574–1680."

250 (1–5). Loudun.

251 (40). Marans.

260 (10). Niort.

261 (21). Parthenay.

262 (8). "Estat de la religion en Poictou."

262 (204–207). Exoudun.

271 (24), 2. St. Savin en Berry.

271 (21). Saint-Quentin.

Bibliothèque municipale d'Orléans

Ms. 916. "Recueils pour l'histoire generalle en abbregé de touttes les missions des capuçins depuis le commencement de la reforme jusques l'an 1673."

Bibliothèque municipale de Poitiers

Fonds Fonteneau

Vol. 14: p. 233. "Deposition des [*sic*] la rupture d'une porte de l'eglise de Boufferé par des gentilhommes protestants pour faire l'inhumation d'une religionnaire" (27 May 1613).

Vol. 37. pp. 261–63. "Consistoire de Niort."

Vol. 64 (2). p. 673. "Ordonnance du lieutenant général de Fontenay-le-Comte aux fins de donner aux protestants dans le bourg de Luçon une sepulture separée" (3 January 1622).

Vol. 68. pp. 223–431. Documents on Niort.

Vol. 78. "Histoire civile et ecclésiatique du Poitou," par D. Fonteneau.

Vol. 79. pp. 303–306. Parthenay contract.

pp. 281–88. "Articles proposés par les deputtez du clergé, en l'assemblée générale des états contre ceux de la religion."

Bibliothèque du protestantisme français

Ms. 579 (1). *Collection Auzière:* Synodes et Colloques du Poitou.

Ms. 868 (5). Notes on the Huguenot prisoners of the donjon of Niort.

Ms. 869 (1). *Papiers Maillard*

Parthenay: contract establishing temple (1600).

"Articles contenants des plaintes des habitants catholiques de la ville de Loudun pour estre présentés à M.M. les commissaires députés pour l'exécution des edits" (1611).

"Remonstrances addresses par les religionnaires de ladite ville de St. Maixent à Messieurs de Vic & de Saint-Germain" (15 April 1612).

Réponse des habitants catholiques aux plaintes de ceux de la r.p.r. . . ." (12 May 1612) (Saint-Maixent).

"Réponse des députés" (16 July 1612) (Saint-Maixent).

"Sermon sur ces paroles: 'Je cognoist Ô Eternel que tes jugements ne sont que justice'" (Niort).

Ms. 870 (1). *Papiers Guitton*

Summary of a letter from Marie de Medici to Poitiers' city council (12 January 1612).

"Requête des protestants de Luçon aux commissaires du roi pour obtenir l'exercise public de leur religion" (6 March 1627).

"Acte de Mr de Melleville commissaire en l'instance et poursuite par la religion prétendue reformée du retablissement de l'exercise de leur religion au lieu de Luçon" (28 May 1627).

"Lettres adressées de 1585–1625 à Marc-Antoine Marreau de Boisguérin, governeur de Loudun (letters of 7 November 1610 and 6 July 1615), and notes on the 'Mémoires' of René de Brilhac, Sieur du Parc)."

"Requête des maire, échevins, bourgeois, et habitants catholiques de la ville de Saint-Maixent au sujet de la révolte et violence des religionnaires, présenté à nos seigneurs les députés par sa majesté en ce pays et province de Poitou" (undated).

"Réponse des habitants catholiques aux plaintes de ceux de la r.p.r. . . ." (12 May 1612).

Copy of letter from Flandrine de Nassau, abbesse de Sainte-Croix de Poitiers, à sa soeur Madame de la Trimouille, duchesse de Thouars (18 December 1628).

Ms. 1500/6 (Fonds Dez, Maillard, and Société des Antiquaires de l'Ouest, Melle consistory, 7 April 1673).

Ms. 1500/6/1. Vanzay, Extraits des Registres Catholiques.

Ms. 1500/6/i. Lusignan, Extraits des Registres Catholiques.

Ms. 1956, No. 3 bis. J. Rivierre, "Six cents procédures et arrêts anti-protestants en Poitou, 1678–1730."

Bibliothèque provinciale des Capuçins. Paris

Ms. 22. Lepré-Balain, "La vie du R. Père Joseph de Paris prédicateur de l'ordre des pères capucins, commissaire apostolique des missions étrangères fondateur des religieuses réformées de S. Benoist sous le tiltre de la Congrégation de Nostre Dame sur le Calvaire."

Ms. 43, fols. 109, 151, 159. "Memorabilia provincia turonensis capucinorum."

Ms. 180, fols. 92, 154. Untitled.

Bibliothèque Sainte-Geneviève

Ms. 3249, fol. 278. Letter of Père Joseph de Paris to Cardinal La Rochefoucauld (undated).

PUBLISHED SOURCES

Aldenburg, Charlotte Amélie, Princess of. *The Autobiography of Charlotte Amélie, Princess of Aldenburg, née Princess de la Trémoille, 1652–1732*. Edited by Aubrey Le Blond. London: Eveleigh Nash, 1913.

Babu, Jean. *Églogues poitevines sur différentes matières de controverse, pour le vulgaire du Poitou*. Niort: L. Favre, 1875.

———. *Poésies de Jean Babu, curé de Soudan, sur les ruines des temples protestants de Champdeniers, d'Exoudun, de La Mothe-Saint-Héraye (1663–1682)*. Edited by A. Richard. Poitiers: P. Blanchier, 1896.

Benoist, Elie. *Histoire de l'Edit de Nantes contenant les choses les plus remarquables qui se sont passées en France avant & après sa publication. . . .* 5 vols. Delft: Adrien Beman, 1693–1694.

Benoist, René. *Briefve proposition des admirables conversions à la vraye foy, eglise & religion catholique de S. Paul & de S. Augustin . . . envoyée & dediée à l'Altesse de très sage, très vertueuse & magnanime princesse, Madame la duchesse de Bar, soeur unique du roy très chrestien*. Paris: Pierre Chevallier, 1601.

Camus, Jean-Pierre. *Des missions ecclésiastiques*. Paris: G. Alliot, 1643.

Clouet, François. *Declaration du Sr François Clouet cy-devant appellé Pere Basile de Rouën, Predicateur Capucin & Missionaire du Pape, où il déduit les raisons qu'il a euës de se separer de l'Eglise Romaine pour se ranger à la Reformée*. Sedan: Jean Jannon, 1639.

Colbert de Croissy, Charles. *État du Poitou sous Louis XIV: Rapport au roi et mémoire sur le clergé, la noblesse, la justice et les finances*. Edited by Charles Dugast-Matifeux. Poitiers: Le Bouquiniste, 1976.

La conversion de Monseigneur le duc D'esdiguières à la Religion Catholique, Apostolique & Romaine ensemble le Brevet de l'Estat de Connestable de France à luy envoyé par sa Majesté le 7ème de ce mois de juillet 1622. Paris: Pierre Rocollet, 1622.

Conversion de Monsieur de la Trimoüille; Dicours [sic] *theologique sur la conversion de Monsieur le duc de la Trimoüille, à la Religion Catholique, Apostolique & Romaine, contenant une sommaire narration des raisons & motifs qui l'ont porté à ce changement*. Paris: J. Bessin, 1628.

La conversion de Monsieur de la Trimoüille duc et pair de France faitte en l'armée du roy devant La Rochelle le 18 iour de juillet mil six cens vingt-huict. Paris: Toussainct du Bray, 1628.

La conversion de Monsieur Jarrige cy-devant Jesuite confesseur et pere spirituel de la maison des Jesuistes à la Rochelle Admoniteur du Recteur & Predicateur Ordinaire. Charenton: Louis Vendosme, 1648.

La conversion du Sieur Cotiby ministre de Poictiers, faite entre les mains de Monseigneur l'Evesque de Poictiers, le jeudy de la semaine saincte: Ensemble la Conversion de plusieurs autres personnes de la R.P.R. qui ont suivy son exemple. Paris: Estienne Maucroy, 1660.

La conversion du Sieur de Parabere Faicte à Rome le premier Janvier 1617, addressée a Monsieur de Parabere, Gouverneur pour le Roy en la ville & chasteau de Niort, son Pere. Paris: Edme Martin, 1617.

La conversion du Sieur Mestayer cy-devant ministre du Lusignan, faicte en la ville de Poitiers le 23 jour de mars 1617. Poitiers: I. Mesnier, 1617.

Cottiby, Samuel. *Lettre de M. Cottiby, envoyée le XXV Mars au Pasteurs et Anciens de l'Eglise Reformée de Poictiers*. Published with Jean Daillé, *Lettre escrite a Monsieur Le Coq Sieur de la Talonnière sur le changement de religion de M. Cottiby*. Charenton: Louis Vendosme, 1660.

Declaration chrestienne du pere Charles Andrieu iadis cordelier de l'ordre pretendu de S. François natif de la ville de Murat en Auvergne & reduit en la ville de Figeac en Quercy le 27 mars 1602. Pontorson: Jean Le Fevre, 1602.

Declaration de Maistre Daniel Dusert, natif de Cinte-gavelle prés Thoulouse, cy-devant Religieux de la Reforme selon la reigle de S. Francoys, contenant l'abiuration de la doctrine de l'Eglise Romaine & la protestation de vivre & mourir en celle de l'Eglise Reformee, qu'il a faite publiquement en l'Eglise de Melle le vingt-deuxiesme Decembre 1602. La Rochelle: Pierre Prunier, 1603.

Declaration de Maistre François Cupif cy-devant curé de Contigné diocese d'Angers, Docteur en Theologie de la Faculté de Paris, ou il deduict les raisons qui l'ont meu à se separer de l'Eglise Romaine pour embrasser la Reforme, addressee a Monsieur l'Evesque d'Angers. Charenton: Melchior Mondiere, 1637.

Declaration de Maistre Olivier Enguerrand de Mante sur Seine, cy-devant ministre en l'Eglise pretendue reformée de Chef-Boutonne en Poictou contenant l'abiuration de l'heresie Lutherienne & Calvinique & la protestation de vivre & mourir en la doctrine de l'Eglise Catholique Apostolique & Romaine, qu'il a faict & prononcée publiquement dans l'Eglise de Mairé l'Eveschaut. . . . Bordeaux: Arnaud du Brel, 1607.

Declaration du Sieur Pierre Jarrige cy-devant Jesuite Profez du Quatrième Voeu & Predicateur, Prononcé dans le Temple de l'Eglise Française de Leide, le 25 mars 1648. Leiden: Jean Dupré, 1648.

Declaration du Sr. Michel Le Camus cy-devant appellé Pere Eusebe de S. Michel de l'ordre des Carmes Reformez predicateur & prestre en l'Eglise Romaine: Contenant les moyens de sa conversion à la religion reformée addressee a Messieurs de l'Eglise Romaine avec les paroles de son abjuration & profession prononcée par luy, en l'Eglise Reformée de Bloys, sur le poinct de la Sainte Communion. Charenton: Louis de Vendosme, 1640.

Declaration et manifeste des principaux suiets et motifs qui ont poussé & induit Maistre M. du Tertre Sr. de la Mothe Luyne, autrefois predicateur en l'ordre des capucins sous le nom de P. Firmin, à s'en retirer de l'Eglise Romaine pour se ranger joindre & unir aux Reformées de ce Royaume & en icelles professer la pureté de l'Evangile. Saumur: Thomas Portau, 1616.

La declaration que fait M. Charles Roy notaire royal, à Loudun contenant les raisons qui l'ont induict à se retirer de l'Eglise Romaine moderne pour se rejoindre & unir aux Eglises Reformées. Saumur: Thomas Portau, 1603.

Demaillasson, M. "Journal de M. Demaillasson, avocat du roi à Montmorillon (1643–1694)." In *Archives historiques du Poitou*, 36–37 (Poitiers, 1907, 1908).

Denesde, Antoine. "Journal d'Antoine Denesde et de Marie Barré, sa femme (1628–1687)." In *Archives historiques du Poitou*, edited by E. Bricaud, 15 (1885): 51–332.

Dictionnaire de l'Académie française (1694). Available online at *http://www.lib.uchicago.edu/efts/ARTFL/projects/dicos/ACADEMIE/PREMIERE/*

Drelincourt, Charles. *Avertissement sur les disputes et le procédé des missionaires*. Charenton: Louis Vendosme, 1654.

Drouhet, Jean. *Les oeuvres de Jean Drouhet, maître apothicaire à Saint-Maixent*. Edited by Alfred Richard. Poiters: E. Druincaud, 1878.

Dumoulin, Pierre. *Le capucin traitté auquel est descrite et examiné l'origine des capucins, leurs voeux, reigles, et disciplines*. N.p., 1641.

———. *Conseil fidele et salutaire sur les mariages entre personnes de contraire religion*. La Rochelle: G. Delchaux, 1620.

———. *Trois sermons faits en presence des peres Capucins qui les ont honorez de leur presence*. Paris: Samuel Petit, 1641.

Exomologese de Samuel Paul de Mugod, Docteur en Medicin, retiré par la grace de Dieu de l'heresie de Calv. à la foy catholique Faicte au pieds du souverain pontife Paul V en l'an 1608 lors que le . . . Prince Charles de Gonzague de Cleves, Duc de Nivernois . . . estoit à Rome Ambassadeur du Roy Tres-Chretien Henry le Grand. Paris: Charles Sevestre, 1611.

Filleau, Jean. *Décisions catholiques ou recueil general des arrests rendus dans toutes les cours souveraines de France en éxécution, ou interpretation, des edits, qui concernent l'exercise de la religion pret. reformée avec les raisons fondamentales desdits arrests, tirées de la doctrine des pères de l'eglise, des conciles, & des loix civiles & politiques du royaume*. . . . Poitiers: J. Fleuriau, 1668.

Genève, P. Charles de. *Trophées sacrés ou missions des capucins en Savoie, dans l'Ain, la Suisse Romande et la vallée d'Aoste, à la fin du XVIe et au XVIIe siècle*. Edited by Félix Tisserand. 3 vols. Lausanne: Société d'Histoire de la Suisse Romande, 1976.

L'heureuse conversion de Noble Homme Benoist Berault, Escuyer Sieur de Fraisne, premier pair de La Rochelle & premier tresorier des deniers de laditte ville; de Iacques Blamont Escuyer Sieur de la Faye, Ministre; de Maistre Paul Groüard, Iuge de la Prevosté de Loudun; de Maistre Paul Aubry, Advocat à Loudun; . . . & de plusieurs autres qui en ces derniers mois ont abiuré l'heresie & protesté de la Religion Catholique, Ap. & Rom. Instruits & absout par le R. Pere Athanase Molé, Capucin. . . . Paris: Pierre Ramier, 1623.

Les justes motifs de l'heureuse conversion à la religion catholique de Madame la Baronne de Courville faite en une conference tenue en la maison de Monsieur du Moulin ministre de Charenton, qui plus que tres-ignominieusement prist la fuite; entre Monsieur de Raconis professeur en theologie & predicateur & le Sieur la Miltiere, substitué en la place du fuyard du Moulin. . . . Rouen: Richard Allemant, 1618.

Lettre de conversion d'une Damoiselle de Poictou, vefve d'un des plus anciens ministres pretendus. Lyon: Jacques Roussin, 1600.

Lettre escrite a Monseigneur l'Evesque de Nismes par Monsieur le Prieur Villevielle, sur l'heureuse reduction de Mademoiselle sa mere à la religion Catholique. N.p., 1625.

Manifeste de l'abiuration publique de la Religion pretendue reformée faicte en la Ste Chapelle de Nostre Dame de Garaison par Madame & Mademoiselle de Fontrailles le jour de la Nativité de Sainct Jean Baptiste 24 juin 1618. . . . Toulouse: n.p., 1618.

Le manifeste de Monsieur de Bouillon envoyé à messieurs de la religion. N.p., 1622.

Martin, Arnoul. *Declaration des causes qui ont meu Arnoul Martin jadis ministre entre les calvinistes, d'embrasser la foy catholique*. Paris: Jean le Blanc, 1601.

Mestayer, Jacques. *Conversions signalées depuis peu de iours par l'entremise des pères capucins de la mission de Poictou, d'un de plus anciens ministres et autres notables personnes de la R.P.R*. . . . Paris: N. Rousset, 1620.

Meynier, Bernard. *De l'éxécution de l'Edit de Nantes dans les provinces de Guyenne, Poitou, Angoumois, Xaintonge et Aunis*. . . . Poitiers: J. Fleuriau, 1665.

———. *De l'éxécution de l'Edit de Nantes en Guienne et en Poitou*. Cahors: P. Dalvy, 1665.

Migault, Jean. *Le journal de Jean Migault: Les dragonnades en Poitou et Saintonge*. Edited by N. Weiss and H. Clouzot. Paris, 1910; reprint, Le Poiré-sur-Vie: Editions UPCP, 1988.

"La ministresse Nicole. Dialogue Poictevin de Josué et de Jacot, ou l'histoire ou vray de ce qui arriva chez le ministre Dusou et dans le temple des Huguenots de Fontenay le premier jour de may 1665." Niort: Favre, 1882.

Molé, P. Athanase. *Lettre envoyée aux ministres de Charenton par un des leurs nouvellement converty, & receu la veille de la pentecoste en l'église catholique, apostolique, & romaine par le Reverend Père Athanase Molé, predicateur capuçin*. Paris: n.p., 1621.

Montaigne, Michel de. *The Complete Essays of Montaigne*. Translated by Donald M. Frame. Stanford, Calif.: Stanford University Press, 1958.

Les motifs de la conversion du Sieur de La Mothe, ministre, envoyez à Messieurs de la Religion pretenduë reformée. Paris: François Muguet, 1665.

Les motifs qui ont obligé M. de Clermont d'Amboise Marquis de Garlande de faire abiuration de la Rpr & profession de la foy Cath., Ap. & Rom. entre les mains du reverend Pere Hyacinthe de Paris Predicateur Capucin. Paris: Sebastien Cramoisy, 1638.

Nassau, Flandrine de. "Lettres de Flandrine de Nassau, abbesse de Sainte-Croix de Poitiers à Charlotte-Brabantine de Nassau, duchesse de La Trémoille, sa soeur." In *Archives historiques du Poitou*, edited by P. Marchegay, 1 (1872): 203–96.

Le nouveau restablissement de la ville de Sainct-Jean-d'Angely, avec la conversion de plus de huit mille personnes à la religion catholique, apostolique et romaine, fait par les pères capucins de la Mission, le jour et les fêtes de la Pentecôte dernière 1623. Paris: A. Saugrain, 1623.

La nouvelle conversion du Sieur Durand ministre de Loudun à la religion catholique. Bordeaux: François Buclier & Arnaud du Breil, 1601.

Paris, P. Albert de. *Manual de la mission à l'usage des capucins de la province de Paris*. Troyes: J. Oudot, 1702.

Protestation chrestienne de Francoys Goupil cy-devant Cordelier au Couvent de Chasteau-roux, prononcée publiquement en l'Eglise Reformée de Thouars le Dimanche neufiefme Septembre, mil six ces un. Niort: René Troismailles, 1601.

Les raisons qui ont meu monsieur de Fiebrun chevalier, Conseiller du Roy . . . Et son Seneschal en Poictou, Civray, & Sainct Maixant, lequel a esté instruict & absou avec Madame sa femme, Mademoiselle leur fille, Monsieur des Essain, Escuyer & Valet de Chambre de sa Majesté avec dix autres, par le Reverend Père Athanase Molé, Predicateur Capucin. . . . Paris: Jean Bessin, 1622.

Retraction du Pere Pierre Jarrige de la Compagnie de Jesus retiré de sa double apostasie par le misericorde de Dieu. Antwerp: n.p., 1650.

Richeome, Louis, S.J. *L'idolatrie huguenote figurée au patron de la vieille payenne divisée en huict livres & desdiée au roy très chrestien de France et de Navarre Henry IIII*. Montpellier: J. Gillet, 1607.

Rigaud, Benoist. *Forme d'abiuration d'heresie & confession de foy qui doivent faire les desvoyez de la foy pretandans estre recevez en l'Eglise*. Paris: M. Roffet, 1572.

Rouen, Basile de. *Le retour au giron de l'Eglise du Pere Basile cy-devant Apostat & maintenant Capucin contenant 25 articles de ses Protestations & dernieres volontez faites par luy estant en son lict malade*. La Rochelle: Toussaincts de Govy, 1648.

La saincte messe restablie a Mouchamp & Vanderene par les pères capucins de la mission de Poictou, & de l'authorité du roy ou elle n'avoit esté dite depuis soixante ans. Avec la conversion de Madame de Rohan de messieurs des anfans & d'un grande nombre d'huguenotz. Fontenay: J. Petit, n.d. [1622].

Sales, Saint Francis de. *Introduction to the Devout Life*. Translated and edited by John K. Ryan. New York: Harper, 1950.

Schurman, Anna Maria van. *Whether a Christian Woman Should Be Educated and Other Writings from Her Intellectual Circle.* Translated and edited by Joyce L. Irwin. Chicago: University of Chicago Press, 1998.

Sponde, Henri de. *Les cimetières sacrez*. Lyon: J. Pillehotte, 1598.

Tallement des Réaux, Gédéon. *Les historiettes de Tallemant des Réaux*. 3rd ed. 10 vols. Paris: Delloye, 1840–1861.

La Tour d'Auvergne, Marie de. "Mémoire de Marie de la Tour d'Auvergne." In *Mémoires de la Société des Antiquaires de l'Ouest*, edited by H. Imbert, 32 (1867): 89–129.

La Trémoille, Henri-Charles de, Prince de Tarente. *Mémoires de Henri-Charles de la Trémoille, Prince de Tarente*. Liege: J. F. Bassompierre, 1767.

La verification de Vincent du Jordain natif de Bourges en Berry cy-devant Predicateur Cordelier, demeurant au couvent des Cordeliers de la ville de Xainctes, suivant la protestation qu'il en a publiquement faicte en l'Eglise reformée de Soubize le 20 janvier 1602. Pontorson: Jean Le Fevre, 1602.

La verité de la conversion de Madame de Frontenac, de Dimanche 27 may 1618. Paris: Bertrand Martin, 1618.

SECONDARY MATERIAL

Armogathe, Jean-Robert. *Croire en liberté: L'église catholique et la révocation de l'Édit de Nantes*. Paris: O.E.I.L., 1985.

———. "De l'art de penser comme art de persuader." In *La conversion au XVII siècle. Actes du XIIe Colloque de Marseille (janvier 1982)*, edited by Roger Duchene, 29–43. Marseilles: Centre méridional de recontres sur le XVIIe siècle, 1983.

Armstrong, Brian G. *Calvinism and the Amyraut Heresy: Protestant Scholasticism and Humanism in Seventeenth-Century France*. Madison: University of Wisconsin Press, 1969.

Audisio, Gabriel. "Se marier en Luberon: Catholiqes et protestants vers 1630." In *Histoire sociale, sensibilités collectives et mentalités: Mélanges Robert Mandrou*, 231–45. Paris: Presses Universitaires de France, 1985.

Bainton, Roland H. "The Bible in the Reformation." In *The Cambridge History of the Bible*, edited by S. L. Greenslade, 3 vols., 3:1–37. Cambridge, U.K.: Cambridge University Press, 1975.

Barth, Fredrik. "Boundaries and Connections." In *Signifying Identities: Anthropological Perspectives on Boundaries and Contested Values*, edited by Anthony P. Cohen, 17–36. London: Routledge, 2000.

———, ed. *Ethnic Groups and Boundaries: The Social Organization of Culture Difference*. London: Allen & Unwin, 1969.

Beckford, James A. "Accounting for Conversion." *British Journal of Sociology* 29 (1978): 249–62.

Beisel, Nicola. "Constructing a Shifting Moral Boundary: Literature and Obscenity in Nineteenth-Century America." In *Cultivating Differences: Symbolic Boundaries and the Making of Inequality*, edited by Michèle Lamont and Marcel Fournier, 104–28. Chicago: University of Chicago Press, 1992.

Bell, Catherine. *Ritual Theory, Ritual Practice*. New York: Oxford University Press, 1992.

Bels, Pierre. *Le mariage des protestants français jusqu'en 1685: Fondements doctrinaux et pratique juridique*. Paris: Librairie générale de droit et de jurisprudence, 1968.

Benedict, Philip. *Christ's Churches Purely Reformed: A Social History of Calvinism*. New Haven, Conn.: Yale University Press, 2002.

———. "Confessionalization in France? Critical Reflections and New Evidence." In *The Faith and Fortunes of France's Huguenots, 1600–85*, 309–25. Aldershot, U.K.: Ashgate, 2001.

———. *The Huguenot Population of France, 1600–1685: The Demographic Fate and Customs of a Religious Minority*. Transactions of the American Philosophical Society 81, pt. 5. Philadelphia: American Philosophical Society, 1991.

———. "La population réformée française de 1600 à 1685." *Annales: Économies, sociétés, civilisations*, no. 6 (November–December 1987): 1433–65.

———. *Rouen during the Wars of Religion*. Cambridge, U.K.: Cambridge University Press, 1981.

———. "*Un roi, une loi, deux fois:* Parameters for the History of Catholic-Reformed Co-existence in France, 1555–1685." In *Tolerance and Intolerance in the European Reformation*, edited by Ole Peter Grell and Bob Scribner, 65–93. Cambridge, U.K.: Cambridge University Press, 1996.

Benoist, André. "Catholiques et protestants en 'Moyen-Poitou' jusqu'à la révocation de l'Édit de Nantes, 1534–1685." *Bulletin de la société historique et scientifique des Deux-Sèvres*, 2nd ser., 16, no. 1 (1983): 235–434.

———. "Les populations rurales du 'Moyen-Poitou' protestant de 1640 à 1789: Économie, religion, société dans une groupe de paroisses de l'éléction de Saint-Maixent." Thèse de 3e cycle, Université de Poitiers, 1983.

Bercé, Yves-Marie. *History of Peasant Revolts: The Social Origins of Rebellion in Early Modern France*. Translated by Amanda Whitmore. Ithaca, N.Y.: Cornell University Press, 1990.

Bérenger, Jean. *Tolérance ou paix de religion en Europe centrale (1415–1792)*. Paris: Honoré Champion, 2000.

Bergeal, Catherine, and Antoine Durrleman, eds. *Protestantisme et libertés en France au 17e siècle de l'Édit de Nantes à sa révocation, 1598–1685*. Carrières-sous-Poissy: La Cause, 1985.

Berriot-Salvadore, Evelyne. *Les femmes dans la société française de la renaissance*. Geneva: Droz, 1990.

Bertheau, Solange. "Le consistoire dans les églises réformées du Moyen-Poitou au XVIIe siècle." *Bulletin de la société d'histoire du protestantisme français* 116, no. 3 (July–September 1970): 332–59, and 116, no. 4 (October–November 1970): 513–49.

Berthelot du Chesnay, Charles. *Les missions de Saint Jean Eudes: Contribution à l'histoire des missions en France au XVIIe siècle*. Paris: Procure des Eudists, 1967.

Billacois, François. *Le duel dans la société française des XVIe–XVIIe siècles: Essai de psychologie historique*. Paris: Éditions de l'École des Hautes Études en Sciences Sociales, 1986.

Binski, Paul. *Medieval Death: Ritual and Representation*. Ithaca, N.Y.: Cornell Unversity Press, 1996.

Blaisdell, Charmarie Jenkins. "Calvin's Letters to Women: The Courting of Ladies in High Places." *Sixteenth Century Journal* 13, no. 3 (1982): 67–84.

———. "Renée de France between Reform and Counter-Reform." *Archive for Reformation History* 63 (1972): 196–225.

Blet, Pierre. *Le clergé de France et la monarchie: Étude sur les assemblées générales du clergé de 1615–1666*. 2 vols. Rome: Presses de l'Université Grégorienne, 1959.

Boissonade, P. *Histoire de Poitou*. Paris: Boivin, 1926.

Bossy, John. "The Counter-Reformation and the People of Catholic Europe." *Past and Present* 47 (May 1970): 51–70.

———. "The Social History of Confession in the Age of the Reformation." *Transactions of the Royal Historical Society*, 5th ser., 25 (1975): 29–38.

Bourdieu, Pierre. *Distinction: A Social Critique of the Judgement of Taste*. Translated by Richard Nice. Cambridge, Mass.: Harvard University Press, 1984.

Brémond, Henri. *Histoire littéraire du sentiment religieux en France depuis la fin des guerres de religion jusqu'à nos jours*. 11 vols. Paris: Bloud et Gay, 1921.

Brereton, Virginia Lieson. *From Sin to Salvation: Stories of Women's Conversions, 1800 to the Present*. Bloomington: Indiana University Press, 1991.

Brunelle, Gayle K. "Dangerous Liaisons: *Mésalliance* and Early Modern French Noblewomen." *French Historical Studies* 19, no. 1 (Spring 1995): 75–103.

Burke, Peter. "How to Be a Counter-Reformation Saint." In *The Historical Anthropology of Early Modern Italy: Essays on Perception and Communication*, 48–62. Cambridge, U.K.: Cambridge University Press, 1987.

Bynum, Carolyn Walker. "Jesus as Mother and Abbot as Mother: Some Themes in Twelfth-Century Cistercian Writing." In *Jesus as Mother: Studies in the Spirituality of the High Middle Ages*, 110–69. Berkeley and Los Angeles: University of California Press, 1982.

Calmette, M. "Un épisode de la Contre-Réforme: La mission des capuçins dans la province de Poitou." *Bulletin de la société polymathique du Morbihan* (1937): 38–39.

Cameron, Keith, Mark Greengrass, and Penny Roberts, eds. *The Adventure of Religious Pluralism in Early Modern France: Papers from the Exeter Conference, April 1999*. Bern: Peter Lang, 2000.

Capot, Stéphane. *Justice et religion en Languedoc au temps de l'Édit de Nantes: La chambre de l'édit de Castres (1579–1679)*. Paris: École des Chartres, 1998.

Carmona, Michel. *Les diables de Loudun: Sorcellerie et politique sous Richelieu*. Paris: Fayard, 1988.

Certeau, Michel de. *The Mystic Fable*. Vol. 1, *The Sixteenth and Seventeenth Centuries*. Translated by Michael B. Smith. Chicago: University of Chicago Press, 1992.

———. *The Possession at Loudun*. Translated by Michael B. Smith. Chicago: University of Chicago Press, 2000.

Chareyre, Philippe. "'The Great Difficulties One Must Bear to Follow Jesus Christ': Morality at Sixteenth-Century Nîmes." In *Sin and the Calvinists: Morals Control and the Consistory in the Reformed Tradition*, Sixteenth Century Essays and Studies 32, edited by Raymond A. Mentzer, 63–96. Kirksville, Mo.: Sixteenth Century Journal Publishers, 1994.

Châtellier, Louis. *La religion des pauvres: Les sources du christianisme moderne, XVIe–XIXe siècle*. Paris: Aubier Montaigne, 1993.

———. *Tradition chrétienne et renouveau catholique dans le cadre de l'ancien diocèse de Strasbourg (1650–1770)*. Paris: Ophrys, 1981.

Chevalier, Françoise. "Les difficultés d'application de l'Édit de Nantes d'après les cahiers des plaintes (1599–1660)." In *Coexister dans l'intolérance: L'Édit de Nantes (1598)*, edited by Michel Grandjean and Bernard Roussel, 302–20. Geneva: Labor et Fides, 1998.

———. *Prêcher sous l'Édit de Nantes: La prédication réformée au XVIIe siècle en France*. Geneva: Labor et Fides, 1994.

Chrisman, Miriam. "Family and Religion in Two Noble Families: French Catholic and English Puritan." *Journal of Family History* 8, no. 2 (Summer 1983): 190–210.

Christian, William A., Jr. *Moving Crucifixes in Modern Spain*. Princeton, N.J.: Princeton University Press, 1992.

Christin, Olivier. *La paix de religion: L'autonomisation de la raison politique au XVIe siècle*. Paris: Seuil, 1997.

Clendinnen, Inga. "Landscape and World View: The Survival of Yucatec Maya Culture under Spanish Conquest." *Comparative Studies in Society and History* 22, no. 3 (July 1980): 374–93.

"Le clergé de Chartres et les enterrements huguenots (1600)." *Bulletin de la société d'histoire du protestantisme français* 47 (1898): 524–25.

"Le clergé de Langres et les enterrements huguenots (1602)." *Bulletin de la société d'histoire du protestantisme français* 47 (1898): 523–24.

Cohen, Anthony P. *The Symbolic Construction of Community*. London: Tavistock, 1985.

Collins, James M. *The State in Early Modern France*. Cambridge, U.K.: Cambridge University Press, 1995.

Comaroff, Jean, and John Comaroff. *Of Revelation and Revolution: Christianity, Colonialism, and Consciousness in South Africa*. 2 vols. Chicago: University of Chicago Press, 1991 and 1997.

Cottret, Bernard. *1598, L'Édit de Nantes: Pour en finir avec les guerres de religion*. Paris: Perrin, 1997.

Crouzet, Denis. "A Woman and the Devil: Possession and Exorcism in Sixteenth-Century France." In *Changing Identities in Early Modern France*, edited by Michael Wolfe, 191–215. Durham, N.C.: Duke University Press, 1997.

———. *Les guerriers de Dieu: La violence au temps des troubles de religion, vers 1525–1610*. 2 vols. Seyssel: Champ Vallon, 1990.

Curry, Kate. "Degrees of Toleration: The Conjuncture of the Edict of Nantes and Dynastic Relations between Lorraine and France, 1598–1610." In *The Adventure of Religious Pluralism in Early Modern France: Papers from the Exeter Conference, April 1999*, edited by Keith Cameron, Mark Greengrass, and Penny Roberts, 231–44. Bern: Peter Lang, 2000.

Cuthbert, Father, O.S.F.C. *The Capuchins: A Contribution to the History of the Counter-Reformation*. 2 vols. London: Sheed & Ward, 1928.

Davis, Natalie Zemon. "Boundaries and the Sense of Self in Sixteenth-Century France." In *Reconstructing Individualism: Autonomy, Individuality, and the Self in Western Thought*, edited by Thomas C. Heller, Morton Sosna, and David E. Wellbery, 53–63. Stanford, Calif.: Stanford University Press, 1986.

———. "Ghosts, Kin, and Progeny: Some Features of Family Life in Early Modern France." *Daedalus* 106 (Spring 1977): 87–114.

———. "The Sacred and the Body Social in Sixteenth-Century Lyon." *Past and Present*, no. 90 (1981): 40–70.

———. *Society and Culture in Early Modern France*. Stanford, Calif.: Stanford University Press, 1975.

———. *Women on the Margins: Three Seventeenth-Century Lives*. Cambridge, Mass.: Harvard University Press, 1995.

Debon, René. "Religion et vie quotidienne à Gap." In *Le protestantisme en Dauphiné au XVIIe siècle: Religion et vie quotidienne à Mens-en-Trièves, Die et Gap (1650–1685)*, edited by Pierre Bolle, 91–170. Poët-Laval: Curandera, 1983.

Dedouvres, L. *Le Père Joseph polémiste, ses premiers écrits, 1623–1626*. Paris: Alphonse Picard, 1895.

———. *Politique et apôtre: Le Père Joseph de Paris, Capucin: L'éminence grise*. 2 vols. Paris: Beauchesne, 1922.

DeJean, Joan. *Tender Geographies: Women and the Origins of the Novel in France*. New York: Columbia University Press, 1991.

Delumeau, Jean. *Le catholicisme entre Luther et Voltaire*. Paris: Presses Universitaires de France, 1979.

Desgraves, Louis. *Répertoire des ouvrages de controverses entre catholiques et protestants en France (1598–1685)*. 2 vols. Geneva: Droz, 1984.

———. "Un aspect des controverses entre catholiques et protestants, les récits de conversion (1598–1628)." In *La conversion au XVII siècle. Actes du XIIe Colloque de Marseille (janvier 1982)*, edited by Roger Duchene, 89–110. Marseilles: Centre méridionale de rencontres sur le XVIIe siècle, 1983.

Deslandres, Dominique. *Croire et faire croire: Les missions françaises au XVIIe siècle (1600–1650)*. Paris: Fayard, 2003.

Desplat, Christian. "Sépulture et frontière confessionelle: Protestants et catholiques de Béarn (XVI–XVIIe siècle)." *Revue de Pau et du Béarn* 23 (1996): 67–75.

Deyon, Solange. "La destruction des temples." In *La révocation de l'Édit de Nantes et le protestantisme français en 1685. Actes du colloque de Paris (15–19 octobre 1985)*, edited by Roger Zuber and Laurent Theis, 239–59. Paris: Société d'Histoire du Protestantisme Français, 1986.

Dez, Pierre. *Histoire des protestants et des églises réformées du Poitou*. La Rochelle: Imprimerie de l'Ouest, 1936.

Diefendorf, Barbara B. *Beneath the Cross: Catholics and Huguenots in Sixteenth-Century Paris*. New York: Oxford University Press, 1991.

———. "Discerning Spirits: Women and Spiritual Authority in Counter-Reformation France." In *Culture and Change: Attending to Women*, edited by Margaret Mikesell and Adele Seeff, 241–65. Newark: University of Delaware Press, 2003.

———. "Houses Divided: Religious Schism in Sixteenth-Century Parisian Families."

In *Urban Life in the Renaissance*, edited by Susan Zimmerman and Ronald F. E. Weissman, 80–99. Newark: University of Delaware Press, 1989.

Dolan, Frances E. *Whores of Babylon: Catholicism, Gender and Seventeenth-Century Print Culture*. Ithaca, N.Y.: Cornell University Press, 1999.

Dompnier, Bernard. *Enquête au pays des frères des anges: Les capucins de la province de Lyon au XVIIe et XVIIIe siècles*. Saint-Etienne: Université de Saint-Etienne, 1993.

———. "L'histoire religieuse chez les controversistes réformés du début du XVIIe siècle: L'apport de Du Plessis Mornay et Rivet." In *Historiographie de la Réforme*, edited by Philippe Joutard, 16–36. Paris: Delachaux & Niestle, 1977.

———. "La logique d'une destruction: L'église catholique, la royauté et les temples protestants (1680–1685)." In *Révolution française et "vandalisme révolutionnaire." Actes du colloque international de Clermont-Ferrand, 15–17 décembre 1988*, edited by Simone Bernard-Griffiths, Marie-Claude Chemin, and Jean Ehrard, 343–51. Paris: Universitas, 1992.

———. "Mission et confession au XVIIe siècle." In *Pratiques de la confession: Des pères du desert à Vatican II, Quinze études d'histoire*, 201–22. Paris: Cerf, 1983.

———. "Mission lointaine et mission de l'intérieur chez les capuçins français de la première moitié du XVIIe siècle." In *Les réveils missionaires en France du moyen-âge à nos jours (XIIe–XXe siècles). Actes du colloque de Lyon, 29–31 Mai 1980*, edited by Guy Duboscq and André Latreille, 91–106. Paris: Beauchesne, 1984.

———. "Le missionaire et son public: Contribution à l'étude de la prédication populaire." In *Journées Bossuet: La prédication au XVIIe siècle. Actes du Colloque de Dijon 2–4 décembre 1977*, edited by Thérèse Goyet and Jean-Pierre Collinet, 105–28. Paris: A. G. Nizet, 1980.

———. "Pastorale de la peur et pastorale de la séduction: La méthode de conversion des missionnaires capucins." In *La conversion au XVII siècle. Actes du XIIe Colloque de Marseille (janvier 1982)*, edited by Roger Duchene, 257–81. Marseilles: Centre méridionale de rencontres sur le XVIIe siècle, 1983.

———. "Un aspect de la dévotion eucharistique dans la France du XVIIe siècle: Les prières des Quarante-Heures." *Revue d'histoire de l'église de France* 67 (January–June 1981): 5–31.

———. *Le venin de l'hérésie: Images du protestantisme et combat catholique au XVIIe siècle*. Paris: Le Centurion, 1985.

Donia, Robert J., and John V. A. Fine, Jr. *Bosnia and Hercegovina: A Tradition Betrayed*. New York: Columbia University Press, 1994.

Douglas, Mary. *Purity and Danger*. Harmondsworth, U.K.: Penguin Books, 1966.

Duchene, Roger, ed. *La conversion au XVII siècle. Actes du XIIe Colloque de Marseille (janvier 1982)*. Marseilles: Centre méridionale de rencontres sur le XVIIe siècle, 1983.

Dumonceaux, Pierre. "Conversion, convertir, étude comparative d'après les lexicographes du XVIIe siècle." In *La conversion au XVII siècle. Actes du XIIe Colloque de Marseille (janvier 1982)*, edited by Roger Duchene, 7–17. Marseilles: Centre méridionale de rencontres sur le XVIIe siècle, 1983.

Durand, J. *La réforme à Lusignan en Poitou des origines à la révolution (1559–1789)*. Paris: Ch. Noblet, 1907.

Durand, R. *Saint-Gelais au péril des dragons, 1681–1981*. Niort: Soulisse et Cassegrain, 1981.

Epstein, Cynthia Fuchs. "Tinkerbells and Pinups: The Construction and Reconstruction of Gender Boundaries at Work." In *Cultivating Differences: Symbolic Boundaries and the Making of Inequality*, edited by Michèle Lamont and Marcel Fournier, 232–56. Chicago: University of Chicago Press, 1992.

Esmein, A. *Le mariage en droit canonique*. 2 vols. Paris: Librairie du Recueil Sirey, 1929.

Eurich, S. Amanda. "'Speaking the King's Language': The Huguenot Magistrates of Castres and Pau." In *Society and Culture in the Huguenot World, 1559–1685*, edited by Raymond A. Mentzer and Andrew Spicer, 117–38. Cambridge, U.K.: Cambridge University Press, 2002.

Fagniez, Gustave. *Le Père Joseph et Richelieu (1577–1638)*. 2 vols. Paris: Hachette, 1894.

Favre, L. *Histoire de la ville de Niort depuis son origine jusqu'en 1789*. Niort: Imprimerie de L. Favre, 1880.

Favreau, Robert, ed. *Histoire de Poitiers*. Toulouse: Privat, 1985.

Félice, Paul de. "Les abjurations de catholiques dans les temples Huguenots." *Bulletin de la société d'histoire du protestantisme français* 45 (1896): 561–72.

———. *Les protestants d'autrefois: Vie intérieure des églises, moeurs et usages*. 4 vols. Paris: Fischbacher, 1896–1898.

Fillon, B. *Recueil de notes sur les origins de l'église réformée de Fontenay-le-Comte et sur ses pasteurs*. Niort: P. Rebuchon, 1888.

Finley-Crosswhite, S. Annette. "Engendering the Wars of Religion: Female Agency during the Catholic League in Dijon." *French Historical Studies* 20, no. 2 (Spring 1997): 127–54.

———. *Henry IV and the Towns: The Pursuit of Legitimacy in French Urban Society, 1589–1610*. Cambridge, U.K.: Cambridge University Press, 1999.

Formon, Marcelle Gabrielle. "Un évêque de la Contre-Réforme: La Rocheposay et le diocèse de Poitiers, 1612–1651." Thèse de doctorat, Université de Poitiers, 1951.

Forster, Marc. *Counter-Reformation in the Villages: Religion and Reform in the Bishopric of Speyer, 1560–1720*. Ithaca, N.Y.: Cornell University Press, 1992.

François, Etienne. *Protestants et catholiques en Allemagne: Identités et pluralisme Augsbourg, 1648–1806*. Paris: Albin Michel, 1993.

Frazee, Charles A. *Catholics and Sultans: The Church and the Ottoman Empire, 1453–1923*. Cambridge, U.K.: Cambridge University Press, 1983.

Fredriksen, Paula. "Paul and Augustine: Conversion Narratives, Orthodox Traditions, and the Retrospective Self." *Journal of Theological Studies*, n.s., 37, pt. 1 (April 1986): 3–34.

Freitag, Sandria B. *Collective Action and Community: Public Arenas and the Emergence of Communalism in North India*. Berkeley and Los Angeles: University of California Press, 1989.

Gachignard, Pierre. *Dictionnaire du patois du marais poitevin: Particulièrement celui du canton de Maillezais et des communes voisines de Vendée, Charente-Maritime, et Deux-Sèvres*. Marseille: J. Lafitte, 1983.

Garrisson, F. *Essai sur les commissions d'application de l'Édit de Nantes, première partie: Règne de Henri IV*. Montpellier: P. Dehan, 1964.

Garrisson, Janine. *L'Édit de Nantes et sa révocation: Histoire d'une intolerance*. Paris: Seuil, 1985.

———. *Les protestants au XVIe siècle*. Paris: Fayard, 1988.

Garrisson-Estèbe, Janine. *L'homme protestant*. Paris: Hachette, 1980.

Geertz, Clifford. *The Interpretation of Cultures*. New York: Basic Books, 1973.

Gibson, Wendy. *Women in Seventeenth-Century France*. London: Macmillan, 1989.

Gittings, Claire. *Death, Burial and the Individual in Early Modern England*. London: Croom Helm, 1984.

Goodwine, Rev. Joseph G. *The Reception of Converts: Commentary with Historical Notes*. The Catholic University of America Canon Law Studies 198. Washington, D.C.: The Catholic University of America Press, 1944.

Gordon, Bruce, and Peter Marshall, eds. *The Place of the Dead: Death and Remembrance in Late Medieval and Early Modern Europe*. Cambridge, U.K.: Cambridge University Press, 2000.

Grandjean, Michel. "Présentation." In *Coexister dans l'intolérance: L'Édit de Nantes (1598)*, edited by Michel Grandjean and Bernard Roussel, 7–14. Geneva: Labor et Fides, 1998.

Grandjean, Michel, and Bernard Roussel, eds. *Coexister dans l'intolérance: L'Édit de Nantes (1598)*. Geneva: Labor et Fides, 1998.

Gregory, Brad S. *Salvation at Stake: Christian Martyrdom in Early Modern Europe*. Cambridge, Mass.: Harvard University Press, 1999.

Grell, Ole Peter, and Bob Scribner, eds. *Tolerance and Intolerance in the European Reformation*. Cambridge, U.K.: Cambridge University Press, 1996.

Haag, Eugène, and Emile Haag. *La France protestante*. 10 vols. Paris: J. Cherbuliez, 1846–1859.

Haase-Dubosc, Danielle. *Ravie et enlevée: De l'enlèvement des femmes comme stratégie matrimoniale au XVIIe siècle*. Paris: Albin Michel, 1999.

Haase-Dubosc, Danielle, and Eliane Viennot, eds. *Femmes et pouvoirs sous l'ancien régime*. Paris: Rivages, 1991.

Halbertal, Moshe, and Avishai Margalit. *Idolatry*. Translated by Naomi Goldblum. Cambridge, Mass.: Harvard University Press, 1992.

Hall, Basil. "Biblical Scholarship: Editions and Commentaries." In *The Cambridge History of the Bible*, edited by S. L. Greenslade, 3 vols., 3:38–93. Cambridge, U.K.: Cambridge University Press, 1975.

Hanley, Sarah. "Engendering the State: Family Formation and State Building in Early Modern France." *French Historical Studies* 16, no. 1 (Spring 1989): 4–27.

———. "Family and State in Early Modern France: The Marriage Pact." In *Connecting Spheres: Women in the Western World 1500 to the Present*, edited by Marilyn J. Boxer and Jean H. Quataert, 53–63. New York: Oxford University Press, 1987.

———. "Social Sites of Political Practice in France: Lawsuits, Civil Rights, and the Separation of Powers in Domestic and State Government, 1500–1800." *American Historical Review* 102, no. 1 (February 1987): 27–52.

———. "Women in the Body Politic of Early Modern France." In *Proceedings of the Annual Meeting of the Western Society for French History* 16 (1989): 408–14.

Hanlon, Gregory. *Confession and Community in Seventeenth-Century France: Catholic and Protestant Coexistence in Aquitaine*. Philadelphia: University of Pennsylvania Press, 1993.

———. *L'univers des gens de bien: Culture et comportements des élites urbaines en Agenais-Condomois au XVIIe siècle*. Bordeaux: Presses Universitaires de Bordeaux, 1989.

Hardwick, Julie. *The Practice of Patriarchy: Gender and the Politics of Household Authority in Early Modern France*. University Park: Pennsylvania State University Press, 1998.

———. "Seeking Separations: Gender, Marriages, and Household Economies in Early Modern France." *French Historical Studies* 21, no. 1 (Winter 1998): 157–80.

Harran, Marilyn J. *Luther on Conversion: The Early Years*. Ithaca, N.Y.: Cornell University Press, 1983.

Harrington, Joel F., and Helmut Walser Smith. "Confessionalization, Community, and State Building in Germany, 1555–1870." *Journal of Modern History* 69 (March 1997): 77–101.

Hefner, Robert W. "Introduction: World Building and the Rationality of Conversion." In *Conversion to Christianity: Historical and Anthropological Perspectives on a Great Transformation*, edited by Robert W. Hefner, 3–44. Berkeley and Los Angeles: University of California Press, 1993.

Heyberger, Bernard. *Les chrétiens du Proche-Orient au temps de la réforme catholique (Syrie, Liban, Palestine, XVIIe–XVIIIe siècles)*. Rome: École française de Rome, 1994.

Hickey, Daniel. "Enforcing the Edict of Nantes: The 1599 Commissions and Local Elites in Dauphiné and Poitou-Aunis." In *The Adventure of Religious Pluralism in Early Modern France: Papers from the Exeter Conference, April 1999*, edited by Keith Cameron, Mark Greengrass, and Penny Roberts, 65–83. Bern: Peter Lang, 2000.

———. "Living in France under the Edict of Nantes: Confessional Conflict and Coexistence in Poitou and Aunis, 1598–1685." Forthcoming.

———. "Le rôle de l'état dans la réforme catholique: Une inspection du diocèse de Poitiers lors des Grands Jours de 1634." *Revue historique* 307, no. 4 (October–December 2002): 939–61.

Hoffman, Philip T. *Church and Community in the Diocese of Lyon, 1500–1789*. New Haven, Conn.: Yale University Press, 1984.

Holt, Mack P. *French Wars of Religion, 1562–1629*. Cambridge, U.K.: Cambridge University Press, 1995.

———. "Putting Religion Back into the Wars of Religion." *French Historical Studies* 18, no. 2 (Fall 1993): 524–51.

Hsia, R. Po-chia. *Social Discipline in the Reformation: Central Europe, 1550–1750*. London: Routledge, 1989.

———. *Society and Religion in Münster, 1535–1618*. New Haven, Conn.: Yale University Press, 1984.

———. *The World of Catholic Renewal, 1540–1770*. Cambridge, U.K.: Cambridge University Press, 1998.

Huxley, Aldous. *The Devils of Loudun*. Harmondsworth, U.K.: Penguin Books, 1971.

———. *Grey Eminence*. New York: Carroll & Graf, 1941.

Imbert, Hugues. *Histoire de Thouars*. Niort: Clouzot, 1871.

———. *Registre de correspondance et biographie du Duc Henri de La Trémoille, 1649–1667*. Poitiers: Imprimerie de Dupré, 1867.

Iriarte, Lazaro, OFMCap. *Franciscan History: The Three Orders of St. Francis of Assisi*. Chicago: Franciscan Herald Press, 1982.

James, William. *The Varieties of Religious Experience*. Vol. 15 of *The Works of William James*. Cambridge, Mass.: Harvard University Press, 1985.

Jordan, Constance. *Renaissance Feminism: Literary Texts and Political Models.* Ithaca, N.Y.: Cornell University Press, 1990.

Juster, Susan. "In a Different Voice: Male and Female Narratives of Religious Conversion in Post-Revolutionary America." *American Quarterly* 41 (1989): 34–62.

Kappler, Emile. "Conférences théologiques entre catholiques et protestants en France au XVIIe siècle." 2 vols. Thèse de 3e cycle, Université de Clermont II, 1980.

Kintz, Jean-Pierre, and Georges Livet, eds. *350e anniversaire des Traités de Westphalie, 1648–1998: Une genèse de l'Europe, une société à reconstruire. Actes du colloque international tenu à l'Université Marc Bloch, Université des Sciences humaines et de la Ville de Strasbourg.* Strasbourg: Presses Universitaires de Strasbourg, 1999.

Klaits, Joseph. *Servants of Satan: The Age of the Witch Hunts.* Bloomington: Indiana University Press, 1985.

Koslofsky, Craig M. *The Reformation of the Dead: Death and Ritual in Early Modern Germany, 1450–1700.* New York: St. Martin's Press, 2000.

Krumenacker, Yves. *Les protestants du Poitou au XVIIIe siècle (1681–1789).* Paris: Honoré Champion, 1998.

Laborie, Jean-Claude. *La mission jésuite du Brésil: Lettres et autres documents (1549–1570).* Paris: Chandeigne, 1998.

Labrousse, Elisabeth. "Conversion dans les deux sens." In *La conversion au XVII siècle. Actes du XIIe Colloque de Marseille (janvier 1982),* edited by Roger Duchene, 161–77. Marseilles: Centre méridionale de rencontres sur le XVIIe siècle, 1983.

———. "La conversion d'un huguenot au catholicisme." *Revue d'histoire de l'église de France* 64, no. 172 (January–June 1978): 55–68 and no. 173 (July–December 1978): 251–52.

———. "Les mariages bigarrés: Unions mixtes en France au XVIIIe siècle." In *Le couple interdit, entretien sur le racisme: La dialectique de l'altérité socio-culturelle et la sexualité. Actes du colloque tenu en mai 1977 au Centre Culturel International de Cerisay-la-Salle,* edited by Léon Poliakov, 159–76. Paris: Mouton, 1980.

———. "Religious Toleration." In *Dictionary of the History of Ideas,* 4 vols., 4: 112–21. New York: Scribners, 1973.

———. *"Une foi, une loi, un roi?": Essai sur la révocation de l'Édit de Nantes.* Geneva: Labor et Fides, 1985.

Lamont, Michèle, and Marcel Fournier. *Cultivating Difference: Symbolic Boundaries and the Making of Inequality.* Chicago: University of Chicago Press, 1992.

La Trémoïlle, Charles-Louis, duc de. *Les La Trémoïlle pendant cinq siècles.* 5 vols. Nantes: Émile Grimaud, 1895.

Leahey, Margaret J. "'Comment peut un muet prescher l'évangile?': Jesuit Missionaries and the Native Languages of New France." *French Historical Studies* 19, no. 1 (Spring 1995): 105–31.

Lecler, Joseph, S.J. *Histoire de la tolérance au siècle de la réforme.* Paris: Montaigne, 1955; reprint, Paris: Albin Michel, 1994.

Le Goff, Jacques, and Jean-Claude Schmitt, eds. *Le charivari. Actes de la table ronde organisée à Paris (25–27 avril 1977).* Paris: Mouton, 1981.

Léonard, Emile G. *Histoire générale du protestantisme.* 3 vols. Paris: Presses Universitaires de France, 1961; reprint, Paris: Presses Universitaires de France, 1988.

Levi, A. H. T. "La psychologie de la conversion au XVIIe siècle: De François de Sales à Nicole." In *La conversion au XVII siècle. Actes du XIIe Colloque de Marseille (janvier 1982)*, edited by Roger Duchene, 19–28. Marseilles: Centre méridionale de rencontres sur le XVIIe siècle, 1983.

Lièvre, Auguste-François. *Histoire des protestants et des églises réformées du Poitou.* 3 vols. Paris: Grassart, 1856–1859.

———. *Les martyrs poitevins.* 1874; reprint, La Mothe-Saint-Héray: Italiques, 1984.

Ligou, Daniel. *Le protestantisme en France de 1598 à 1715.* Paris: Société d'Édition d'Enseignement Supérieur, 1968.

Loats, Carol L. "Gender, Guilds, and Work Identity: Perspectives from Sixteenth-Century Paris." *French Historical Studies* 20, no. 1 (Winter 1997): 15–30.

Lougee, Carolyn C. *Le Paradis des Femmes: Women, Salons, and Social Stratification in Seventeenth-Century France.* Princeton, N.J.: Princeton University Press, 1976.

Love, Ronald S. *Blood and Religion: The Conscience of Henri IV, 1553–1593.* Montreal: McGill-Queen's University Press, 2001.

Luria, Keith P. "Cemeteries, Religious Difference, and the Creation of Cultural Boundaries in Seventeenth-Century French Communities." In *Memory and Identity: The Huguenots in France and the Atlantic Diaspora*, edited by Bertrand Van Ruymbeke and Randy J. Sparks, 58–72. Columbia: University of South Carolina Press, 2003.

———. "The Counter-Reformation and Popular Spirituality." In *Christian Spirituality: Post-Reformation and Modern*, edited by Louis Dupré and Don E. Saliers, 93–120. Vol. 18 of *World Spirituality: An Encyclopedic History of the Religious Quest.* New York: Crossroad, 1989.

———. "The Politics of Protestant Conversion to Catholicism in Seventeenth-Century France." In *Conversion to Modernity: The Globalization of Christianity*, edited by Peter van der Veer, 23–46. New York: Routledge, 1996.

———. "Rituals of Conversion: Catholics and Protestants in Seventeenth-Century Poitou." In *Culture and Identity in Early Modern Europe (1500–1800): Essays in Honor of Natalie Zemon Davis*, edited by Barbara B. Diefendorf and Carla Hesse, 65–81. Ann Arbor: University of Michigan Press, 1993.

———. "Separated by Death?: Burials, Cemeteries, and Confessional Boundaries in Seventeenth-Century France." *French Historical Studies* 24, no. 2 (Spring 2001): 185–222.

———. *Territories of Grace: Cultural Change in the Seventeenth-Century Diocese of Grenoble.* Berkeley and Los Angeles: University of California Press, 1991.

MacFarlane, Graham. "'It's not as simple as that': The Expression of the Catholic and Protestant Boundary in Northern Irish Rural Communities." In *Symbolising Boundaries: Identity and Diversity in British Cultures*, edited by Anthony P. Cohen, 88–104. Manchester, U.K.: Manchester University Press, 1986.

Maclean, Ian. *Woman Triumphant: Feminism in French Literature, 1610–1652.* Oxford, U.K.: Clarendon Press, 1977.

Maillard, Jacques. "La mission du Père Honoré de Cannes à Angers en 1684." *Annales de Bretagne et des Pays de l'Ouest* 81, no. 3 (July 1974): 501–16.

Mandrou, Robert. *Magistrats et sorciers en France au XVIIe siècle: Une analyse de psychologie historique.* Paris: Seuil, 1980.

Marcadé, Jacques, and Marie-Louise Fracard. "Le XVIe siècle: Le temps des crises." In

Le diocèse de Poitiers, edited by Robert Favreau, 114–34. Paris: Beauchesne, 1988.

———. "Le XVIIe siècle: Un triomphe difficile." In *Le diocèse de Poitiers*, edited by Robert Favreau, 135–55. Paris: Beauchesne, 1988.

Margolf, Diane C. "Adjudicating Memory: Law and Religious Difference in Early Seventeenth-Century France." *Sixteenth Century Journal* 27 (1996): 399–418.

———. "The Edict of Nantes's Amnesty: Appeals to the *Chambre de l'Edit*, 1600–1610." In *Proceedings of the Annual Conference of the Western Society for French History* 16 (1988): 49–55.

———. *Religion and Royal Justice in Early Modern France: The Paris Chambre de l'Edit, 1598–1665*. Sixteenth-century Essays and Studies 67. Kirksville, Mo.: Truman State University Press, 2003.

Marion, Marcel. *Dictionnaire des institutions de la France aux XVIIe et XVIIIe siècles*. Paris, 1923; reprint, New York: Burt Franklin, 1968.

Mauzaize, Jean. "Le rôle et l'action des capucins de la province de Paris dans la France religieuse du XVIIème siècle." Thèse, Université de Paris, 1977. 3 vols. Lille: Atelier Reproduction des Thèses, 1977.

Méjan, François. *Discipline de l'église réformée: Annotée et précédée d'une introduction historique*. Paris: Éditions "Je Sers," 1947.

Mentzer, Raymond A. *Blood and Belief: Family Survival and Confessional Identity among the Provincial Huguenot Nobility*. West Lafayette, Ind.: Purdue University Press, 1994.

———. "Marking the Taboo: Excommunication in French Reformed Churches." In *Sin and the Calvinists: Morals Control and the Consistory in the Reformed Tradition*, Sixteenth Century Essays and Studies 32, edited by Raymond A. Mentzer, 97–128. Kirksville, Mo.: Sixteenth Century Journal Publishers, 1994.

———. "Morals and Moral Regulation in Protestant France." *Journal of Interdisciplinary History* 31, no. 1 (2000): 1–20.

———, ed. *Sin and the Calvinists: Morals Control and the Consistory in the Reformed Tradition*. Sixteenth Century Essays and Studies 32. Kirksville, Mo.: Sixteenth Century Journal Publishers, 1994.

Mentzer, Raymond A., and Andrew Spicer, eds. *Society and Culture in the Huguenot World, 1559–1685*. Cambridge, U.K.: Cambridge University Press, 2002.

Moote, A. Lloyd. *Louis XIII: The Just*. Berkeley and Los Angeles: University of California Press, 1989.

Morán, Manuel, and José Andrés-Gallego. "The Preacher." In *Baroque Personae*, edited by Rosario Villari, translated by Lydia G. Cochrane, 126–59. Chicago: University of Chicago Press, 1995.

Morrison, Karl F. *Conversion and Text: The Cases of Augustine of Hippo, Herman-Judah, and Constantine Tsatsos*. Charlottesville: University Press of Virginia, 1992.

———. *Understanding Conversion*. Charlottesville: University Press of Virginia, 1992.

Motley, Mark. *Becoming a French Aristocrat: The Education of the Court Nobility, 1580–1715*. Princeton, N.J.: Princeton University Press, 1990.

Mours, Samuel. *Les églises réformées en France: Tableaux et cartes*. Paris: Librairie protestante, 1958.

———. *Essai sommaire de géographie du protestantisme français au XVIIe siècle*. Paris: Librairie protestante, 1966.

Mousnier, Roland. *The Assassination of Henri IV: The Tyrannicide Problem and the Consol-*

idation of the French Absolute Monarchy in the Early Seventeenth Century. Translated by Joan Spencer. New York: Scribners, 1973.

Muir, Edward. *Ritual in Early Modern Europe*. Cambridge, U.K.: Cambridge University Press, 1997.

Naphy, William G., and Penny Roberts, eds. *Fear in Early Modern Society*. Manchester, U.K.: Manchester University Press, 1997.

Nirenberg, David. *Communities of Violence: Persecution of Minorities in the Middle Ages*. Princeton, N.J.: Princeton University Press, 1996.

Orcibal, Jean. *Louis XIV et les protestants: La cabale des accommodeurs de religion; la caisse des conversions; la révocation de l'Édit de Nantes*. Paris: Vrin, 1951.

Pannier, Jacques. *L'église réformée de Paris sous Henri IV: Rapport de l'église et de l'état, vie publique et privée des protestants*. Paris, 1911; reprint, Geneva: Slatkine-Megariotis, 1977.

———. *L'église réformée de Paris sous Louis XIII de 1621 à 1629 environ*. 2 vols. Paris: Honoré Champion, 1932.

Paris, Charles B. *Marriage in XVIIth Century Catholicism: The Origins of a Religious Mentality. The Teaching of l'École française*. Tournai: Desclée, 1975.

Parker, David. *La Rochelle and the French Monarchy: Conflict and Order in Seventeenth-Century France*. London: Royal Historical Society, 1980.

Pellegrin, Nicole. "L'androgyne au XVIe siècle: Pour une relecture des savoirs." In *Femmes et pouvoirs sous l'ancien régime*, edited by Danielle Haase-Dubosc and Eliane Vienot, 11–48. Paris: Rivage, 1991.

Pérouas, Louis. *Ce que croyait Grignion de Montfort et comment il a vécu sa foi*. Tours: Mame, 1973.

———. "La 'Mission de Poitou' des capuçins pendant le premier quart du XVIIe siècle." *Bulletin et mémoires de la société des antiquaires de l'ouest et des musées du Poitiers*, 4th ser., 7, no. 1 (1964): 349–362.

———. *Le diocèse de La Rochelle de 1648 à 1724: Sociologie et pastorale*. Paris: École Pratique des Hautes Études, 1964; reprint, Paris: École des Hautes Études en Sciences Sociales, 1999.

———. "Missions intérieures et missions extérieures françaises durant les premières décennies du XVII siècle." *Paroles et mission* 7, no. 27 (October 1964): 644–59.

Piat, Colette. *Le Père Joseph: Le maître de Richelieu*. Paris: Bernard Grasset, 1988.

Pignon, J. *La gente poitevinrie: Recueil des texts en patois poitevin du XVIe siècle*. Paris: D'Artrey, 1960.

Plattard, J. "Un étudiant ecossais en France en 1665–1666: Journal de voyage de Sir John Lauder." *Mémoires de la Société des Antiquaires de l'Ouest*, 3rd ser., vol. 12 (1935): 1–129.

Popkin, Richard H. *The History of Skepticism from Erasmus to Descartes*. New York: Humanities Press, 1964.

Poton, Didier. "Le consistoire protestant au XVIIe siècle: Un tribunal des moeurs?" In *Ordre moral et délinquance de l'antiquité au XXe siècle. Actes du colloque de Dijon, 7–8 octobre 1993*, edited by Benoît Garnot, 411–17. Dijon: Éditions Universitaires de Dijon, 1994.

———. "Les déliberations consistoriales: Une source pour l'histoire de la violence au XVIIe siècle." In *Histoire et criminalité de l'antiquité au XXe siècle: Nouvelles approaches.*

Actes du colloque de Dijon-Chenove, 3–5 octobre 1991, edited by Benoît Garnot, 67–73. Dijon: Éditions Universitaires de Dijon, 1992.

Prosperi, Adriano. "The Missionary." In *Baroque Personae*, edited by Rosario Villari, translated by Lydia G. Cochrane, 160–94. Chicago: University of Chicago Press, 1995.

Quéniart, Jean. *La révocation de l'Édit de Nantes: Protestants et catholiques français de 1598 à 1685*. Paris: Desclée de Brouwer, 1985.

Questier, Michael C. *Conversion, Politics and Religion in England, 1580–1625*. Cambridge, U.K.: Cambridge University Press, 1996.

Rabut, Elisabeth. *Le roi, l'église et le temple: L'exécution de l'Édit de Nantes en Dauphiné*. Grenoble: Éditions de la Pensée Sauvages, 1987.

———. "Vie religieuse et vie de la cité: Catholiques et protestants en Dauphiné au lendemain de l'Édit de Nantes." In *Renaissance européenne et phénomènes religieux, 1450–1650*, 317–24. Montbrison: Association du Centre Culturel de la Ville de Montbrison, 1990.

Rambo, Lewis R. *Understanding Religious Conversion*. New Haven, Conn.: Yale University Press, 1993.

Ramsey, Ann W. *Liturgy, Politics, and Salvation: The Catholic League in Paris and the Nature of Catholic Reform, 1540–1630*. Rochester, N.Y.: University of Rochester Press, 1999.

Ranger, Terence. "Taking Hold of the Land: Holy Places and Pilgrimages in Twentieth-Century Zimbabwe." *Past and Present*, no. 117 (1987): 158–94.

Rapley, Elizabeth. *The Dévotes: Women and Church in Seventeenth-Century France*. Montreal: McGill-Queen's University Press, 1990.

Rapley, Robert. *A Case of Witchcraft: The Trial of Urbain Grandier*. Montreal: McGill-Queen's University Press, 1998.

Read, Charles. "Cimetières et inhumations des huguenots principalement à Paris aux XVIe, XVIIe, et XVIIIe siècles (1563–1792)." *Bulletin de la société d'histoire du protestantisme français* 11 (1862): 132–50, 351–59.

———. "Cimetières et inhumations des huguenots principalement à Paris aux XVIe, XVIIe, XVIIIe siècles (1563–1792)." *Bulletin de la société d'histoire du protestantisme français* 12 (1863): 33–41, 141–48, 274–84, 367–75.

Rézeau, Pierre. *Dictionnaire du français régional de Poitou-Charentes et de Vendée*. Paris: Bonneton, 1990.

———. *Le "Vocabulaire poitevin" (1803–1825) de Lubin Mauduyt: Édition critique d'après Poitiers, Bibl. Mun., ms. 837*. Tübingen: M. Niemayer, 1994.

Richard, Michel-Edmond. *La vie des protestants français de l'Édit de Nantes à la Revolution (1598–1789)*. Paris: Éditions de Paris, 1994.

Roberts, Penny. "Contesting Sacred Space: Burial Disputes in Sixteenth-Century France." In *The Place of the Dead: Death and Remembrance in Late Medieval and Early Modern Europe*, edited by Bruce Gordon and Peter Marshall, 131–48. Cambridge, U.K.: Cambridge University Press, 2000.

———. "Religious Pluralism in Practice: The Enforcement of the Edicts of Pacification." In *The Adventure of Religious Pluralism in Early Modern France: Papers from the Exeter Conference, April 1999*, edited by Keith Cameron, Mark Greengrass, and Penny Roberts, 31–43. Bern: Peter Lang, 2000.

Roelker, Nancy L. "The Appeal of Calvinism to French Noblewomen in the Sixteenth Century." *Journal of Interdisciplinary History* 2 (1972): 391–418.

———. "The Role of Noblewomen in the French Reformation." *Archive for Reformation History* 63 (1972): 168–95.

Romane-Musculus, Paul. "L'église réformée de Pouzauges de l'Édit de Nantes à sa révocation." *Bulletin de la société d'histoire du protestantisme français* 125 (1979): 9–46.

Roper, Lyndal. *The Holy Household: Women and Morals in Reformation Augsburg*. Oxford, U.K.: Clarendon Press, 1989.

———. *Oedipus and the Devil: Witchcraft, Sexuality and Religion in Early Modern Europe*. London: Routledge, 1994.

Rosa, Susan. "The Conversion to Catholicism of the Prince de Tarente, 1670." *Historical Reflections/Reflexions Historiques* 21, no. 1 (1995): 57–75.

———. "'Il était possible aussi que cette conversion fût sincère': Turenne's Conversion in Context." *French Historical Studies* 18, no. 3 (Spring 1994): 632–66.

———. "Seventeenth-Century Catholic Polemic and the Rise of Cultural Rationalism: An Example from the Empire." *Journal of the History of Ideas* 57, no. 1 (January 1996): 87–107.

Roussel, Bernard. "'Ensevelir honnestement les corps': Funeral Corteges and Huguenot Culture." In *Society and Culture in the Huguenot World, 1559–1685*, edited by Raymond A. Mentzer and Andrew Spicer, 193–208. Cambridge, U.K.: Cambridge University Press, 2002.

Rowell, Geoffrey. *The Liturgy of Christian Burial: An Introductory Survey of the Historical Development of Christian Burial Rites*. London: Alcuin Club, 1977.

Sahlins, Peter. *Boundaries: The Making of France and Spain in the Pyrenees*. Berkeley and Los Angeles: University of California Press, 1989.

Sallmann, Jean-Michel. *Naples et ses saints à l'âge baroque (1540–1750)*. Paris: Presses Universitaires de France, 1994.

Sauzet, Robert. *Contre-réforme et réforme catholique en Bas-Languedoc: Le diocèse de Nîmes au XVIIe siècle*. Louvain: Nauwelaerts, 1979.

———. "Prédication et missions dans le diocèse de Chartres au début du XVIIe siècle." *Annales de Bretagne et des Pays de l'Ouest* 81, no. 3 (July 1974): 491–500.

Sawyer, Jeffrey K. *Printed Poison: Pamphlet Propaganda, Faction Politics, and the Public Sphere in Early Seventeenth-Century France*. Berkeley and Los Angeles: University of California Press, 1990.

Sayce, R. A. "Continental Versions to c. 1600: French." In *The Cambridge History of the Bible*, edited by S. L. Greenslade, 3 vols., 3:113–22. Cambridge, U.K.: Cambridge University Press, 1975.

Sceaux, Raoul de [Jean Mauzaize]. *Histoire des frères mineurs capucins de la province de Paris, 1601–1660*. Blois: Éditions Notre-Dame de la Trinite, 1965.

———. "Le Père Honoré de Cannes: Capucin missionaire au XVIIe siècle." *XVIIe siècle* 7 (1958): 349–74.

Schilling, Heinz. "Confessionalization in the Empire: Religious and Societal Change in Germany between 1555 and 1620." In *Religion, Political Culture and the Emergence of Early Modern Society: Essays in German and Dutch History*. Leiden: E. J. Brill, 1992.

———, ed. *Kirchenzucht und Sozialdisziplinierung im frühneuzeitlichen Europa*. Berlin: Duncker & Humblot, 1994.

Schmidt, Heinrich Richard. "Sozialdisziplinierung? Ein Plädoyer für das Ende des Etatismus in der Konfessionalisierungsforschung." *Historische Zeitschrift* 265 (December 1997): 639–82.

Scribner, Bob. "Preconditions of Tolerance and Intolerance in Sixteenth-Century Germany." In *Tolerance and Intolerance in the European Reformation*, edited by Ole Peter Grell and Bob Scribner, 32–47. Cambridge, U.K.: Cambridge University Press, 1996.

Sedgwick, Alexander. *The Travails of Conscience: The Arnauld Family and the Ancien Regime*. Cambridge, Mass.: Harvard University Press, 1998.

Selwyn, Jennifer D. "'Procur[ing] in the Common People These Better Behaviors': The Jesuits' Civilizing Mission in Early Modern Naples, 1550–1620." *Radical History Review* 67 (Winter 1997): 4–34.

Sheriff, Mary D. *The Exceptional Woman: Elisabeth Vigée-Lebrun and the Cultural Politics of Art*. Chicago: University of Chicago Press, 1996.

Silverman, Lisa. *Tortured Subjects: Pain, Truth, and the Body in Early Modern France*. Chicago: University of Chicago Press, 2001.

Sluhovsky, Moshe. "The Devil in the Convent." *American Historical Review* 107, no. 5 (December 2002): 1379–1411.

Soergel, Philip M. *Wondrous in His Saints: Counter-Reformation Propaganda in Bavaria*. Berkeley and Los Angeles: University of California Press, 1993.

Solé, Jacques. "Le débat confessionel français entre 1598 et 1685: Esquisse de bilan." In *La controverse religieuse: XVIe–XIXe siècles. Actes du premier colloque Jean Boisset, VIème colloque du Centre d'histoire de la réforme et du protestantisme*, edited by Michel Péronnet, 17–23. Montpellier: Université Paul Valéry, 1980.

———. *Le débat entre protestants et catholiques français de 1598 à 1685*. 2 vols. Lille: Atelier National Reproduction des Thèses, 1985.

Spellman, W. M. *The Latitudinarians and the Church of England, 1660–1700*. Athens: University of Georgia Press, 1993.

Spicer, Andrew. "'Qui est de Dieu oit la parole de Dieu': The Huguenots and Their Temples." In *Society and Culture in the Huguenot World, 1559–1685*, edited by Raymond A. Mentzer and Andrew Spicer, 175–92. Cambridge, U.K.: Cambridge University Press, 2002.

———. "'Rest of their Bones': Fear of Death and Reformed Burial Practices." In *Fear in Early Modern Society*, edited by William G. Naphy and Penny Roberts, 167–83. Manchester, U.K.: Manchester University Press, 1997.

Stegmann, André, ed. *Édits des Guerres de Religion*. Paris: J. Vrin, 1979.

Steinberg, Sylvie. "Le mythe des amazons et son utilization politique de la renaissance à la Fronde." In *Royaume de fémynie: Pouvoirs, contraintes, espaces de liberté des femmes de la renaissance à la Fronde*, edited by Kathleen Wilson-Chevalier and Eliane Viennot, 261–73. Paris: Champion, 1999.

Stephens, Winifred. *From the Crusades to the French Revolution: A History of the La Trémoille Family*. London: Constable, 1914.

Stocquart, Emile. "Le mariage des protestants en France." In *Aperçu de l'évolution juridique du mariage*, 115–61. Brussels: Oscar Lamberty, 1905–1907.

Strayer, Brian E. *Huguenots and Camisards as Aliens in France, 1598–1789: The Struggle for Religious Toleration*. Lewiston, N.Y.: Edwin Mellen Press, 2001.

Taylor, Charles. *Sources of the Self: The Making of Modern Identity*. Cambridge, Mass.: Harvard University Press, 1989.

Thibaut-Payen, Jacqueline. *Les morts, l'église et l'état: Recherches d'histoire administrative sur la sépulture et les cimetières dans le ressort du parlement de Paris aux XVIIe et XVIIIe siècles*. Paris: F. Lanore, 1977.

Thiollet, Denise. "Les capucins et la Congrégation de la Propagande d'après le mss 112 conservé chez les pères capucins (1624–1647)." *Revue historique* 280, no. 2 (October–December 1988): 387–93.

Thomas, Keith. *Religion and the Decline of Magic: Studies in Popular Beliefs in Sixteenth- and Seventeenth-Century England*. Harmondsworth, U.K.: Penguin Books, 1973.

Timmermans, Linda. *L'accès des femmes à la culture (1598–1715): Un débat d'idées de Saint François de Sales à la Marquise de Lambert*. Paris: Honoré Champion, 1993.

Traver, Emilien. *Histoire de Melle*. 1938; reprint, Marseilles: Lafitte, 1980.

Turner, Victor. *Dramas, Fields, and Metaphors: Symbolic Action in Human Society*. Ithaca, N.Y.: Cornell University Press, 1974.

———. *The Ritual Process: Structure and Anti-Structure*. Ithaca, N.Y.: Cornell University Press, 1969.

"Usage en commun d'un cimetière entre catholiques et protestants en 1609." *Bulletin de la société d'histoire du protestantisme français* 2 (1853): 502–5.

Varshney, Ashutosh. *Ethnic Conflict and Civic Life: Hindus and Muslims in India*. New Haven, Conn.: Yale University Press, 2002.

Vaumas, Guillaume de. *L'éveil missionaire de la France: D'Henri IV à la fondation du Séminaire des Missions Etrangères*. Lyon: Imprimerie Express, 1942.

Venard, Marc. "Le démon controversiste." In *La Controverse religieuse: XVIe–XIXe siècles. Actes du premier colloque Jean Boisset, VIème colloque du Centre d'histoire de la réforme et du protestantisme*, edited by Michel Péronnet, 45–60. Montpellier: Université Paul Valéry, 1980.

———. "L'église catholique bénéficiare de l'Édit de Nantes: Le témoignage des visites épiscopales." In *Coexister dans l'intolérance: L'Édit de Nantes (1598)*, edited by Michel Grandjean and Bernard Roussel, 283–302. Geneva: Labor et Fides, 1998.

———. *Réforme protestante et réforme catholique dans la province d'Avignon au XVIe siècle*. Paris: Cerf, 1993.

———. "'Vos Indes sont ici.': Missions lointaines (et) (ou) missions intérieures dans le catholicisme français de la première moitié du XVIIe siècle." In *Les réveils missionaires en France du moyen-âge à nos jours (XIIe–XXe siècles). Actes du colloque de Lyon, 29–31 Mai 1980*, edited by Guy Duboscq and André Latreille, 83–89. Paris: Beauchesne, 1984.

Viénot, John. *Histoire de la réforme française de l'Édit de Nantes a sa révocation*. Paris: Fischbacher, 1926.

Vogler, Bernard. "La législation sur les sépultures dans l'Allemagne protestante au XVIe siècle." *Revue d'histoire moderne et contemporaine* 22 (April–June 1975): 191–232.

Vray, Nicole. *Catherine de Parthenay, duchesse de Rohan: Protestante insoumise (1554–1631)*. Paris: Perrin, 1998.

———. *Protestants de l'ouest: Bretagne, Normandie, Poitou, 1517–1907*. Rennes: Éditions Ouest-France, 1993.

Wallace, Peter G. *Communities and Conflict in Early Modern Colmar: 1575–1730*. Atlantic Highlands, N.J.: Humanities Press, 1995.

Wanegffelen, Thierry. *Ni Rome ni Genève: Des fidèles entre deux chaires en France au XVIe siècle*. Paris: Honoré Champion, 1997.

Warmbrunn, Paul. *Zwei Konfession en einer Stadt: Das Zusammenleben von Katholiken und Protestantischen in den Paritätischen Reichsstädten Augsburg, Biberach, Ravensburg und Dinkelsbühl von 1548 bis 1648*. Wiesbaden: F. Steiner, 1983.

Weinstein, Donald, and Rudolph M. Bell. *Saints and Society: Two Worlds of Western Christendom, 1000–1700*. Chicago: University of Chicago Press, 1982.

Weissman, Ronald F. E. *Ritual Brotherhood in Renaissance Florence*. New York: Academic Press, 1982.

Wiesner, Merry E. *Women and Gender in Early Modern Europe*. 2nd ed. Cambridge, U.K.: Cambridge University Press, 2000.

Wilson-Chevalier, Kathleen, and Eliane Viennot, eds. *Royaume de fémynie: Pouvoirs, contraintes, espaces de liberté des femmes de la renaissance à la Fronde*. Paris: Honoré Champion, 1999.

Wolfe, Michael. *The Conversion of Henri IV: Politics, Power, and Religious Belief in Early Modern France*. Cambridge, Mass.: Harvard University Press, 1993.

INDEX

Sacred Boundaries: Religious Coexistence and Conflict in Early-Modern France was designed and composed in Dante by Kachergis Book Design of Pittsboro, North Carolina. It was printed on 60-pound Natural Offset by McNaughton & Gunn Lithographers of Saline, Michigan, and bound by John Dekker & Sons, of Grand Rapids, Michigan.

www.ingramcontent.com/pod-product-compliance
Lightning Source LLC
LaVergne TN
LVHW090147080826
844660LV00013B/699/J

* 9 7 8 0 8 1 3 2 1 4 1 1 5 *